MW01517938

GREENING DEMOCRACY

Greening Democracy explains how nuclear energy became a seminal political issue and motivated new democratic engagement in West Germany during the 1970s. Using interviews, as well as the archives of environmental organizations and the Green Party, the book traces the development of anti-nuclear protest from the grassroots to the parliaments. It argues that worries about specific nuclear reactors became the basis for a widespread anti-nuclear movement only after government officials' unrelenting support for nuclear energy caused reactor opponents to become concerned about the state of their democracy. Surprisingly, many citizens thought transnationally, looking abroad for protest strategies, cooperating with activists in other countries, and conceiving of "Europe" as a potential means of circumventing recalcitrant officials. At this nexus between local action and global thinking, anti-nuclear protest became the basis for citizens' increasing engagement in self-governance, expanding their conception of democracy well beyond electoral politics and helping to make quotidian personal concerns political.

STEPHEN MILDER is Assistant Professor of Politics and Society in the Department of European Languages and Cultures at the University of Groningen.

NEW STUDIES IN EUROPEAN HISTORY

Edited by

PETER BALDWIN, University of California, Los Angeles
CHRISTOPHER CLARK, University of Cambridge
JAMES B. COLLINS, Georgetown University
MIA RODRÍGUEZ-SALGADO, London School of Economics and Political Science
LYNDAL ROPER, University of Oxford
TIMOTHY SNYDER, Yale University

The aim of this series in early modern and modern European history is to publish outstanding works of research, addressed to important themes across a wide geographical range, from southern and central Europe, to Scandinavia and Russia, from the time of the Renaissance to the present. As it develops, the series will comprise focused works of wide contextual range and intellectual ambition.

A full list of titles published in the series can be found at: www.cambridge.org /newstudiesineuropeanhistory

GREENING DEMOCRACY

*The Anti-Nuclear Movement and Political
Environmentalism in West Germany
and Beyond, 1968–1983*

STEPHEN MILDER

CAMBRIDGE
UNIVERSITY PRESS

CAMBRIDGE
UNIVERSITY PRESS

University Printing House, Cambridge CB2 8BS, United Kingdom

One Liberty Plaza, 20th Floor, New York, NY 10006, USA

477 Williamstown Road, Port Melbourne, VIC 3207, Australia

4843/24, 2nd Floor, Ansari Road, Daryaganj, Delhi – 110002, India

79 Anson Road, #06–04/06, Singapore 079906

Cambridge University Press is part of the University of Cambridge.

It furthers the University's mission by disseminating knowledge in the pursuit of education, learning, and research at the highest international levels of excellence.

www.cambridge.org
Information on this title: www.cambridge.org/9781107135109
DOI: 10.1017/9781316471401

First published 2017

Printed in the United States of America by Sheridan Books, Inc.

A catalogue record for this publication is available from the British Library.

ISBN 978-1-107-13510-9 Hardback

For Valerie Rousse, Linda Cole, and Patricia Sullivan,
three teachers who opened the world to me.

Contents

Illustrations

Acknowledgments

In August 1999, I began a year as an exchange student in Sulzheim, a tiny Franconian village in the shadow of the Grafenrheinfeld nuclear reactor. "It's best to live so close," my host mother told me without a hint of sarcasm in her voice. "That way we'll go nice and quick if anything ever happens," she explained. Like most Germans of her generation, she had a good idea of what a nuclear accident might be like. She remembered giving up on fresh produce, checking the dates of ultra-pasteurized milk, and stopping her children from playing in sandboxes in order to protect them from radioactive fallout after the Chernobyl disaster, which had taken place some 1,600 kilometers away. The consequences of a meltdown at Grafenrheinfeld had been laid out with no lack of detail for Germans of all ages by Gudrun Pausewang in her children's book, *Die Wolke*. Like my host mother and her neighbors, I too learned to live with the nuclear reactor down the road, and the potential disaster it represented. Only years later did I realize the extent to which the experience of living with the reactor and watching its influence on both daily life and high politics guided my work on this book.

My year as an exchange student provided the point of departure for this project, but I would never have gone to Sulzheim or considered researching the history of a social movement without having been taught by three inspiring teachers beforehand. Valerie Rousse taught me German and opened the world to me by helping me to imagine a world far beyond suburban Boston, and then pushing me to become an exchange student and explore that world myself. Linda Cole and Patricia Sullivan inspired me to think about the past and the way it shaped the present by teaching me the history of the Civil Rights Movement. This book, which was deeply influenced by their transformative teaching, is dedicated to them.

I learned to use the tools required to analyze the anti-nuclear movement after I returned from Sulzheim and began my studies. As an undergraduate, I was mentored by Andrei Markovits, who has remained a close friend ever since I took his unforgettable seminar on the European Left in the spring of 2003. In graduate school, where I began to work on this project in earnest, I benefited from the influence of supportive friends, thoughtful colleagues, and dedicated teachers. Alex and Adri Jacobs, Ben Carroll, Ana Maria Reichenbach, Philipp Stelzel, Friederike Brühöfener, Patrick Tobin, Lawrence Goodwyn, and Don Reid provided inspiration, encouragement, and much needed opportunities for commiseration. Konrad Jarausch, who supervised my doctoral dissertation, encouraged me to continue studying green politics and environmentalism when I was considering other topics. His emphasis on the need to take concrete realities and ordinary lives into account in order to understand big historical transformations informs the approach to history taken in this book. Christof Mauch went far out of his way to make me feel welcome at the Rachel Carson Center in Munich. During my year there, I had the opportunity to conduct the bulk of the research used in this book, but also to come into contact with leading environmental historians from all around the world.

Without the support of Philipp Stelzel, Jocelyn Olcott, and Bill Donahue, I would never have secured my first tenuous foothold in the miserable academic job market. Since I left Chapel Hill for my first temporary job, James Chappel has read numerous drafts and offered thoughtful and helpful comments on my writing time and again. Don Reid, Tom Lekan, Astrid Eckert, and Silke Mende read chapter drafts, provided valuable feedback, and generously shared their expertise. Karrin Hanshew, Andrew Tompkins, Dolores Augustine, Jan Hansen, Kyle Harvey, Peter Caldwell, and Astrid Kirchhof provided important feedback at conferences and workshops. Sylvia Paletschek, Jan-Henrik Meyer, and Jacob Eder offered valuable opportunities to present my project at colloquia in Freiburg, Berlin, and Jena.

Seth Koven, Judith Surkis, Jennifer Mittelstadt, Lynn Shanko, James Delbourgo, and Toby Jones provided important insights into the publishing process and offered intellectual and personal support during a very productive year at the Rutgers Center for Historical Analysis. I can hardly begin to thank Belinda Davis for her friendship and willingness to help me overcome challenges of many sorts. She read drafts of several chapters of this book with unmatched attention to detail, helped me to better understand popular politics in postwar Germany, and offered invaluable assistance and mentorship in extended discussions and frantic email exchanges. Finally, Stefan Couperus made my transition from New Jersey to the Netherlands a breeze, and encouraged me to keep going during the tedious final round of revisions on my manuscript.

My thanks are due to Michael Watson at Cambridge University Press, who took a chance on a new author, as well as to Julie Hrischeva and Vel Murugan, who guided me through the uncharted territory of academic publishing. The two anonymous readers engaged by the press provided important comments and feedback on the manuscript, which I have used to improve the text.

The research that comprises this book would not have been possible without generous grants from many sources. The German Academic Exchange Service, the University of North Carolina's EU Center of Excellence, the German–American Fulbright Commission, the Andrew W. Mellon Foundation, as well as the Duke University German Department, the Groningen Research Institute for the Study of Culture, and the Mulerius Foundation of the University of Groningen all supported my work on this project.

Like most historians, I am deeply indebted to archivists, and also to other researchers I met in the archives. Getting to know archivists like Volkmar Vogt, Christoph Becker-Schaum, Robert Camp, Anne Vechtel, Wolfgang Hertle, Gerd Auer, and Sophie Barrat was one of the benefits of spending such a long time researching this book. They opened new archival collections to me, introduced me to interviewees, took time to discuss my project, and offered invaluable advice. I am particularly grateful for their help finding elusive references and providing access to the illustrations I have included in this book long after I returned home from the archives. Saskia Richter, who happened to be conducting research at the Archiv Grünes Gedächtnis during one of my early visits there, went out of her way to help me get my bearings at the archive. Her friendly demeanor and collegial approach to research, as well as her important insights into green politics and public participation, will be sorely missed.

The most rewarding part of researching this book was meeting and interviewing the many people involved in the movements it seeks to describe. Though I can only mention a few of my interviewees by name here, I am grateful to everyone who took the time to discuss the anti-nuclear movement with me over the years. Günter and Ute Sacherer hosted me several times and even helped me stop to smell the roses by taking me on a tour of the breathtaking Kaiserstuhl vineyards. Michel Fernex hosted me at his home in Biederthal, showed me his sons' farm, and allowed me access to his late wife's voluminous papers. Walter Mossmann opened the world of the Freiburg Left to me and helped me gain my first insights into the nature of Franco-German cooperation in the Upper Rhine valley. His dogged determination to tell the story of Wyhl to anyone who would listen will be missed in the years ahead.

Conducting research and presenting it at conferences required the generosity of friends like Jacob Comenetz, Susann Minter, and the Rilling, Thurn, and Werner families, who opened up their homes time and again.

My parents, Sara and Forrest Milder, who took me to my first protest (in support of increased funding for the Needham Public Schools), have supported me in every way, made my education possible, and helped me find my way to this topic. My sister, Elinor Milder, and my brother-from-another-mother, Grant Ellis, provided characteristically sarcastic responses to life's inevitable ups and downs. Their witty encouragement helped me to keep up with this project and put my travails into perspective. My partner, Jamie Snow, has been a steadfast source of love and support for more than a decade, living with this project from the time we moved to Chapel Hill to our first visits to archives in Detmold and Karlsruhe, to its completion here in Groningen. Taking the journey together with her has added so many wonderful moments and enriched my life in ways I could never have imagined. The final work on this manuscript was completed just before our son, Henry, was born. It is my hope that the story of popular politics and personal engagement it tells will remind us that we can – and must – work towards a better future for his generation.

Note on Translations and Acronyms

Unless otherwise noted, all translations into English are my own. Except in cases where foreign-language names are widely accepted in English or almost identical to English names (e.g. Paris Ecologie and Electricité de France), I have translated the names of the copious businesses, organizations, and anti-nuclear groupings described in this book into English. When introducing organizations with non-English names, I have provided the foreign-language acronym by which the group is known. After each group has been introduced for the first time, I use either its foreign-language acronym or its English name when referring to it. There is one important exception to this rule: I have used "Die Grünen" and "the Greens" interchangeably when referring to the German Green Party. Finally, I have left the names of books, journals, newspapers, and press agencies (all of which are italicized) in the original languages, but provided translations where these seem useful.

The following acronyms are used in this book (acronyms used to refer to archives are listed in the bibliography):

AEG	Allgemeine Elektricitäts-Gesellschaft
AFRPN	Federated Regional Association for the Protection of Nature (Association Fédérative Régionale pour la Protection de la Nature)
ARD	*Arbeitsgemeinschaft der öffentlich-rechtlichen Rundfunkanstalten der Bundesrepublik Deutschland*
AUD	Action Community of Independent Germans (Aktionsgemeinschaft Unabhängiger Deutscher)
BBU	Federal Association of Citizens' Initiatives for Environmental Protection (Bundesverband Bürgerinitiativen Umweltschutz)
BGL	Bremen Green List (Bremer Grüne Liste)

BKA	League of Communist Workers (Bund Kommunistische Arbeiter)
BuLi	Rainbow List – Defend Yourselves (Bunte Liste – Wehrt Euch)
BUU	Lower Elbe Citizens' Initiatives for Environmental Protection (Bürgerinitiativen Umweltschutz Unterelbe)
BZ	*Badische Zeitung*
CDU	Christlich Demokratische Union
CEA	Commission for Atomic Energy (Commissariat à l'Énergie Atomique)
CLINs	Local Nuclear Information Committees (Comités Locale d'Information Nucléaire)
CRIN	Regional Nuclear Information Committee (Comité Régional d'Information Nucléaire)
CRS	Republican Security Companies (Compagnies Républicaines de Sécurité)
CSFR	Committee to Protect Fessenheim and the Rhine Valley (Comité pour sauvegarde de Fessenheim et de la Plaine du Rhin)
CWM	Munich Chemical Works (Chemische Werke München)
DKP	German Communist Party (Deutsche Kommunistische Partei)
DLB	Democratic Movement for the Protection of Life (Demokratische Lebenschutzbewegung)
EDF	Electricité de France
EE	Europe Écologie
EEB	European Environmental Bureau
EEC	European Economic Community
EP	European Parliament
FoE	Friends of the Earth (Amis de la Terre)
FRG	Federal Republic of Germany
FSU	Free Social Union (Freie Soziale Union)
GAF	Nonviolent Action Freiburg (Gewaltfreie Aktion Freiburg)
GAK	Nonviolent Action Kaiseraugst (Gewaltfreie Aktion Kaiseraugst)
GAZ	Green Action Future (Grüne Aktion Zukunft)
GDR	German Democratic Republic
GLH	Hessian Green List (Grüne Liste Hessen)
GLSH	Schleswig Holstein Green List (Grüne Liste Schleswig-Holstein)

GLU	Green List for Environmental Protection (Grüne Liste Umweltschutz)
GLU-HH	Hamburg Green List for Environmental Protection (Grüne Liste Umweltschutz – Hansestadt Hamburg)
IFOR	International Fellowship of Reconciliation
JEF	Young European Federalists (Junge Europäische Föderalisten)
KB	Communist League (Kommunistischer Bund)
KBW	Communist League of West Germany (Kommunistischer Bund Westdeutschland)
KPD/ML	Communist Party of Germany/Marxists-Leninists (Kommunistische Partei Deutschlands/Marxisten-Leninisten)
KWU	Kraftwerk-Union
ME	Ecological Movement (Mouvement Ecologique)
MEP	Political Ecology Movement (Mouvement d'Ecologie Politique)
MRP	Popular Republican Movement (Mouvement Républicain Populaire)
NASA	National Aeronautics and Space Administration
NATO	North Atlantic Treaty Organization
NSM	New Social Movements
OAPEC	Organization of Arab Petroleum Exporting Countries
PCF	Communist Party of France (Parti Communiste Français)
RAF	Red Army Faction (Rote Armee Faktion)
SA	Sturmabteilung
SB	Socialist League/Socialist Office (Sozialistischer Bund/ Sozialistisches Büro)
SDS	Socialist German Students' League (Sozialistische Deutsche Studentenbund)
SPD	Social Democratic Party of Germany (Sozialdemokratische Partei Deutschlands)
SPV	Alternative Political Association: The Greens (Sonstige Politische Vereinigung: Die Grünen)
SVB	United People's Movement (Solidarische Volksbewegung)
SWR	*Südwestrundfunk*
taz	*die tageszeitung*
TMI	Three Mile Island
UK	United Kingdom
USA	United States of America

USP	Environmental Protection Party (Umweltschutz Partei)
VDEW	Association of Electricity Suppliers (Verband der Elektrizitätswirtschaft)
WDR	*Westdeutsche Rundfunk*
WFCC	Wyhl Forest Community College (Volkshochschule Wyhler Wald)
WSL	World Federation for the Protection of Life (Weltbund zum Schutze des Lebens)
WWW	*Was Wir Wollen*

Introduction: Taking the Democratic Dimensions of Anti-Nuclear Activism

On 11 July 1974 at Wyhl on the Rhine, a village of some 2,000 inhabitants nestled just north of the renowned vineyards of the Kaiserstuhl Hills, citizens publicly mourned the passing of democracy. Late in the afternoon, as government officials concluded a licensing hearing on a nuclear power plant that the Badenwerk utility company intended to build outside the village, a funeral cortège entered the meeting hall. From their seats on the dais, officials looked on in disbelief as a group of citizens filed past bearing a black coffin marked "DEMOCRACY." Back on the streets, these mourners paraded solemnly to the village mayor's home, where they eulogized the deceased. Their observance of democracy's demise had not been prompted by an authoritarian seizure of power, the suspension of free elections, or any obvious threat to the functions of parliament. Instead, they had been moved to act when officials excluded them from the bureaucratic and technical reactor licensing hearing by suddenly switching off the audience microphones.

Several weeks later, the Reverend Peter Bloch, himself active in the "citizens' actions" that opposed the reactor project, sent an open letter to the local newspaper explaining what had happened. The pastor began by detailing the "exceptionally dedicated work and . . . substantial sacrifice of money and time" that underpinned the grassroots challenge to the reactor project. Bloch's flock had gathered tens of thousands of petition signatures, patiently explained their concerns to local officials, and attended numerous hearings and public debates. After such widespread, popular engagement in the licensing process, officials' sudden, unilateral decision to suspend debate at the 11 July hearing was an affront. Forebodingly, Bloch predicted that, "if the hearing that took place in Wyhl is allowed to serve as an example in our Federal Republic, wide circles of the population will lose their trust in the democratic order of our state."[1] The mock funeral and

---

[1] Bloch, "Nicht gegen den Willen der Bevölkerung durchsetzen," *Badische Zeitung*, 14 August 1974.

I

Bloch's letter evidenced reactor opponents' complicated relationship with democracy. Paradoxically, they showed their reverence for the democratic order at the same time as they voiced their distrust of long-revered, democratically elected officials.

Not least because of the capricious history of democracy in twentieth century central Europe, the idea that environmental concerns had motivated rural citizens to identify with the democratic system – and that officials' minor abuses of power threatened their trust in that same system – was surprising. After all, there had been no mock funeral in the Upper Rhine valley forty years earlier when democracy was suspended by the National Socialist regime. And though voter turnout was very high in the 1950s and 1960s, suggesting that local people accepted democracy after 1945, going to the polls did not mean that voters saw democratic participation as a means of defending their own interests. Instead, as Claudia Gatzka has recently shown, the practice of going out to vote evidenced West Germans' support for a "quiet, unified, celebratory, worthy," democracy "that hardly accepted conflict."[2] So why did plans to build a nuclear reactor motivate Rhenish people to think of the liberal democratic order as the appropriate forum for their conflict with the Badenwerk, and also to proclaim democracy itself as the best means of safeguarding their particular interests?

Though the anti-nuclear movement has been the subject of a great deal of research, this question has gone unanswered because it challenges the way we think about both democracy and environmental activism. In their zeal to classify and explain the social movements of the 1970s, social scientists consistently separated the material protests of workers demanding fair treatment and better social conditions from "post-material" environmental activism, which addressed only quality-of-life issues.[3] The labor movement has been hailed for its role in "forging democracy."[4] Yet, looking only at the nominal aims of movements dedicated to stopping

[2] Claudia Gatzka, "Des Wahlvolks großer Auftritt. Wahlritual und demokratische Kultur in Italien und Westdeutschland nach 1945," *Comparativ* 23, no. 1 (2013): 72.

[3] See, for example: Dieter Rucht, "Anti-Atomkraftbewegung" in Roland Roth and Dieter Rucht, eds., *Die Sozialen Bewegungen in Deutschland seit 1945. Ein Handbuch* (Frankfurt/New York: Campus, 2008). William Tucker's *Progress and Privilege* (Garden City, NY: Anchor/Doubleday, 1982) famously claims that environmentalism is a post-material concern of the well-to-do. Though Tucker's thesis has been refuted in various scholarly studies, the idea that "only people in rich countries are concerned about the environment" retains enormous traction, as discussed by Steven Brechin and Willett Kempton in "Global Environmentalism: A Challenge to the Postmaterialism Thesis" in *Social Science Quarterly* 75, no. 2 (June 1994): 245–269.

[4] Geoff Eley, *Forging Democracy: The History of the Left in Europe, 1850–2000* (Oxford: Oxford University Press, 2002).

nuclear reactors or saving particular neighborhoods from development justified the dismissal of "post-material," "single issue" movements as selfish and apolitical; it is assumed that they could hardly have had to do with such basic matters as democratic inclusion. Thus, the democratic concerns of the protesters at Wyhl are rarely taken seriously because they were uttered in a rural village, had to do with the way a single nuclear reactor project would impact a handful of remote communities, and seemed far afield from the matters of high politics debated in parliament.

Despite the supposed divergence between democracy and environmental issues, protesters' sustained engagement in arcane licensing processes, their frequent references to the highhandedness of public officials, and their criticisms of the stagnancy of civic debate all evidenced links between environmental concerns and democratic praxis. These links were made explicit after the July 1974 Wyhl hearing, when protesters mourned democracy's loss and identified themselves as its unlikely defenders.[5] References to the state of democracy soon became commonplace amongst Rhenish activists. When they occupied the Wyhl construction site in 1975, protesters from Alsace, Baden, and Northwest Switzerland justified the direct action protest by denouncing the state government of Baden-Württemberg as a dictatorship comparable to the Nazi regime or East Germany's socialist government.[6] In 1977, the Austrian journalist Robert Jungk coined the term "atomic state" to describe this connection between nuclear matters and a sort of creeping abuse of government authority, which limited democracy by asserting that citizens were not equipped to debate nuclear energy and thus unable to govern themselves in an age of high technology.[7] The open-ended, frequently transnational communities' anti-nuclear activists organized through their protests, by contrast, embodied a sort of grassroots democracy dependent on individuals' engagement for its very survival. The present study asserts, therefore, that concerns about democracy, which ran like a red thread through Rhine valley anti-reactor protests, enabled that locally rooted movement against nuclear energy to grow

---

[5] This process has clear parallels to the one Karrin Hanshew has proposed that Germans underwent as they moved to defend West German democracy after it proved itself reformable through its struggle with the Red Army Faction. Hanshew, *Terror and Democracy in West Germany* (Cambridge: Cambridge University Press, 2012).

[6] Frederic Mayer, "Ein Elsässer fühlt sich wie im dritten Reich" in Bernd Nössler and Margret de Witt, eds., *Wyhl. Kein Kernkraftwerk in Wyhl und auch sonst nirgends. Betroffene Bürger berichten* (Freiburg: Dreisam Verlag, 1976).

[7] Robert Jungk, *Der Atomstaat: vom Fortschritt in die Unmenschlichkeit* (Munich: Kindler, 1977).

across Western Europe and take on particular resonance in high politics within the Federal Republic of Germany (FRG).

One explanation of the relationship between anti-nuclear protest and West German democracy – and its significance – can be found in the assessments of contemporary observers, who saw in environmental activism an enchanting alternative to previous protest movements. Though he initially dismissed anti-reactor protest as too distant from the post-oil shock reality to be taken seriously, the social movements expert Professor Theodor Ebert soon changed his tune, praising the protests against the Wyhl reactor as "the most significant explicitly nonviolent campaign since the founding of the Federal Republic."[8] His ringing endorsement came despite the issues at stake, since he remained unsure that nuclear energy threatened rural communities' futures or their inhabitants' agricultural livelihoods. Ebert was focused instead on the movement's form and the expansive coalition that participated in it; the same aspects of environmental protest were praised in France by Jean-Paul Sartre, who declared the movement against the expansion of the Larzac military base the "most beautiful struggle of our twentieth century."[9] These endorsements of environmental protest depended on its position outside politics-as-usual: in effect, on its rejection of standard political praxis. Later analyses noted environmental activists' affinity for flat organizational structures and participatory processes, reinforcing the perceived separation between hierarchical, formulaic liberal democracy and the beautiful, bottom-up cooperation of environmental activism.[10]

Such emphasis on environmental activism's alternative forms implies a stark separation between participatory democracy and the liberal democratic, parliamentary systems by which Western European states were governed after 1945. To the extent that environmental protest is linked with liberal democracy at all, the relationship is typically described as a sort of feedback loop. After environmental protests "capture the attention of large publics and occupy prominent media spaces," they go on to "alter the entire political discourse," compelling "all the parties . . . to offer solutions

---

[8] Theodor Ebert, "Als Berliner in Wyhl: Friedensforschung und Konfliktberatung vor Ort," *Gewaltfreie Aktion*, Nr. 23, 24, 25 (1975). Ebert's journal *Gewaltfreie Aktion* focused closely on anti-nuclear protests as a potent form of nonviolent action during the mid and late 1970s.

[9] "Jean-Paul Sartre et les paysans du Larzac," *Libération*, 28 October 1978.

[10] See, for example: Wolfgang Beer, *Lernen im Widerstand. Politisches Lernen und politche Sozialisation in Bürgerinitiativen* (Hamburg: Verlag Association, 1978); Barbara Epstein, *Political Protest and Cultural Revolution: Nonviolent Direct Action in the 1970s and 1980s* (Berkeley: California, 1991); and Michael Hughes, "Civil Disobedience in Transnational Perspective: American and West German Anti-Nuclear-Power Protesters," *Historical Social Research* 39, no. 1 (2014): 236–253.

to these problems."[11] But, scholars argue, such broad consensus actually limited the extent of environmentalism's advance. Far from fundamentally transforming society – not to mention democracy – environmentalism has become yet another problem that could be addressed through technical solutions amenable to mainstream politics. As Michael Bess has shown, France became a "light green society" by the 1990s, where environmental rhetoric was widespread but any impetus for the sort of radical action necessary to solve deep-seated environmental problems was absent.[12] Even in the Federal Republic of Germany, whose newfound identity as "the greenest nation" has been explored by Frank Uekötter, the rapid march of environmental progress was best evident in technical solutions to particular problems, not fundamental changes to political practice, the social order, or democracy.[13]

Perhaps environmentalists' influence on the fundamental framework of democracy, beyond the introduction of new topics to the platforms of political parties and the widespread acceptance of particular pieces of environmental legislation, is underestimated because it has proven hard to chart. The green parties founded across Western Europe in the 1970s and 1980s are the most frequently cited evidence of a bigger transformation of the political brought about by environmentalists.[14] But like the environmental themes they advocate, green parties are now widely considered purveyors of limited reformist projects, not advocates of fundamental systemic change.[15] In fact, though they were received apprehensively at first, green parties were quickly reconceived as minor additions to existing parliamentary systems, which continued apace.[16] That the West German state, for example, can be said to have "eventually managed to channel [the] new social movements back into regular politics through the foundation of a new [green] political party" suggests that in the FRG,

---

[11] Rob Burns and Wilfried van der Will, *Protest and Democracy in West Germany: Extra-Parliamentary Opposition and the Democratic Agenda* (Basingstoke: Palgrave, 1988), 15.

[12] Michael Bess, *The Light Green Society: Ecology and Technology in Modern France, 1960–2003* (Chicago: University of California Press, 2003).

[13] Frank Uekötter, *The Greenest Nation? A New History of German Environmentalism* (Cambridge, MA: MIT Press, 2014).

[14] This is the approach taken, for example, in Andrei S. Markovits and Philip S. Gorski's landmark study *The German Left: Red, Green, and Beyond* (Oxford: Oxford University Press, 1993).

[15] See, for example: Joachim Jachnow, "What's Become of the German Greens?" *New Left Review* 81 (May–June 2013).

[16] German politicians and the mainstream media, for example, raised alarmist warnings about the Greens during the 1980 and 1983 Bundestag campaigns. See Stephen Milder, "Petra Kelly and the Power of the Green Alternative in the United States," in Frank Reichherzer, Jan Hansen, and Christian Helm, eds., *Making Sense of the Americas: How Protest Related to America in the 1980s and Beyond* (Frankfurt: Campus, 2015); See also: Chapter 6.

a well-entrenched parliamentary system absorbed a weak extra-parliamentary movement.[17] But this apparent absorption into "regular politics" in the early 1980s came nearly a decade after Rhenish reactor opponents declared their identification with democracy in 1974, and was itself a departure from the alternative, transnational approaches to politics that environmentalists deployed in the mid-1970s. Moreover, the idea that the state itself channeled protest movements back into parliament overlooks the agency of the activists themselves, many of whom were uninterested in helping build new political parties, and hoped instead to realize a hybrid form of participatory democracy that combined extra-parliamentary activism with allegiance to liberal democratic electoral processes and parliamentary rule.

Precisely because it seeks to measure anti-nuclear protest's democratic impact, therefore, this book emphasizes the years surrounding Rhenish activists' forceful declaration of their identification with democracy in 1974. In the mid-1970s, I argue, grassroots activists changed the course of democracy's development in Western Europe. They forced open new debates, engaged new people in politics, and confronted elected officials with their inability to adequately address their concerns about nuclear energy within the liberal democratic order. Western Europe's green parties, which sought to take up these activists' mantle in the 1980s, aimed at institutionalizing this challenge by incorporating environmental concerns and the new forms of participation they inspired directly into the parliamentary framework of liberal democracy. It would be incorrect to propose that the Greens had little effect on West German democracy. But it is important not to overlook the achievements and the radical potential of 1970s activism – the point from which many "founding Greens" claimed to depart.[18] The turning point in democracy's development that these activists caused – what I refer to in this book as the greening of democracy – came as they simultaneously identified with the liberal democratic order and engaged in extra-parliamentary activism. Environmental issues, which motivated this new wave of engagement, proved well-suited to the creation

---

[17] Konrad Jarausch, *After Hitler: Recivilizing Germans 1945–1995* trans. Brandon Hunziker (Oxford: Oxford University Press, 2006), 178. In their classic study of the rise of the Greens, *The German Left: Red, Green and Beyond*, Andrei Markovits and Philip Gorski provide much evidence for Jarausch's point by tracing the roots of the Greens from discontented SPD members to the student movement of the 1960s, through the New Social Movements of the 1970s. Markovits and Gorski, *The German Left* 30. The thesis is also supported in Paul Hockenos's *Joschka Fischer and the Making of the Berlin Republic: An Alternative History of Postwar Germany* (Oxford: Oxford University Press, 2008).

[18] The term "founding Greens" was coined by Silke Mende: *"Nicht rechts, nicht links, sondern vorn." Eine Geschichte der Gründungsgrünen* (Munich: Oldenbourg Wissenschaftsverlag, 2011), 6.

of links between liberal democratic institutions and extra-parliamentary action precisely because they seemed so distant from democracy matters. Over time, therefore, anti-nuclear activism itself changed the way its protagonists practiced democracy.

Creating Political Environmentalism, Expanding Democratic Participation

Greening Democracy addresses the relationship between environmentalism and democracy in three specific ways in order to show the anti-nuclear movement's radical democratic potential and evaluate the ways it changed democratic praxis in West Germany. First, and most fundamentally, in showing how activists probed the perceived boundary between environmental affairs and high politics, this book challenges the notion that the protest movements of the 1970s were primarily significant as markers of the turn away from meaningful, "material" politics, or as evidence of the disintegration of the mass parties that shaped the mid-twentieth-century political order.[19] Second, by showing the myriad ways in which environmentalists thought beyond political, social, and even geographic boundaries, *Greening Democracy* considers what it means to "think globally and act locally," and questions national politics' absence from this oft-repeated environmentalists' mantra.[20] In so doing, it also emphasizes the importance of conceiving the mid-1970s as a time when new options opened in political activism and democratic praxis. Finally, by studying the larger goals of the broad coalitions built by citizens concerned with particular local environmental problems, like individual nuclear reactor projects, this book reassesses the nature of the social fracturing that is said to epitomize

---

[19] I am of course in conversation here with Ronald Inglehart, but also authors like Geoff Eley and Tony Judt, who have emphasized the breakdown of mass parties – particularly the mass parties of the working class – after 1968. See: Inglehart, *The Silent Revolution* (Princeton: Princeton University Press, 1977); Geoff Eley, *Forging Democracy: The History of the Left in Europe, 1850–2000* (Oxford: Oxford University Press, 2002); Tony Judt, *Postwar: A History of Europe since 1945* (New York: Penguin, 2005).

[20] Studies of the 1980s anti-nuclear weapons movement in Germany and the United States by Susanne Schregel and Byron Miller have shown the importance of scales of protest for activists' ability to recruit others to their cause. Michael Foley has made similar arguments for a range of American social movements in the 1970s and 1980s. Schregel, *Der Atomkrieg vor der Wohnungstür. Eine Politikgeschichte der neuen Friedensbewegung in der Bundesrepublik, 1970–1985* (Frankfurt/Main: Campus, 2011); Miller, *Geography and Social Movements: Comparing Anti-nuclear Activism in the Boston Area* (Minneapolis: University of Minnesota Press, 2000); Foley, *Front Porch Politics: The Forgotten Heyday of American Activism in the 1970s and 1980s* (New York: Hill and Wang, 2013).

the final third of the twentieth century.[21] In contrast to the hypothesis that the breakdown of the social democratic Left diminished opportunities for meaningful progressive politics, the present study shows that the growing significance of localized and individualized approaches to democratic participation also had the potential to foster new, heterogeneous coalitions and thus to increase inclusion and participation.[22]

Between Local Environmental Concerns and High Politics

The book begins with the first attempts to "nuclearize" the Upper Rhine in the late 1960s. A close look at protests in the Rhine valley reveals the ways in which grassroots activists developed a new, politicized sort of environmentalism in the 1970s: one capable of probing the boundaries of high politics. Government officials' efforts to license the construction of a "pearl necklace" of reactors between Basel and Strasbourg motivated protests that crossed national borders and asserted the significance of individuals' particular concerns for centralized decision-making processes, effectively challenging the limits of high politics. This story runs contrary to the common narrative of environmentalism's sudden emergence around 1970, which focuses on the growing awareness of environmental problems by international organizations, evidenced in 1972 by the UN's Stockholm Conference on the Human Environment as well as the publication of the Club of Rome's *Limits to Growth*.[23] Instead, these grassroots anti-reactor protests built on farmers' concerns about their crops, and inhabitants' worries that unchecked nuclear development would cause them to be resettled from their homes in the Rhine valley to the hills of the Black Forest or the Vosges.[24] The protests were carried out by people who remembered well the devastation of the Second World War, and they

[21] Daniel Rodgers, *Age of Fracture* (Cambridge, MA: Harvard University Press, 2011). Tony Judt and Timothy Snyder suggest a similar trajectory for Western Europe in *Thinking the Twentieth Century* (New York: Penguin, 2012).

[22] On this point I am in agreement with Andrei Markovits, who has proposed the "politics of compassion" as a cypher for the ways in which the post-1968 Left has sought to expand inclusion in democracy – even without the framework for the mass social democratic party. See, for example: Markovits and Katherine N. Crosby, "Introduction," in *From Property to Family: American Dog Rescue and the Discourse of Compassion* (Ann Arbor: University of Michigan Press, 2014), 1–34.

[23] Thus, the development of environmental awareness at the grassroots level developed along a different track than did the international consciousness of environmental issues described by Kai F. Hünemörder, *Die Frühgeschichte der deutschen Umweltpolitik (1950–1973)* (Stuttgart: F. Steiner, 2004).

[24] In Baden, the concerns were prompted by a 1972 editorial in the state-sponsored *Staatsanzeiger für Baden-Württemberg*, and were linked to local people's evacuation to the Black Forest during the Second World War. In Alsace, the concerns were based on a plan by Etienne Juillard to create

followed up on earlier efforts to protect local fisheries in the industrialized Rhine.[25] In this sense, these first anti-reactor protests might be said to follow on the work of pioneering nineteenth-century ecologists and even the local nature protection movements of the postwar "miracle years."[26]

But there was something new about the environmentalism of the 1970s. Henri Jenn, the first self-proclaimed "ecologist" to run for the National Assembly in France, earned his stripes as an advocate of bird protection before his 1973 campaign. He differentiated between an old "green" ecology concerned with protecting birds and other animals, and a new "grey" environmentalism concerned with questions of pollution.[27] Though attempts to deal with air pollution, in particular, have a history that long predates the 1970s, many historians agree with Jenn that something significant changed in the ways Western Europeans thought about nature and environmental protection around 1970.[28] German historiography juxtaposes the term Naturschutz, or the protection of nature, with Umweltschutz, or the protection of the environment, to explain this shift.[29] The historian Michael Bess summed up this transformation by describing the emergence of environmentalism in France as the adoption of a "new vision of the human place within nature, a cultural transformation of nearly Copernican proportions."[30]

This book proposes that grassroots anti-reactor activists themselves – in the very process of building their movement against nuclear energy – changed the meaning of environmentalism, rethinking not only the human place within nature but also nature's place in politics. At the local

---

a "French Ruhr" on the Upper Rhine. Elisabeth Schulthess, *Solange l'insoumise: écologie, féminisme, non-violence*, (Barret-sur-Méouge: Y. Michel, 2004) 75. For more on these plans, see Chapter 1.

[25] Balthasar Ehret, "Fischerei am Oberrhein," in *Wyhl* (see note 6).

[26] See, for example: Raymond Dominick, *The Environmental Movement in Germany: Prophets & Pioneers, 1871–1971* (Bloomington: Indiana University Press, 1992); Sandra Chaney, *Nature of the Miracle Years: Conservation in West Germany, 1945–1975* (New York: Berghahn Books, 2008); Frank Uekötter, *Naturschutz im Aufbruch Eine Geschichte des Naturschutzes in Nordrhein-Westfalen, 1945–1980* (Frankfurt am Main: Campus, 2004); Jonas Kaesler, "'Ein vordringlich europäisches Problem?' Industrielle Verschmutzung und die Entstehung saarländischer Umweltproteste im deutsch-französischen Grenzgebiet, 1957–1959," in Birgit Metzger, Annette Lensing, and Olivier Hanse, eds., *Die Ökologie im linken und rechten Spektrum: Konvergenzen und Divergenzen zwischen Deutschland und Frankreich von 1970 bis heute* (Hamburg: Peter Lang, forthcoming).

[27] Henri Jenn, interview with author. Mulhouse, 21 March 2016.

[28] On histories of attempts to deal with pollution, particularly in German-speaking Central Europe, see: Frank Uekötter, *Umweltgeschichte im 19. Und 20. Jahrhundert* (Munich: Oldenbourg, 2007), 62–63.

[29] Thomas Lekan discusses the meanings of these terms in *Imagining the Nation in Nature: Nature Preservation and German Identity 1885–1945* (Cambridge, MA: Harvard University Press, 2004), 257. Raymond Dominick describes the transformation from Naturschutz to Umweltschutz in *Prophets and Pioneers*, 138.

[30] Bess, *Light Green Society*, 61.

level, as Rev. Bloch explained in his letter to the *Badische Zeitung*, government officials' tactless responses to popular complaints altered citizens' relationships with the democratic system. The coalescence of personal interests and the democratic order shifted the protection of nature from a local issue to one that affected citizens regardless of their proximity to a particular environmental hazard. At the same time, deep-seated personal transformations, which occurred on account of the anti-reactor struggle and motivated vintners to adopt organic farming techniques and electricians to experiment with solar energy, prompted the turn to a seemingly post-materialist language that made the protection of nature not just a particular local problem but a geographically diffuse social issue. In so doing, the new environmentalism of the 1970s linked specific, local concerns with far-reaching high politics.[31]

Between Global Thinking and Local Action

The motto "think globally, act locally" has been called the founding myth of the environmental movement.[32] Despite the importance of the emergence of green parties for our understanding of the environmental movement's development, it was no accident that this slogan failed to mention national politics. The path that West German anti-nuclear protesters took down the Rhine from Wyhl to Karlsruhe, where Die Grünen was founded in 1980, therefore, was not nearly as direct as the river's rectified course. Nor was René Dumont's landmark 1974 campaign for the French Presidency evidence that French ecologists thought solely in national terms. Instead, these events revealed the meanderings of anti-nuclear activists in grassroots, transnational, and regional politics. In fact, a whole host of different possibilities for future action opened up as grassroots anti-reactor protests garnered attention across Western Europe in the mid-1970s. Even as activists in parts of France and West Germany formed the insurgent "green" candidates' lists and parties that preceded the national green parties, Die Grünen and Les Verts, many anti-reactor activists remained reticent to formally enter electoral

---

[31] Chapter 2 considers in far more detail the ways that the growth of the environmental movement opened up the potential for new coalitions at the same time as it contributed to the fracturing of old ones. Susanne Schregel's excellent study of the 1980s peace movement shows, in fact, how the links between individualized local concerns and high politics established by anti-reactor activists in the 1970s were deployed by anti-missile activists in the 1980s. Schregel, *Der Atomkrieg vor der Wohnungstür*.

[32] Brendan Prendiville, *Environmental Politics in France* (Boulder: Westview Press, 1994), 91–93.

politics.[33] These grassroots activists' frustrating experiences at licensing hearings and their futile attempts to express their concerns to government officials had imbued them with a deep distrust of politicians, even if they now saw democratic processes as means by which they ought to be able to defend their interests. They continued to vote – many even became ardent democrats – but their inability to effectively defend their interests caused these concerned citizens to express themselves in public alongside the established democratic process. Because they prioritized the continuance of extra-parliamentary activism alongside formal liberal democratic praxis, they considered the founding of green parties no reason for celebration.

Thus, the greening of West German democracy was not a straightforward, Whiggish journey from lonely places like Wyhl to state legislatures and eventually the Bundestag. Instead, transnational routes and seeming detours must be conceived as essential stages – perhaps even the foremost accomplishments – in this process, because it was the journey itself which revealed that there was more to democratic praxis than elections and parliamentary debates. The exploration of connections with France was particularly important in this regard, both amongst anti-reactor campaigners at the local level, and in terms of political concepts and models of protests that passed back and forth across the Rhine.[34] It is unsurprising then, that the highpoint of environmentalism's influence on democracy was to be found during the mid-1970s. Not only did French and German activists cooperate most effectively during those years, it was also the time when reactor opponents most productively considered the relationship between environmental concerns and democracy matters, and the moment when many citizens expanded their conception of democratic praxis beyond the ballot box for the first time. Significantly, all of these developments took place without any explicit connection to partisan politics, and seemed far afield even from elections and thus from liberal democracy. In this sense, though the 1970s are frequently considered the time in "which the seeds of future crises were sown," it is important also to separate the 1970s from an eternal present.[35] The possibilities for transnational

---

[33] See, for example: Walter Mossmann, *realistisch sein: das unmögliche verlangen. Wahrheitsgetreu gefälschte Errinerungen* (Berlin: der Freitag, 2009), 248. This is discussed further in Chapter 6.

[34] Andrew Tompkins has charted three particular ways in which anti-nuclear activists in France and West Germany influenced one another across borders. Andrew Tompkins, "Grassroots Transnationalism(s): Franco-German Opposition to Nuclear Energy in the 1970s," *Contemporary European History* 25, no. 1 (February 2016): 117–142.

[35] Niall Ferguson, "Crisis, What Crisis?" in Ferguson et al, eds., *The Shock of the Global: The 1970s in Perspective* (Cambridge, MA: Harvard University Press, 2010) 18. Here I am referencing the argument that Konrad Jarausch and I made in our essay on the rise of Green politics in West

action, or the openness between Left and Right that contemporaries noticed, are not the same today.[36] Hence, the formation of national political parties was only one outcome of the anti-reactor protest movements that began with grassroots action and local thinking. The present study, therefore, incorporates the space "beyond" the FRG into its account of the transformation of West German democracy because even this ultimately national process would not have been possible without local campaigners' openness to transnationalism – and their initial avoidance of national politics.

Between Extra-Parliamentary Activism and Liberal Democratic Praxis

The hard-won moment of radical democratic possibility that occurred in the mid-1970s stands at the core of this study. That moment did not initiate the wholesale reform of existing liberal democracies or their replacement with a new, transnational democratic order. It was a time, nonetheless, when citizens linked engagement in extra-parliamentary activism with allegiance to the liberal democratic order. This link had powerful effects. Perhaps most significantly, it underpinned popular challenges to politicians' attempts to rein in or circumvent liberal democratic procedures and it diminished voters' support for the parties of the establishment. The idea that environmental protest was wholly separate from the liberal democratic order, but also the seemingly more hopeful argument that the founding of Western Europe's green parties finally incorporated the protagonists of extra-parliamentary protest into parliamentary systems, neglect some of the most important ways in which environmentalism's emergence influenced democracy's progress in postwar Europe.

Correcting these countervailing explanations' shortcomings requires looking at individuals' growing identification with democracy as both an idea and a practice. But it also requires thinking about the consequences of

---

Germany, that the "founding greens" ought no longer to be studied as part of the present but rather from the perspective of "history of the present," which posits a difference between even the recent past and the present in order to allow for critical reflection. See: Milder and Jarausch, "Introduction: Renewing Democracy: The Rise of Green Politics in West Germany," *German Politics and Society* 33, no. 4 (Winter 2015): 4–5.

[36] Here I am in agreement with Andrew Tompkins, who has proposed that the transnationalism of the 1970s was unique. See, Tompkins, "A specifically 1970s kind of transnationalism," paper presented at *Transformationen der Ökologiebewegung*, Berlin (November 2014); and Tompkins, "Grassroots Transnationalism(s)." Silke Mende made related comments at the conference, *Die Ökologie im linken und rechten Spektrum: Konvergenzen und Divergenzen zwischen Deutschland und Frankreich von 1970 bis heute*, Saarbrücken and Metz (November 2015).

this new outlook for the existing democratic order, since increased individual involvement went hand in hand with new criticisms of the parties and practices of the postwar establishment. In marked contrast to the thinkers and intellectual traditions which shaped postwar democracy in Western Europe, democracy's entrenchment in Europeans' minds and their daily practices remains understudied.[37] Only a handful of histories of protest during the 1960s have brought personal stories into debates about democratic transformation.[38] These histories propose that "1968" was the seminal moment when democracy was "deepened and widened" throughout Western Europe, and when the Federal Republic of Germany finally became a democratic state through a "second founding."[39] Yet, this literature focuses on a narrow band of activists who are perceived to have "marched through" democracy's institutions in order to improve and open them. Missing from these accounts are the "ordinary" people who comprised Western Europe's polities, and without whose assent the democratic system could never truly become socially entrenched. New research, including Claudia Gatzka's study of democracy as a local practice in the FRG and Italy, and Karrin Hanshew's history of the Federal Republic's confrontation with Left-wing terrorism, has begun to show how individuals were transformed through their engagement in popular politics.[40]

Ordinary people, and the ways in which their experiences as activists changed them and caused them to see themselves as democrats, are at the heart of the present book.[41] Engagement in anti-reactor protest, as the case of the farmers and vintners who protested against the Wyhl reactor exemplifies, was one significant cause of individuals' changing perceptions of democracy. Rather than continuing to foster economic development as it had since 1945, the struggle's protagonists came to believe that their

---

[37] Important recent studies of postwar democracy's intellectual foundations include Udi Greenberg, *Weimar Century: German Emigres and the Ideological Foundations of the Cold War* (Princeton: Princeton University Press, 2015); and also, Noah Strote, *Lions and Lambs: Chaos in Weimar and the Creation of Post-Nazi Germany* (New Haven: Yale University Press, 2017). Claudia Gatzka has worked on the popular components in her dissertation on "Demokratie als lokale Praxis. Bürger, Politik und urbane Wahlkampfkultur in Italien und der Bundesrepublik, 1945–1976" (PhD Dissertation, Humboldt Universität zu Berlin, 2015).

[38] This approach is exemplified in Hockenos's *Joschka Fischer and the Making of the Berlin Republic*, which closely links Fischer's life to big political changes in the FRG. Belinda Davis's forthcoming monograph *The Internal Life of Politics*, which is based on numerous interviews with activists, will expand this approach to a much wider group.

[39] See: Manfred Görtemaker, *Geschichte der Bundesrepublik Deutschland. Von der Gründung bis zur Gegenwart* (Munich: Beck, 1999); and Norbert Frei, *1968: Jugendrevolte und Globaler Protest* (Munich: Deutscher Taschenbuch Verlag, 2008).

[40] Claudia Gatzka, "Demokratie als lokale Praxis;" and: Hanshew, *Terror and Democracy*.

[41] Barbara Cruikshank, *The Will to Empower* (Ithaca: Cornell University Press, 1999).

democracy had begun eating its children. As they saw it, the democratically elected government was threatening all of their most essential interests by attacking their crops, their villages, and their health. Thus, Rhenish anti-reactor protestors did more than simply reject the dismissive actions taken by government officials at licensing hearings. In fighting against the fact that they themselves, the "affected population," were not included in decision-making processes, they linked their particular local interests with high politics and the democratic order.

Precisely because its most powerful ramifications affected individuals' approach to democracy, popular political participation has proven difficult to assess. A first wave of studies, in fact, emphasized the departure from pre-existing concepts of the political within the so-called "New Social Movements" (NSM) of the 1970s in order to better classify the movements and their objectives, but also to propose that they might harm the postwar democratic order.[42] Following Ronald Inglehart's value change hypothesis, much of this scholarship linked personal transformations to the NSM by explaining their emergence as products of individuals' turn away from important, material issues.[43] As a result, the protest movements of the 1970s were cast as ideologically limited projects directed towards the "post-material" realm of "reproduction."[44] Much research conducted in the New Social Movements paradigm, therefore, implies that the NSM were focused only on increasing "quality of life" in comparison to the more fundamental and more transformative economic goals of the labor movement, or even the emancipatory aspirations of the student movement. In contrast to the radical potential of other earlier movements, then, New Social Movements were presented as the watered down pet projects of well-to-do reformists.

And yet, regardless of the issues on which the NSM nominally focused, the sort of grassroots activism that underpinned them and the engagement

---

[42] This literature is taken up by Claus Offe in "New Social Movements: Challenging the Boundaries of Institutional Politics," *Social Research* 52, no. 4 (Winter 1985): 817–868. Though Offe himself argues against the "neo-conservative" project of dividing politics from "nonpolitical spheres" such as the family, the market, and science, he too proposes that the movements of the 1970s addressed a "new paradigm" and sought to "politicize the institutions of civil society" in order to emancipate civil society from the state. Offe, "New Social Movements," 821.

[43] Inglehart's value change thesis is described in his pathbreaking 1971 article "The Silent Revolution in Europe: Intergenerational Change in Post-Industrial Societies" (*The American Political Science Review* 65, no. 4 (December 1971): 991–1017) and laid out more fully in his classic 1977 work *The Silent Revolution: Changing Values and Political Styles Among Western Publics* (Princeton: Princeton University Press, 1977).

[44] Karl-Werner Brand begins one of his many articles on the New Social Movements by explaining their remarkable origins: they were motivated, he explains, not by the "newly polarized questions of capitalist order, but rather from problems of social reproduction." In Roth and Rucht, *Neue Soziale Bewegung in der Bundesrepublik Deutschland*, 30.

they represented have long been celebrated by critics of liberal democracy's shortcomings. Benjamin Barber famously argued, for example, that rather than the particular issues under discussion, self-government itself, "carried on through institutions designed to facilitate ongoing civic participation in agenda-setting, deliberation, legislation, and policy implementation (in the form of 'common work')" is the key to transforming "thin" representative democracy, into "strong" participatory democracy. His is a model for "the creation of a political community capable of transforming dependent private individuals into free citizens and partial and private interests into public goods."[45] This "both/and" approach is an apt framework for a movement that began with an uproar over the ways that particular nuclear reactors, designed to power exponential economic growth and thus benefit society as a whole, might threaten a handful of farmers' livelihoods or denigrate the quality of life in several villages with a few thousand total inhabitants. By exploring the vital link between partial and public interests and the connection between liberal, parliamentary democracy and extra-parliamentary advocacy, *Greening Democracy* builds on recent analyses of "popular politics" in order to explain how privately motivated, immediately local environmental protest precipitated widespread identification with democracy as not only a system of government but also a way of life in postwar Western Europe, and the Federal Republic of Germany in particular.[46]

From the Upper Rhine to. . .

The book first approaches the movement from the grassroots level, looking closely at the Upper Rhine valley, where Western Europe's first significant anti-reactor protests took place. These protests' location was no accident. The Upper Rhine comprised an abundant source of vital cooling water. It also formed the border between France, West Germany, and Switzerland, making it an excellent site for potentially hazardous projects that planners sought to locate far from capital cities and population centers. In Chapter 1, I show that fears about radiation poisoning and potential meltdowns did not motivate these early protests. Instead, local people feared that steam discharge from the cacophony of reactor projects planned by the three governments competing to exploit the river's resources would

---

[45] Benjamin Barber, *Strong Democracy* (Berkeley: University of California Press, 1984), 151.

[46] I draw here particularly on Belinda Davis "What's Left? Popular Political Participation in Postwar Europe" *The American Historical Review* 113, no. 2 (April 2008): 363–390; and Davis, *The Internal Life of Politics* (forthcoming); as well as Foley, *Front Porch Politics*.

create fog and block out the sun. Nuclear energy production was, therefore, an imminent, material threat to this renowned winegrowing region, but it was also the focus of a budding transnational cooperation that linked communities that had allowed the Rhine to separate them since 1945.

The second chapter looks at how activists in the Upper Rhine valley built on these first transnational contacts and used them to transform local anti-reactor protests into a diverse, multi-faceted, regional movement against nuclear energy. West Germany, France, and Switzerland's competing ambitions to "nuclearize" the Rhine showed local people that nuclear reactors' negative effects were not limited by political boundaries. At the same time, government officials' unwillingness to address local vintners' concerns caused fears about steam discharge to develop into criticisms of bureaucrats' behavior. Cross-border cooperation fostered probing questions about officials' motivations and enabled protesters to exchange strategies and broaden local anti-reactor coalitions. By seeing themselves as a transnational "Alemannic community" local people overstepped political boundaries, proved to themselves that local matters were of political importance, and thus empowered themselves in their nascent struggle against their governments.

I show in Chapter 3 that the 1975 occupation of the Wyhl reactor construction site, frequently described as the catalyst of West Germany's powerful anti-nuclear movement, existed in two very different contexts. Locally, the occupation was rooted in years of transnational anti-reactor struggle, including earlier site occupations at Kaiseraugst, Switzerland and Marckolsheim, France. Moreover, local people contributed to the nine-month occupation at Wyhl by cooking, learning, and socializing on the site, thus making anti-nuclear protest part of their daily routine. Nationally, however, sensational press reports made the occupation appear unprecedented. Precisely because of its place between the local (yet transnational) and national contexts, the Wyhl occupation exemplified the transformation of protest and of the relationship between protest and politics that was underway in the mid-1970s.

Wyhl's influence on protests elsewhere was immediate. After learning about the Wyhl occupation, protesters attempted to create "many Wyhls" by contesting other reactor projects; all the while, they sought to build a bigger anti-nuclear movement. In Chapter 4, I show how attempts to build on the Wyhl occupation took two different forms. While mass protests intended to affect national politics became more commonplace in West Germany, locally focused grassroots actions continued unabated in France. Though they were harder to understand as a national movement than bombastic mass protests, disparate grassroots anti-reactor campaigns had broad effects. Such protests did not stop nuclear energy production – or even prevent many of the individual reactors they targeted from being built. Nonetheless, experiences protesting nuclear energy at the grassroots level fostered community-building efforts and changed individual citizens, causing them to become deeply concerned about a host of ecological matters, and also more engaged in democratic processes. Focusing too closely on mass occupation attempts obscures these regional and personal transformations.

The tragic July 1977 showdown at the Super-Phénix site in Malville and the string of Left-wing terror attacks comprising the "German Autumn" dramatically shifted the context – and the effectiveness – of site occupation as a protest tactic in the FRG. As occupation attempts were repeatedly brutally suppressed by police forces outfitted with military hardware, many reactor opponents gave up on occupation as a means of protest. I argue in Chapter 5 that the idea of political environmentalism took root as activists struggled amongst themselves to devise a workable means of promoting their interests. Amidst many different potential strategies, grassroots reactor opponents sought a respectable method of defending themselves and their interests from the capriciousness of government officials. This outlook led them away from combative protests and towards direct challenges to politicians at the ballot box; it soon became the basis for anti-nuclear activists' attempts to win seats in local, state, and even national parliaments.

In 1979, the near-meltdown at the Three Mile Island nuclear power station in Pennsylvania, together with German officials' plans to build a nuclear waste storage and reprocessing center in Gorleben, and the first direct election to the European Parliament, all challenged anti-nuclear activists' ideas about the proper framework for their activism. Chapter 6 shows how transnational frameworks provided space for the nationalization of green politics in the FRG. The French and West German campaigns for the European parliament were a particularly important moment in this transformation of the anti-nuclear movement. Despite some leading activists' determination to use the European election as a stepping stone towards the withering away of the nation-state and the creation of transnational democracy, impressive returns excited many Greens about domestic elections. While the European election's results short-circuited elite activists' efforts to reimagine politics on the European level and to create a new more participatory, ecological Europe, it also helped anti-nuclear protest to gain pride of place in West German high politics. Thus, the

European perspective brings the Greens' difficult path to national political relevance into view, but it also reinforces the significance of the broader movement of which the Green Party was but one part. Only by considering the Green Party alongside grassroots anti-nuclear activism does the way in which political environmentalism shifted parliamentary democracy come into view.

As the Greens shed their participatory idealism and transnational approach, their interactions with the liberal democratic system shaped the salience that nuclear energy has taken in German politics today. Die Grünen became a small but vocal opposition party, which seemed to have a fighting chance at influencing policy, but also chafed during the 1980s at giving up its anti-establishment mantra. Thus, the Greens helped many West Germans feel enfranchised and persuaded them to commit themselves to a long battle against nuclear energy within the country's liberal democratic order, even as technical fixes to environmental problems proliferated. Though these sorts of transformations and inclusions are rightfully celebrated in histories of democratization, they fell short of the potential for strong democratic participation evident in the grassroots anti-nuclear actions of the mid-1970s. Though the Greens played a meaningful part in the broadening of democracy, they must be viewed within the framework of the broader impetus towards popular democratic engagement that was already underway during the mid-1970s, when citizens connected particular threats to their lives and livelihoods with matters of democratic praxis and public participation.

CHAPTER I

"Today the Fish, Tomorrow Us": The Threatened Upper Rhine and the Grassroots Origins of West European Environmentalism

A retrospective on "six years of conflict over nuclear energy on the Upper Rhine" in Freiburg's *Badische Zeitung* (*BZ*) began by describing a noteworthy failure. In May 1971, a country doctor by the name of Engelhard Bühler organized a meeting in order to inform his fellow physicians about the dangers of nuclear power. Apparently unconcerned about the risks to the local population and even the German genetic heritage that Bühler and the Freiburg nuclear physicist Walther Herbst attributed to reactors at the gathering, those present did not "allow themselves to be motivated to resistance." Nevertheless, the Rhenish anti-nuclear movement later flourished beyond Bühler's wildest dreams. As Michael Doelfs of the *BZ* reported, "when people began to think about wine, the spark caught."[1]

In part, Doelfs considered the doctors' meeting an isolated failure because he had allowed the Rhine, which divided German Baden from Northwest Switzerland and French Alsace, to bound his perspective. Had he looked just across the river, the reporter might have noticed that more than 1,000 reactor opponents – including 150 Freiburgers – had marched through the Alsatian village of Fessenheim less than a month before Bühler's meeting. He might also have seen that Walther Herbst, the Freiburg physicist who explained the nuclear threat to the Badensian doctors, had been invited to discuss the same topic with the residents of Kaiseraugst, Switzerland two years earlier. Concerned inhabitants of the Upper Rhine valley were beginning to think beyond the same boundaries that Doelfs's account reaffirmed because they had realized that the borderland in which they lived was slated for

[1] Michael Doelfs, "Erst beim Wein sprang der Funke über," *Badische Zeitung*, 26 January 1977; see also: "Wie gefährlich können Kernkraftwerke sein?" *Badische Zeitung*, 3 May 1971.

"nuclearization" by government planners in each of the three countries it included.[2]

Though he overlooked its transnational scope, Doelfs was correct to note the centrality of wine to the emergence of a powerful anti-nuclear movement along the Upper Rhine. The specifics of nuclear energy production were unknown to most Europeans in 1970. But people who lived along the Upper Rhine – particularly on Southern Baden's Kaiserstuhl, a striking outcropping of volcanic rock considered a "unique production area for European wines of the highest quality" – were well versed in the art of viticulture.[3] As one proud craftsman put it, "wine-grapes are a very work-intensive, highly sensitive specialty crop. Many people can earn their livelihoods working vineyards in a relatively small space."[4] Describing the dangers of nuclear power in terms of viticulture – rather than emphasizing the invisible danger of radiation or using the more abstract language of atomic physics – was the key to attracting interest in the topic. This fact is often overlooked in analyses of Rhenish anti-nuclear activism, perhaps because vintners' concerns seem peripheral to fears about radiation voiced by doctors, scientists, and environmentalists.[5]

---

[2] Though, scientifically speaking, the Upper Rhine ends at Basel, where navigation on the river becomes far more difficult, and the stretch of the river between Basel and Lake Constance is known as the High Rhine (and though inhabitants of southern Baden, Alsace, and Northwest Switzerland certainly were aware of, and acknowledged, this distinction), the Kaiseraugst reactor was frequently included in descriptions of anti-nuclear activism in the "Upper Rhine valley." Still, since Kaiseraugst was sixty kilometers upriver from the short fifteen kilometer stretch between Fessenheim and Breisach where both France and Germany planned to build reactors, the Kaiseraugst project and the opposition to it had a less straightforward relationship to the other reactors. This sometimes contradictory relationship will be explored and described throughout the text. On the classification of the Rhine's sections, see: Mark Cioc, *The Rhine: An Eco-Biography, 1815–2000* (Seattle: University of Washington Press, 2006), 23ff.

[3] Interessengemeinschaft der Kaiserstuhl- und Tuniberggemeinden to Das Wirtschaftsministerium Baden-Württemberg, 28 September 1972. St A-EN III. A 842, 1971–1974.

[4] Josef Reinauer, "Der Weinbau am Kaiserstuhl," in Bernd Nössler and Margret de Witt, eds., *Wyhl. Kein Kernkraftwerk in Wyhl und auch sonst nirgends. Betroffene Bürger berichten* (Freiburg: Dreisam Verlag, 1976), 16–19.

[5] The significant role of economic motivations in early anti-nuclear activism has been overlooked, in particular, by New Social Movements theory, which places anti-nuclear activism as part of a "larger whole" of social movements that emerged early in the 1970s focused only on problems of social reproduction. See, for example: Roland Roth and Dieter Rucht, eds., *Neue soziale Bewegungen in der Bundesrepublik Deutschland* (Frankfurt: Campus, 1987). More recent treatments, such as Jens Ivo Engels's important study *Naturpolitik in der Bundesrepublik: Ideenwelt und politische Verhaltensstile in Naturschutz und Umweltbewegung, 1950–1980* (Paderborn: Schöningh, 2006), buck this trend, arguing that seeing value change as a motivation for environmental activism during the 1970s explains little about why environmental concerns developed when they did and makes little sense given the increasing focus on restoring economic growth since the end of the postwar boom in the late 1960s.

Viticultural concerns did not motivate anti-nuclear activism on the Upper Rhine on their own.[6] But they exemplify the means by which pioneering activists made the nebulous threat of nuclear energy more tangible in order to promote anti-nuclear protest, creating an instance of what the historian Michael Foley has referred to as "front porch politics."[7] The importance of this approach for the development of anti-nuclear activism in the region is evident in the movement's slow and unsteady initial growth. The first nuclear debates in Swiss Kaiseraugst, early protests in French Fessenheim, and Bühler's doctors' meeting all failed to foster widespread anti-nuclear sentiment. But a series of grassroots protests that challenged the *Badenwerk*'s plans for a reactor in German Breisach on the basis of viticultural concerns caused the movement to gain wide support – even if they fell far short of derailing the plans for reactor development in the region.

How, then, can the plodding development of Rhenish anti-reactor protest in the late 1960s and early 1970s be reconciled with the widely held notion that environmentalism emerged fully formed in 1970 with the first Earth Day celebrations in the United States and the launch of the United Nations' Man and the Biosphere research program?[8] A closer look at the lives and ideas of pioneering anti-nuclear activists reveals the circularity of chalking environmental activism's emergence up to value change and the sudden development of widespread environmental consciousness.

---

[6] Jens Ivo-Engels notes that only 13 percent of the population of Landkreis Emmendingen was engaged in agriculture. Engels, *Naturpolitik*, 356. This figure is nonetheless significant because it is more than one-and-a-half times the federal rate of 8.4 percent employed in agriculture in 1970. Nevertheless, it is clear that even in a rural area, agriculture was not a personal concern for 100 percent of the population. Statisches Bundesamt, "Arbeitsmarkt" www.destatis.de/DE/ZahlenFakten/Indikatoren/LangeReihen/Arbeitsmarkt/lrerwo13.html (accessed 23 September 2014).

[7] Michael Foley, *Front Porch Politics: The Forgotten Heyday of American Activism in the 1970s and 1980s* (New York: Hill and Wang, 2013).

[8] J. R. McNeill, *Something New Under the Sun: An Environmental History of the Twentieth Century World* (New York: Norton, 2000), 336–339. In his impressive history of the first Earth Day, Adam Rome attributes immense transformative power to the event itself. He emphasizes how Earth Day changed, first and foremost, its organizers because "they often devoted months to their task, and they had to answer question after question as they worked out what kind of event Earth Day would be." This argument helps to explain the way that engagement changed people in the 1970s, but it does not completely depart from the idea that April 1970 marked a sort of environmental awakening. Rome, *The Genius of Earth Day: How a 1970 Teach-in Unexpectedly Made the First Green Generation* (New York: Hill and Wang, 2013), 273. Frank Uekötter has challenged this idea in his history of German environmentalism. He writes there that, "Depicting the history of environmentalism as a grand awakening makes for a strangely diffuse narrative that is devoid of actors, interests, and turning points. Thus, for anyone reflecting on the underlying causes, it is imperative to treat the rise of environmentalism as an uncertain and perhaps even unlikely turn of events." Uekötter, *The Greenest Nation? A New History of German Environmentalism* (Cambridge, MA: MIT Press, 2014), 101–102.

A well-documented, longstanding respect for nature did motivate some early anti-reactor protesters along the Upper Rhine, particularly in Alsace.[9] But in the early 1970s, the region's most successful organizers portrayed nuclear energy as a threat to the local economy, to public health, and to traditional ways of life – not as an environmental concern. Thus, the emergence of the Rhenish anti-reactor movement shows how citizens developed environmental consciousness through activism, not a sudden, silent shift in values.

International Industry, National Interest, and Local Nuclear Development

Though the first public anti-reactor protests along the Upper Rhine did not take place until the early 1970s, the stage for the nuclear debate was set by the global surge in excitement about nuclear energy production during the 1960s. Thus, global developments influenced plans to "nuclearize" the Upper Rhine, which were often perceived as matters of national interest. This bigger picture also underscores the challenges pioneering opponents of nuclear energy faced as they sought to merge their more general concerns about nuclear energy with the specificities of local conditions. From its very beginnings, the struggle over nuclear energy in the Upper Rhine valley was shaped by global developments and national interests even though it was playing out in a rural region on the fringes of three countries.

Approaching the Upper Rhine through its global context reveals how the postwar economic boom motivated demand for the development of nuclear energy production throughout Western Europe well before the 1973 oil shock.[10] Nuclear technology gained support at the height of the

---

[9] In his acclaimed environmental history of the twentieth-century world, *Something New Under the Sun*, J. R. McNeill very clearly shows that "there has never been anything like the twentieth century" in terms of human alteration of the global environment. Yet, he argues, "environmental politics and policies, as such, began only in the 1960s." McNeill, *Something New*, 3 and 349. This idea is echoed in Raymond Dominick's impressive history of German environmentalism, where he describes the long legacies of "preservationism" and "conservationism" that preceded the emergence of the modern "environmental" movement at the beginning of the 1970s. Raymond Dominick, *The Environmental Movement in Germany: Prophets and Pioneers, 1871–1971* (Bloomington: Indiana University Press, 1992), x–xi. I argue here that such preservationists and conservationists were present at the outset of the Rhenish anti-nuclear movement, but that it was in the course of this movement itself that the oft-touted environmentalists of the 1970s emerged.

[10] That the oil shock drastically changed the way that France and Germany thought about energy policy, as Sandra Tauer has clearly shown in her impressive study *Störfall für die gute Nachbarschaft? Deutsche und Franzosen auf der Suche nach einer gemeinsamen Energiepolitik (1973–1980)* (Göttingen: Vandenhoeck & Ruprecht, 2012), does not preclude an earlier infatuation with nuclear energy.

boom because it seemed well-matched to the era's soaring economic growth rates, not because affordable energy sources were lacking. In fact, Middle Eastern oil was cheap and readily available. But, as US Atomic Energy Commission Chairman Lewis Strauss famously pronounced in 1954, nuclear energy would fuel industrial production at a cost "too cheap to meter."[11] In an era of big ideas and mega-projects, nuclear energy was perceived as the biggest, most complex, and therefore most prestigious, of all. By the end of the 1960s, a global building boom evidenced this excitement, which was dampened neither by consistently low oil prices, nor the controversial relationship between the "peaceful" use of atomic fission and nuclear weapons tests.[12] In the United States alone, fifty-eight reactors were ordered in 1966 and 1967.[13] The rural Upper Rhine valley became a dreamland for nuclear engineers because the river, which discharged 1,100 cubic meters of water per second near Basel, was one of Western Europe's most significant sources of cooling water.[14] Moreover, the fast-flowing river's location along the boundaries of Switzerland, France, and West Germany, had established it as an ideal dumping ground for dangerous effluents. When officials in all three countries targeted the region for nuclear development, they instigated a three-way race for the Rhine's precious cooling water that was a microcosm of international nuclear development and a focal point for national energy strategies.[15]

On the contrary, it helps us to understand how European governments' interest in nuclear energy before 1973 was not so much a matter of meeting immediate energy needs as it was a means of building national prestige and proving technological prowess. N.J.D. Lucas, in fact, argues that the Electricité de France began promoting nuclear energy during the late 1960s as a means of self-preservation. Lucas, *Energy in France* (London: Europa Publications, 1979), 140–141.

[11] The phrase was coined by Lewis Strauss, Chairman of the US AEC during a 1954 speech. Although he actually said it in reference to the prospects for hydrogen fusion, the phrase "too cheap to meter" has come to be associated with traditional fission-based nuclear energy production. Richard Pfau, *No Sacrifice Too Great: The Life of Lewis L. Strauss* (Charlottesville: University of Virginia Press, 1984), 187.

[12] Though studies by Ernest Sternglass and then by John Gofman and Arthur Tamplin had linked Nevada nuclear tests to increased infant mortalities as early as the 1950s (and though Gofman and Tamplin later conducted another study showing that reactors would lead to further deaths), this research was hardly a hot conversation topic. Foley, *Front Porch Politics*, 122.

[13] Patrick Kupper, *Atomenergie und gespaltene Gesellschaft: Die Geschichte des gescheiterten Projektes Kernkraftwerk Kaiseraugst* (Zürich: Chronos, 2003), 71. Two years later, the US Atomic Energy Commission reported that twenty-five megawatts of nuclear capacity had been ordered for each and every currently operating megawatt. See: Steve Cohn, *Too Cheap to Meter: An Economic and Philosophical Analysis of the Nuclear Dream* (Albany: State University of New York Press, 1997), 47.

[14] Cioc, *The Rhine*, 31. French planners considered the Rhine one of the few rivers in the country suitable for cooling nuclear reactors. See: Tauer, *Störfall*, 251–252.

[15] "Wettlauf um Atomstrom hat begonnen: Auch Frankreich und Schweiz planen Kernkraftwerke im Baden-Württembergischen Einzugsgebiet," *Rhein-Neckar-Zeitung*, 14 August 1968.

The international connections that underpinned the nuclear industry also served to link plans for nuclear development on the Upper Rhine to the widespread nuclear euphoria of the 1950s and 1960s. Soaring US demand influenced European utilities interested in purchasing "turn-key reactors" from American firms. The SKK consortium, which planned to build and operate a reactor on the Rhine near Kaiseraugst, Switzerland, was told that due to high domestic demand, General Electric was willing to fulfill its order only if SKK enlarged its project from 300 to 600 MW.[16] As GE and Westinghouse cashed in, European firms clamored for experience in building reactors at home in order to win market share abroad. Thus, the boom itself pushed European governments to approve more, bigger reactor projects.[17] Such mega-projects were particularly well suited to rural stretches of the mighty Rhine: remote borderlands where space and cooling water were readily available.[18]

The expense and the scale of the reactor projects proposed during the late 1960s made almost every nuclear plant an international undertaking. Even as Electricité de France (EDF) committed to a 50 percent stake in the Swiss Kaiseraugst reactor, for example, representatives of Swiss utilities firms and the German Badenwerk utility considered purchasing stakes in EDF's planned reactor park at Fessenheim.[19] Such collaborations were not only about financing and insuring a market for the copious amounts of energy the new power stations would generate. West German officials considered cooperation with France the key to creating a "European" reactor line that could compete with Westinghouse and GE.[20] The director of the Swiss consortium building at Kaiseraugst saw the inclusion of EDF as a "trump card" that would get the project off the ground, because EDF's involvement would foster the transfer of French design and engineering expertise into Switzerland.[21] And despite the rhetorical linkage of nuclear

---

[16] Kupper, *Atomenergie*, 72–3.

[17] Joachim Radkau, *Aufstieg und Krise der deutschen Atomwirtschaft, 1945–1975. Verdrängte alternative in der Kerntechnik und der Ursprung der nuklearen Kontroverse* (Reinbek bei Hamburg: Rowohlt, 1983), 210.

[18] Though the government of Baden-Württemberg, for example, pursued reactor projects on other rivers, there were considered "regional" reactors, in contrast to the massive reactor parks that could be built along the mighty Rhine. Wirtschaftsministerium to Staatsministerium, 20 January 1969. HSAS EA 1/924 Bü 1728.

[19] Kupper, *Atomenergie*, 67–70. See also: "Des sociétés suissés participeront pour 30% à la construction de la central de Fessenheim," *L'Alsace*, 12 February 1972, reprinted in *Ionix*, "Special Marche" (7 May 1972), 17.

[20] In a January 1970 letter to French Prime Minister Chaban-Delmas, German Chancellor Willy Brandt pushed for Franco-German cooperation in order to "set a decidedly European accent" on nuclear development. Quoted in Tauer, *Störfall*, 248.

[21] Kupper, *Atomenergie*, 75.

technologies with energy independence, which became especially fierce after the 1973 oil shock, almost all of the uranium that fueled European reactors was mined – and, if need be, enriched – overseas.[22] Internationally financed fast-breeder reactors and reprocessing facilities were conceived as a means of minimizing the need to import uranium.[23]

Despite the international nature of reactor construction and fuel processing, competing national interests wrinkled nuclear cooperation. In addition to providing energy, the mastery of civil nuclear technology was a status symbol. More ominously, it was closely linked with the development of nuclear weapons. The French nuclear weapons program justified especially close central government control of the state-run EDF utility's plans for the development of nuclear energy as part of what the historian Gabrielle Hecht has termed the postwar struggle to restore the "radiance of France."[24] Regardless of Konrad Adenauer's 1955 nonnuclear pledge, West German officials, too, saw in the development and mastery of nuclear reactor technology a means to prove the Federal Republic's mettle. Bellicose politicians like Franz-Josef Strauß, who served as the FRG's first Minister for Atomic Affairs, even continued to prioritize the development of reactors as tools to produce the plutonium needed to eventually create a nuclear bomb.[25] These sorts of motivations help to explain why, well before the 1973 oil shock allowed for arguments promoting nuclearization as an economic necessity in a time of crisis, nuclear energy was a hotly pursued technology.

While economic growth in France and Germany during the boom years benefited from cheap oil, the race to nuclearize the Upper Rhine was initiated by Swiss utilities firms, which were desperate to supplement the country's limited hydropower resources. Already by the summer of 1966, they had devised plans for no fewer than six reactor parks along the High Rhine and its major tributary, the Aar.[26] The concerned Swiss government

---

[22] On the basis of documents from the German and French foreign ministries, Sandra Tauer shows the geopolitical calculations inherent in plans for national reactor development and European enrichment and reprocessing facilities. Tauer, *Störfall*, 43ff.

[23] Kupper, *Atomenergie*, 72.

[24] Gabrielle Hecht, *The Radiance of France: Nuclear Power and National Identity after World War II* (Cambridge, MA: MIT Press, 1998).

[25] The pledge was a precondition for West German accession to NATO in 1955. Mark Cioc, *Pax Atomica: The Nuclear Defense Debate in West Germany during the Adenauer Era* (New York: Columbia University Press, 1988), xix. On officials' reasons for pursuing nuclear technology, see Radkau, *Aufstieg und Krise*, 188–194. The Federal Republic's lack of a nuclear weapons program caused German officials to emphasize fuel reprocessing as a means of showing German nuclear expertise. Radkau, *Aufstieg und Krise*, 294.

[26] Marc Landry has shown that although construction of hydropower capacity in Switzerland reached its height between 1955 and 1970, the tremendous new amounts of energy required by the postwar boom made other energy sources necessary to Swiss planners. Marc Landry, "Europe's Battery:

organized a commission chaired by Friedrich Baldinger of the Federal Office for Water Protection to study and report on the effects that such intensive nuclear development might have on Swiss waterways.[27] The steam that nuclear reactors produced in quantities far greater than their turbines could turn into electricity was the Baldinger Commission's primary focus. Cooling down excess steam was essential to maintaining safe operations. Typically, cooling water was used to condense the steam, which was then returned – heated – to the river from which it had been drawn.[28] By calling for strict limitations on riverine "thermal pollution," the Baldinger report ratcheted up competition amongst Swiss utilities firms, which were now forced to jockey for limited cooling water capacity.

The report stoked tensions between Swiss and German authorities, too.[29] Government officials in Baden-Württemberg, the FRG's large southwest state, were concerned by the late 1960s that they lagged well behind their Swiss neighbor in the race to exploit the Rhine.[30] Thus, Ministerial Director Herbert Hochstetter began a January 1968 statement about the importance of pursuing nuclear development by reminding the state parliament's Committee for Planning, Land Use, and Housing that, "Baden-Württemberg has long suffered on account of its distance from the coalfields." In order to insure a brighter energy future, he explained, "The Ministry of Economics will, therefore, do everything to insure that the two large utilities companies in our state create a joint commission to consider where on the High Rhine and Upper Rhine reactors could be sited."[31]

The Making of the Alpine Energy Landscape, 1870–1955" (PhD Dissertation, Georgetown, 2013), 219. Swiss village councils' direct democratic control over zoning and licensing on their territory made it all but impossible for utilities to build oil and coal plants. As a result, Swiss utilities gravitated quickly towards nuclear energy, which they were careful to portray as a means of avoiding hazardous sulfur dioxide and fluoride emissions. Kupper, *Atomenergie*, 37, 64, 65.

[27] Ibid., 85.

[28] This problem was common to fossil fuel-fired power plants as well as nuclear reactors; but the reactors of the 1960s used the steam they had generated to drive their turbines 40–50 percent less efficiently than fossil fuel-fired plants. J. Samuel Walker, "Nuclear Power and the Environment: The Atomic Energy Commission and Thermal Pollution, 1965–1971," *Technology and Culture* 30, no. 4 (October 1989), 971. For more on the sorts of reactor cooling systems used in the 1970s, see Bonnie Osif, Anthony Baratta, and Thomas Conkling, *TMI 25 Years Later: The Three Mile Island Nuclear Power Plant Accident and Its Impact* (University Park: Pennsylvania State University Press, 2004), 7–11.

[29] Kupper, *Atomenergie*, 86–87.

[30] On the state energy plan, see: "Stuttgart bringt licht in Energieschatten: Landesgutachten schafft Grundlage für die Planungen," *Handelsblatt* 139 (23 July 1968). In 1968, the economics ministry's clippings file was already bulging with articles on the imminent scarcity of Rhine cooling water. HSAS EA 1 / 107 Bü 743.

[31] 4. LT von Ba-Wu. Auschuss für Landesplanung, Raumordnung und Wohnungswesen. 33. Sitzung. Monday, 8 January 1968. Min. Dr. Hochstetter. Building reactors along the Upper Rhine seemed particularly practical after the discovery of the Federal Republic's most significant uranium reserves

Hochstetter's ministry had to push hard for a search for sites on the Rhine because the executives of the state's two quasi-public utilities firms were hesitant to build reactors in a rural region so far from Baden-Württemberg's industrial core around Stuttgart.[32] In the end, it was due primarily to the influence of the state's Premier and its Minister of Economics, who served respectively as chair and vice chair on the board of the Badenwerk utility, that the firm's director finally agreed to move ahead with site explorations that he had originally intended to put off until the 1980s.[33]

Baden-Württemberg officials felt an imperative to move ahead quickly with nuclear development on the Upper Rhine not only because of the extensive plans of Swiss utilities, but also on account of the directives of Paris, which closely controlled all aspects of nuclear development in France. In December 1967, the Interministerial Council on Energy Matters selected the Alsatian village of Fessenheim, less than sixty kilometers downriver from Kaiseraugst, as a site for two new 750 MW gas-graphite reactors.[34] In 1970, the EDF formally announced the Fessenheim project, which had by then been upscaled to comprise two 925 MW pressurized water reactors.[35] A month later, the utility proudly announced plans to install a reactor every thirty kilometers along the Rhine in Alsace; a statement that implied it would build four more reactors in the region.[36]

The Rhine's obvious inability to provide enough cooling water for the six proposed Swiss nuclear parks, five French power stations, and the still inchoate plans of Baden-Württemberg's quasi-public utilities to build two

in the nearby Black Forest village of Menzenschwand. Radkau, *Aufstieg und Krise*, 170. See also: Armin Simon, *Der Streit um das Schwarzwald-Uran: Die Auseinandersetzung um den Uranbergbau in Menzenschwand im Südschwarzwald, 1960–1991* (Bremgarten: Donzelli-Kluckert, 2003).

[32] Vorstand Badenwerk Aktiengesellschaft, "Gesichtspunkte für und gegen einen Standort zur Errichtung eines Kernkraftwerkes am Hochrhein," 6 May 1969. See also: Badenwerk Vorstand to Minister of Economics Schwarz, 16 February 1970. HSAS EA 1/924 Bü 1728.

[33] The Ministry of Economics constantly sugar-coated the statements of the Badenwerk in its communications with other Ministries in order to make an exploration of the Rhine for reactor sites sound imminent. See, for example: Wirtschaftsminister Schwarz to Staatsministerium, 25 February 1970. HSAS EA 1/924 Bü 1728. State officials were also far more eager to pursue nuclear development on the Upper Rhine than their federal counterparts. In a response to a question from a Bundestag Member from Southern Baden, Federal Minister for Research, Gerhard Stoltenberg, said there were no plans to develop a reactor on the German side of the Upper Rhine in 1967. Tauer, *Störfall*, 247.

[34] Thierry Jund, *Le nucléaire contre l'Alsace* (Paris: Syros, 1977), 24.

[35] The change was linked to the government's decision to purchase American pressurized water reactors rather than pursuing its own French gas graphite reactor. Tauer, *Störfall*, 49. See also: Lucas, *Energy in France*, 146; and Jund, *Le nucléaire*, 24.

[36] Jund, *Le nucléaire*, 25. Sandra Tauer has found that by 1974 the four additional sites (Marckolsheim, Gerstheim, Sundhausen, and Lauterbourg) had been selected and that EDF was planning to proceed as quickly as possible with reactor construction at each of them. By 1976 at the latest the sites had been made known to the West German government. Tauer, *Störfall*, 260.

or more reactors of their own brought these nuclear projects into direct competition with one another. German and Swiss planners met several times during the late 1960s, in a failed effort to craft an agreement that would allot each country a share of the Rhine's cooling water.[37] Such negotiations were even more difficult between Germany and France, since the resources of the Rhine itself had been hotly contested in the three wars those countries had fought since 1870. In the aftermath of both of the World Wars, in fact, the French government had moved quickly to divert significant portions of the Rhine into a "Grand Canal d'Alsace" (known as the Rhine Lateral Canal in English) that powered a series of hydroelectric plants.[38]

The three countries' competing nuclearization projects could, perhaps, be considered little more than a new chapter in the struggle over the Rhine's limited resources, which had long been linked with separate national identities.[39] Paradoxically, however, the competition also fostered the idea that the Upper Rhine valley comprised a single unit. Government officials' failed negotiations on cooling water rights were premised on the idea that the Rhine could provide only a certain amount of cooling water, regardless of the state in which the reactors using it operated. And despite the competition amongst their governments, utilities firms gladly involved themselves in reactor projects in all three countries. For farsighted industrialists and planners, this collaboration marked the beginning of the transformation of the rural and politically divided Upper Rhine into an economic axis for the European Economic Community (EEC).[40] Individuals concerned about radiation and other potential dangers of nuclear energy, too, saw in international nuclear development a certain form of integration. For them, however, this integration created a sense of collective jeopardy. From either perspective, the combination of conflicting national interests and international economic cooperation in the Upper Rhine valley fostered the idea that the region, though it contained three countries with competing nuclear programs, would have a single fate in the nuclear age.

---

[37] While the Swiss maintained that the Rhine's tributaries were domestic waterways, the Germans wanted water drawn from the Aar to be counted against the Swiss allotment from the Rhine. Kupper, *Atomenergie*, 87.

[38] Cioc, *The Rhine*, 66–67.

[39] On the particular role of the Rhine in the German national imaginary, see: Thomas Lekan, *Imagining the Nation in Nature: Landscape Preservation and German Identity, 1885–1945* (Cambridge, MA: Harvard University Press, 2004), especially pp. 24–30.

[40] "Meinungen zur Landespolitik," *Staatsanzeiger für Baden-Württemberg* 21, no. 76 (23 September 1972).

Caught Between the Upper and Nether Millstones: "Kitchen Table" Activism Framed by Uninterest and Abstraction

Though the race to exploit the river's cooling water exercised utilities' executives and obsessed government officials during the late 1960s, it never quite became front page news.[41] Accordingly, plans to nuclearize the Upper Rhine initially caught the attention of individuals who had a pre-existing interest in nuclear matters. Though such concerned citizens were few and far between, the many reactor projects proposed for the short stretch of the Rhine from Kaiseraugst to Strasbourg – and the growing sense that they were interlinked – enabled a small group of pioneering activists in the Rhine valley to find one another. The projects' staggered construction schedule offered these pioneers opportunities to try out and then to refine protest strategies. The trans-local nature of this developing anti-nuclear community differentiated it from groupings of reactor opponents elsewhere in Europe, who had typically focused on a single, immediately local reactor project.[42] Such localized concerns tended to motivate protests focused not on nuclear energy as such, but rather on the potential ramifications of a particular reactor project for a single community.

The numerous reactors planned for the Upper Rhine, however, allowed individuals with a pre-existing interest in nuclear energy to raise more general nuclear concerns, and thus suggested the potential for a larger and more explicitly "anti-nuclear" movement rather than targeted anti-reactor protests. The Salzburg-based World Federation for the Protection of Life (WSL), which had been founded in 1958 by the Austrian forester Günther Schwab, provided the initial link between the reactor opponents along the Upper Rhine. Having joined both the Nazi Party and its Sturmabteilung (SA) in 1930, Schwab was a Nazi "old fighter," and the WSL's anti-nuclear rhetoric was frequently couched in rhetoric that belied its founder's background. Going without nuclear energy, he argued at a WSL congress in 1965 for example, was a prerequisite for the development and survival of "a biological elite of the human species."[43] Though Schwab's reasoning revealed that his ideology had changed little after 1945, the WSL influenced and brought together concerned inhabitants of the Upper Rhine valley because it was one

---

[41] See the articles on this subject in the Economics' Ministry's "Energiewirtschaft" clippings file. HSAS EA 1 / 107 Bü 743.

[42] Radkau, *Aufstieg und Krise*, 439ff.

[43] Peter Bierl, "Lebensschutz und Rassenhygiene: Zu den ideologischen Grundlagen des Weltbundes zum Schutz des Lebens (WSL)" [unpublished manuscript, dated 1 August 2011].

of the only organizations openly critical of nuclear energy in German-speaking Central Europe.

Schwab's criticisms of nuclear energy posed difficulties for pioneering activists not only because of his motivations, but also because he emphasized the idea that radiation was an invisible, sinister killer. In his well-known 1958 novel *Der Tanz mit dem Teufel*, for example, the devil gloats that nuclear technology will destroy humanity and ruin the earth because "drops of water containing only a small amount of radioactive isotopes cause seemingly harmless burns that later develop into skin cancer." Though they served the devil's sinister purposes well, it was difficult to raise widespread consciousness of dangers posed by invisible isotopes and "seemingly harmless burns." The WSL's monthly publication *Der Stille Weg*, which linked together far-flung anti-nuclear activists, echoed Schwab's approach to the nuclear topic, drawing on völkisch sentiments and emphasizing the nebulous threat of radiation. It called the protection of nature a "cultural duty," for example, regularly featured articles advocating eugenics, and reported on a lawsuit brought against the Gundremmingen reactor in Bavaria because of its potential to leak Krypton-98.[44] Given their primary source of information, pioneering anti-nuclear activists along the Upper Rhine struggled to make their concerns about the opaque subject of nuclear energy production understandable, not to mention palatable, to neighbors, friends, and colleagues. They found themselves caught between the abstraction of their own nuclear concerns and the uninterest of their neighbors. The steady stream of individual reactor projects planned for the Upper Rhine, which offered repeated opportunities for activists to apply general concerns to their specific situation and thus created new openings for discussions with neighbors, proved a saving grace for pioneering activists who were hard-pressed to convince their neighbors of their nuclear concerns' severity.

The Swiss village of Kaiseraugst, where the Motor-Columbus Utilities Company made public its intention to build and operate a reactor in March 1966, was the first place in the Upper Rhine valley where citizens were confronted with a concrete reactor project. In one sense, Kaiseraugst was an unlikely site for the region's first reactor, because its inhabitants had torpedoed Motor-Columbus's plans to site a coal or oil-fired plant in their village barely two years earlier.[45] Yet, when utilities executives returned to announce their plans for a nuclear reactor, an initial public hearing was

---

[44] Arne Boyer, "Er Kämpft gegen ein Atomkraftwerk," *Der Stille Weg* 18, no. 1–2 (Frühling 1966), 27.
[45] The town's residents voted 171 to 24 against the proposed power plant. Kupper, *Atomenergie*, 40.

surprisingly cordial. While the pollutants emitted by traditional thermal power plants had become a major concern in Northwest Switzerland due to the damage emissions from an Alusuisse plant had wreaked on nearby agricultural land and forests, well-prepared utilities spokesmen portrayed nuclear energy as clean and safe. They handily dismissed the concerns of the village's main dissenter, Nora Casty, who quoted one of Schwab's essays in her effort to warn her neighbors against the proposal.[46]

The local population's lack of concern about the sorts of dangers Casty linked with nuclear technology was obvious in the aftermath of a February 1967 public forum on the subject. Villagers invited Schwab and the Freiburg nuclear physicist Walther Herbst, whose research on the dangers of radiation was discussed in *Der Stille Weg*, to present anti-nuclear arguments in a debate with the reactor's supporters.[47] Schwab, it turned out, could not present his anti-nuclear arguments any more effectively in person than Casty already had. Perhaps more surprisingly even Herbst, whose identification of a radioactive cloud over the FRG in 1951 had helped motivate the founding of the West German Commission for Radiation Protection, had little effect on the villagers.[48] Instead, they voted overwhelmingly to approve the construction of a reactor the following year.[49] The Kaiseraugst project had overcome its initial local opposition rather easily, but opponents of nuclear energy in the Upper Rhine valley did not have to wait long for a new opportunity to focus their nuclear concerns on a particular reactor project. In December 1967, President Charles de Gaulle's Interministerial Council on Energy Matters selected the Alsatian village of Fessenheim as the region's second reactor site; less than three years later, EDF made the plans for Fessenheim public.

Activists in Alsace were aware of the struggles Casty had faced in Kaiseraugst, and they took a decidedly different tack in their opposition to the Fessenheim project, making use of Alsace's recent history in crafting their arguments against the reactor. The three wars fought over Alsace in the last century shaped many Alsatians' outlook after 1945. Having grown up in a war-torn region, and having had fathers, uncles, brothers, and grandfathers die for both Germany and France in the two World Wars, Alsatians were particularly likely to see war as futile and pointless.[50]

---

[46] Ibid., 62 and 112.
[47] "Sektion Österreich. Jahreshauptversammlung," *Der Stille Weg* 17, no. 7–8 (Winter 1965), 18.
[48] "Die Herbst-Wolke," *Der Spiegel* (31 October 1956): 24–25.
[49] The vote was 97–14. Kupper, *Atomenergie*, 94.
[50] See, for example: Jean-Jacques Rettig, "Der Regionalismus der 1970er Jahre. Der Oberrhein: weithinstrahlender Leuchtturm der Ökologiebewegung," (Lviv: 22 May 2001). Translated by Walter Mossmann; see also: Esther Peter-Davis, interview with the author, Strasbourg, 8 May 2014.

Moreover, Alsatians' conflicted relationship with the French government in Paris – which was perceived as both a protector from German brutality and a harsh colonial overlord – fostered local campaigns to protect Alsace from unchecked development.[51]

Alsace's recent history was a useful tool for the handful of dedicated activists who spread concerns about the Fessenheim reactor throughout the region. Esther Peter-Davis, one of the reactor's first opponents, had herself become a lifelong peace activist after she survived the allied bombing of Strasbourg as a girl. She also happened to be related to the mayor of Fessenheim, who excitedly told her about the project before a public announcement was made. The news brought to mind the warning about nuclear energy's dangers that she had heard from Frederic Joliot-Curie, the former director of France's Commission for Atomic Energy (CEA), during a chance encounter at the 1950 People's World Convention in Geneva.[52] Living near the Swiss border, and aware of the Kaiseraugst reactor's smooth approval process, Peter-Davis looked for ways to elucidate her longstanding nuclear concerns and to build a protest movement in the region. Rather than reaching across the Rhine to Schwab's WSL, Peter-Davis looked across the Atlantic. Her in-laws, whom she visited frequently in New York City, introduced her to the UC Berkeley molecular biologist and prominent opponent of nuclear energy, John Gofman.[53] On the basis of critical scientific research, journalistic reports, and even personal experiences garnered during visits to US reactor sites, Peter-Davis prepared a sixty-page pamphlet on the nuclear threat, which she entitled *Fessenheim vie ou mort de l'Alsace.* Her pamphlet offered few editorial comments, but it was bursting with translated US press reports, statements from critical nuclear scientists like Gofman, and other hard-to-find information on the nuclear threat.

Her engagement in the peace movement enabled Peter-Davis to distribute her research, too. In May 1970, she attended a meeting of the French, Belgian and Swiss sections of the International Fellowship of Reconciliation (IFOR) at Mulhouse to speak about the threat posed by the planned Fessenheim reactor.[54] There, she met Jean-Jacques Rettig,

---

[51] Jean, *Elsass, Kolonie in Europa* (Berlin: K. Wagenbach, 1976).

[52] Peter-Davis, interview. Joliot-Curie was famously dismissed from his post for saying that he would not "give a scrap of [his] science to make war against the Soviet Union." M. Goldsmith, *Frederic Joliot-Curie: A Biography* (London: Lawrence and Wishart, 1976), 163. See also: Hecht, *Radiance*, 60–61.

[53] The women were E. Peter-Davis, A. Albrecht, and F. Bucher. *Fessenheim vie ou mort de l'Alsace* (Mulhouse-Riedelsheim: Schmitt-Lucos, 1970), 1. See also Jean-Jacques Rettig, interview with the author, Freiburg, 8 March 2010.

[54] Ester Davies [sic], "L'Environnement Nucleaire de Mulhouse," *Cahiers de la Reconciliation* (Special issue: Deshonorer L'Argent de la violence et la domination de l'argent") no. 6/7 (June–July, 1970), 55.

a teacher of German from the nearby village of Saales. Like Peter-Davis, he had come to the IFOR conference to share deeply held concerns about the rumored Fessenheim reactor project. Rettig's concerns about Fessenheim stemmed from his background in nature protection. He had long been involved in the Federated Regional Association for the Protection of Nature (AFRPN), which was founded already in 1965 as one of France's first regional environmental organizations.[55] Rettig's interest in nature protection extended well beyond the boundaries of Alsace. Through his work translating correspondence between German-speaking WSL chapters and French conservationist groups, Rettig had familiarized himself with the former group's concerns about nuclear energy.[56]

When plans for the Fessenheim reactor were finally formally announced in July 1970, activists like Rettig and Peter-Davis were well prepared to respond. On 11 August, together with three neighbors, Rettig sent an open letter to the Minister of Industrial and Scientific Development protesting the plans for the reactor.[57] The group established itself as the Committee to Protect Fessenheim and the Rhine Valley (CSFR) and worked with Peter-Davis to republish her pamphlet.[58] With his wife Inge, Jean-Jacques Rettig distributed the publication to the mayors of each of the more than 900 towns and villages in Alsace.[59] On the basis of the copious scientific research that comprised Peter-Davis's brochure, this impressive canvassing effort diverged from the sorts of völkisch concerns about radiation-poisoning emphasized by the WSL and raised the first significant concerns about nuclear energy along the French bank of the Rhine. Peter-Davis and the Rettig's hard work, however, failed to create an immediate groundswell of opposition to the Fessenheim project. Particularly in Fessenheim itself, where the local government promised villagers significant benefits from the project, dissent was muted.

---

[55] On AFRPN, which was founded in 1965 and became Alsace Nature in 1991, see: Jean-Luc Bennahmias and Agnès Roche, *Des verts de toutes les couleurs* (Paris: Albin Michel, 1992), 33–34; and: Alsace Nature, "30 ans pour la protection de la nature en Alsace," Supplement to *Alsace Nature Infos* 22 (Autumn 1995).

[56] Jean-Jacques Rettig, Walter Mossmann, and Marie-Reine Haug, interview with the author, Freiburg, 8 March 2010.

[57] "Qu'est-ce que le C.S.F.R.?" *Ionix* 1 (October 1971): 1.

[58] Ibid.; see also: Nelkin and Pollak, *The Atom Besieged: Extraparliamentary Dissent in France and West Germany* (Cambridge, MA: MIT Press, 1981), 58. Peter-Davis published the first edition in June 1970 using donated paper, donated ink, and a volunteer printer. Peter-Davis, interview. See also: Tauer, *Störfall*, 256.

[59] Rettig, Mossmann and Haug, interview.

Figure 1.1 Jean-Jacques Rettig on the occupied site in Marckolsheim,
16 November 1974. © Meinrad Schwörer.

The first public protest against reactors in the Upper Rhine valley,
a CSFR-organized march against the Fessenheim reactor that took place
in April 1971, exemplified the disconnect between the few dedicated
activists' concerns about the nuclear threat and local interests. On the
one hand, the march failed to attract the majority of the local population to
the movement or to move public opinion. Three members of Lanza del
Vasto's Community of the Ark helped the CSFR organize the march, and

their strict adherence to Gandhian principles of nonviolence dominated the protest. A postcard inviting Alsatians to participate described the action as a "silent ceremony" against "insidious radioactive pollution."[60] Participants were required to sign a pledge of nonviolence and reminded to remain silent at all times.[61] The peculiar procession's passage through the center of Fessenheim provided the town's inhabitants with little means to engage with the movement and little ammunition to question EDF's guarantee that the plant would provide new jobs and be perfectly safe.[62] Nor did the march block the construction of the Fessenheim reactor, which began on schedule the following September.[63]

Though its effects in Fessenheim itself were muted, the march proved that Rettig and Peter-Davis's research and canvassing had not fallen on deaf ears. More than 1,000 demonstrators participated, including some 150 who came by bus and carpool from Freiburg, as well as small groups of activists from Nancy, Paris, Grenoble, Toulouse, Great Britain, and the United States, making the Fessenheim march the largest anti-reactor protest yet to occur in Western Europe.[64] The Fessenheim march and the public debates that had accompanied the licensing process in Kaiseraugst, in other words, were clear evidence that nuclear energy was slowly becoming a subject of public interest along the Upper Rhine. Writing for the alternative *Charlie-Hebdo*, Pierre Fournier went so far as to call the march "all joking aside, an event that is no more than the storming of the Bastille an event for itself, it is the start of great things."[65]

Engelhard Bühler's doctor's meeting, which the journalist Michael Doelfs remembered as an isolated failure, takes on a different meaning in light of the simultaneous developments in Alsace and Northwest Switzerland. Not only were the happenings across the Rhine important precedents for Bühler's meeting, they also helped to explain why it had few

---

[60] Comité pour sauvegarde de Fessenheim et de la Plaine du Rhin, "Invitation: 12 Avril, Ceremonie Silencieuse, Fessenheim – 68." ASB "Wyhl—Die Anfänge," 18413.

[61] Rettig, Mossmann, and Haug, interview.

[62] Jean de Barry, interview with the author, Strasbourg, 3 March 2010. The persistence of this view amongst the people of Fessenheim further supports the idea that spreading anti-nuclear knowledge played a key part in building anti-reactor sentiment and recruiting local people to the anti-nuclear cause. Unlike the Badensian side of the Rhine, where an entire year of information sessions preceded the first public protests, the Fessenheim march was organized with little such preparation.

[63] Wolfgang Hertle, "Skizze der französischen Ökologiebewegung," *Gewaltfreie Aktion* 26/27 (4th Quarter 1975/1st Quarter 1976): 47.

[64] Ibid.; see also: Press release of the Freiburger BI gegen Kernenergieanlagen in response to attack against the occupiers at Heiteren (July 1977). AGG E.04/81; see also: Pierre Fournier, "Une bonne journée au grand air," *Charlie-Hebdo*; 26 April 1971.

[65] Fournier, "Une bonne journée."

tangible results. Bühler, who had conducted racial science research at the Kaiser-Wilhelm-Institut in Rome during the Second World War, was chiefly concerned about the threat he believed nuclear radiation posed to the German genetic inheritance.[66] His approach to questions of nuclear energy was even more deeply stained by its links with Nazism than was Schwab's. In a repeat of his performance in the Kaiseraugst debate four years earlier, the Freiburg nuclear physicist Walther Herbst also proved unable to motivate to resistance the rural doctors whom Bühler had called together with scientific arguments. That such perspectives failed to attract many West Germans – let alone French or Swiss – to anti-nuclear activism in the late 1960s and early 1970s is hardly surprising. Instead, Bühler's situation exemplified the problems other early reactor opponents faced.

The concerns about genetics and the specialized scientific findings at the center of early anti-nuclear efforts on the Upper Rhine were disconnected from the everyday lives and interests of the vast majority of the region's inhabitants. This made them unwieldy tools for activists interested in recruiting their neighbors to the anti-reactor struggle. If the collapse of the anti-nuclear weapons movement in West Germany during the 1950s can be attributed, at least in part, to the fact that "nuclear annihilation was an abstract threat to Germans"[67] – even amidst NATO simulations which suggested that a nuclear exchange between the superpowers would obliterate the Federal Republic – it seems reasonable to assume that the destructive potential of "peaceful" reactors was detached from public consciousness two decades later.[68]

All Politics Is Local: From "Abstract Peril" to "Front Porch Politics"[69]

The divide between nuclear matters and everyday life trapped anti-nuclear pioneers around what Lawrence Goodwyn referred to as the "kitchen table" of social activism, a "domestic setting" where would-be activists

---

[66] Engelhard Bühler to Reichsführer SS, 4 August 1939. Bundesarchiv Berlin NS/21/1138. For more information on Bühler's research during the Third Reich, see Benno Müller-Hill's interview with Bühler in Benno Müller-Hill, *Tödliche Wissenschaft. Die Aussonderung von Juden, Zigeunern, und Geisteskranken, 1933–1945* (Reinbek bei Hamburg: Rowohlt, 1993), 149–151.

[67] Cioc, *Pax Atomica*, 140.

[68] On the NATO exercises, see Holger Nehring, *The Politics of Security: British and West German Protest Movements and the Early Cold War, 1945–1970* (Oxford: Oxford University Press), 54.

[69] Michael Foley uses the term "front porch politics" to describe the struggles of local people confronted with real evidence of pollution such as occurred in Love Canal, NY. Foley, *Front Porch Politics*, 137ff.

"think together, drink coffee or wine or some other national drink, argue, interpret power, and pull their chairs closer together for comfort in their isolation."[70] Though early opponents of nuclear energy claimed that, "the goal of our work is to inform a broader social stratum, one which can be assumed to have little more than an elementary knowledge of these matters,"[71] achieving this far-reaching goal proved difficult. It was one thing to spread information to like-minded friends or a few familiar neighbors, or even to hold a modest protest march. It was quite another, however, to turn the majority of the region's population against nuclear energy. "To get out of the kitchen and connect with the larger society," Goodwyn asserted, has long been the "most maddening challenge" facing "private insurgents."[72] For Rhenish activists, articulating nuclear concerns in a more concrete and more palatable way was the key to making this connection.

Amidst activists' struggles to inform a broader social stratum, the competitive nature of nuclear development along the Upper Rhine helped bridge the divide between generalizable nuclear concerns and the specific situation in the valley. The release of the Baldinger Commission's Report in 1968, which had ignited the intergovernmental competition for the Rhine's cooling water, gave credence to the idea that the Rhine was seriously threatened by "thermal pollution." It formed the basis for a conversation about nuclear energy that was very different from the discussions of invisible radiation found in *Der stille Weg*. As a result of the Baldinger report, fishermen worried about their catch while shipping firms raised concerns that a warmer Rhine would generate more fog and impair riverine traffic.[73] Even people whose economic interests were not directly linked to the river saw the impending "biological death" of the region's defining physical feature as a reason to stop and think about the consequences of nuclear development.[74] Concern for the Rhine was longstanding, and linked with the region's war-torn past. Even in the immediate postwar period, as Badensians and Alsatians struggled to rebuild their shattered communities, plans to divert the river into the Rhine Lateral Canal had raised the hackles of the river's Badensian neighbors, particularly local fishermen.

---

[70] Lawrence Goodwyn, *Breaking the Barrier: The Rise of Solidarity in Poland* (Oxford: Oxford University Press, 1990), 110.
[71] Dr. B. Kromayer Rektor to Hans-Helmuth Wüstenhagen, 17 May 1972. GLA S Umweltschutz 152.
[72] Goodwyn, *Breaking the Barrier*, 110.
[73] Badenwerk to Wasser und Schifffahrtsdirektion Freiburg, 17 August 1972. SAFR, P 680/21. Balthasar Ehret, "Fischerei am Oberrhein," in *Wyhl* (see note 4), 22–24.
[74] Bundesverband Bürgerinitiativen Umweltschutz, "Kernenergie und Umwelt," 4.

In the 1970s, fishermen and shippers' concerns about the ill-effects of cooling water discharge could be solved with technology. Engineers proposed cooling towers as a means of dissipating excess heat without harming Father Rhine.[75] Already in December 1971, just a few months after construction had begun on the region's first reactor at Fessenheim, the chairman of the German Commission for the Prevention of Pollution in the Rhine called for all reactors built along the river to be equipped with cooling towers.[76] Since even cooling towers might create fog over the river, however, one utility company informed the Freiburg Water and Shipping Office that cooling towers would have to be between 110 and 160 meters high so as not to hinder barge traffic.[77] The problem of discharging excess heat, and the increasingly grandiose solutions to it envisioned by engineers, became the touchstone of the nuclear debate along the Upper Rhine.

It was on account of the back-and-forth over heat dissipation, in fact, that a young electrician named Dieter Berstecher was able to make the connection between nuclear energy and local viticulture that Doelfs emphasized in his retrospective newspaper article. Berstecher knew very little about nuclear power when he learned of plans for the Breisach reactor, which was to be built just a few kilometers from the renowned vineyards of South Baden's Kaiserstuhl. His professional background piqued his interest in the project, however. After reading a pamphlet entitled *Atom Reaktoren für den Frieden – Todesfälle der Zukunft* (Atomic Reactors for Peace – Causes of Death in the Future), his curiosity developed into concern.[78] To make the scientific evidence cited in the pamphlet more relevant to his neighbors, Berstecher creatively applied it to the local context. "If a nuclear power plant or radioactive particles come into connection with wine," he told the village council in his native Burkheim, "then the game will be up here."[79]

The link Berstecher proposed between nuclear radiation and the centerpiece of the local economy enabled activists to connect their isolated kitchen table conversations to "ominous forces" that their neighbors could see "encroaching" on their lives and livelihoods. In essence, linking

[75] Wirtschaftsministerium Baden-Württemberg to Staatliche Weinbauinstitut (20 November 1972). SAFR, G1115/1 Nr. 7.
[76] "Chronik Breisach." ABEBI Göpper Siegfried 95GS3.
[77] Badenwerk to Wasser und Schifffahrtsdirektion Freiburg, 17 August 1972. SAFR P 680 / 21.
[78] David S. Cooper, *Atom Reaktoren für den Frieden – Todesfälle der Zukunft* (Mannheim: Waerland-Verlagsgenossenschaft, n.d.); and: Dieter Berstecher, email message to author, 29 April 2011.
[79] Dieter Berstecher and Günter Sacherer, interview with the author, Oberrotweil, 18 February 2010.

nuclear energy with wine allowed local activists to turn their abstract concerns about radiation into a case of "front porch politics."[80] With the support of the Burkheim village council, whose members his warnings had sufficiently awed, and the help of a few "like-minded friends," Berstecher mass-produced a flyer detailing the threat and dropped it in mailboxes all over the Kaiserstuhl.[81] Vintners and the many others who relied on the viticultural industry for their livelihoods were suddenly full of questions about the Breisach reactor and its potential to affect the region's precious and sensitive crops. Though viticulture was not the foremost personal interest of everyone in the Upper Rhine valley, Breisach's proximity to the Kaiserstuhl's renowned vineyards made that project the focal point of a local anti-reactor movement that quickly expanded beyond activists' kitchen tables and affected the way nuclear energy was discussed throughout the region.

Beginning in the summer of 1971, meeting halls, pubs, and even school auditoriums and gymnasiums in winegrowing villages became key sites in the debate over the nuclearization of the Upper Rhine. Government officials and opponents of nuclear power, as well as political foundations, churches, and community groups, organized information sessions at which they described nuclear reactors' potential to affect the region to anyone who would listen. Unlike the 1967 public forum at Kaiseraugst, where Herbst and Schwab failed to sway public opinion, opponents of nuclear power gained the upper hand in the nuclear debate by late 1971 because they argued convincingly that reactor construction would cripple local agriculture. Hans von Rudloff, a meteorologist at Freiburg's State Weather Office and the author of a 450-page book on European climate trends since the seventeenth century, played a leading part in reframing the nuclear debate.[82] By arguing that steam discharged from reactor cooling towers would create dense fog that would be trapped in the valley and block out its

---

[80] Michael Foley uses the phrase "front porch politics" to describe how American "No Nukes activists" learned that "if a campaign could not make the invisible dangers of nuclear power less abstract, it would be almost impossible to stop the building of a nuclear power plant." He contrasts the abstract nuclear danger with "evidence of pollution in the air, on the ground, and in the water," which he writes, "Americans could see from their front porches." Foley, *Front Porch Politics*, 148 and 150.

[81] Ibid., 5.

[82] "Atomkraftwerk Breisach in der Diskussion," *Freiburger Wochenbericht*, 9 November 1972, 5. "Die Besten Jahre sind vorüber. SPIEGEL-Gespräch mit dem Freiburger Meteorologe Hans von Rudloff über Wetter und Wettervorhersage," *Der Spiegel*, 30 May 1966. Von Rudloff later took a job as the meteorologist at the Bremgarten military airport. See also: Kurt Rudzinski, "Wenn ein Kernkraftwerk schlechtes Wetter macht," *Frankfurter Allgemeine Zeitung*, 5 October 1974.

precious sunlight, he turned the abstract peril of radiation into the concrete threat of damp, dark days.[83]

Local vintners and farmers saw this fog as nothing less than an "existential threat." Ernst Jenne, who raised tobacco in the village of Weisweil, explained that:

> We have here not only the warmest region in Germany, but also the most humid one and we have the most foggy days ... the cooling towers would have the following effect: more fog and thus more fungal diseases, more hail and thus more damage to the tobacco, corn and wheat crops.[84]

Jenne's concerns were far from baseless. A firm that purchased local corn, for example, threatened to stop buying the crop if the reactor were built, since steam discharge would cause an "inferior ripening process and thus an inferior quality."[85] The threat to viticulture was particularly grave. One report expected a 30 percent reduction in light intensity, which would lower the amount of sugar in grapes by ten degrees on the Öchsle scale. A loss of even one degree would have degraded much of the local vintage from "fine wine" status to "table wine," drastically reducing its value.[86] With their livelihoods at stake, "interested vintners and citizens" reached out to professional scientists and university students in order to get additional information.[87] "From day to day," one vintner reported, "more and more negative facts [about nuclear power] came to light." By the end of the year, informal discussions of nuclear energy on the Kaiserstuhl had grown into "proper meetings of more than 100 persons."[88]

Growing anti-reactor sentiment did not stop the reactor's supporters from wading unflinchingly into the quickly expanding nuclear debate. They did their best to convince farmers and vintners that the reactor

---

[83] Steam discharge was quantifiable, as well. One report stated that the cooling towers of a single 1,200 MW nuclear reactor would release an amount of steam equivalent to that emitted by "one tenth the surface area of Lake Constance" into an area with a circumference of only 100 meters. BBU, "Kernenergie und Umwelt," 4.

[84] Ernst Jenne, "Kernkraftwerk – meine Existenzbedrohung!" in *Wyhl* (see note 4), 19–21.

[85] Albert Bär (LC Nungesser, KG) to Siegfried Göpper, 8 June 1974. ABEBI Göpper Siegfried 107GS15.

[86] Norbert J. Becker, "Beiträge zur Standortforschung an Reben <Vitis vinifera L.>: Ergebnisse eine Erhebungsuntersuchung im Rheingau" (PhD Dissertation, Gießen, 1967), quoted in Arbeitskreis Umweltschutz an der Universität Freiburg, "Bedrohung der Landwirtschaft durch das KKW Wyhl" (Freiburg: January 1976), 7.

[87] Ernst Schillinger "Breisach – Der Kampf beginnt," in *Wyhl* (see note 4), 29–33. Although Gerd Auer, a student in Freiburg and native of Emmendingen, did not consider himself particularly familiar with the topic of nuclear energy, he was asked by rural citizens' initiatives to speak on various aspects of it. Gerd Auer, interview with the author, Emmendingen, 22 February 2010.

[88] Schillinger, "Breisach."

posed no threat to local agriculture. Yet government statements did little to allay rural people's fears because they seemed to contradict both the growing wealth of critical meteorological studies and farmers' common sense. At times, government statements even contradicted themselves. While French officials asserted that steam from the Fessenheim reactor would blow eastward into Baden, German officials maintained that steam from the Breisach reactor would be carried westward by the winds and end up in Alsace.[89] The growing number of contradictory reports and rumors circulating on the Kaiserstuhl made the information presented by government officials seem increasingly open to question.

With the veracity of their reports already in doubt, the patronizing manner in which government spokesmen addressed the public further decreased local people's willingness to take seriously government arguments. At one January 1972 hearing, recalled the vintner and poet Ernst Schillinger, a single speaker succeeded in doing "what no silver-tongued spokesperson against these eerie, insane projects had yet achieved."[90] That speaker, Professor Sigel from the Agricultural Meteorology Department at the University of Mainz, explained in a "brash and impertinent manner" that "wine certainly could not be considered a 'sun crop' since the potato requires more sun to flourish than does the grape." The vintners were incensed.[91] The idea that Sigel, "simply because he was a professor . . . had to tell the dumb people where the wind came from, when the sun shines," was too much for vintners to bear.[92] The attempts of the president of the Wine Growers' Association to quiet their "scornful laughter and chorus of whistles" and to chastise the vintners for their "emotional derailment" of the proceedings revealed to them "what they ought to think about such expert blather in the future." And with that, Schillinger concluded, "the majority of the population was mobilized."[93]

Professor Sigel's comments may well have played a decisive part in mobilizing vintners, but Schillinger's description of the event reveals the importance of the months of information-seeking and public meetings that preceded the professor's appearance on the Kaiserstuhl. When it came to their crops, vintners were extremely knowledgeable. After all,

---

[89] Wolfgang Beer, *Lernen im Widerstand. Politisches Lernen und politische Sozialisation in Bürgerinitiativen* (Hamburg: Verlag Association, 1978), 89.
[90] Concerned by the critical meteorological reports, the vintners had flooded the Badensian Winegrowers' Association with complaints and "pushed [the Association] finally to take a position on this issue." These demands resulted in the Winegrowers' Association joining with the state government in order to schedule the January hearing. Schillinger, "Breisach."
[91] Ibid.   [92] Berstecher, interview.   [93] Schillinger, "Breisach."

a single lifetime growing grapes provided more than enough experience to acquaint the average vintner with this delicate crop's need for sunlight. Yet, vintners' knowledge of the local climate stretched back much further, having been passed down from generation to generation.[94] The scientific information about the local climate that vintners had discussed with meteorologists for much of the past year bolstered this practical wisdom and linked it to the reactor project. More importantly, however, it helped them to see that government representatives and their scientific advisors were anything but infallible. As a result, it was much more difficult for government and industry spokesmen to convince farmers and vintners that reactors were harmless. Thus, Sigel's appearance did not change the facts about how the Breisach reactor would affect local viticulture, but rather the very idea that government officials had winegrowers' interests in mind.

With their interests apparently endangered and unprotected, vintners took their first anti-nuclear steps. Rather than mounting an all-out attack on the Breisach project, they appealed for more time so that an informed decision about the reactor and its effects on local agriculture could be made.[95] In letters to state and federal officials, villagers pleaded for further studies of steam discharge. They challenged the Breisach project on a series of specific, technical concerns ranging from the costs of the proposed reactor to the lacking coordination between French and German officials. An August 1972 newspaper report summed up the technical nature of rural concerns, noting that reactor opponents were "not principally against the use of nuclear energy to produce electricity. What they do not want is a technologically second-class solution for the disposal of excess heat."[96] Far from the racial and biological arguments of Schwab and Bühler, or even the scientific evidence shared by Peter-Davis, the arguments that found widespread support on the Kaiserstuhl portrayed nuclear energy as an immediately local matter of "front porch politics." In a way, then, these first anti-nuclear steps may seem to have been taken in the wrong direction. Rather than addressing nuclear energy itself or acting boldly against utilities companies and government planners, activists had pinned their protest campaign to trivial local concerns.

[94] Berstecher, interview.
[95] "Kernkraftwerk im Kreuzfeuer," *Badische Zeitung* [n.d., likely March 1972]. ASB Wyhl—Die Anfänge, 18173.
[96] Werner Gutmann, "Bürger wehren sich gegen Reaktor-Boom am Hochrhein," [unknown newspaper (likely *Badische Neueste Nachrichten*), hand-dated August 1972]. GLA S Umweltschutz 762.

From the Front Porch Across the Rhine, Telegraphing Local Activism

The technical arguments that reactor opponents used to challenge the Breisach reactor made the nuclear debate on the Upper Rhine seem limited and provincial, especially after government officials began to couple their avowals of the project's importance for Baden-Württemberg's energy future with assurances that the reactor would have no effect on the quality of Badensian wine.[97] Such arguments were intended to further trivialize reactor opponents' complaints by implicitly describing them as small-minded and misinformed – both when it came to the state's energy needs and to their own professions. And yet, government officials' statements contained their own brand of provincialism. Though officials considered individual reactors part of a larger whole, that whole was strictly delimited by Baden-Württemberg's political boundaries, regardless of the international cooperation – and competition – that underpinned the nuclear industry. Though their own arguments were often locally focused, however, Rhenish anti-nuclear activists intentionally disregarded the national borders that cleaved their region in three as they sought to convince their neighbors that the Kaiseraugst, Fessenheim, and Breisach projects were closely linked. As a result, the emergent debate over the nuclearization of the Upper Rhine also became a forum for considerations of provincialism and transnationalism.

The university town of Freiburg was a central node in the debate over the Rhenish anti-reactor movement's purported provincialism. Members of the city's educated middle-class, organized by Margot Harloff, recruited their neighbors to the struggles against both the Fessenheim and Breisach projects, which were approximately equidistant from the city center.[98] A single mother and homemaker, Harloff had herself been drawn into the anti-nuclear struggle by an advertisement for a Spring 1971 WSL-sponsored meeting that described the series of reactors proposed for the Upper Rhine as a "pearl necklace." Though she had "no knowledge of reactors and their effects" and claimed not even to know much about pearls, she was well aware that pearl necklaces were "tightly packed." A disturbing mental image of reactors packed like pearls along the Rhine convinced her to attend the meeting and made the nuclear threat real for her.[99] Soon afterwards, she

---

[97] See, for example: "Drehscheibe der Gasversorgung: Wirtschaftsminister Schwarz zerstreut Freiburger gedanken," *Stuttgarter Nachrichten*, 1 February 1972.

[98] Beate de Barry, interview with the author, Strasbourg, 3 March 2010.

[99] Margot Harloff, "Eine 'Perlenkette' von Atomkraftwerken entlang des Rheins!" in *Wyhl* (see note 4), 25.

accepted an invitation from Jean-Jacques Rettig, whom she knew due to a shared interest in Waldorf education, to participate in the April 1971 silent march through Fessenheim.[100] Building on the years of work carried out by the region's pioneering anti-reactor activists, Harloff founded the Freiburg Action Group against Environmental Threats Posed by the Breisach and Fessenheim Reactors (Freiburger Aktionsgemeinschaft gegen Umweltgefährdung durch die AKW Breisach und Fessenheim – Aktionsgemeinschaft) six months later.[101]

The Aktionsgemeinschaft drew Freiburgers into the anti-nuclear struggle by connecting the nuclear debate with the view from city-dwellers' "front porches" – or perhaps their balconies. Its approach was exemplified by a poster that juxtaposed a pair of reactor cooling towers with the spire of Freiburg's beloved Minster.[102] Harloff described the image, which had been drawn perfectly to scale, as depicting the "small and wimpy" Minster wedged in "between those two colossuses."[103] Because the reactors at Breisach and Fessenheim were to be built nearly thirty kilometers from Freiburg, however, their towers would not actually dwarf the Minster. Thus, volunteers in Freiburg mixed the figurative and the technical in order to bring the proposed reactors closer to home for urbanites. The Aktionsgemeinschaft's first major campaign, carried out in the Spring of 1972, aimed at forging a more corporeal connection between the two nearby reactor projects by recruiting Freiburgers to participate in an anti-reactor march from Vogelgruen, an Alsatian village located just across the Rhine from the proposed Breisach reactor site, to Fessenheim.[104]

Despite the march organizers' obvious interest in connecting the French and German reactor projects, their transnational aspirations have been overlooked by scholars, causing the action's resonance to seem muted. The march was difficult to organize from the start. The French authorities, who viewed criticism of nuclear reactor projects as a threat to the force de frappe, sought to prevent the action from even taking place, going so far as to detain some of its key organizers.[105] Moreover, the inhabitants of Fessenheim strongly favored the reactor and refused to join in the march.

---

[100] Rettig, interview.

[101] The group later changed its name to Freiburger Aktionsgemeinschaft gegen Umweltgefährdung durch Atomkraftwerke. Harloff, "Eine 'Perlenkette'," 25.

[102] "Alarm am Oberrhein," *Badische Zeitung*, 25 May 1974.   [103] Harloff, "Eine 'Perlenkette'."

[104] See, for example: Freiburger Aktionsgemeinschaft gegen Umweltgefährdung durch die Atomkraftwerke in Breisach und Fessenheim, "Wir rufen auf zum Marsch nach Fessenheim am 7. Mai 1972." ASB Wyhl – die Anfänge 17587.

[105] Peter-Davis, interview. See also: Tauer, *Störfall*, 257–258.

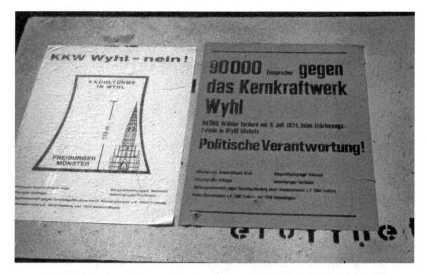

Figure 1.2 Two posters created by local opponents of the Wyhl reactor: Left: A cooling tower planned for the Wyhl reactor is compared to the Freiburg Minster; Right: An advertisement for the July 1974 public hearing on the Wyhl reactor. © Meinrad Schwörer.

The marchers themselves, who came from neighboring villages in Alsace but also from Freiburg and the Kaiserstuhl, could do little to stop a project that had already been underway since Fall 1971.[106] As a result, despite the fact that it attracted more than 10,000 participants, even sympathetic French scholars have attributed little significance to the march. Alain Touraine concluded, for example, that the protest at Fessenheim was both "isolated" and largely irrelevant because it "had no imitators in other regions of France."[107]

A perspective that transcends the Rhine, however, changes the march's meaning. For one thing, Rettig, Peter-Davis and the other CSFR activists who organized the march were in contact with reactor opponents across France and as far afield as Austria and the United States. Their geographically broad perspective was evident in a pair of international meetings they organized in 1971 and 1972. For two days in December 1971, the CSFR hosted some 100 reactor opponents representing forty local groups from

---

[106] Hertle, "Skizze der französischen Ökologiebewegung," 47.
[107] Alain Touraine, *Anti-Nuclear Protest: The Opposition to Nuclear Energy in France* (Cambridge: Cambridge University Press, 1983), 20.

France, Germany, Austria, Sweden, and Belgium.[108] Though this conference was clearly intended to bring together local anti-reactor fights as part of an international struggle, it was internally divided. While the Alsatian hosts and their German and Swiss guests pushed for a patient, legalistic approach, French activists of the "Gallic type" had little interest in formality or in abiding by the rules.[109] Another meeting of fifteen French and German anti-nuclear groups held over Pentecost in 1972 – shortly after the march from Vogelgruen to Fessenheim – was more productive. It led to the formation of a new, international anti-reactor group called Rhine Valley Action (Rheintalaktion) that brought together opponents of the Fessenheim reactor with a group of activists further down the Rhine in Karlsruhe, who had grown concerned about the development of a research reactor there in the 1950s.[110] The string of international anti-nuclear meetings taking place in Alsace revealed that the region had become a gathering place for reactor opponents from across Western Europe, even if local activists had little success stopping Fessenheim and seemed ineffective to some French observers. Likewise, the exponential growth from 1,000 to 10,000 activists in a year's time convinced local anti-nuclear activists that their movement was moving forward, even if it seemed unlikely to stop construction at Fessenheim.[111] In the early 1970s, they had already begun to develop an approach to anti-nuclear activism that blurred together local, regional, and transnational contexts – and therefore confused observers.

The march also found imitators across the Rhine. Hence, the German activist Georg Löser argued that even if it came too late to stop Fessenheim, the march was held "at the right moment for Breisach."[112] The march's participants, who came from both sides of the Rhine, used it as a springboard to develop new strategies and organize further protests against the Breisach reactor. According to one German scholar, the very difficulty in opposing the Fessenheim reactor project once it had gotten underway motivated Alsatian activists to involve themselves in anti-reactor actions

---

[108]   Tauer, *Störfall*, 250; see also: *Ecologie* June–July 1975, no. 1. Cited in Fagnani, *Nucleopolis*, 50; and: "Strasbourg, 28–29. XII. 71," *Ionix* 1 (February 1972).

[109]   Hertle, "Skizze der französischen Ökologiebewegung," 46.

[110]   The Karlsruhe group was headed by the later founder of the BBU, Hans-Helmuth Wüstenhagen. Thus, Rheintalkation was the key predecessor of the West German Bundesverband Bürgerinitiativen Umweltschutz, meaning that that important national organization had distinctly transnational roots.

[111]   See the cover of *Ionix* 3 (November 1972), which is headlined "La longue marche pourque triomphe la sagesse."

[112]   Georg Löser, "Die Badisch-Elsässischen Bürgerinitiativen," in *Lieber heute aktiv als morgen radio-aktiv* (Hamburg: Laika-Verlag, 2011), 24.

across the Rhine as early as possible.[113] Already in the fall of 1972, the march's resonance across the Rhine became clear. On Saturday, 16 September, more than 500 farmers and vintners from the Kaiserstuhl staged a long-distance march of their own, parading their tractors through a dozen winegrowing villages. Organized by vintners who had marched to Fessenheim the previous May, the parade emphasized their concerns about their crops. Slogans like, "He who builds a cooling tower here/Will sow the wind and reap the whirlwind" emphasized the rural population's readiness to respond actively to a reactor project that would threaten its interests.[114] Though quite different from its French precursor, the tractor parade marked the debut in Baden of the sort of street protest that had been taking place in Alsace for the past two years, exemplifying the ways that activists influenced one another across the Rhine but also the different ways that they deployed similar tactics.[115]

The tractor parade came amidst an anti-reactor petition drive, which further evidenced Badensian activists' newfound willingness to take to the streets in opposition to reactor projects. During a four-week window in fall 1972, the drive's organizers gathered 60,000 signatures throughout Southern Baden.[116] They achieved particularly remarkable success rates on the Kaiserstuhl, where the electrician Dieter Berstecher and his childhood friend Günter Sacherer went door-to-door to ask their neighbors to sign the complaint. In Sacherer's village of Oberrotweil, 1021 of the 1090 voters signed; in Burkheim, Berstecher's hometown, 889 of 891 voters added their names.[117] In neighboring villages, too, public officials reported that upwards of 90 percent of eligible voters had signed the petition.[118] Yet, the drive was not only successful among vintners and others dependent on the viticultural industry. Energized by their engagement in the Fessenheim march, Harloff's Aktionsgemeinschaft collected the signatures

---

[113] Wolfgang Hertle also noted the march's importance in developments across the Rhine, because its inefficacy changed Alsatian activists' ideas about how to oppose reactors. Hertle, "Skizze der französischen Ökologiebewegung," 47.

[114] Schillinger, "Breisach," 30–31.

[115] On transnationalism as a process of transformation, see: Daniel Rodgers, *Atlantic Crossings: Social Politics in a Progressive Age* (Cambridge, MA: Harvard University Press, 1998), 362. Andrew Tompkins takes up the same theme, in the specific case of 1970s anti-nuclear protest: Tompkins, "Grassroots Transnationalism(s): Franco-German Opposition to Nuclear Energy in the 1970s," *Contemporary European History* 25, no. 1 (2016): 117–142.

[116] "Fast 60 000 Unterschriften gegen Kernkraftwerk Breisach," *Badische Zeitung*, 3 October 1972.

[117] "50 000 Unterschriften gegen das Kernkraftwerk Breisach," *Badische Zeitung*, 2 October 1972.

[118] "Fast 60 000 Unterschriften," *Badische Zeitung*.

Figure 1.3 Günter Sacherer at a demonstration in Freiburg. © Günter Sacherer.

of tens of thousands of Freiburgers at its booths in front of the Minster and around city hall. A series of informational meetings in Freiburg were packed with urbanites interested in better understanding technical aspects of the nuclear threat. Scientists like Walther Herbst articulated these problems to much more receptive audiences than they had found just a year or two earlier.[119] The heated nuclear debate on the Kaiserstuhl and the protests against the Fessenheim reactor project had affected people in Freiburg, who now believed that the spate of nuclear development planned for the Rhine jeopardized their city's future.

Building on the apparent failure of the protests in Fessenheim, the campaign against the Breisach reactor attracted the project's immediate neighbors, who were concerned about their agricultural livelihoods, as well as Freiburgers, who felt that their city and the region as a whole were threatened by the massing of reactors. Though they went beyond the immediate threat to grapes and other sensitive crops, these protests still seemed confined to Southern Baden; observers who failed to look across the Rhine and investigate the ways that Alsatian activists had participated in

---

[119] "Gegen Atomkraftwerke," *Badische Zeitung*, 24 September 1972.

Badensian protests were particularly unlikely to note the broader networks of which these local protests were part. From the perspective of Stuttgart officials, who rarely looked across the Rhine, Badensian anti-nuclear protests seemed provincial and short sighted, especially because the protesters rejected an important opportunity to develop the "underdeveloped" Upper Rhine valley and thus move the state of Baden-Württemberg forward.

Though local activists had developed a sort of localized transnationalism that emphasized connections between protests against the Fessenheim and Breisach reactors and even drew on the region's nascent anti-nuclear prominence to attract protesters from elsewhere to organizing meetings, outsiders from government officials to scholars and even dogmatic Leftists continued to see these protests as isolated, far-flung, and self-interested. From these latter viewpoints, Rhenish anti-nuclear protests may have effectively recruited and mobilized many local people, but the marches and petition drives that grassroots activists organized were short-sighted provincial struggles with little resonance elsewhere.

Conclusion

The competing understandings of Rhenish anti-reactor protests that had emerged by late 1972 raise questions about the relationship between local activism and high politics – a relationship that is not satisfactorily addressed by the idea of front porch politics alone. In the United States, Michael Foley has shown, debates over certain front porch issues like toxic waste caused elected officials to act because the threat became so clear and was so widespread. Most local struggles, however, had little effect on national politics, which continued its Rightward drift. Grassroots struggles coexisted with the "Reagan revolution" because activists were increasingly devoted to local issues, and had come to see national politics as a "spectator sport." This interpretation could be said to buttress the arguments made by government officials and utilities' executives about Rhenish reactor opponents' lacking understanding of the bigger issues connected to local nuclear development. In fact, this same debate about real political salience has long dogged the environmental movement. While its proponents believe that environmental activism is concerned with the fate of the earth, and therefore of humanity, critics consider environmental themes too separate from real political issues, like work and wages.[120] Moreover, these critics allege, environmentalists are

---

[120] See, for example: Tony Judt, *Postwar* (New York: Penguin, 2005), 493. Jan-Werner Müller, too, sees environmentalism as patently apolitical. He writes that "if there ever was such a thing as an end of

interested only in preserving their own backyards; a criticism that could easily be leveled against Rhenish reactor opponents in the early 1970s.

In essence, these criticisms of the environmental movement hinge on its classification as a new sort of politics that is alien to traditional, "material" politics. The Rhenish anti-reactor struggle had many novel and confusing aspects, but they did not amount to the sort of rejection of meaningful politics assumed by some of the environmental movement's most strident critics. Instead, the confusing anti-nuclear coalition developing in the Upper Rhine during the early 1970s exemplifies the "political expression . . . outside of formal channels and involving broad populations," that Belinda Davis has referred to as "popular politics." Given its incredible diversity, which included vintners and farmers, students, scientists and middle-class Freiburgers as well as Alsatian environmentalists, rural Christian Democratic Union (CDU) members, and even incompletely rehabilitated ex-Nazis, the Rhenish movement supports her interdiction that historians must look "beyond national boundaries but also across more conventional cultural barriers" in order to describe political engagement since 1945.[121]

Despite these novel aspects, however, it would be incorrect to classify the Rhenish anti-reactor protests of the early 1970s as a wholly "new" sort of politics. The concerns about the fate of the region's most significant cash crop that motivated early protests gave them an obvious materialist framework. These protests should not, in other words, be explained away as a retreat from meaningful politics, or even as an example of the effects of value change and the widespread adoption of post-material concerns. While non-material matters clearly motivated some pioneering anti-nuclear activists, apprehensions about the German gene pool and the perils of invisible radiation failed to mobilize the vast majority of the region's population. Instead concerns about the future of local agriculture made nuclear power a salient issue in the Upper Rhine valley. In standing up for their own economic self-interest, Rhenish farmers and vintners were not exactly post-materialist trailblazers. They were, however, extremely effective community organizers. The grassroots anti-reactor campaign they created became the basis for a reimagination of the Rhenish community and thus for fundamental changes to common conceptions of democratic participation in the Upper Rhine valley.

---

ideology (at least in Europe), it could be found [in environmentalism]." Müller, *Contesting Democracy: Political Ideas in Twentieth Century Europe* (New Haven: Yale University Press, 2011), 212.

[121] Belinda Davis, "What's Left? Popular Political Participation in Postwar Europe," *American Historical Review* 113, No. 2 (April 2008), 376.

CHAPTER 2

A Different Watch on the Rhine: How Anti-Nuclear Activists Imagined the Alemannic Community and United a Region in Resistance

In Alsace and in Baden
Was long a time of woe
We shot each other in the wars,
Killed each other for our lords
Now we're fighting for ourselves
In Wyhl and Marckolsheim
Here we are together
A different watch on the Rhine

—Walter Mossmann,
Die Wacht am Rhein (The Watch on the Rhine)[1]

In the fall of 1974, the Freiburg singer-songwriter Walter Mossmann penned a 14-verse ballad recounting recent protests in the Upper Rhine valley. He borrowed his composition's title, "The Watch on the Rhine," from an anthem sung by patriotic Germans during the Franco-Prussian War.[2] But Mossmann took the melody from an American strike song and wrote fresh lyrics describing a new and different effort to protect the river.[3] Rather than encouraging his countrymen to defend the "German Rhine" from the French hereditary enemy, Mossmann's song urged the inhabitants of the Upper Rhine valley to join together in order to save themselves and protect the river from their own governments. His song's contrast to

[1] Song text copyright © Walter Mossmann, reprinted with permission from his estate.
[2] The original version was written by Max Schneckenberger during the Rhine Crisis of 1840, and became popular during the Franco-Prussian War. See: James Brophy, "The Rhine Crisis of 1840 and German Nationalism: Chauvinism, Skepticism, and Regional Reception," *Journal of Modern History* 85, No. 1 (March 2013): 2. On Schneckenberger's song's relationship to Germans' imaginings of the Rhine, see: Thomas Lekan, *Imagining the Nation in Nature: Landscape Preservation and German Identity, 1885–1945* (Cambridge, MA: Harvard University Press, 2004), 27. For more on Mossmann's version of the song, see: Walter Mossmann and Peter Schleunig, *Alte und neue politische Lieder. Entstehung und Gebrauch, Texte und Noten* (Reinbek bei Hamburg: Rowohlt, 1978).
[3] Mossmann took the melody from Florence Reece's 1931 song, "Which Side are you on?," a song sung by striking coal miners in Harlan County, Kentucky. Reece had taken her melody, in turn, from another song, likely the Baptist Hymn, "Lay the Lily Low." Timothy P. Lynch, *Strike Songs of the Depression* (Jackson: University of Mississippi Press, 2001), 66–68 and 141–142.

the nineteenth-century anthem was striking, but the tale of transnational resistance was also alien to the atmosphere along the Rhine in the early 1970s. Though rural people on both riverbanks still spoke the Alemannic dialect, the stigma of German defeat and the success of Paris's efforts to Frenchify Alsace had fostered distinct identities and caused transborder traffic to dwindle to the point where no one noticed that the region's few border crossings closed each night at 10 pm.[4]

Sung at protests by a motley crew of Germans and French, rural conservatives and urban Leftists, Mossmann's ballad embodied the unlikely community that Rhenish activists built by reconceiving Baden and Alsace as a single unit threatened by a cacophony of industrial projects. Through their collaboration, farmers and vintners adopted new forms of action while Leftists came to see anti-reactor protests as a means of escaping their post-1968 malaise. The new watch on the Rhine was shorthand for an effort to build community and broaden the immediately individual interests that motivated the first Rhenish anti-reactor protests. Yet, in turning their backs on the traditional structures of national politics and emphasizing local issues, activists also created the sorts of limited "communities of virtue and engagement" that Daniel Rodgers considers essential to the disaggregation of US society since the 1970s.[5] Tony Judt posits a parallel process of fracturing and fragmentation in European politics as mass parties based around "abstract ... principles and objectives" lost ground to narrowly conceived "single-issue" parties.[6] The discrepancy between Mossmann's description of anti-reactor protesters as a vibrant community and Rodgers and Judt's lamentations of a society cleaved into Burkeian "little platoons" forces a reconsideration of focused local engagement in the final third of the twentieth century.

Myopic narratives of societal disaggregation and narrowing interests cannot properly explain the diverse groups that came together around new political focus points. Instead, despite the seventies' reputation as the opening decade of a new era of interconnectedness and globalization,[7]

---

[4] Postwar efforts to rebuild the French nation sought to reincorporate Alsace into France without the strife of the interwar period; they were remarkably successful. Robert Gildea, *France since 1945* (Oxford: Oxford University Press, 2002), 156. See also: Sarah Farmer, *Martyred Village* (Berkeley: University of California Press, 1999), 146 and 167. On the creation of distinct identities in Baden and Alsace, see: Hermann Bausinger, "Die 'Alemannische Internationale.' Realität und Mythos," *Recherches Germaniques* 8 (1978): 147. On border crossings, see: Walter Mossmann, *realistisch sein: das unmögliche verlangen. Wahrheitsgetreu gefälschte Erinnerungen* (Berlin: edition der Freitag, 2009), 194.

[5] Daniel Rodgers, *Age of Fracture* (Cambridge, MA: Harvard University Press, 2011), 198.

[6] Tony Judt, *Postwar: A History of Europe since 1945* (New York: Penguin, 2005), 486.

[7] Jürgen Osterhammel and Niels P. Petersson describe the era "since the end of the 1960s" as the "beginning of the most recent phase of globalization" because it marked the state of the end of the

the New Social Movements have become emblematic of disconnection and dissolution.[8] Even internationalism has come to be counted as evidence of a movement's retreat from high politics, which is implicitly national.[9] And yet, the growing anti-reactor movement in the Upper Rhine valley created a new community that was far more diverse than the constituencies of "class or occupation" that supported mass parties before the 1970s.[10] In contrast to these large but homogenous groupings, the Rhenish anti-nuclear movement appealed to a shared dialect and to distant histories in order to help the local population overcome deep divisions and to "imagine" a new Alemannic community.[11] Transnational community-building and the sharing of ideas across borders had significant ramifications for the efficacy of anti-reactor protests.[12] Perhaps most significantly, and rather paradoxically, Rhenish transnationalism prompted a new understanding of nuclear policy as a local matter.[13]

Just as front porch politics in the USA had its heyday amidst waxing apathy and the ascendancy of the Reagan revolution, the heterogeneous

---

"bipolar" Cold War order, the start of the era of the crisis of the welfare state, and the start of the present globalized economic order. Osterhammel and Petersson, *Globalization: A Short History* (Princeton: Princeton University Press, 2005), 141.

[8] Most works on the New Social Movements start from the premise of disaggregation by looking at each of the movements separately, rather than noting their myriad links, in terms of personnel, roots, and objectives. Perhaps the best known proponents of this approach are Dieter Rucht and Roland Roth. Their handbook of social movements, which painstakingly differentiates, for example, the anti-nuclear energy and environmental movements, exemplifies it. Dieter Rucht and Roland Roth, *Die Soziale Bewegungen in Deutschland seit 1945. Ein Handbuch* (Frankfurt am Main: Campus, 2008).

[9] Samuel Moyn, *The Last Utopia: Human Rights in History* (Cambridge, MA: Harvard University Press, 2010), 8.

[10] Judt, *Postwar*, 486.

[11] Benedict Anderson famously argues that all communities "larger than primordial villages" are imagined because "the members ... will never know most of their fellow-members ... yet in the minds of each lives the image of their communion." The importance for him, therefore, is in the act of "creating" such a community, which is what Rhenish activists did through their protests. Benedict Anderson, *Imagined Communities* (New York: Verso, 1983), 6.

[12] Such uses of transnationalism are evident in recent histories of the student movement. See, for example: Jeremy Varon, *Bringing the War Home: The Weather Underground, the Red Army Faction, and Revolutionary Violence in the Sixties and Seventies* (Berkeley: University of California Press, 2004); Martin Klimke, *The Other Alliance: Student Protest in West Germany and the United States during the Global Sixties* (Princeton: Princeton University Press, 2010); and Quinn Slobodian, *Foreign Front: Third World Politics in Sixties West Germany* (Durham, NC: Duke University Press, 2012).

[13] In this sense, the sort of grassroots transnationalism deployed in the Upper Rhine valley was perhaps a hybrid between what Andrew Tompkins has called "thinking transnationally" and "acting transnationally," since transborder cooperation both allowed protesters to reimagine particular local contexts, and served as a source of ideas and inspiration. Tompkins, "Grassroots Transnationalism(s): Franco-German Opposition to Nuclear Energy in the 1970s," *Contemporary European History* 25, no. 1 (February 2016): 117–142.

networks that anti-reactor activists built along the Upper Rhine co-existed with a nuclear building boom – dozens of new reactor projects in France, West Germany, and Switzerland broke ground during the 1970s.[14] In the eyes of the government officials and utilities executives who opposed them then and the scholars who critique them now, anti-reactor activists were too closely focused on trivial matters, too aloof from the liberal democratic process, and thus ultimately irrelevant. But emphasizing trivial matters rather than national nuclear policy exemplified the movement's kaleido-scopic embodiment of competing traits and identities. The very existence of this diverse, multifaceted, transnational movement displaces one-sided explanations of social disaggregation that find the NSMs selfish, inwardly focused, and distant from meaningful high politics. So how was the Rhenish anti-reactor movement at once provincial and cosmopolitan? How was this same closely focused movement driven by rural conserva-tives, but appealing to urban Leftists? And if the anti-reactor movement's proponents were so concerned with matters of democracy, why did they operate beyond liberal democratic boundaries? Seeking answers to these questions opens up reconsiderations of focused activism's significance for high politics and its potential to foster widespread change in "fractured" societies.

Vintners into Democrats

The idea that rural anti-reactor protesters were deeply interested in matters of democracy fits neither typical accounts of the anti-nuclear movement nor broader narratives of 1970s politics.[15] This is hardly surprising. Despite deepening concerns about the proposed Breisach reactor, the pro-nuclear Christian Democratic Union – which governed Baden-Württemberg from 1953 until 2011 – actually increased the total number of votes it received in the Upper Rhine valley by nearly 50 percent in the April 1972 state parliament election, suggesting a sharp distinction between grassroots

---

[14] Michael Foley, *Front Porch Politics: The Forgotten Heyday of American Activism in the 1970s and 1980s* (New York: Hill and Wang, 2013).

[15] On the anti-nuclear movement, see: Dieter Rucht, *Von Wyhl nach Gorleben. Bürger gegen Atomprogramm und nukleare Entsorgung* (Munich: C. H. Beck, 1980); and Jens-Ivo Engels, *Naturpolitik in der Bundesrepublik. Ideenwelt und politische Verhaltensstile in Naturschutz und Umweltbewegung, 1950–1980* (Paderborn: Schöningh, 2006). On the 1970s, see: Judt, *Postwar*; see also: J. R. McNeill, "The Environment, Environmentalism, and International Society in the Long 1970s," in Niall Ferguson, et al., eds., *The Shock of the Global: The 1970s in Perspective* (Cambridge, MA: Harvard University Press, 2011).

protest and political decision-making.[16] Likewise, in Alsace, postwar elections were dominated by conservative parties, first the Christian
Democratic Popular Republican Movement (MRP) and then the
Gaullists.[17] Since conservatives in both countries supported nuclear development, citizens' concerns about nuclear energy seemed separate from
their behavior in the voting booth. Even when rural Badensians took
their concerns to the streets, they managed only to plead for "help" from
Rudolf Eberle, Baden-Württemberg's minister of economics.[18] Regardless
of their continued support for the parties of government, however, rural
reactor opponents' trusting and deferential attitude towards revered
elected officials was decaying beneath the surface.

Disputes over grandiose development plans exemplified growing tensions between government and society – and showcased government
officials' failure to notice their constituents' rising discontent. At the
same time as grassroots activists collected signatures against the Breisach
reactor, the state-sponsored *Staatsanzeiger für Baden-Württemberg* featured
an op-ed that set "Environmental Protection" at loggerheads with "Energy
Provision." Published in a newspaper that was intended primarily to
transmit technical information to government bureaucrats, the bombastic
piece described the Breisach reactor as part of a much larger development
plan that would turn the "the Upper Rhine valley between Frankfurt and
Basel" into the European Economic Community's new "primary
economic axis." To achieve this transformation, it asserted, "lowlands
should be held free for commercial and industrial use while the functions
'living,' 'recreation,' etc. should be re-settled to the 'pre-mountainous
zone' and the side-valleys of the Rhine."[19] Though it may have seemed

---

[16] The CDU governed Baden-Württemberg uninterruptedly from 1953 until 2011, and received the
largest share of the vote in every Landtag election in Baden-Württemberg from 1952 (when the state
was founded) until 2016. Nevertheless, 1972 marked the first time it received an absolute majority of
votes for the Landtag. "Endgültigte Ergebnisse der Wahl zum Landtag von Baden-Württemberg am
23. April 1972," *Statistische Berichte des Statistischen Landesamts Baden-Württemberg* B VII 2 (9 May
1972). The gains in total votes were due in part to significant growth in the number of eligible voters
between 1968 and 1972, and in part to the NPD's decision not to campaign after having received
9.8 percent of the vote in 1968.

[17] It was only after François Mitterrand was elected French President in 1981 that the Lower Rhine
Department sent its first Socialist to the National Assembly. Marc Burg, *Les Gauches face aux Droites
dans le Bas Rhin sous la Ve Republique, 1958–1988* (Strasbourg, 1988), 406.

[18] "500 Kaiserstühler Bauern demonstrieren gegen Kernkraftwerk," *Klassenkampf. Extra Blatt*,
19 September 1972. ASB "Wyhl—Die Anfänge," 3581.

[19] "Meinungen zur Landespolitik: Umweltschutz oder Energiedarbietung?" *Staatsanzeiger für Baden-
Württemberg* (No. 76), 23 September 1972, reprinted in Gerhard A. Auer and Jochen Reich,
"Gebrannte Kinder. Vorgeschichten vom Kampf gegen das Atomkraftwerk Wyhl," *'s Eige zeige'
Jahrbuch des Landkreises Emmendingen für Kultur und Geschichte* 15 (2001): 97.

harmless from a professional planner's perspective, the article resonated far beyond the newspaper's normal readership because it addressed a technical issue in language that matched rural people's experiences.[20] Ida Tittmann, who as a young woman during the Second World War had been evacuated from her hometown of Weisweil "to the so-called pre-mountainous zone of the Black Forest," recalled how unnerved she and her neighbors were by the offhand reference to their wartime evacuation site.[21] Now their own government, not allied artillery, threatened all that they had "toiled for and achieved – one's own four walls and a roof over one's head."[22] From Tittmann's perspective, at least, the CDU government seemed to be attacking the very prosperity that it sought to make synonymous with its time in government.[23] All at once, it was no longer obvious to rural Badensians that their representatives in Stuttgart had their best interests in mind.

A similar debate, also influenced by the border-region's recent history as well as dreams of developing the Rhine into Europe's new economic axis, unfolded on the river's French bank. Motivated by a desire to stop Germans from "re-conquering Alsace" by "opening factories, buying up country homes, and competing with the businessmen in Strasbourg and Mulhouse with their ultra-modern shopping centers and mail order establishments," French planners sought to build up French industry, and improve infrastructural connections from Alsace into central France.[24] In his role as a government planning consultant, the Strasbourg geographer Étienne Juillard proposed a "French Ruhr" along the Upper Rhine, which would include two intercontinental airports, as well as "factories, nuclear reactors, highways, not to mention the expanded Rhine-Rhône canal," and thus foster economic development at the same time as it bound the region

---

[20] Gerhard Auer, interview with the author, Emmendingen, 22 February 2010.

[21] Ida Tittmann, quoted in Auer and Reich, "Gebrannte Kinder," 96. Memories of the evacuation were coupled, of course, with memories of returning to bombed out villages after the War. Weisweil was 90 percent destroyed. Heinz Ehrler (director, Museum der Geschichte von Weisweil), interview with the author, Weisweil, 23 February 2010; see also: "'Wir protestieren mit Nachdruck' Offener Brief der Weisweiler Frauen an Filbinger," *Badische Zeitung*, 19 July 1974.

[22] Auer and Reich, "Gebrannte Kinder," 96. The *Staatsanzeiger* prefaced this article with a note that it came from the "viewpoint" of "the *sws* Press Service, which has close connections to industry." Yet this disclaimer was overlooked or considered immaterial by local people, who were infuriated that such an inflammatory piece had appeared in a state-sponsored publication. Moreover, similar plans were being promoted by the Strasbourg geographer and government planning consultant Étienne Juillard in Alsace, who spoke of pushing the population into the Vosges to make way for a "French Ruhr" in the Rhine Valley. Elisabeth Schulthess, *Solange l'insoumise: ecologie, feminisme, non-violence*, (Barret-sur-Méouge Y. Michel, 2004), 75.

[23] "Im Südwesten ein achtes Weltwunder?" *Der Spiegel*, 17 April 1972.

[24] "Le plan de destruction de l'Alsace," *Le Sauvage* 37 (January 1977): 67; and: "Deutsche Gefahr," *Der Spiegel*, 7 April 1969.

to France and made it the economic heart of Europe.[25] As in Germany, the ruminations of an overexcited planner led to growing concern amongst local people about far-off politicians' control over their destiny.

But combatting Juillard's plans proved difficult. By January 1973, when a handful of Alsatian ecologists met around Solange Fernex's dining-room table in the remote village of Biederthal, they had been fighting against proposals to develop Alsace for half a decade; since the Fessenheim reactor and the expansion of the Rhine–Rhône canal were progressing, they seemed to be making little headway. Fernex, who was born in interwar Strasbourg and lost her father in the Second World War, moved to Biederthal in 1963 after spending several years in Africa with her husband, the Swiss physician Michel Fernex. After they painstakingly restored it, the Fernexes' spacious home – Biederthal's former chateau – became a central node of activism in Alsace. Able to support their family of six from Michel's salary, Solange became a full-time activist, but both Solange and Michel were involved in the AFRPN and the couple co-founded the preservation-ist group Peasant Homes of Alsace (Maisons Paysannes d'Alsace).[26] Younger activists in the region came to think of the couple as their "spiritual guides."[27] The January 1973 meeting brought the Fernexes together with two ecologists from Mulhouse, Henri Jenn, a 32-year-old technician and ardent supporter of bird protection, and Antoine Waechter, a 23-year-old activist who had organized Young Friends of Animals (Jeunes amis des animaux).[28] Frustrated by their inability to stop the Fessenheim reactor or the expansion of the Rhine–Rhône canal, the group decided that it was time to "announce and assert the political existence of environmental matters on their own terms."[29] They founded an organization called Ecology and Survival (Écologie et Survie) and convinced Jenn to run for a National Assembly seat in Mulhouse; Fernex served as his alternate.

The organizers treated the campaign as an opportunity to publicize their concerns about plans to turn Alsace into an "industrial suburb" or, worse

---

[25] Schulthess, *Solange l'insoumise*, 75. Juillard's 1968 study of the Rhine noted the missed opportunities for development along the Upper Rhine, and analyzed the region's potential in a Europe that was increasingly linked together by the Rhine and its tributaries. Étienne Juillard, *L'Europe Rhénane. Géographie d'un grand espace* (Paris: Libraire Armand Colin, 1968).

[26] Schulthess, *Solange l'insoumise*, 73, 75.

[27] Raymond Schirmer, interview with the author, Ferette, 19 March 2016.

[28] Schulthess, *Solange l'insoumise*, 92.

[29] Gregoire Gauchet, "Implantation Politique et Associative des Ecologistes en Alsace," (Master's Thesis, Université Robert Schuman de Strasbourg, 1991), 12–13; see also: Henri Jenn, email to author (4 June 2015); and: Mouvement Ecologie et Survie, "Henri Jenn" (election pamphlet), [undated (1973)]. In the possession of the author.

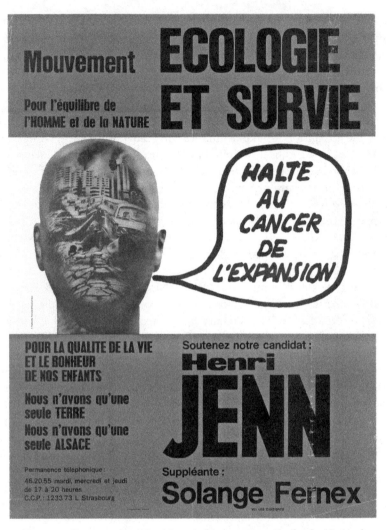

Figure 2.1 Poster used by Henri Jenn in his 1974 campaign for the National
Assembly from Mulhouse. © Henri Jenn.

yet, "Europe's trash can." Jenn himself hung up hundreds of posters showing a human head covered in highways and smokestacks, and adorned with
the phrase, "Stop the cancer of expansion."[30] Visits from nationally known

---

[30] Schulthess, *Solange l'insoumise*, 93.

ecologists Robert Hainard and Philippe Lebreton each drew several hundred interested Mulhousians, and forced the inexperienced candidate to learn public speaking on the fly. Even as he pasted campaign posters and made stump speeches, however, the National Assembly was not really on Jenn's mind; he did not aspire to be elected, and his campaign was intended primarily to force Alsatian politicians to address problems of concern to local environmentalists.[31] It is hardly surprising, then, that one of his campaign's slogans, "We only have one earth! We only have one Alsace!" skipped over the national level altogether in order to assert the link between the local campaign and global – rather than French – politics.[32] With 2.7 percent of the vote, Jenn came nowhere close to winning a seat in parliament, but his campaign was perceived as a victory by its organizers because it opened a new forum for their advocacy.[33] As Fernex put it, elections could be made part of a "multi-strategy" that called for "action everywhere ... outside of parliament, within parliament (within the established parties *and* as environmental groups)."[34] The multi-strategy evidenced a broad notion of activism that brought specific concerns about nuclear energy and unchecked development – which had previously been pursued only via extra-parliamentary action – into the regulated framework of liberal democracy.

In Baden, reactor opponents had no plans to run candidates for office in the early 1970s, but government officials' insensitivity caused their concerns to become ever more closely linked with democratic praxis. The single incident that best evidenced the fusion of personal concerns and the workings of democracy came late in 1972, when government officials scheduled a public hearing on the proposed Breisach reactor. Citizens' hackles were raised as soon as they learned that the hearing would take place on 31 October, at the height of the grape harvest.[35] Many vintners were unable to leave their vines for the day in order to participate; those who could were upset by the "arrogant and overbearing" manner in which an official sent from Stuttgart chaired the meeting. When he abruptly switched off the audience microphone, disregarding a long queue of reactor

---

[31] Henri Jenn, interview with the author, Mulhouse, 21 March 2016.
[32] Mouvement Ecologie et Survie, "Halte au cancer de l'expansion," (poster). In the possession of the author.
[33] Schulthess, *Solange l'insoumise*, 91–93.
[34] Solange Fernex, "Konzept der Multistrategie," *BBU-Aktuell* 9 (May–June 1979): 32–33. Emphasis from the original.
[35] Josef Reinauer, "Der Weinbau am Kaiserstuhl," in Bernd Nössler and Margret de Witt, eds., *Wyhl. Kein Kernkraftwerk in Wyhl und auch sonst nirgends. Betroffene Bürger berichten* (Freiburg: Dreisam-Verlag, 1976), 16–18.

opponents who had waited patiently for their chance to speak, the would-be complainants realized their irrelevance to government officials. Unable to express their concerns verbally, incensed farmers stormed the podium and lobbed rotten tomatoes. Government officials responded in kind, calling upon a waiting state police unit to halt the melee.[36]

Had they planned to take their constituents' worries seriously, government officials would hardly have felt the need to prevent patient reactor opponents from speaking their minds, nor would they have had police troopers on standby. Nonetheless, Minister of Economics Rudolf Eberle, whose office held primary responsibility for the reactor project, suggested that the issues raised by rural reactor opponents would now be taken more seriously when he announced immediately after the hearing that his ministry, "would take the necessary time to study the issues" related to the Breisach project. At least one local media outlet understood this statement as evidence "that construction will not be permitted to begin too hastily."[37] In fact, Baden-Württemberg's Minister of the Interior had taken a strong stance against Breisach as a potential reactor site at a cabinet meeting months before the hearing. At that time, Eberle had agreed with his colleague that the "possible negative effects of the cooling towers on agriculture and viticulture" were reason enough to abandon Breisach. Instead of "formally repudiating the Breisach site," and thereby appearing to acquiesce to the protesters' will, however, Eberle continued to promote the project in public.[38] His conscious efforts to downplay popular concerns amounted to a carefully devised strategy of ignoring and misinforming his constituents in order not to give credence to their concerns in a way that might sabotage future reactor projects. Such behavior revealed the government's assumptions about rural people's political ineptitude, and thus reinforced reactor opponents' own doubts about government officials' intentions and even the democratic order itself.

Freiburg's Action Group against Environmental Threats Posed by the Breisach and Fessenheim Reactors responded to Eberle's equivocal statement in an angry open letter addressed to "Those responsible in our democracy." The letter carefully described several particular, technical

[36] Ernst Schillinger, "Breisach – der Kampf beginnt," in *Wyhl* (see note 35), 29–33.

[37] "Atomkraftwerk Breisach in der Diskussion," *Freiburger Wochenbericht*, 9 November 1972.

[38] Sibylle Morstadt explains that the Interior Ministry (IM) had never been enamored with the Breisach project for two reasons. First, its "State Development Plan" had set aside the proposed construction site as a recreation area, and second it was concerned about the potential effect on local agricultural production. Despite these concerns, the IM did not make a final decision against the reactor until July 1972. Sibylle Morstadt, "Die Landesregierung von Baden-Württemberg und der Konflikt um das geplante Kernkraftwerk in Wyhl," (Diplomarbeit, Freiburg, 2002), 21–22.

concerns about the Breisach project, but it emphasized the fact that despite a plethora of formal complaints, including 60,000 petition signatures, a warning signed by thirty scientists, and the concerns voiced at the hearing itself, government officials had provided "no certainty that all necessary scientific data will actually be collected and published." To remedy this situation, the Aktionsgemeinschaft demanded that the government give "independent citizens' groups . . . the right to participate in the decision-making process in all aspects (environmental protection, zoning and energy distribution planning, information, etc.)."[39] Even well-heeled citizens in a region long regarded as a CDU stronghold were second-guessing governing politicians now that these trusted representatives had so blatantly failed to heed their concerns. Despite these misgivings, however, activists remained keen to participate in the democratic process, which they still believed offered a means to improve their situation.

The apparent inability of citizens and government officials to communicate without resorting to direct electoral competition, bombastic op-eds, blunt open letters, hurled rotten tomatoes, or police truncheons linked the limited, localized struggle over the Breisach reactor with democratic praxis. Rural people's concerns about the reactor projects proposed for their region began with perceived threats to the microclimate and to their valuable vines, making it easy to consider them separate from high politics. Such an interpretation allowed for the minimization of the protests and for the presumption of a clean break between provincial nuclear concerns and the important work of government. Yet, it was precisely because distant Stuttgart officials insisted on addressing nuclear energy as a particular local issue – and dismissing local people's concerns about their lives and livelihoods – that reactor opponents linked the issue with problems of the democratic order. Increasing Christian Democratic dominance in Stuttgart, growing identification with France in Alsace, and reactor opponents' linkage of nuclear energy, planning initiatives and democracy matters appear to be contradictory narratives. But their coexistence was essential for the anti-reactor movement's emergence and early growth. Similarly, defining NSMs like the anti-nuclear movement as wholly novel and alien from high politics takes only one side of the nuclear debate on the Upper Rhine into account. Such an approach implicitly dismisses the subtle ways in which participation in anti-reactor protest began to reshape activists' opinions of government officials and caused them to aspire to more democratic participation. Not only Alsatian

[39] Aktionsgemeinschaft gegen Umweltgefährdung durch Atomkraftwerke, "Atomkraftwerk Breisach. An die Verantwortlichen unserer Demokratie." ASB "Wyhl—die Anfänge," 17577.

activists' attempt to influence politicians by competing with them at the ballot box but also the Freiburg Aktionsgemeinschaft's call for more involvement of citizens' groups in licensing and zoning processes are simply left out. Emphasizing the "newness" and "extra-parliamentary" nature of NSMs fails to explain how reactor opponents began to engage with the democratic order. At the same time, claiming that NSMs focused solely on new, postmaterial matters makes explaining why anti-reactor activism began to appeal to social activists of many stripes in the early 1970s rather difficult.

Seeking New Modes of Protest in the "Leaden" Seventies[40]

In a January 1974 article that pushed for more engagement, the West German anarchist publication *graswurzelrevolution* (grassroots revolution) openly questioned the efficacy of its readers' activism:

> One cannot say that the *graswurzel*-groups are out of work; but it would be just as difficult to say that they are—at the moment, at least—bubbling with activity. They are all searching for a field of political work that transcends anti-militarist busywork at the local level and leads to trans-regional initiatives.[41]

The periodical's proposed remedy for its readership's unproductive activist "busywork" was an "ecology campaign." The idea was surprising at first glance because it seemed to diverge so significantly from the *graswurzel*-groups' previous focus on anti-militarism. Yet for the publication's editor, Wolfgang Hertle, looking for inspiration where others did not was a conscious strategy. To this end, his journal had, since its first issue in 1972, carried reports on all sorts of nonviolent activism, "especially from abroad," and featured "model actions and concrete action plans, which may not be universal, but will offer new ideas for the struggle here in the FRG."[42]

---

[40] On the idea of the 1970s as a "leaden" decade, see: Christiane Peitz, "Die Bleikappe des Schweigens. Margarethe von Trotta über ihren Ensslin-Film, das Sympathisantentum und deutsche Kontinuitäten," *Der Tagesspiegel*, 28 April 2007.

[41] [Michael Schroeren], "'Damit wir auch morgen noch kraftvoll zubeißen können...' Notizen zu einer 'Ökologie-Kampagne,'" *graswurzelrevolution* 7 (January 1974): 2.

[42] Untitled [Editorial Statement], *graswurzelrevolution* 0 (1972): 1. The Larzac became one such exemplary struggle. Reports in *graswurzelrevolution* analyzed it, described key actors and important influences, and kept readers abreast of the latest developments on the plateau. Reports on Larzac appeared in almost every issue of *graswurzelrevolution* during the mid-1970s. The May 1975 issue featured a seven-page special section on Larzac entitled, "Larzac: vom gewaltlosen Widerstand der 103 Bauern gegen einen Truppenübungsplatz zum Erntefest der 103 000 für die dritte Welt." *graswurzelrevolution* 14/15 (May 1975).

Though it included groupings far more ideologically rigid than the *graswurzel*-groups, the variegated post-1968 Left was nonetheless open to new influences.[43] Early in the 1970s, some of the communist cells or "K-groups" that had formed after the dissolution of the Socialist German Students' League (SDS) in 1969 adhered closely to strict interpretations of Marxist dogma. Among them was Freiburg's League of Communist Workers (BKA), which dismissed the first protests against the Breisach reactor as the work of "doctors and big vintners," effectively attacking anti-reactor protests for being on the wrong side of the class struggle.[44] Others on the Left, including many Social Democratic Party of Germany (SPD) politicians, were disinterested in anti-nuclear protest because of the difficulty "for thinkers and political parties of an ultimately Marxist inspiration to break with a belief in the beneficial nature of industrial production."[45] But even the best known K-groups, including the Communist League (KB) and the Socialist League/Socialist Office (SB) were searching for new inspiration where they could find it by the mid-1970s; with time, they found themselves able to reconsider their beliefs about the necessity of industrial production for the proletarian revolution. Some of the activist groups that proved themselves most interested in anti-reactor protest seemed focused particularly on specific issues. The *graswurzel*-groups and the Young European Federalists (JEF), whose own *Forum E* magazine published articles primarily on European integration, were quick to identify links between nuclear issues and their own projects. All of these groups were motivated not by a sudden interest in environmental issues in and of themselves, but rather by a conception of environmental issues as a means of continuing their own struggle. Linking environmental campaigns with

---

[43] Recent studies suggest that this search for new approaches to politics and new areas of activism had to do with activists' emotional concerns and personal perceptions. Sven Reichardt argues that the 1970s New Left connected its "theoretical debates about revolutionary social change with a sense of emotional concern." Reichardt, *Authentizität und Gemeinschaft. Linksalternatives Leben in den siebziger und frühen achtziger Jahren* (Berlin: Suhrkamp, 2014), 218. Gerd Koenen claims that themes "from the grand coalition to the emergency laws, to the far-off war in Vietnam" did not motivate the West German New Left to take action in the 1970s in and of themselves, but did so instead because of the "particular *resonance* that they found in the youthful audiences." It was the activists' "hallucination of an 'historical moment' in which good and bad trajectories were crossing and mixing" that made this resonance possible. Koenen, *Das rote Jahrzehnt. Unsere kleine deutsche Kulturrevolution, 1967–1977* (Cologne: Kiepenheuer and Witsch, 2001), 476.

[44] "500 Kaiserstühler Bauern demonstrieren gegen Kernkraftwerk," *Klassenkampf. Extra Blatt*, 19 September 1972. ASB "Wyhl—Die Anfänge," 3581.

[45] Jan-Werner Müller, *Contesting Democracy: Political Ideas in Twentieth Century Europe* (New Haven: Yale University Press, 2011), 211.

the democratic order was essential for this conception of anti-reactor activism's significance.

As was apparent not just in the pages of *graswurzelrevolution*, but also amongst activists in Freiburg, West German Leftists were even more open to new influences when they came from outside the country.[46] A frustration with West German activism, fed in part by adherence to preconceived notions about what constituted protest, added to the attraction of foreign protest campaigns. Despite Freiburg's geographic proximity to the wine-growing villages where protests against the Breisach reactor were brewing in the early 1970s, a significant ideological divide and a surprising psychological distance initially separated urban Leftists from rural reactor opponents. Even in 1977, by which time he had become deeply involved in the local anti-reactor struggle, the Freiburg singer-songwriter and radio journalist Walter Mossmann emphasized the distance between the city and the rural centers of Rhenish anti-nuclear activism. "Joining in," he explained, "meant a lot of work because we don't live there, but rather thirty kilometers away."[47] Mossmann considered his relationship to student activism complicated, and he was no longer a student himself by the mid-1970s, but his budding interest in Rhenish anti-reactor protests exemplified the means by which the 68er generation became interested in anti-reactor protest in particular and environmentalism more generally. Mossmann had become engaged in the student movement in February 1968 when he stumbled upon a demonstration against a public transit fare hike in Freiburg. The campaign was organized by the University of Freiburg's SDS Chapter, and Mossmann joined the group, despite being put-off by the theory-laden pronouncements of national SDS leaders like Hans-Jürgen Krahl.[48]

Given his entrance into the student movement via a local issue, it was ironic that a detour to central France's Larzac plateau opened Mossmann's mind to Rhenish anti-reactor protests. The Larzac, a desolate region where shepherds made their livelihoods selling sheep's milk to be made into Roquefort cheese, was since 1970 the site of a protracted struggle over government plans to expand a military base.[49] In January 1973, as Rhenish reactor opponents waited to see how Minister Eberle would follow up on

---

[46] On the roots of this infatuation with extra-German influences, see: Slobodian, *Foreign Front*.

[47] Mossmann, "Die Bevölkerung ist Hellwach!" 10.

[48] Mossmann, *realistisch sein*, 96–98. Belinda Davis's oral histories show that this is hardly as atypical as Mossmann makes it sound. Davis, *The Internal Life of Politics: The New Left in West Germany, 1962–1983* (forthcoming).

[49] Wolfgang Hertle, *Larzac 1971–1981. Der Gewaltfreie Widerstand gegen die Erweiterung eines Truppenübungsplatzes in Süd-Frankreich* (Kassel: Weber, Zucht, und Co., 1982), 20.

his pledge to evaluate the data before proceeding with the Breisach reactor project, Larzac farmers drove their tractors more than 700 kilometers to protest in Paris. That August, they welcomed 80,000 visitors to a harvest festival on their farmsteads.[50] The protests on the Larzac were not well known in the FRG, and they drew on intellectual currents like Lanza del Vasto's Gandhism, which were far removed from the Marxian traditions of the European Left. For those German Leftists who encountered them, therefore, the Larzac protests seemed radically different from the ineffective domestic protests of the leaden 1970s. Most significantly, the campaign on the Larzac seemed to link together environmental concerns, anti-militarism, and criticisms of central government officials.

Precisely because it remained beyond the ken of West German main-stream culture, many activists' initial encounters with the Larzac were rather personal. Mossmann first stumbled upon the Larzac movement early in the summer of 1973 during a rambling roadtrip through France with his friend and fellow *Südwestrundfunk* (SWR) correspondent Freia Hoffmann. On a whim, the pair decided to visit Hoffmann's sister and her husband in Millau, near the rural epicenter of the Larzac protests. Over dinner, Hoffmann's brother-in-law informed his guests about the struggle of the shepherds, who had organized themselves as the "Committee of the 103."[51] The story's "numerical magic," by which he linked the 103 farmers with the Chicago 7 and other infamous bands of activists, enchanted Mossmann.[52] Hoffmann's interest was more pragmatic, but nonetheless evidenced the young Leftist's concerns about liberal democratic praxis; she recalled that her "lack of confidence in the types of political engagement that were possible through parties" turned her attention to the autono-mously organized protests. After a brief visit to the Larzac plateau, the duo returned to Freiburg where they decided to produce a radio program that would introduce SWR listeners to the shepherds' autonomous organiza-tion as "an alternative form of political action."[53]

In the process of producing their radio show, Mossmann and Hoffmann realized that there were autonomously organized "citizens' initiatives" active all over the Federal Republic – even in their own backyard.[54]

---

[50] Ibid., 264–267.   [51] Mossmann, *realistisch sein*, 176–177.

[52] In his memoir, Mossmann also linked the Committee of the 103 with Nena's 99 Red Air Balloons, though the song wasn't released until a decade after he first visited the Larzac. Mossmann, *realistisch sein*, 179.

[53] Freia Hoffmann, interview with the author, Bremen, 17 June 2010.

[54] Peter Cornelius Mayer-Tasch, *Die Bürgerinitiativbewegung. Der aktive Bürger als rechts- und poli-tikwissenschaftliches Problem* (Reinbek bei Hamburg: Rowohlt, 1976).

Rather than returning to the Larzac in order to gather material, the two Freiburgers decided to seek out West German organizations similar to the Committee of the 103.[55] By August, Mossmann had contacted members of rural citizens' initiatives working against nuclear development on the Upper Rhine. An interview that he and Hoffmann conducted in the village of Weisweil became the basis for a longstanding cooperation with rural reactor opponents, but building that relationship took time. In fact, his initial request for information caused Lore Haag, chair of the Weisweil Citizens' Initiative, to write to SWR headquarters in Baden-Baden in order to confirm that Mossmann and Hoffmann did indeed work with the broadcaster.[56] Two months later, when the Freiburgers returned to the village to listen to the broadcast of their program together with the rural activists whom they had interviewed, Haag advised her colleagues to be on guard "that we are not stabbed in the back from different sides."[57] Long-haired Freiburg activists simply were not the sort of people with whom concerned rural citizens expected to cooperate in their struggle against reactor development.

Nor was the unusual group of activists that Mossmann and Hoffman encountered in Weisweil comprised of the sort of people with whom they typically practiced politics. Nonetheless, in the conclusion to their radio program, Mossmann and Hoffmann linked the Weisweilers to the student movement. Citizens' initiatives, they reasoned,

> have taken hold of one of the [student movement's] ideas and developed it further: the consciousness that active politics can be conducted outside of institutionalized politics, outside of the political parties and beyond the act of voting.[58]

By associating the citizens' initiatives with their own extra-parliamentary political vision, Mossmann and Hoffman construed the Rhenish anti-nuclear movement as a people's rebellion, not a single issue movement. That description made cooperation between the 68ers and the rural anti-reactor movement conceivable.

---

[55] Wolfgang Hertle, the editor of *graswurzelrevolution* suggested that many West German Leftists had similar experiences. Visiting the Larzac, however, inspired the two Freiburgers to make more out of the smaller-scale German protests, which they reinterpreted in its light. Wolfgang Hertle, in conversation with the author, Hamburg, July 2010.

[56] "Am 28.8.73 in Gemeindehaus Weisweil," ABEBI Haag Lore 2HL2. See also "Informationsmaterial an Walter Moosmann [sic], Freiburg," ABEBI Haag Lore 2HL2.

[57] "Am 7.8 [sic] trafen wir uns in dem Fischerinsel," Lore Haag. ABEBI Haag Lore 2HL2.

[58] Freia Hoffmann and Walter Mossmann, "Bürger werden Initiativ – Vier Beispiele," transcript (Broadcast 7 October 1973), 24. ASB "Wyhl—Die Anfänge," 17517.

Mossmann and Hoffmann's personal encounters with rural activism may not have been as unusual as they seemed at the time, but the Freiburg journalists were pioneers amongst veterans of the student movement. For many of their erstwhile comrades, concerns about particular nuclear reactor projects still seemed apolitical and misguided in the early 1970s. Much as Mossmann had become involved in protests over the Freiburg tram fare hike despite the fact that he commuted to the city by car, his and Hoffmann's praise for the citizens' initiatives' operation "outside of the political parties and beyond the act of voting," emphasized the potential in the movement's form of activism rather than its content. Their interpretation, which drew on student activists' deep discontent with established parties and their open-ended search for alternatives, overcame discrepancies between Marxist logics and local environmental protest by simply ignoring them. It was not a productivist vision or an interest in the class struggle that drew the two Freiburg journalists to Weisweil, but rather excitement about "people's rebellion." Mossmann and Hoffmann realized that something big was happening in the Kaiserstuhl hills near Breisach. And that something, they believed, was an important example of "active politics."

A Movement of Provincials

Despite growing excitement from the likes of Mossmann and Hoffmann, reactor opponents' relentlessly local focus appeared all the more detached from high politics after the 1973 oil shock, which made energy policy a hot political topic all across Western Europe. The German Bundestag's speed limit reduction and Sunday driving ban made a marginal difference in efforts to ease the oil shortage's material effects, but such initiatives had special symbolic significance in a country known for its Fahrvergnügen.[59] French Prime Minister Pierre Messmer took a practically bold, but also symbolically powerful, initiative in March 1974 when he announced the new "Messmer Plan," which aimed to make France tout electrique, tout nucléaire by starting the construction of sixteen new reactors in the next two years and thirty-two more over the following decade.[60] Having thrown

---

[59] Jens Hohensee, *Der erste Ölpreisschock 1973–74. Die politischen und gesellschaftlichen Auswirkungen der arabischen Erdölpolitik auf die Bundesrepublik Deutschland und Westeuropa* (Stuttgart: Steiner Verlag, 1996), 156.

[60] Michael Bess, *The Light Green Society: Ecology and Technological Modernity in France, 1960–2000* (Chicago: University of Chicago Press, 2003), 95. See also: N.J.D. Lucas, *Energy in France: Planning, Politics, and Policy* (London: Europa Publications, 1979), 148–149.

the European economy from the heights of the "thirty glorious years" of unchecked growth to the depths of its first prolonged postwar recession, the oil shock was clear evidence that decisions as to whether or not reactors were to be built along the Upper Rhine had real economic significance – not to mention an important place in national politics. Such visible policies, one might presume, ought to have led Rhenish anti-nuclear protesters to shed their quaint, provincial image and connect their activism with high politics.

In one sense, French ecologists did organize themselves at the national level as Prime Minister Messmer was dictating the country's nuclear future. After the unexpected death of President Georges Pompidou on 2 April 1974, the Paris-based French branch of Friends of the Earth (FoE) reignited earlier discussions of running a candidate for President and convinced the agronomist René Dumont to run on an ecological ticket in the hastily organized May election to replace Pompidou. The reluctant candidate may have been convinced by Parisian activists to run in the first place, but his campaign was anything but a typical centralized, national campaign for the French Presidency.[61] For one thing, many mainstream, nationally organized environmental groups were reticent to support Dumont's upstart candidacy.[62] His frenzied month-long campaign relied instead on regional organizations and local committees, which coordinated Dumont's campaign stops and promoted his candidacy on the ground.

In Alsace, Dumont's 1974 presidential campaign was an undoubtedly local effort that built directly on recent activism.[63] Together with Jean-Jacques Rettig's anti-nuclear Committee to Protect Fessenheim and the Rhine Valley (CSFR), Ecology and Survival – which had been organized in support of Henri Jenn's 1973 National Assembly campaign – coordinated volunteers in Alsace and organized Dumont's 26 April visit to the region.[64]

---

[61] Members of the association of Journalists and Writers for the Protection of Nature and the Environment discussed the possibility of a presidential campaign at a Paris meeting in December 1973. After President Georges Pompidou's unexpected death on 2 April 1974, the Friends of the Earth reignited this discussion and selected René Dumont as their candidate for the May elections to replace Pompidou. René Dumont, *La campagne du René Dumont et du mouvement Écologique. Naissance de l'Écologie Politique* (Paris: Jean-Jacques Pauvet, 1974), 11. The Dumont campaign was only launched after the Leftists Charles Piaget and Michel Rocard determined not to run and no other suitable ecological candidate could be found. Yves Frémion, *Histoire de la révolution écologiste* (Paris: Hoëbeke, 2007), 121–122.

[62] Brendan Prendiville, *Environmental Politics in France* (Boulder: Westview Press, 1994), 19.

[63] Solange Fernex, "Elsaß-Lothringen werden sie nicht kriegen," in Claus Leggewie and Roland de Miller, *Der Wahlfisch. Ökologiebewegungen in Frankreich* (Berlin: Merve-Verlag, 1978), 121.

[64] Claude-Marie Vadrot, *L'écologie, histoire d'une subversion* (Paris: Syros, 1977), 41.

Dumont's tour of Alsace began in Eglingen, where he ate breakfast at a family-owned restaurant and talked with villagers about their ongoing struggle against the expansion of the Rhine–Rhône canal.[65] Later that morning, on a gravel parking lot in the Vosges mountain town of Saales, the candidate held an impromptu press conference on nuclear safety along-side Rettig. In the afternoon, Dumont biked through Mulhouse with hundreds of young cyclists. He concluded the day with a stump speech that attracted an audience of 800, a far larger crowd than attended a simultaneous rally in support of the Socialist Presidential candidate, François Mitterrand.[66] By dining, biking, and discussing local environmental issues with Alsatians, Dumont deployed retail politics to engage locally focused activists in the Presidential election.[67] The results of his campaign confirmed the importance of local issues for voters' attitudes towards the ecological candidate: Dumont received only 1.32 percent of the vote across France, but scored "almost 30% of the votes" in the two Alsatian villages that would be most affected by Rhine–Rhône canal.[68]

Though Dumont spoke frequently of the global context of his candidacy, his visit to Alsace hinted at the importance of local organizations and local environmental issues for the campaign. Dumont's disdain for the traditional, centralized structure of national politics in France began with his platform, which called for the decentralization of power at every geographic level.[69] Accordingly, Dumont described his insurgent candidacy as dependent on a convergence of outsider groups, including "women . . . immigrant workers, Occitanians and Alsatians, feminists, students, pacifists, pedestrians, vache-quiriphobes, and the shepherds of the Larzac."[70] Much like Jenn's legislative campaign, in other words, Dumont's run for the Presidency was premised on the outlandish proposition that peripheral places like Alsace and people typically regarded as outsiders were central to discussions about national and even global environmental issues.

Despite these examples of the links between local activism and national politics, the oil shock and the policies that the French and West German governments pursued in response to it did not deeply affect Rhenish anti-nuclear protest. In part, this is because even a policy as grandiose as the Messmer Plan had limited effects on the development of Europeans' attitudes towards nuclear energy. In fact, as Michael Bess has argued, "by and large, with the exception of a sometimes sizable minority," the French

---

[65] Schulthess, *Solange l'insoumise*, 94.
[66] Dumont, *La campagne*, 5; and: Schulthess, *Solange l'insoumise*, 94.
[67] Dumont, *La campagne*, 32–33.   [68] Fernex, "Elsaß-Lothringen," 199.
[69] Dumont, *La campagne*, 44.   [70] Ibid., 100–101.

people simply accepted the plan.[71] The decision to go all nuclear, made by the prime minister without even a single debate in the National Assembly, was taken on a completely different level than the anti-nuclear protests of the early 1970s, which referenced particular reactor projects and their local effects. In its technocratic nature and distance from the electorate, in fact, the Messmer Plan embodied what scholars have called the crisis of 1970s politics.[72] There is no question that the oil shock shifted the context in which nuclear reactors were built, giving nuclear energy pride of place in official pronouncements. Nonetheless, the changing rationale with which government officials justified reactor development, and the increasing tenacity with which they promoted nuclear projects did not immediately change the facts on the ground at reactor construction sites. Rhenish anti-nuclear activists remained focused on individual reactor projects – most of which had been planned well before 1973 – not central government policies.

The dissonance between local anti-reactor protest and the bold strokes of the Messmer Plan supports the argument that grassroots protesters really were operating in a separate sphere from high politics, even when they helped organize a campaign for the Presidency. Though local people had come to realize that government officials were not taking their concerns seriously, and begun to criticize the democratic order as a result, they had done little to engage themselves in the sorts of high-level decision-making from which policies like the Messmer Plan, which would dictate the construction of further reactors at Fessenheim among numerous other sites, emerged. Activists' persistent local focus, despite important changes in the national debate, revealed how effective insurgent political campaigns developed beneath a veneer of inaction and disinterest. Even amidst the Dumont campaign, an early, limited foray into "high politics," grassroots activists remained focused on visceral local matters rather than national policies. In so doing, they enabled themselves to build a broad coalition despite the quickly increasing political and economic significance of nuclear development.

From the perspective of locally focused Rhenish reactor opponents, there-fore, the biggest shock of 1973 was not the Organization of Arab Petroleum Exporting Countries' announcement of production cuts and embargoes against supporters of Israel – though that policy led directly to the

[71] Bess, The Light Green Society, 98.
[72] Gabriele Metzler, "Staatsversagen und Unregierbarkeit in den siebziger Jahren?" in Konrad Jarausch, ed., Das Ende der Zuversicht? Die siebziger Jahre als Geschichte (Göttingen: Vandenhoek und Ruprecht, 2008), 243–260.

Messmer Plan the following year. Instead, 1973's most shocking statement came from an SWR newscaster, who informed the public at 7:15 pm on 19 July that state government officials and Badenwerk executives had agreed to site a nuclear reactor some twenty kilometers downriver from Breisach, near the village of Wyhl.[73] The announcement shifted the regional anti-reactor movement's center of gravity overnight. Though most people were caught completely off guard, an organizing meeting was underway in Weisweil, Wyhl's closest neighbor, within half an hour of the news bulletin.[74] By 11 pm, the Weisweilers had sent an incredulous telegram to Baden-Württemberg's Premier, Hans Filbinger. Their message trotted out yet again the issue of disrespect at the hands of government officials by explaining that the people of Weisweil had been "alienated by the manner in which planning for this mass project had proceeded" and planned, therefore, to "protest against [Filbinger's] undemocratic behavior."[75] The group met again the very next day and made good on its pledge to continue protesting by organizing itself as the Citizens' Initiative Weisweil. The village, with its well-organized Citizens' Initiative, quickly became an important center in the movement against nuclear energy in Baden and Alsace.

Yet the Weisweilers' reaction to the Wyhl announcement, and thus the movement's shifting focal point, was not as spontaneous as it seemed. The Weisweilers responded promptly because they had been recruited to the anti-reactor struggle long before July 1973. Their preparations for the Wyhl struggle, which were made deep in the grassroots and dependent on local conditions, arguably predated even the first plans for nuclear development on the Upper Rhine. A rare Protestant village in an overwhelmingly Catholic region, Weisweil's inhabitants had long felt embattled. Because the Catholic inhabitants of neighboring villages voted for the Catholic Center Party before 1933 and the CDU after the war, Weisweilers supported the SPD so as "to vote against Catholicism," regardless of their misgivings about socialism.[76]

---

[73] Bernd Nössler, "Die Auseinandersetzung um das Kernkraftwerk Wyhl," in *Wyhl* (see note 35), 34–44.

[74] Balthasar Ehret, quoted in Hoffmann and Mossmann, "Bürger werden Initiativ."

[75] "Atomkraftwerk jetzt in Wyhl," (Flyer, July 1973). ASB "Wyhl—Die Anfänge," 18171.

[76] Lore Haag, quoted in Auer and Reich, "Gebrannte Kinder," 88. The shallowness of Weisweilers' support for the SPD was made evident in the 1930s, when it vanished in favor of the Nazis "from one day to the next." Nevertheless, the SPD regained its support in the village after the war. Walter Biselin, quoted in Auer and Reich, "Gebrannte Kinder," 88. See also: Milder, "Protest and Participation: The Transformation of Democratic Praxis in the FRG, 1968–1983," forthcoming in Michael Meng and Adam Seipp, eds., *German History in Transatlantic Perspective* (New York: Berghahn).

Though they were separated from one another by no more than a few kilometers, the villages around the Kaiserstuhl had long been "closed units." What few relationships existed between them were deeply influenced by each village's reputation, which was shaped in turn by its inhabitants' confession, the sort of crops they grew, and their level of economic prosperity.[77] Wyhl and Weisweil, located on flat land right along the Rhine, were both less affluent than the neighboring winegrowing villages situated on the Kaiserstuhl's steep slopes. Weisweil's fishermen and its tobacco farmers made it slightly more prosperous than Wyhl, but it was nonetheless tainted by its inhabitants' Protestantism, their support for the SPD, and the presence of the active German Communist Party (DKP) member Balthasar Ehret. As the owner of the Fischerinsel pub, Ehret was easily the region's best-known Communist. His prominence had long motivated the condescension of Weisweil's neighbors. Wyhl, on the other hand, stood to gain prestige, grow its economy, and thus bound past Protestant, Socialist Weisweil in the local pecking order as the site of a new nuclear reactor.[78]

That the new reactor project fit so easily into longstanding animosities proved helpful in mobilizing opposition, but the Weisweilers' quick response to the Wyhl announcement relied on several years of purposeful anti-nuclear recruiting work in the village. Together with a few other local notables, Siegfried Göpper, Weisweil's gristmill owner and largest landholder, had seen to it that his fellow villagers were not only aware of the earlier struggles against the Fessenheim and Breisach reactors, but also involved in them.[79] Göpper's work against the Wyhl reactor began already in December 1971, long before such a project really even existed. An unknown caller swore Göpper to secrecy early Christmas morning before informing him that Wyhl's Mayor Zimmer had offered the village to Minister of Economics Eberle "as an alternative site for the contested reactor planned for Breisach."[80] Göpper, who had been laughed out of

---

[77] Auer, interview.

[78] Interessengruppe KKW Ja Wyhl, "Wyhler – habt Ihr eigentlich noch Ehre im Leib?" StA-EN III. A 842.

[79] Martin Kaul, "Die Wunden von Wyhl," *die tageszeitung*, 18 September 2010.

[80] Göpper organized a meeting with Zimmer two days later at which he asked the Mayor point blank "whether he had written a letter to the Ministry of Economics in Stuttgart offering the Wyhl forest as an alternative site for a nuclear reactor." Zimmer "sprang up" from his chair in response to this question and asked indignantly how Göpper had come upon this information that "no more than five people in all of Baden-Württemberg knew about." The mayor's response confirmed Göpper's suspicions, but he kept his pledge not to share the information with anyone else. "Wirtschaftsminister Eberle erhielt 1971 einen brisanten Brief," *Badische Zeitung*, 24 February 2005; also: Siegfried Göpper, interview with the author, Weisweil, 16 February 2010.

Figure 2.2 Balthasar Ehret on the occupied site at Wyhl. © ABEBI.

a physics lecture at the University of Karlsruhe in the 1950s for asking why a miniature reactor could not be used to power a gristmill like his family's, had been deeply suspicious of nuclear energy ever since.[81] He was also deeply engaged in local affairs and committed to protecting his interests from what he perceived as the bungling interventions of government officials. Though he made good on his word, Göpper did not allow his promise of confidentiality to stop him from working discretely against the potential Wyhl reactor.[82] Even though Weisweil was a good twenty kilometers from Breisach, then the nearest proposed reactor site, Göpper recruited the support of Weisweil's Protestant Pastor, Reverend Richter, and of the church elders in order to organize an information session that was rather ominously entitled "Weisweil's

[81] Attending the lecture while visiting a cousin, Göpper had asked why his family gristmill could not be powered by nuclear energy. As the audience laughed, the Professor responded that nuclear energy was far too dangerous to be distributed so widely. This experience stuck with Göpper. Göpper, interview.

[82] Göpper was fiercely protective of his property rights, and became embroiled in several disputes with officials, including one over a water treatment plant as a result. Göpper, interview.

Figure 2.3 Siegfried Göpper (center) speaks to a reporter. © ABEBI.

future in the shadow of a nuclear reactor."[83] Not long after the meeting, which featured a presentation by the retired atomic physicist Dr. Hans Klumb, the citizens of Weisweil drafted a letter to Chancellor Willy Brandt decrying the Breisach project.[84]

Göpper's efforts to recruit his neighbors depended on local knowledge and the structures of village life. It was the village's unique position in the region geographically, confessionally, and politically – that made it a point

[83] Günter Richter, "Chronologie der Auseinandersetzungen mit den in Wyhl geplanten Reaktoren." ABEBI Richter Günter 123RG1. Göpper went so far as to personally invite Mayor Zimmer to the meeting. The Mayor only remained for half of the program and when he left, Göpper followed him out to his car. As the Mayor climbed into the driver's seat, Göpper asked him if he would still have promoted Wyhl as a potential reactor site had he known then what he knew now. "His answer, given over the hum of the running motor, was 'perhaps not,'" Göpper recalled. "Wirtschaftsminister Eberle erhielt 1971 einen brisanten Brief," *Badische Zeitung*, 24 February 2005; also: Göpper, interview.

[84] Jagdgenossenschaft Weisweil to Bundeskanzler Willi [sic] Brandt, 23 March 1972. ABEBI 101GS9 047. The Jagdgenossenschaft, which was chaired by Göpper, was an organization of all the village's landowners (and thus almost all of its inhabitants), which had been formed in order to lease hunting rights on their land. It was a major source of income for the villagers; Göpper was able to redirect some of these funds towards the anti-nuclear struggle. Göpper, interview.

of convergence after the Wyhl project was announced in July 1973. The village's outsider status made it easier for local officials like Mayor Nicola, a Social Democrat, to position themselves against the reactor. The leading citizens who pushed forward the movement, like the Protestant Pastor Reverend Richter and the Communist pub owner Ehret, also hailed from outside the region's mainstream. These characteristics, not to mention its proximity to Wyhl, made the village an ideal point of convergence for urban and rural activists, Badensians and Alsatians, Leftists and conservatives.

Yet, bringing so many people together relied on focused work by local reactor opponents, too. Based on their previous experiences, veterans of the campaigns against the Fessenheim and Breisach reactors had committed themselves to the task of getting a broader cross section of the population involved in anti-nuclear protest after the Wyhl project was announced. Rural veterans of the Breisach struggle wrote to the region's mayors, urging them to file objections against the Wyhl project on behalf of their communities. To expedite this arduous technical process, the activists provided village officials with detailed technical data upon which their objections could be based.[85] As a result of these efforts, Weisweil and three other villages filed formal complaints against the project, as did 300 individuals.[86]

Activists considered a petition drive against the Wyhl reactor their best chance to show the strength of the local opposition. From Freiburg, Harloff's Aktionsgemeinschaft sent personal letters to pastors requesting that they make petition sheets "available at religious services and other community events."[87] But, as one activist later wrote, once the drive got underway it was not only the pastors who "collect signatures before and after services." In addition:

> Pupils collect the signatures of upperclassmen in the high schools. Students collect them in the university, teachers collect them from their colleagues, entire enterprises in the Kaiserstuhl area sign against the reactor together. Farmers' wives go from door to door, every house is visited. Even the Black Forest Club (Schwarzwaldverein) helps out.[88]

[85] Hans Erich Schött to Bürgermeister Eitenbenz (Endingen am Kaiserstuhl), 1 June 1974. StA-EN III. A 842.

[86] The other villages were Sasbach, Endingen, and Lahr. Bernd Nössler, "Genehmigungsverfahren," in *Wyhl* (see note 35), 45.

[87] Illegible signature (for the Aktionsgemeinschaft gegen Umweltgefährdung durch Atomkraftwerke) to Evangelische Pfarramt, 6 June 1974. ASB "Wyhl—Die Anfänge," 3423.

[88] Nössler, "Das Genehmigungsverfahren," 45.

Figure 2.4 Margot Harloff submits 90,000 signatures collected by the citizens initiatives against the Wyhl reactor to Emmendingen county officials. © SAFR. W 134 No 096726b. Photographer: Willy Pragher.

With such deep, grassroots involvement, protesters were able to gather 90,000 petition signatures during the Wyhl project's month-long comment period – a figure equivalent to the entire population of rural Emmendingen county, where the reactor was to be built.[89] Opponents of the Wyhl project wasted no opportunity to accentuate the breadth of anti-reactor sentiment. Harloff made a show of piling the signatures into her laundry basket in order to deliver them to the county executive's office in Emmendingen. The official who accepted the signatures shamelessly downplayed this Herculean achievement, refusing to discuss the project with Harloff or the press.[90] Even such an impressive effort was quickly dismissed as a provincial undertaking, certain to be unimportant to higher-ups.

Reactor opponents themselves did little to dislodge the idea that their concerns were provincial. Their protest campaigns all targeted individual reactor projects and had little resonance outside the region. The public hearing on the Wyhl reactor, which took place a month after Harloff

[89] Of course, many of the signatures came from the city of Freiburg, which was outside Emmendingen County. "Nicht gegen den Willen der Bevölkerung durchsetzen," *Badische Zeitung*, 14 August 1974.
[90] "Bürgerinitiativen kamen mit dem Wäschekorb: Landrat Dr. Mayer als 'Briefträger,'" *Badische Zeitung*, 20 June 1974.

delivered the signatures and drew hundreds to the village, exemplified this local focus and the movement's hokey provincialism. The hearing was held in Wyhl's public gymnasium, the largest meeting space in town, and it drew people from all over the Kaiserstuhl. As they streamed into the gym, they passed two men on horseback dressed as the grim reaper. Once underway, the hearing devolved quickly into a showdown between farmers who felt they were being ignored and government officials who sought to downplay popular concerns in order to push through the project as quickly as possible. Once again, the hearing's chairman acted with dictatorial authority:

> He condescendingly suggested to an excited farmer that he should simply submit his concerns in writing. Or he made it apparent that he was only listening to an environmentalist's chit-chat for the sake of form. Or he switched off all the microphones in the hall.[91]

In response to the chair's obvious lack of compunction about ignoring or dismissing comments that did not suit him, Hans-Helmuth Wüstenhagen of the Federal Association of Citizens' Initiatives for Environmental Protection (BBU) stood up and denounced the event as a "show trial." He proclaimed that, "We are leaving and we will see to it that our democratic claims are fulfilled at a higher level!"[92] Silently, in Wüstenhagen's wake, "the complainants almost unanimously left the hall."[93]

Still, the curtain failed to drop, because "the Badenwerk's shock troops, the police, and 'the big-wigs' on the podium" simply remained in their places on the dais.[94] As Stuttgart officials shepherded the hearing to a hasty conclusion before a sea of empty seats, a band of protesters returned to the virtually empty meeting hall bearing a black coffin onto which they had painted the word "Democracy."[95] Yet the ultimate target of their protest was not the Stuttgart bureaucrats, but rather Wyhl's Mayor Zimmer, who had spent only a few minutes at the hearing that morning before returning home. The mock cortège marched to the Mayor's home where protesters made short speeches while the mayor sunbathed behind his

---

[91] Walter Mossmann, "Die Bevölkerung ist hellwach!" *Kursbuch* 39 (April 1975). Walter Mossmann and Cornelius Schwehr, eds., reprinted in *Die Störung. Tonstück und Texte zur Anti-AKW-Bewegung* (Emmendingen: verlag die brotsuppe, 2000), 12. All page references here are to the reprinted edition.
[92] "Weil die Wyhler kein Atomkraftwerk wollen," *Lahrer Zeitung*, 12 July 1974.
[93] "Nicht gegen den Willen der Bevölkerung durchsetzen," *Badische Zeitung*, 14 August 1974.
[94] "Weil die Wyhler," *Lahrer Zeitung*.   [95] Nössler, "Genehmigungsverfahren," 50.

Figure 2.5 Local reactor opponents carry a coffin with the word
"democracy" written on it through the public hearing on the Wyhl reactor,
9 July 1974. © Meinrad Schwörer.

garden wall.[96] Even this symbolically freighted protest, which linked
the development of nuclear energy with the shortcomings of democracy,
found a place for itself within the local framework by targeting
Zimmer. Despite the oil shock and the nationalization of the nuclear debate,
Rhenish anti-nuclear activists ultimately directed their bitter critiques of the
state of democracy in Baden-Württemberg towards local officials.

Nevertheless, stepping outside the licensing process's legalistic framework and condemning the narrow interpretation of public discourse
embodied in government officials' actions was a momentous move for anti-
nuclear protesters. The *BZ* took immediate note of this change in protesters' attitude, headlining its story on the hearing, "Environmentalists

---

[96] Ibid. See also: Wüstenhagen, *Bürger gegen Kernkraftwerke*, 51; and "Weil die Wyhler," *Lahrer Zeitung*. The *KVZ* estimated that 150 protesters took part. See: P.A., OG Freiburg and H.B., OAG Emmendingen, "Der Widerstand der Wyhler wächst. Die Anhörungstermin wurde zu einer Niederlage für die Landesregierung," *Kommunistische Volkszeitung*, 24 July 1974.

maneuvered themselves out of bounds."[97] The charge exposed anti-nuclear protesters to a barrage of new attacks. In another article, for example, the *BZ* argued that protesters' "departure from the hall proved itself to be a boomerang for them and all those who were more interested in provocation than discussion."[98] Following their dramatic action, in other words, anti-nuclear activists were blamed for the lack of debate at the hearing; Stuttgart officials were taken off the hook.

Yet the response of the Kraftwerk-Union (KWU), the subsidiary of Siemens and AEG that was to build the proposed Wyhl reactor, suggested that reactor proponents felt from the beginning that debate was neither realistic nor desirable with the vast majority of complainants. The KWU reckoned that while only one quarter of the complainants were "earnestly interested citizens," the other three-quarters were comprised of "demonstrators and organized groups who spared no means in order to feign 'righteous indignation' about the proposed project." The firm's conclusion that the vast majority of the public was not really outraged was bolstered by its finding that making documents about the project available had, "as predicted," led only to "boisterous criticisms on account of incompleteness, too short a period to look at it, or manipulation." Far from soliciting public comment and promoting healthy debate, in other words, the KWU expected numerous problems and sought the path of least resistance. In fact, the firm's recommendations for future public hearings included an admonition not to issue numbers or compose long speakers' lists, because doing so "means that the opponents can, at any time, prove how many speakers have yet to be heard."[99]

Though Rhenish reactor opponents localized their anti-reactor activism and willingly maneuvered themselves out of bounds, their dissociation from national politics was not simply a matter of provincialism. Instead, the reactor's supporters, from Minister Eberle, who coyly shielded his hand, to the KWU, which actively sought to discourage public debate, wanted little part in a political debate with concerned citizens. Their dismissals of local knowledge played an important part in grassroots anti-reactor protests' consignment to political irrelevance. In such a hostile environment, fraught inter-village relationships and symbolic protests brought local people into the movement. Even if such local foci could not immediately connect the growing insurgency with national politics, they produced

[97] "Umweltschützer haben sich selbst ins Aus manövriert," *Badische Zeitung*, 12 July 1974.
[98] "Hitzköpfe im Aus," *Badische Zeitung*, 12 July 1974.
[99] "Ein Internes Papier der Kraftwerk-Union," Erlangen, 15 July 1974. ASB "Wyhl—Die Anfänge," 2968.

a potent movement with local significance since reactor opponents targeted local and state officials.

International Independence

In the Spring of 1974, as Badensian opponents of the Wyhl reactor were gathering petition signatures, the Munich Chemical Works (CWM) announced plans to build a lead stearate processing facility in the Alsatian village of Marckolsheim, directly across the Rhine from the proposed reactor site. The struggle against the lead plant fostered new, deeper links amongst activists from both sides of the Rhine, and shifted the way they perceived the Upper Rhine valley. These transnational links and reconceptions of the region drew on the nature of the threat posed by the CWM plant since, in contrast to the more mysterious dangers associated with nuclear energy production, "the names of towns like Stolberg and Nordenham," where lead plants caused cattle to drop dead in the fields, were already "synonyms for contamination of the environment."[100] Badensian activists' protests against the proposed Breisach and Wyhl reactors helped make cooperation across the Rhine conceivable. The protest movement itself also played an important role in sustaining the new cooperations. Activists imagined a new, transnational community as they struggled together to defend their livelihoods, their home towns, and their health.

Given widespread knowledge of the effects of lead plant emissions, it was hardly a surprise that the announcement of plans for the Marckolsheim plant caused Strasbourg professors to issue warnings about the threat it would pose to public health, and drew the ire of Alsatian anti-nuclear groups.[101] The most vigorous response came from Marckolsheim itself, where "respected citizens," including "vets, pharmacists, dentists, even the

---

[100] Mossmann, *realistisch sein*, 195. Widespread knowledge of these disasters helped foment strong local opposition to the plant now proposed for Marckolsheim in five other towns where the CWM had previously attempted to build it. Fernex, "Non-Violence Triumphant," *The Ecologist* 5, no. 10 (December 1975), 373. See also "Die Bauplatzbesetzung in Marckolsheim dauert an," *Badische Zeitung*, 8 October 1974.

[101] Fernex, "Non-Violence Triumphant," 378. Even before their involvement in the anti-nuclear movement, however, these same Alsatian conservationists had launched a petition drive to protect the Vosges mountains, which had garnered some 40,000 signatures in 1970. Solange Fernex, "Non-Violence Triumphant," 372–373. The groups included S.O.S. Plaine du Rhin, Comité pour Sauvegarde de Fessenheim et de la Plaine du Rhin, and the Association Fédérative pour la Protection de la Nature. Georg Löser, *Grenzüberschreitende Kooperation am Oberrhein. Die Badisch-Elsässischen Bürgerinitiativen* (Stuttgart: Landesarchivdirektion Baden-Württemberg, 2003), 108.

vicar," founded a citizens' initiative to fight against the project.[102] Even the village council sided with the project's opponents, voting 11–10 to reject the plans. When Prefect Jean Sicurani overturned the vote and ordered construction to proceed as planned, the eleven opposed councilors resigned in protest.[103] Locally, at least, a high stakes fight over the project was brewing.

Despite the heated debate in Alsace, the announcement of plans for the lead plant did not initiate an immediate surge of interest in Baden. On its face, the lack of response from the Rhine's right bank was hardly surprising. Though marches against the Fessenheim reactor in 1971 and 1972 had momentarily brought together activists from Alsace and Baden, the three wars fought between France and Germany since 1871 had deeply divided the Upper Rhine valley.[104] There were "ample reasons for emotional distance; German was after all the language of Kaiser Wilhelm [and] the language of Hitler."[105] Memories of allied artillery barrages of the Badensian Rhine villages could not easily be set aside, either.[106] The Rhine itself, which was traced on its left bank by the Maginot Line and on its right by the Westwall during the 1930s and 1940s, remained more of a scar than a piece of connective tissue after the war. Given the division between the two regions, in fact, it was more surprising that the anti-reactor activists in Baden and Alsace had briefly cooperated than that Badensians had no immediate response to Marckolsheim.

Despite their disinclination to transnational engagement, however, their own struggles to make their concerns heard eventually sparked rural Badensians' interest in the fate of the Marckolsheim project. Farmers and vintners became more willing to heed the "tidings of horror" from Alsace after the failed Wyhl hearing shook their confidence in Baden-Württemberg officials who maintained that the lead plant would have no ill effects in Baden.[107] When the harried farmers organized yet another round of information sessions, where they shared information about the potential impact of lead processing on public health and agricultural

---

[102] The citizens' initiative was called the Groupemont d'Information pour la Sauvegarde de l'Environment de Marckolsheim (G.I.S.E.M.). Fernex, "Non-Violence Triumphant," 373.

[103] Ibid., 373–374.

[104] Hermann Bausinger argues that the Rhine "for a long time did not create separation, but rather neighborliness." It was the "preponderance" of "state-territorial, economic, trade, religious, and natural and cultural contacts" that allowed the feeling of neighborliness, however tenuously, to hang on. Bausinger, "Die 'Alemannische Internationale,'" 144.

[105] Ibid., 152.   [106] Auer and Reich, "Gebrannte Kinder".

[107] Nössler, "Genehmigungsverfahren," 51.

production, they made new realizations about the relationship between reactor construction and the grandiose proposals to rapidly develop industrial enterprises in the region. Because the meetings were conducted in the Alemannic dialect, which was spoken by rural people on both banks of the Rhine, they were accessible to Badensians and Alsatians alike. Farmers and vintners began once again to make use of the Rhine crossing that linked Sasbach with Marckolsheim to attend the sessions, sometimes even sneaking over the border after it had closed for the night at 10 pm.[108]

A pair of protest marches in the summer of 1974 revealed how Alsatians and Badensians' growing concerns about the two projects were causing them to see both banks of the Rhine as a single, integrated region. The first protest took place in late July. Some 2,000 activists from Baden and Alsace marched through Marckolsheim and assembled on the proposed lead plant site, from which they "could see just a few hundred meters away the vineyards [across the Rhine] in Sasbach."[109] The view made obvious the extent to which inhabitants of both Alsace and Baden would be affected by the plant's emissions. To emphasize this fact, the activists concluded their protest by planting a tree "as a symbol of the shared struggle ahead."[110] A similar crowd gathered a month later for the second march, which took place at Wyhl. "Hundreds of banners and signs, some of them written in French," as well as "a loudspeaker car, a smoke machine . . . even a team of donkeys" evidenced the breadth of the opposition.[111] At a peaceful gathering in the Wyhl forest that followed the march, entire families enjoyed the beautiful summer day as they listened to greetings from Swiss and Alsatian anti-reactor groups, and heard speeches that described how the Upper Rhine valley as a whole was threatened by the Wyhl and Marckolsheim projects.[112]

Symbolically and verbally, the marches and speeches linked Wyhl and Marckolsheim and outlined an emergent transnational community. Yet planting trees, driving donkeys through the streets, and gathering on remote construction sites could easily be dismissed as empty symbolic

---

[108] Mossmann, *realistisch sein*, 194.

[109] Nössler, "Genehmigungsverfahren," 51–52. See also: Fernex, "Non-Violence Triumphant," 374; and Löser, *Grenzüberschreitende Kooperation*, 111.

[110] Ibid. The tree was later ripped out of the ground by the Mayor of Marckolsheim, who favored the lead plant. "Jean," *Elsass. Kolonie in Europa* (Wagenbach: Berlin, 1976), 82.

[111] Mossmann, *realistisch sein*, 191. See also: "2.000 Teilnehmer beim Sternmarsch," *Badische Zeitung*, 26 August 1974.

[112] Bürgerinitiativen am Kaiserstuhl und Breisgau, "AUFRUF zum Sternmarrsch gegen das geplante Atomkraftwerk in Wyhl und Bleiwerk in Marckolsheim" [undated, likely August 1974]. ASB "Wyhl—Die Anfänge," 2883; see also: "2.000 Teilnehmer," *Badische Zeitung*.

protest rather than politically meaningful action. A planning session held immediately after the Wyhl march, in contrast, initiated a more traditional organizing effort by bringing together significant numbers of activists from Baden and Alsace to debate how the projects could be stopped. This meeting, which Mossmann described as "a regional independence day," led to the development of real transnational coordination. Finally, activists from both sides of the Rhine "decided to give up their national loyalties and work together across the border to prevent the construction of the Wyhl reactor and the Marckolsheim lead plant."[113] Delegates from ten Alsatian and eleven Badensian anti-nuclear groups founded an umbrella organization, the Association of Badensian and Alsatian Citizens' Initiatives, to coordinate future protests.

In a statement they entitled "The Declaration of the 21 Citizens' Initiatives to the Badensian-Alsatian Population," the alliance's members explained that in learning "that [they] had to defend their own interests together and with determination" they empowered themselves to have a say in projects on both sides of the border. Having realized that neither government would respond to concerns expressed via liberal democratic processes, but no longer willing to accept "disrespect for our rights," the statement's "dynamite" conclusion proclaimed that the twenty-one citizens' initiatives

> have decided to jointly occupy the construction sites for the Wyhl reactor and the Marckolsheim lead factory, as soon as construction commences. We are determined, to passively resist the violence that is being done to us through these projects, until the governments come to their senses.[114]

Georg Löser, a Freiburg chemist, said the conclusion was both an "unmistakable declaration of war against the planned projects and the self-empowerment of the initiatives vis-à-vis the government."[115] By referring to the "Badensian-Alsatian population" as a single unit and addressing their appeal to the people, rather than to elected officials or those responsible for the projects against which they had "declared war," the activists once again maneuvered themselves outside the bounds of the liberal democratic order and promoted the people of the Rhine valley as an alternative authority.

---

[113] Mossmann, *realistisch sein*, 196. From the Alsatian perspective, Fernex called the event an "historical meeting." Fernex, "Non-Violence Triumphant," 374.

[114] Badisch-Elsässische Bürgerinitiativen, "Erklärung der 21 Bürgerinitiative an die Badisch-elsässische Bevölkerung" [undated, August 1974]. ASB "Wyhl—Die Anfänge," 17652

[115] Löser, *Grenzüberschreitender Kooperation*, 114.

In order to take up direct communications with the newly imagined region's population, they printed 30,000 copies of their declaration in German and French and distributed them throughout the Upper Rhine valley. The green-and-white document was hung "on barn doors, in the windows of bakeries, at the pharmacy, at second hand stores, at the electrician's, in the wine growers' cooperative, at school, at the inn, at town hall."[116] Though it was ubiquitous, the text proved surprisingly easy to misunderstand, particularly for advocates of the industrial projects. Many readers struggled to think outside traditional political frameworks and thus failed to understand the importance of the transnational community that the statement addressed. Government officials stopped short of believing that protesters would actually occupy the sites in Marckolsheim and Wyhl, allowing themselves to "be thoroughly surprised" when activists followed through with their well publicized plans.[117] Even the protesters nervously debated "the 'ifs and buts' of the planned occupations" as they waited for construction to begin.[118] Their uncertainly stemmed from the fact that the tactic of occupation was new to the region, and especially to the rural people who planned to initiate it on the Wyhl and Marckolsheim sites.

Protesters' unilateral decision to act transnationally meant that if they had previously "maneuvered out of bounds," they would now engage in illegal protest, and exit liberal democracy's legalistic framework altogether. In fact, transnational cooperation provided not only a means of acting outside the liberal democratic order, but also the mechanism by which new tactics like occupation reached Rhenish activists. As it had been for Mossmann and others in the West German Left, the shepherds' struggle on the Larzac remained a key point of reference. A group of young Alsatian farmers received a practical primer in occupation when they traveled to central France in December 1973 in order to help set up the illegal La Blaquiere farm on land controlled by the French Army.[119] Building up the farmstead – a project with which rural Alsatians were well acquainted – revealed the importance of constructing the infrastructure of everyday life in order to maintain an occupation.[120] At about the same time, a dozen nonviolent Swiss activists organized a five-day "trial-squat" at the proposed

---

[116] Mossmann, *realistisch sein*, 199.   [117] Ibid., 200.

[118] Badisch-Elsässische Bürgerinitiativen, "Wir wenden uns an Sie..." (1 September 1974). ASB "Wyhl—Die Anfänge," 2882. See also, Nössler, "Das Genehmigungsverfahren," 52–53.

[119] Solange Fernex, "Non-Violence Triumphant," 373; see also: Jean-Jacques Rettig, interview with the author, Freiburg, 8 March 2010.

[120] Anna Feigenbaum, Fabian Frenzel, and Patrick McCurdy, *Protest Camps* (London: Zed Books, 2013), 56–59; see also Chapter 3 for more about the infrastructure of occupation at Marckolsheim and Wyhl.

reactor site in Kaiseraugst, a mere eighty kilometers from Freiburg.[121] Though the temperature hovered around –10°C, the squat lasted from 26 until 30 December, attracting 400 visitors, and creating a "wide echo" in the press.[122] Though it differed from the long-term approach taken on the Larzac, the trial-squat proved that occupation could happen in the Upper Rhine valley. Even the *BZ* reported in early 1974 that Nonviolent Action Kaiseraugst (GAK) had announced plans to carry out a full-fledged occupation in the fall on the basis of the action's success.[123]

These first experiences with occupation at Larzac and Kaiseraugst inspired activists to consider the tactic of occupation in their struggles at Marckolsheim and Wyhl, but they did not suddenly make it common-place. Immediately after the July protest march, Solange Fernex solicited written pledges from fifty Alsatian conservationists willing to occupy the Marckolsheim site.[124] At the founding meeting of the Association of Citizens' Initiatives the following month, this group pushed hard to ensure that the declaration threatened occupations of the two sites should con-struction begin.[125] Still, activists remained conflicted about just how to proceed. At an emergency planning meeting the night after construction began at Marckolsheim, "everyone, poised on the brink, was afraid to take the final step." Fernex and a handful of other activists worked late into the night, delivering flyers calling on supporters to, "Come one and all to the construction site in Marckolsheim!"[126] Only a few dozen protesters had assembled on the site by 7 am, but Fernex seized the "dramatic moment," pulling a bundle from her car and assembling "a small, ugly tent."[127] Soon, another woman pitched her own tent on the site. By 10 am, more than one hundred activists were on the construction site, which was now dotted with tents.[128]

---

[121] These activists were members of the newly formed Nonviolent Action Kaiseraugst, which quickly became one of the so-called *graswurzel* groups affiliated with the nonviolent, anarchist publication *graswurzelrevolution*.

[122] Michael Schroeren, *z. B. Kaiseraugst. Der gewaltfreie Widerstand gegen das Atomkraftwerk: Vom legalen Protest zum zivilen Ungehorsam* (Zürich: Schweizerischer Friedensrat, 1977), 32–33. Marc Häring, "NAK – GAK – GAGAK – Versuch einer Erklärung." AfZ, NL Alexander Eule: NWA GAK AGEA GAGAK etc. 1968–1974 Gründerphase, 10 Jahr-Jubiläum – 1980, 20 Jahr-Jubiläum – 1990.

[123] "Bauplatz-Besetzung im Herbst," *Badische Zeitung*, 11 April 1974.

[124] Fernex, "Non-Violence Triumphant," 374.

[125] Walter Mossmann, interview with the author, Freiburg, 20 February 2010.

[126] "Blei-Alarm," Flyer (19 September 1974). Reprinted in Nössler and de Witt, *Wyhl* (see note 35), 53.

[127] Walter Mossmann, interview with the author, Freiburg, 8 March 2010.

[128] Fernex reports that "two women" were the first to set up their tents. Fernex, "Non-Violence Triumphant," 374.

The small settlement that grew up around Fernex's ugly tent brought construction of the Marckolsheim lead processing plant to a halt. It also became the capital of the nascent "Alemannic Community." In fact, the two functions were closely linked. Though the occupiers quickly convinced the construction workers to leave and got their protest announced on a Radio Luxembourg broadcast at 1 pm, they were uncertain how the occupation would proceed or even how long they could keep it going. They did know, however, that attracting more occupiers would make it more difficult for the police to clear the site. Leon Siegel, the trusted local veterinarian, led a team of dialect speakers that visited local farm families, asked the farmers their opinions of the lead plant, and urged them to come see the site for themselves. Once curious farmers arrived, beverages and nature tours enticed them to stay. When the police failed to intervene the following Monday, Fernex later wrote, she knew the protesters had won and that the occupation would endure.[129]

Figure 2.6 Women knit while they occupy the lead stearate plant construction site in Marckolsheim, fall 1974. © Meinrad Schwörer. AGG FO-01990-01-rp.

[129] Fernex, "Non-Violence Triumphant," 375. Die 21 Bürgerinitiativen, "Liebe Freunde" (Marckolsheim, 20 September 1974). ASB "Wyhl—Die Anfänge," 17801.

In another sense, however, the struggle was just beginning. Having empowered themselves to work together across the Rhine, rural people from both sides of the river imagined themselves as an "Alemannic Community" on the occupied site in Marckolsheim. At a protest on the site, Meinrad Schwörer, a reactor opponent from Wyhl, emphasized the links between rural people on both riverbanks. Using their common Alemannic dialect, he proclaimed, Badensians and Alsatians could "voice so well their mind." What is more, the dialect articulated the distance between rural people and government officials because it was "a language that they do not understand in Paris, that they do not understand in Bonn."[130] After Jean Gilg, an Alsatian German teacher, raised a banner above his tent that read, "Germans and French together, the watch on the Rhine," Walter Mossmann was inspired to write his ballad as an expression of local solidarity against hostile governments.

Though they were loath to come out and say it, politicians in Alsace and in Baden began to realize the significance of this deepening cooperation. Rather than ordering a direct police intervention on the site, Jean Sicurani, prefect of the Upper Rhine Department, attempted to use the protesters' transnational cooperation to his advantage by blaming Badensians for the disorder in Marckolsheim. The Germans were an easy target; preventing the "hereditary enemy," known derisively as le boche, from wreaking havoc fell squarely within the responsibilities of any competent French official. Thus, just one week after the occupation began, Prefect Sicurani ordered two local border crossings closed to Badensians.[131] In response, villagers in Alsace and in Baden rang church bells and set off fire sirens so as to "alarm the entire region" that something was amiss.[132] As Badensian protesters made their way towards the site, they came upon the closed bridges in Sasbach and Breisach. Alsatians, too, were sent from Marckolsheim to the sealed checkpoints. Using tractors, cars, and even their bodies, protesters from both countries blockaded the two bridges for hours.[133] "The border," they declared, "cannot stop poisonous lead particles. It will not hinder our

[130] An audio recording of Schwörer's speech is available on: Badisch-Elsässische Bürgerinitiativen, *Neue Lieder und Gedichte aus Dreyeckland*, Trikont-Verlag (Record). My translation into English is based on "Jean's" transcription of the speech into high German. See: "Jean," *Elsass. Kolonie in Europa*, 87.

[131] "Blei-Alarm Gilt! – Bauplatz seit 2 Wochen besetzt," *Informations-Dienst zur Verbreitung unterbliebener Nachrichten* 51 (6 October 1974), 3.

[132] Mossmann, "Die Bevölkerung ist hellwach!" in *Die Störung* (see note 91), 17; see also: "Wacht am Rhein," *Der Spiegel* (21 October 1974).

[133] "Sperrung des Grenzübergangs auf der Sasbacher Rheinbrücke" (Photograph), in *Wyhl* (see note 35), 55.

Figure 2.7 Protesters blockade the border crossing at Sasbach on
26 September 1974. © Leo Horlacher. ASB.

solidarity!"[134] This stunning display of transnational cooperation on the
part of people who had fought three wars against one another in the past
century forced Sicurani to realize that he could not divide and conquer the
protesters along the lines of Franco-German "hereditary enmity."[135] By the
end of the day, he ordered the border reopened.

Officials in Baden-Württemberg still sought to disassociate the two
projects, however. The state's Minister of Health, who had previously
pooh-poohed public concerns about emissions from across the Rhine,
denounced the Marckolsheim plant as a serious threat to public
health.[136] By late October, the state government had made such a strong
case against the lead plant that the *BZ* ignored the fact that protesters had
halted all progress on the project for the past month by occupying the site
and reported that, "environmentalists east of the Rhine can only hold out

---

[134] "Blei-Alarm Gilt!" *Informations-Dienst.*
[135] Sonia Lemettre, "Erbfeind / Enemi héréditaire," in Astrid Kufer, Isabelle Guinaudeau, and
    Christophe Premat, eds., *Handwörterbuch der deutsch-französischen Beziehungen* (Baden-Baden:
    Nomos, 2009), 69–71.
[136] Shortly after the beginning of the occupation, Minister Griesinger stated that "lead emissions are
    not harmful." Nössler, "Das Genehmigungsverfahren," 58.

hope that Stuttgart or Bonn will be able to influence Paris."[137] The Baden-Württemberg government's intention to portray itself as the lead plant's chief foe depended on its reassertion of the political boundary that divided Marckolsheim and Wyhl. To this end, Premier Filbinger traveled to Paris and lobbied against the Marckolsheim project on the very same day that the Ministry of Economics announced its approval of an initial construction license for the Wyhl reactor.[138] Anti-nuclear activists fought back by deriding Filbinger's mission to Paris as "a trick to push through the reactor in Wyhl."[139] After all, they noted, "it costs the state government nothing to speak out against the lead plant ... it is under the control of the French authorities."[140]

Protesters' responses to government officials' attempts to reassert the Rhine as a political boundary revealed the extent to which Alemannic cooperation opened the border, even as they raised interesting questions about the relationship between transnational cooperation and liberal democratic politics. Addressing the Badensian-Alsatian population and acting outside the bounds of the established liberal democratic order, Rhenish protesters finally caught the attention of government officials and succeeded in delaying construction of the Marckolsheim lead stearate plant. Though their intentions were misread because of the tangled, transnational roots of their chosen protest tactics and their explicit calls to act outside of the liberal democratic order, the Marckolsheim occupation should not be understood solely as evidence that anti-nuclear activists had left the democratic order behind. Instead, the occupation ought also to be seen as a site of community-building. Circumventing deadlocked high politics led to increased discussion of important issues. Rural people's decision to fight back in the name of their own self-interest built community across the Rhine and throughout the region.

Conclusion

By the fall of 1974, conservative rural people in the Upper Rhine valley had become deeply distrustful of their governments. Local Leftists, meanwhile, had begun to see potential for popular rebellion in farmers' "self-interested"

[137] "Tag und Nacht auf der Wacht am Rhein," *Badische Zeitung*, 26 October 1974.
[138] Rudolf Eberle, "Warum das Kernkraftwerk Wyhl genehmigt wird," *Badische Zeitung* (paid advertisement), 6 November 1974; "Proteste halten an," *Badische Zeitung*, 8 November 1974.
[139] Arbeitskreis Umweltschutz an der Universität Freiburg, "Gefährdung durch Kernkraftwerke – Kein KKW in Wyhl!" (Freiburg: Stern-Druck, January 1975), 3.
[140] "Demo in Sasbach," *Was Wir Wollen* 3 (17 November 1974).

protests. And yet, in spite of the oil shock and the 1973 recession, not to mention the Messmer Plan and René Dumont's Presidential candidacy, the most lively debates about nuclear energy and industrial development remained focused on particular projects not central government policies or the state of the national economy. Paradoxically, this pronounced provincialism became codependent with a transnational approach to politics that brought together Alsatians and Badensians in opposition to their governments. Since even the first ecologists to run for office in Alsace disavowed their interest in government, these developments seemed separate from policymaking and party politics. They nonetheless revealed a complicated relationship with liberal democracy.

But there was more to Rhenish anti-reactor protests than first meets the eye. Believing that grassroots protests like those that occurred along the Upper Rhine marked a withdrawal from high politics requires flattening protests that actually took place on multiple levels. Problematically, this flattening dramatically limits our understanding of environmental politics. That Rhenish protesters directed their righteous anger about nuclear development towards the Mayor of Wyhl, a village with 2,500 inhabitants, rather than the Premier of Baden-Württemberg, let alone the authors of West Germany's Federal nuclear law or France's Prime Minister Messmer, is considered evidence of their provincialism and their estrangement from high politics. Yet protesters submitted complaints to their representatives at every level, assisted René Dumont in his Presidential campaign, and even criticized government officials in neighboring countries. In focusing ultimately on officials like Mayor Zimmer, local activists did not mean to take themselves out of political debates but rather to tackle the problem of nuclear energy at the level where a complex technical topic – not to mention the actions of the government itself – became palpable. On account of its proximity and tangibility, seeking to stop a single nuclear reactor seemed more meaningful than advocating amendments to the Atomic Law.

By operating in a manner that seemed peripheral to high politics, however, Rhenish activists created space to work towards their goals in an otherwise inhospitable environment. Those with the power to make decisions, from government officials to industrial executives, had no interest in hearing Rhenish activists' concerns about nuclear energy, which they dismissed as provincial and misinformed. Yet, for local people those concerns were about their survival. The fact that government officials refused to take those existential concerns seriously actually helped activists to recruit their neighbors to the anti-reactor cause and to develop more powerful modes of protest. Because antinuclear activists focused on building new associations at the grassroots level, speaking with neighbors, and organizing symbolic actions, their protests seemed provincial. Given their part in allowing Rhenish people to imagine a new, transnational community, one that overcame old divisions in the struggle to save itself, such efforts can hardly be considered evidence of social atomization.

Creating too firm a division between high politics and provincial protest implies that political environmentalism, too, must fall on only one side of this divide. This invented division obscures the ways that grassroots activism and local engagement can reshape the political, an outlook that makes environmental protest very difficult to understand. The consequences of such preconceptions became clear when Rhenish protesters occupied the Wyhl reactor construction site in February 1975. For observers versed in the action's local precedents and context, it was easy to see it as a political act carried out by well-prepared protesters. From an outside perspective, however, the occupation was incredibly difficult to read. It was dismissed as an unexpected outburst of rural rage, devoid of political meaning. This divided vision of the Wyhl protest shaped both the antinuclear movement's immediate future and the ways it has been interpreted by scholars ever since. The shearing of political significance from grassroots protest continues to define the way we approach environmental matters today, obstructing the manifold – albeit complicated – links between grassroots protest and liberal democratic processes. Yet it was precisely those links that made the anti-nuclear movement meaningful to an ever broader cross section of society and thus made nuclear energy a focal point of West German politics.

CHAPTER 3

Onto the Site and into Significance? The Wyhl Occupation in Its Contexts, from Strasbourg to Kaiseraugst and Constance to Kiel

In August 1974, a member of the Citizens' Initiative Weisweil asked Professor Theodor Ebert to sign a statement of opposition to the Wyhl reactor project. The professor, a renowned expert on social movements, refused the request because he was "not personally certain" that local people's "existence was in fact threatened" by the proposed reactor.[1] Just six months later, however, Ebert rushed from West Berlin to Wyhl so as to offer unsolicited advice and encouragement to anti-reactor activists. The professor had not suddenly become more concerned about the potential dangers of nuclear energy production. Instead, Rhenish protesters' occupation of the Wyhl reactor construction site, which began in February 1975 and endured for nine months, excited him. By using their bodies to take control of the site and thus physically preventing construction, Rhenish anti-reactor protesters made their movement known across the country. Not long after the occupation began, Ebert breathlessly defined the fight against the Wyhl reactor as "surely the most significant explicitly non-violent campaign since the founding of the Federal Republic." He was captivated by "the number of protesters, the significance of the controversy, the scope of the civil disobedience, and the transnational character" of the movement.[2]

In fact, the occupation at Wyhl prompted a sudden interest in Rhenish anti-reactor protest across West Germany – and not just from experts in social movements like Ebert. The influx of attention proved fleeting, but the occupation's effect on West German politics endured. A laudatory entry in the encyclopedia of German memory sites contends that in the minds of West Germans, the 1975 occupation stands in for the years of grassroots anti-nuclear protest that preceded it; Wyhl "gained the profile in

[1] Theodor Ebert to Heinz Siefritz, 3 September 1974. ABEBI Haag Lore 8HL6.
[2] Theodor Ebert, "Als Berliner in Wyhl: Friedensforschung und Konfliktberatung vor Ort," *Gewaltfreie Aktion*, 24/25 (1975): 36–42.

which it went down in West German history on account of the nine month occupation."[3] This perspective reduces the long-winded anti-reactor struggle, which developed out of an even longer history of anti-reactor protest in the Upper Rhine valley, to the 1975 site occupation, an event that has come to be considered, as its place in the encyclopedia of memory sites reminds us, both unprecedented and uniquely West German.

Why did the occupation suddenly interest West Germans in the Rhenish anti-reactor movement, giving a new national dimension to what had previously been a local and transnational movement? What caused this particular action to dominate Germans' collective memory of anti-nuclear protest? And how did the singular occupation affect the meaning of protest and its relationship politics? The first years of the grassroots anti-reactor struggle along the Upper Rhine provided little reason to believe that the goings-on at Wyhl would attract widespread attention or that the village would become the site of one of the most important protests in the FRG's history. Right up until the occupation began, very few observers from outside the region were interested in Rhenish anti-reactor protest, as was evident in Ebert's dismissal of the protestors' goals in the summer of 1974. Part of the occupation's significance was derived from its shock value. Citizens from Constance to Kiel were flabbergasted by footage – broadcast on national television – of middle-aged women and men engaged in a hard-nosed confrontation with police. Members of K-Groups and of a whole host of other activist organizations were motivated by "the example of Wyhl" to renew their activism. Government officials worried that the occupation posed a serious challenge to the country's young democratic order.

Ironically enough, understanding how and why the Wyhl occupation created such a powerful initial shock far away from the Rhine valley, but also changed West Germans' conceptions of protest in the long run, requires viewing the action both within its local context and from beyond the FRG's borders. Locally, the occupation was conceived as a last-ditch effort to halt the reactor project, not an incitement to West Germans to become more politically active, a threat to democracy, or even a call for citizens to re-think their attitudes towards nuclear energy. In France, however, occupation had attained pride of place as a protest tactic since May 1968, when occupation strikes shut down fifty factories. In the early 1970s, the celebrated protests at Larzac, which included squatting on

---

[3] Bernd-A. Rusinek, "Wyhl" in Étienne François and Hagen Schulze, *Deutsche Errinerungsorte II* (Munich: Beck, 2001), 653.

government-owned farmsteads, bolstered occupation's reputation as a serious – not to mention powerful – mode of protest.[4] The Alsatian and Badensian protagonists of the Wyhl struggle could place their actions in this French context, but most West Germans were unfamiliar with the trajectory of occupation protest in France.[5] Instead, scholars argue that Germans still "lacked a self-conscious tradition of civil disobedience as legitimate political action in a democracy" in the 1980s.[6] Within its divergent transnational, local, and national contexts, the Wyhl occupation was simultaneously predictable and shocking, powerful and pathetic. Looking from multiple perspectives reveals how the action's longer-term political significance lay in the ways it caused these disparate contexts to intersect.

An Action Out of Context

The Badenwerk's project managers and the local government officials responsible for the Wyhl reactor surely expected the start of construction to be met with protest. They had experienced a half-decade of grassroots opposition to nuclear energy and read the Declaration of the Badensian and Alsatian Citizens' Initiatives. Nevertheless, the threatened "occupation" at Wyhl remained enigmatic. Officials were familiar with the exploits of the Red Army Faction (RAF), which had ensconced "armed struggle" as the most "vivid expression of the importance of militancy for New Leftists" in the FRG.[7] But applying concepts of militant protest derived from the actions and statements of the RAF did little to help officials understand Rhenish activists' plans. Officials would have been far better off studying

---

[4] Herman Lebovics, *Bringing the Empire Back Home: France in the Global Age* (Durham, NC: Duke University Press, 2004), 48–49.

[5] The most frequently mentioned precedent in West Germany was the "occupation" of the Großer Knechtsand on 8 September 1957. Though some 300 protesters did spend the entire day illegally occupying the Großer Knechtsand, a large sandbank at the mouth of the Elbe River, used by the Royal Air Force as a bombing range, the activists left as planned (and of their own accord) at the end of the day. Anna-Katharina Wöbse, "Die Bomber und die Brandgans. Zur Geschichte des Kampfes um den 'Knechtsand' – eine historische Kernzone des Nationalparks Niedersächsisches Wattenmeer," *Jahrbuch Ökologie* (2008): 195–196; see also: Wolfgang Kraushaar, *Die Protest-Chronik 1949–1959. Eine illustrierte Geschichte von Bewegung, Widerstand, und Utopie* (Hamburg: Zweitausendeins, 1996), 1707–1708. In contrast to France, where occupation strikes had been part of the 1968 "events" and remained in the political lexicon, there had not been a similar development in West Germany.

[6] Michael Hughes, "Civil Disobedience in Transnational Perspective: American and West German Anti-Nuclear-Power Protesters, 1975–1982," *Historical Social Research* 39, no. 1 (2014): 237.

[7] Jeremy Varon, *Bringing the War Home: The Weather Underground, the Red Army Faction, and Revolutionary Violence in the Sixties and Seventies* (Berkeley: University of California Press, 2004), 8.

the ongoing occupation at Marckolsheim. Even the *BZ* was perceptive enough to report in January 1975 that "an occupation of the construction site on the Rhine – following the example of Marckolsheim – is already firmly planned."[8] But Marckolsheim and the longer French history of occupation protests that underpinned it proved a bridge too far for Baden-Württemberg officials, who failed to familiarize themselves with the foreign protest tactic.

Unsure how to prevent an occupation at Wyhl, those responsible for shepherding the reactor project to completion focused on directing attention away from the project and targeting the few local activists they considered capable of "serious" protest. In lieu of a ceremonial ground-breaking, workmen arrived in the Wyhl forest completely unannounced on Monday, 17 February 1975 and began to seal off the site. A pre-emptive police order, nailed to trees throughout the forest, revealed officials' belief that a small group of ringleaders would be responsible for any serious protest. The order forbade "trespassing or loitering on the enclosed construction site," and singled out those who planned to spend an extended period on the site for additional punishment by specifying that the fine of 200 Marks was to "be repeatedly levied" each and every day that offenders remained in the woods. In the event, officials did not even wait to see who might show up when construction began; they pre-emptively levied fines against eight activists whom they presumed would be in the woods and up to no good.[9]

Yet, the very ringleaders whom the authorities pre-emptively held responsible for protest at the reactor site seemed to back down from the threatened occupation altogether once construction began. Leading activists responded to the secretive start of construction at Wyhl by inviting journalists to a press conference at a cabin in the Wyhl Forest. Siegfried Göpper, who had played a central role in fostering anti-reactor sentiment in Weisweil, was the event's primary speaker. He said nothing about an occupation but rather briefed the assembled reporters on pending legal challenges to the reactor project.[10] Göpper was joined on the podium by Hans-Helmuth Wüstenhagen, the chairman of the BBU. On behalf of his

---

[8] Niklas Arnegger, "Die Wyhler sind gleichgültig bis resigniert," *Badische Zeitung*, 8 January 1975.

[9] Local authorities were so certain protesters would show up that they fined the eight protesters even though there were no protests on 17 February and "some of [the eight activists] had proof that they had not set foot in the woods that day." Bernd Nössler, "Es beginnt die Bauerei an dem atomaren Ei," in Bernd Nössler and Margret de Witt, eds., *Wyhl. Kein Kernkraftwerk in Wyhl und auch sonst nirgends. Betroffene Bürger berichten* (Freiburg: Dreisam Verlag, 1976), 85.

[10] "Demonstranten erzwingen Abbruch der Arbeit," *Badische Zeitung*, 19 February 1975.

national umbrella organization's widespread membership, Wüstenhagen calmly asserted that, "the citizens' initiatives will not call for a site occupation."[11] The press conference concluded without any further elucidation of planned protests by the movement's perceived leadership.

The occupation was launched instead by a crowd of 300 reactor opponents, most of them rural women, who had gathered alongside reporters to hear Göpper and Wüstenhagen speak.[12] After the speakers left the podium, one woman suggested a short walk to the construction site. "Confronted by the big machines," the quiet crowd's mood quickly shifted. Reactor opponents began shouting at the Badenwerk's project manager.[13] Their

Figure 3.1 Anti-reactor activists converge on the Wyhl reactor construction site and halt construction, 18 February 1975. © Meinrad Schwörer.

[11] Ibid; and: Nössler, "Es beginnt die Bauerei," 82; see also: KPD/AO, *Rote Fahne Informationsdienst* 1 (18 February 1975). HSAS EA 1/107 Bü 766; Gerd Auer, "Hier wird ein Platz besetzt," in *Wyhl* (see note 9), 86.

[12] The men were "in the vineyards, in the fields, or at work." Maria Köllhofer, "Es war die erste Demonstration in meinem Leben überhaupt," in *Wyhl* (see note 9), 101.

[13] Bernd Nössler, "Es beginnt die Bauerei an dem Atomaren Ei," 83; see also: Westdeutscher Rundfunk, *Vor Ort. Bürger gegen Atomkraftwerk in Wyhl*, DVD, directed by Thomas Schmitt (1975).

frustration increased "when they saw how the forest was being destroyed." Without any command to do so, "protesters broke down the fence and surged onto the site."[14] The emotional response was at odds with commonly held ideas about activism; it contributed to the sense that rural protest was unorthodox and disorganized, but certainly not militant. Its protagonists, the majority of whom were middle-aged women, did not look like student activists, let alone terrorists. They lacked a clear-cut, previously announced plan. None of the protest's presumed ringleaders was anywhere to be seen.

Despite these perceived shortcomings, reactor opponents stopped construction and took control of the site quickly and effectively. A group of Alsatian women "pitched the first tent in front of a bulldozer that had been immobilized when some women from Weisweil climbed onto it."[15] Other activists "jumped onto the shovels of excavators, positioned themselves in front of the treads of the bulldozers, and entered into conversation with the construction workers."[16] Within an hour, "every machine was shut down, [and] the chainsaws were stopped."[17] Though the action seemed unusual or even unprecedented to outsiders, its local roots were remarkably easy to trace. It drew on activists' experience at Marckolsheim, where they had stopped construction just six months earlier. It also built on the long enduring anti-reactor struggle that had been going on in the region since 1971. Maria Köllhofer, a mother of five from Endingen, had never attended a demonstration before, but she strongly opposed the Wyhl reactor project. She had taken to keeping a "fully packed bag containing a warm blanket and provisions" ready by the door at home. Though she was unaware of a specific plan to occupy the site, Köllhofer left for the press conference well provisioned and prepared to spend the night in the Wyhl forest.[18]

Having been told by Wüstenhagen that no occupation would take place, reporters who followed citizens from the press conference to the construction site were flummoxed; "occupation" sounded serious, and so they hesitated to label the commotion they were witnessing as such.

---

[14] Auer, "Hier wird ein Platz besetzt," 86.
[15] Solange Fernex, "Non-Violence Triumphant," *The Ecologist* 5 (no. 10), 376.
[16] Nössler, "Atomaren Ei," 83.   [17] Fernex, "Non-Violence Triumphant," 376.
[18] Her family had even previously agreed that she would participate on their behalf. This was because, unlike her husband, Köllhofer could not be fired, and because she reasoned that "a mother with five kids would not be locked up so quickly." Köllhofer, "Es war die erste Demonstration," 101. This presumption proved incorrect – Köllhofer was among the 54 activists arrested at Wyhl two days later. Gertrud and Emil Friedrich, "30 Weckle und zwei Kannen Kaffee," in Gerd A. Auer, "Siebenunddreißig Wyhl-Geschichten," *'s Eige zeige' Jahrbuch des Landkreises Emmendingen für Kultur und Geschichte* 29 (2015): 232–233.

Figure 3.2 Anti-reactor activists "occupy" a bulldozer on the Wyhl reactor construction site, 18 February 1975. © Meinrad Schwörer.

The reporter projected his uncertainty onto the action's protagonists, claiming that by twelve o'clock, "the demonstrators stood on the site and did not really know if this was now an occupation or not." He went on to conclude that by evening it was clear that no occupation was underway, as protesters had heeded a police order and left the site.[19] But the protesters had not dispersed. Instead, they created an encampment comprised of a few old construction trailers, a covered wagon "reminiscent of the wild west," and a cluster of beat-up tents. The husbands of women who had "'strolled down' to Wyhl in the morning" came to the site in the afternoon "armed with bacon, thermoses full of stew, and bottles of schnapps."[20] The whole group spent the evening eating, drinking, and talking around campfires.

[19] In fact, the report's subtitle was: "The Police Command to Leave the Site was Followed." "Demonstranten erzwingen," *Badische Zeitung.*
[20] Ibid. They were part of an "endless stream of tractors, cars, and bicycles headed towards the construction site." Nössler, "Atomaren Ei," 83.

Like the press, government officials' previous conceptions of protest stopped them from fully comprehending what was happening at Wyhl. Intent on keeping the prestigious project's construction on schedule, Premier Filbinger wasted little time in determining who was responsible for the mess in the Wyhl forest and restoring order. On 19 February, the day after the occupation began, he announced that the "local citizenry is not behind this action [at Wyhl]." By blaming "nationally organized manipulators" for halting construction on the reactor, he recast the protest as a militant struggle against the West German state. Such a struggle matched the purported aims of the Red Army Faction, among other terrorist groups, and could thus be understood by Christian Democratic politicians and, Filbinger presumed, the populace.[21] In a country whose Nazi past caused the term "resistance" to be conceived as a violent effort to overthrow the regime, where the imminent danger of political terrorism dominated public discourse on protest, and where radical parties on both Left and Right had been found unconstitutional and banned by the Federal Constitutional Court, a fine line separated opposition to particular polices from opposition to the democratic order as a whole.[22] Though the people who had initiated the Wyhl occupation had done nothing to suggest that they sought to overthrow the democratic order or endanger the FRG's existence, Filbinger intentionally implied that the action's architects must be radical opponents of West German democracy rather than upstanding citizens. The appropriate penalty for such a "breach of the law," he thundered, would be administered "deliberately and decisively."[23] Filbinger ordered state police to remove protesters from the site immediately. Later that same evening, by which time protesters had occupied the site for nearly thirty-six hours, "a force of 600 policemen ... a police helicopter, two water cannons, two armored vehicles ... and multiple dog teams," assembled near the Wyhl forest.[24]

[21] As evidence, he noted that a Freiburg lawyer had reportedly offered to bus demonstrators out to Wyhl at no cost. "200 Mann stoppen Reaktorbau in Wyhl," *Stuttgarter Nachrichten*, 20 February 1975.

[22] On how Left-wing terrorism shaped discussions of protest in the 1970s, see: Karrin Hanshew, *Terror and Democracy in West Germany* (Cambridge: Cambridge University Press, 2012), esp. Chapter 4. Article 21, paragraph 2 of the West German Basic Law states that political parties that "by reason of their aims or the behavior of their adherents, seek to impair or abolish the free democratic basic order or endanger the existence of the Federal Republic of Germany, shall be unconstitutional," and gives the Federal Constitutional Court the prerogative to "decide on the question of constitutionality." The court used this authority to ban the Right-wing Socialist Reich Party in 1952 and the Communist Party of Germany (KPD) in 1956. Donald P. Kommers, *The Constitutional Jurisprudence of the Federal Republic of Germany* (Durham, NC: Duke University Press, 1997), 218ff.

[23] "200 Mann stoppen Reaktorbau in Wyhl," *Stuttgarter Nachrichten*.

[24] Wolfgang Sternstein, *Überall ist Wyhl. Bürgerinitiativen gegen Atomanlagen. Aus der Arbeit eines Aktionsforschers* (Frankfurt: Haag + Herchen Verlag, 1978), 50–51.

Protesters knew they were breaking the law when they trespassed onto the construction site, but they did not see their protest as the sort of anti-democratic action denounced by their Premier. They did not, in other words, consider themselves nationally organized manipulators bent on destroying the democratic order, and they hardly expected such a forceful response to their last-ditch effort to ensure their survival. Beginning with their declaration to the Badensian and Alsatian population in August 1974, they had justified a potential occupation on account of the government's unwavering support for a project that threatened their very existence.[25] Unlike student activists who had confronted police at street demonstrations with increasing frequency since the late 1960s, rural anti-nuclear protesters still considered the police their "friends and helpers;" they hardly expected a violent police crackdown.[26] Even veterans of the Marckolsheim occupation, which had been ongoing for six months by late February 1975, never faced a police response; French officials had simply allowed the illegal protest to continue. As they huddled around a smoldering campfire, the 150 occupiers, whose ranks included "men, women, children, vintners, students, housewives, priests, and doctors," had difficulty understanding the response to their protest as the prerogative of a democratic government; they could only associate the hundreds of policemen who had encircled their camp with the forces of a brutal dictatorship.[27]

In such a dire situation, activists sought simply to protect themselves as best they could. When an officer ordered them to disperse, the protesters refused. "The answer," one activist recalled, "came spontaneously as if from the mouth of a mighty giant: songs from the occupation at Marckolsheim, where we had already rehearsed everything."[28] As the protesters repeatedly sung "verse after verse" of "The Watch on the Rhine" police deluged them with water cannons.[29] Faced with such intransigent opponents, the police made fifty-four arrests. Targeting those they

---

[25] Badisch-Elsässische Bürgerinitiativen, "Erklärung der 21 Bürgerinitiativen an die Badisch-elsässische Bevölkerung" [undated, August 1974]. ASB "Wyhl—Die Anfänge," 17652.

[26] Michael Hughes has argued that Germans practicing civil disobedience were far less likely to accept punishment or jail time as a justified or reasonable response to their actions. Hughes, "Civil Disobedience in Transnational Perspective," 244.

[27] Sacherer, "Panik erfaßte unsere Herzen," 94–98. While West Germans compared the situation with that of the GDR, French compared it to the Third Reich. Frederic Mayer, "Ein Elsässer fühlt sich wie im Dritten Reich," in *Wyhl* (see note 9).

[28] Mayer "Ein Elsässer fühlt sich wie im Dritten Reich," 91.

[29] Quote is from Annemarie Sacherer, "Panik erfaßte unsere Herzen," 96; also: Günter Sacherer, interview with the author, Oberrotweil, 18 February 2010; Fernex, "Non-Violence Triumphant," 376.

considered most likely to be outside agitators, policemen wrenched anyone who looked young or had long hair from the group, dragged them through the mud, and placed them under arrest.[30] Despite their best efforts not to arrest middle-aged rural people, however, the officers brought in twenty locals from nearby villages in Baden and Alsace along with thirty-three students from Freiburg, Karlsruhe, and Tübingen, and one protester from the Netherlands.[31] Among the locals arrested was Maria Köllhofer, the mother of five who had never participated in a protest before.[32] Those left behind sobbed openly as their friends and neighbors were dragged away. "This is a disgrace," one woman screamed at the top of her lungs. "If you had hearts in your bodies you would never do anything like this!" she howled.[33]

Figure 3.3 Police deploy a water cannon to deluge reactor opponents who are occupying the Wyhl reactor construction site, 20 February 1975. © Gerd Auer.

[30] Köllhofer, "Die erste Demonstration," 102.
[31] Hans-Helmuth Wüstenhagen, *Bürger gegen Kernkraftwerke. Wyhl – der Anfang?* (Reinbek: Rowohlt, 1975), 79.
[32] Gertrud and Emil Friedrich, "30 Weckle und zwei Kannen Kaffee," 232–233.
[33] Westdeutscher Rundfunk, *Vor Ort.*

Figure 3.4 After deploying the water cannon, police arrest reactor opponents still occupying the Wyhl reactor construction site, 20 February 1975. © Gerd Auer.

The raid outraged erstwhile supporters of the Stuttgart government throughout the region. Many publicly disassociated themselves from the ruling CDU, which they held responsible for the police action. Josef Aschenbrenner, who had chaired the party's Sasbach chapter for a quarter century, had long harbored concerns about the reactor project himself, but he had sought "to calm the waves [of opposition] out of solidarity with the government." When "the wife of a candidate for town council was attacked by a water cannon," however, Aschenbrenner became "hot under the collar." The loyal CDU-man announced that he would not seek re-election to his party post. Along with Aschenbrenner, five of the party's eight village council candidates in Sasbach announced that they would no longer run; three resigned from the CDU altogether.[34] The situation was similar across the Kaiserstuhl. The Bischoffingen chapter "voted by an overwhelming majority" to dissolve itself.[35] Twenty

[34] "CDU-Gemeinderatslisten sind gefährdet," *Badische Zeitung*, 25 February 1975.
[35] "CDU Ortsverband wegen Wyhl aufgelöst," *Badische Zeitung*, 25 February 1975.

prominent local people, most of them vintners, took out an advertisement in the *BZ* announcing their resignations from the party on account of the "reprehensible behavior of the state government in union with the utility company through the brutal police actions."[36]

Filbinger's presumption that a powerful police intervention would quickly clear the site proved correct; the deployment also made his charge that the occupation threatened law and order a self-fulfilling prophecy. In addition to causing reactor opponents' faith in their government to evaporate and rural CDU chapters to disintegrate, allegations of police brutality attracted urban activists to a movement that they suddenly considered far more militant. Thanks to the Physics Students' Association, which had participated in rural information sessions on nuclear energy for the past several years, news of the police intervention reached Freiburg quickly. A broad coalition of activist groups, many of whom had previously had little to do with rural anti-reactor protests, called for an immediate demonstration at city hall.[37] The rally's sponsors ran the gamut from student squatters' groups to a third world solidarity organization; they even encompassed the complete spectrum of Freiburg's organized Left, from the DKP to the SPD's youth organization, the Jusos.[38] The rally's organizers had not suddenly become radical opponents of nuclear energy; instead, they were electrified by the reported showdown between police and protesters. Their broad coalition of supporters in Freiburg evidenced both rural anti-reactor protesters' militancy and the brutality of the West German state.[39] Accordingly, handbills advertising

---

[36] "Nit allem sich neige, 's Eige zeige'!" *Badische Zeitung* (paid advertisement), 25 February 1975.

[37] The University of Freiburg's Physics Students' Association, one of the few Freiburg groups that had long supported the rural protesters, became a conduit between the city and the countryside after the brutal showdown. As the physicists received news from the site, "many [students and other members of the institute] drove out to Wyhl in order to personally support the resistance." In a solidarity statement, the physicists pledged to "continue to do everything in our power to convince the members of the institute of the just goals of the struggle and to win them as active supporters." "Fachschaftsrat Physik an die Bürgerinitiativen im Kaiserstuhl," 21 February 1975. ABEBI Haag Lore 12HL12.

[38] Aktion Dritte Welt, AK-Frieden, Bewohner der besetzten Häuser Belfortstr. 34–36, Evangelische Studentengemeinden, Fachschaftsräte Soziologie-Physik-Jura, Gruppe internationaler Marxisten, Gewaltfreie Aktion, Kommunistischer Bund Westdeutschland, Kommunistische Hochschulgruppe, Kommunistischer Studentenverband, Arbeitskreis Umweltschutz an der Universität Freiburg, DKP, "Das KKW wird nicht gebaut!" (20 February 1975). ASB "Wyhl—die Anfänge," 3450. The Jusos published their own flyer, which also focused on police brutality, but without the sensationalism of the other group's flyer. The Jusos' much wordier document described, among other things, the environmental effects that the reactor would have on the region. Jungsozialisten in der SPD, Kreisverband Freiburg, Kreisverband Emmendingen, "Was geschah heute in Wyhl?" (20 February 1975). ASB "Wyhl—Die Anfänge," 3591.

[39] Local Jusos, who co-organized the Freiburg demonstration, referred to capitalist interests as the primary reason for the state's brutality. Karrin Hanshew shows that West German Leftists "invoked Nazism to convey both the extreme criminality and the magnitude of state force confronting

the rally bemoaned the fact that, "Women and children were soaked with water cannons and dragged from the site by their hair."[40] Focusing on the "police intervention and the resistance" rather than nuclear energy, organizers attracted 250 participants to the event within a few hours.[41]

Freiburg activists' speedy response to the police intervention revealed how Filbinger's decision to forcefully disperse the protesters translated the anti-reactor struggle into a more understandable language of protest. Thus, the Jusos decried the raid as "yet another clear sign of the way that the state government and the capitalist groups standing behind it intend to deal with the just interests and legitimate demands of the population."[42] The Communist Party of Germany/Marxists-Leninists (KPD/ML) pushed the same themes further, celebrating the fact that, "the people, who 'only' came to fight against the reactor now see much more clearly the stakes of this struggle: the capitalist system, where there is no democracy for the people, but only for the capitalists."[43] This was the first step towards "a self-conscious struggle against the capitalists and their state apparatus ... against the dictatorship of the capitalist class," which was to be waged by nothing less than "the unified red fighting front of the laborers and working people in our country!"[44]

The Wyhl occupation developed organically out of a French protest tradition filtered through a half-decade of transnational anti-reactor activism in the Upper Rhine valley. Its local precedents – the Marckolsheim occupation and even the Kaiseraugst "trial squat" – had remained peaceful and focused on the particular projects they targeted. They had not incited solidarity protests in nearby cities. But police violence made the Wyhl occupation legible to urban activists as a struggle between the forces of order and militant resistors. At the same time as Filbinger's police deployment helped outsiders fold the Wyhl struggle into their pre-existing concepts of protest and resistance, it also initiated challenges to those ideas. The occupation's protagonists certainly were not the "usual suspects" of

demonstrators" at anti-nuclear demonstrations that took place in Brokdorf the following year (for more on the Brokdorf demonstration, see Chapter 4). Jungsozialisten, "Was geschah;" and: Hanshew, *Terror and Democracy*, 172.

[40] Aktion Dritte Welt et al., "Das KKW wird nicht gebaut!"

[41] "Polizei räumt Kraftwerksgelände in Wyhl," *Badische Zeitung*, 21 February 1975.

[42] Offener Brief der Katholische Junge Gemeinde to Erzdiözese Freiburg and Ministerpräsident Filbinger, 21 February 1975. ABEBI Haag Lore 12HL12. Numerous solidarity statements can be found in: ABEBI Haag Lore 12HL12.

[43] KPD/ML, "Verhindert den bau des KKW!" (23 February 1975), 2. HSAS EA 1/107 Bü 766.

[44] KPD Regional Komitee Baden-Württemberg, "Kein KKW in Wyhl" (23 February 1975). ASB, "Wyhl—Die Anfänge," 3599.

radical activism. Leftists who saw the anti-reactor protest as part of the class struggle jumped to conclusions. Stuttgart officials' unwillingness to acknowledge the potential for rank-and-file Christian Democrats to actively resist unpopular government decisions was also a result of misjudgment. The rural struggle became important in southwestern Germany because it forced a rethinking of ideas about activism and practical politics on both Left and Right.

Grassroots Protest, Great Expectations

The conclusions that outsiders drew from the brutal police raid initiated important changes in the way anti-reactor protest was perceived in West Germany, even if those conclusions had little connection to the actual course of events at Wyhl. This was because outsiders' responses relied on cursory looks at Rhenish protest through distortive ideological lenses, not close analysis of the facts on the ground. Much as the tactic of occupation had wildly different valences in French and German contexts, so too did it appear quite different locally and nationally. As government officials held outside agitators responsible and Leftists celebrated the coming class struggle, the unorthodox tactics of the initial occupation attempt remained unexamined. Believing that it had overcome the threat to law and order by dispersing the radical outsiders who had overtaken the site, the government of Baden-Württemberg drew down its massive police force. Regardless of the K-Groups' high hopes, an "unified red fighting front" with revolutionary ambitions had not coalesced in the Wyhl forest. Just as they had before the police intervention attracted attention to their struggle, local protesters remained focused first and foremost on "preventing the construction of the Wyhl reactor and other reactors, and not starting a revolution."[45]

In the eyes of outsiders, the protests held at Wyhl the day after the police intervention were notable for their subdued nature and apparent lack of militancy. On the morning of 21 February, activists did not even attempt to stop workmen from repairing the fences around the site. That afternoon, a peaceful rally of 6,000 reactor opponents steered clear of the new fortifications. By nightfall, a few tents just outside the gates of the construction site were the only semblance of an occupation.[46] When set

[45] Günter Richter, quoted in "Protokoll der Sitzung des internationalen Komitees der Badisch-Elsässischen Bürgerinitiativen am 24. Mai 1975 von 20.00–23.00 Uhr im Bürgersaal des Rathauses von Weisweil." ABEBI Richter Günter 123RG1.

[46] There were two small encampments outside the site, one comprised of young people and the other of members of Weisweil's SPD Chapter. Sternstein, *Überall ist Wyhl*, 63.

against the site occupation – let alone the model of armed resistance embodied by the RAF, which was on the minds of government officials and members of the organized Left after the recent police intervention – such peaceful gatherings hardly seemed to be of much consequence. They certainly did not pose a serious challenge to the government's authority.

The situation at Wyhl was not nearly as subdued as it seemed, however; the problem was that anyone who relied on preconceived notions of how protest worked, or who listened only to the pronouncements of the movement's purported leaders, had little idea what was actually happening in the communities surrounding the reactor site. Those willing to dig just a little deeper quickly realized that even as rallies continued outside the fence, local activists were plotting to reoccupy the site. Their plan had nothing to do with class struggle and it was not intended to overthrow the government. It relied instead on participants' willingness to break laws and knock down tall fences in order to stop the reactor project and protect their communities. Forty anti-nuclear activists, "men and women, young and old, Badensian and Alsatians," met at the Fischerinsel pub in Weisweil on the evening of Friday, 21 February to plan the reoccupation. Few details crystalized during their meeting, which seemed primarily focused on keeping protesters' intention to reoccupy the site vague.[47] Even Reverend Berger, the Protestant Pastor who was to emcee a mass rally at the reactor site the following Sunday – at which time activists planned to reoccupy the site – was not supposed to know anything about the action.[48] The protesters determined, therefore, to launch the reoccupation via an "encrypted message" at the conclusion of Sunday's demonstration.[49]

Even observers who knew of such informal plans considered them almost laughable amidst a head-on struggle against the powerful West German state. Members of the Nonviolent Action Freiburg (GAF), who had been involved in the anti-reactor campaign for several years, did not doubt that rural people would act on the plans they had hatched at the Fischerinsel, but they were concerned nonetheless. Though the GAF supported the idea of a reoccupation, the group's members worried that

---

[47] Sternstein, who was himself kicked out, considered the meeting focused on ejecting potential spies from the group. Sternstein, *Überall ist Wyhl*, 35–36.

[48] Ibid., 34. In fact, even after some protesters had breached the perimeter fences, Berger called on protesters to stay away from the site's perimeter. "We have nothing to do with what's going on at the moment at the fence!" he reportedly yelled out to demonstrators as they took a "stroll around the site." Wolfgang Kern and Gerd Auer, "Die zweite Besetzung in Wyhl," in *Wyhl* (see note 9), 113.

[49] Sternstein, *Überall ist Wyhl*, 35–36.

the current plans simply were not the stuff of serious protest. They were terrified that:

> too little had been done to prepare for the action, that it was not fully public, that there were no marshals, and that it was possible that the nonviolent character of the action could be jeopardized in a highly visible situation.[50]

Even the GAF, whose members were personally familiar with the longer history of anti-nuclear activism in the region and trained in nonviolent protest, were concerned that plans for the second occupation did not match their conceptions of how protests ought to be organized and how they functioned.

If the clandestine planning session at the Fischerinsel caused GAF activists to consider the action poorly organized and unlikely to succeed, the public preparations for the Sunday, 23 February 1975 rally seemed more likely to beget a country fair than an illegal act of militant resistance. On the morning of the rally, "information booths and sausage stands were set up" along the Rhine while "posters were hung and loudspeakers installed."[51] Perhaps because of its festive atmosphere, the gathering that took place near the construction site on 23 February 1975 was the largest in five years of anti-reactor struggle on the Upper Rhine; the University of Freiburg's student government even asserted that it was the largest protest anywhere in Baden since 1945.[52] At 2:30 pm, as Reverend Berger took the podium, the road leading up to Wyhl was obliterated from view by a stream of people walking towards the site, and "the sides of streets and the paths into the fields were covered by parked cars as far as the eye could see."[53] In total, some 28,000 activists came to Wyhl that day.[54]

Though the call for an occupation in the "Declaration of the Badensian and Alsatian Reactor Opponents to the Population" had by no means been rescinded, nothing in the official promotion of the 23 February rally suggested that a new occupation attempt would commence that day. Many assumed that the failure of the first occupation meant that new

---

[50] Wolfgang Hertle, "Törichtes und Menschliches. Eindrücke von der zweiten Bauplatzbesetzung in Wyhl," *Gewaltfreie Aktion* Nr. 23, 24, 25 (1975), 46.

[51] Sternstein, *Überall ist Wyhl*, 65.

[52] Interestingly, though Freiburg students considered this Baden's largest postwar protest, their estimate of the number of protesters was comparatively low. While other sources stated that as many as 30,000 protesters were present, the students said there were only 10,000. GEW, SHB, LHV, *die den asta tragenden gruppen informieren über DIE LAGE IN WYHL*. ASB "Wyhl—Die Anfänge," 3446.

[53] Sternstein, *Überall ist Wyhl*, 65.

[54] Wüstenhagen claims that the figure of 28,000 – by far the most frequently cited – comes from the police report. See: Wüstenhagen, *Bürger gegen Kernkraftwerke*, 82.

tactics must now be deployed. Police certainly did not expect protesters to make a serious effort to get onto the site; only 250 officers – a force less than half the size of that which had removed the 150 occupiers on 20 February – were at Wyhl that day. Most of the police present on 23 February had not even been issued helmets before the deployment.[55] As the rally began, however, a group of approximately eighty rural reactor opponents, many of whom had attended Friday's clandestine meeting at the Fischerinsel, approached the construction site from the far side.[56] These activists were equipped with wire cutters and a portable sound system. They intended to sneak onto the site and then loudly announce their presence in order to provoke the massive crowd to join them.[57] While the instigators cut holes through the fence and found their way to the center of the sprawling construction site, Meinrad Schwörer, a reactor opponent from Wyhl who worked at the state conservation authority, concluded the mass rally by suggesting that the thousands of protesters take a walk along the Wyhl forest nature trail, which he himself had blazed. Convinced that the rally was now over, some of the participants packed their things and went home.[58]

Many more demonstrators took Schwörer up on his invitation to stroll through the woods. As they walked alongside the site and noticed the group of instigators behind the fence, some of the protesters began pushing their way towards the perimeter to get a better look. Still, no leader ordered protesters to occupy the site, and many demonstrators continued walking along the nature trail, simply observing what was going on around them.[59] Others hastened to get onto the site. When the first protesters attempted to cross the Mühlbach, a small tributary of the Rhine that served as part of the reactor site's boundary, police officers rushed to repel them, pushing several protesters into the icy stream. Self-appointed marshals from the GAF tried in vain to soothe the situation. The GAF activists were likely convinced that their cavalier lack of planning had caught up with the occupation's organizers. Finally, Balthasar Ehret of Weisweil seized a police megaphone and stopped the scuffle by screaming a string of jarring questions at the police: "Do you have no hearts in your bodies? How can

[55] Ibid.; also: Kern and Auer, "Die zweite Besetzung in Wyhl," 115.
[56] Sternstein, *Überall ist Wyhl*, 65.   [57] Hertle, "Törichtes und Menschliches," 47.
[58] Among those who left was the University of Freiburg student Roland Burkhart and his family, who lived in the village of Jechtingen. The Burkhart family had visited the demonstration as a sort of Sunday outing. "Let's go out to Wyhl," one family member suggested, "there's something going on there." Roland Burkhart, interview with the author, Freiburg, 24 February 2010.
[59] Kern and Auer, "Die zweite Besetzung in Wyhl," 112.

you be so awful? Don't you have families?" A police commander who had just arrived on the scene ordered his men to retreat.[60]

Though it created confusing confrontations like the scuffle at the Mühlbach, the loosely planned occupation attempt actually had many tactical advantages. Acting independently of one another, protesters surged towards the site from every direction. Some rolled branches and tree trunks into place and clambered across the stream while others toppled tall barbed-wire fences elsewhere along the site's perimeter. The unprepared and vastly outnumbered police made one last attempt to stop protesters from approaching the construction equipment, which stood idle at the center of the site. But a group of "cheering demonstrators" breached this final cordon of police. Having overrun the site, demonstrators watched in awe as the police fell back, formed their cruisers and buses into an orderly column, and evacuated the forest. It was not until the water cannon was driven past the crowd that the protesters snapped to and began "pounding their fists on the sides of the tank." Before any damage was done, however, an Alsatian climbed atop this embodiment of police brutality and convinced the occupiers to back off. After that, the police evacuation continued unhindered. As dusk settled on the Rhine Valley, demonstrators were once again in full control of the site.[61] With only a few minor exceptions – like the shoving match at the Mühlbach – reactor opponents had reoccupied the site nonviolently.

The action's unorthodox, unplanned nature made it a success. Yet, these same characteristics meant that it capped a week of unusual and unpredictable actions far afield from pre-existing notions of protest and resistance. A press conference became an occupation. Unarmed rural people halted progress on a prestigious reactor project by pitching tents and lighting campfires. A leaderless, poorly coordinated mob over-whelmed 250 policemen and stopped construction yet again. The distance between the notions of resistance that shaped government officials' and activists' responses to the goings-on at Wyhl and the actual occupation reveals how embedded in the grassroots anti-reactor movement it remained; but this same disconnect underlay the action's provocative potential in broader political debates. Premier Filbinger remained convinced that outside agitators had instigated the protests, even if he now believed that rural conservatives were involved, too. In a more conciliatory tone, he offered local reactor opponents four weeks to disentangle themselves from the radical troublemakers who were really

---

[60] Sternstein, *Überall ist Wyhl*, 71–75. [61] Ibid., 76.

behind the occupation.[62] What was actually going on at Wyhl remained difficult to articulate without resorting to such presumptions. The remarkably successful reoccupation had less of an immediate impact than the violent police showdown. The occupation's success surprised observers, but it taught them little about the alternative forms of resistance that Rhenish activists so ably deployed.

The Revolution Will Be Televised (on Tape Delay)

The occupation's lack of resonance beyond the Upper Rhine valley was due in no small part to the fact that people beyond Strasbourg and Kaiseraugst were unaware of what was going on at Wyhl. Finally, six days after the initial occupation attempt, on the evening of Wednesday, 26 February 1975, West German television viewers – from Kiel in the North to Constance in the South – were introduced to the struggle via a forty-five-minute film entitled "Citizens Against the Wyhl Reactor." The primetime special retraced vintners' struggles to protect their livelihoods since the summer of 1974.[63] Even as the broadcast shocked West Germans with footage of the brutal 20 February police intervention, it also provided them with sufficient context to begin rethinking their conceptions of protest and resistance. Specifically, the long-simmering struggle in the Upper Rhine valley caused Germans to reconsider how protest worked, who carried it out, and where it took place. In so doing, the film de-provincialized the Wyhl struggle by initiating an extended series of interactions between local people and outsiders that accounted for what one publication called the

---

[62] Medienwerkstatt Freiburg, *s'Wespennäscht – Die Chronik von Wyhl 1970–1982* (film). In fact, Filbinger learned so little from the first occupation and the brutal police crackdown that he ordered another police action for 25 February, which was only headed off at the last minute by the intervention of the state's Protestant Bishop, Hans Heidland. Wolfgang Sternstein, *Mein Weg zwischen Gewalt und Gewaltfreiheit* (Norderstedt: Books on Demand, 2005), 164–165.

[63] Though the film was broadcast a week after the initial occupation began, mainstream newspapers only began to cover the protests in any depth that same day. "Polizei vertreibt die Umweltschützer von Wyhl. Kein aktiver Widerstand auf dem Bauplatz für das Kernkraftwerk beim Kaiserstuhl," *Frankfurter Allgemeine Zeitung*, 21 February 1975. Finally, on Tuesday, 25 February, two days after the reoccupation, the protests made the *Stuttgarter Zeitung*'s front page, with a report entitled "Uproar in Wyhl." "Aufruhr in Wyhl," *Stuttgarter Zeitung*, 25 February 1975. The next day, the *FAZ* ran a second article on Wyhl and *Die Welt* reported on the topic for the first time. "Seit Jahren sind die Bürger am Oberrhein in besonderer Weise gereizt. Die 'Eskalation' wegen des Atomkraftwerks von Wyhl (Wu.)," *Frankfurter Allgemeine Zeitung*, 26 February 1975; Walter Pfuhl, "Die abenteuerliche Armee im Wald am Kaiserstuhl. Auch nach dem Einlenken der Regierung Filbinger harren die Demonstranten auf dem Wyhl Reaktor-Gelände aus," *Die Welt*, 26 February 1975. The occupation was finally starting to receive limited coverage, but it certainly was not a lead topic in the national news.

occupation's "signal effect."[64] The broadcast, in short, transformed the Wyhl occupation from a subject of interest for Alsatian, Badensians, and Northwest Swiss into a national event in West Germany.

"Citizens Against the Wyhl Reactor" raised difficult questions about protest because it was designed to do so. The film was an episode of director Thomas Schmitt's *Vor Ort* series, which went "on location" to sites of grassroots political engagement using one of only two camera setups in the FRG capable of taping extended live segments without a cumbersome broadcast van. Unlike other political journalists, who focused primarily on developments in Bonn, Schmitt and his team believed that politics took place in out-of-the-way places, too. They had been visiting the Rhine Valley for several years by the time that the Wyhl occupation began, and had even created previous episodes in their series on protests there. But despite Schmitt's crew's hard work, his other films on Rhenish anti-nuclear protest had been broadcast only within the state of North Rhine-Westphalia on the regional broadcaster *Westdeutsche Rundfunk* (WDR) and had not brought the provincial anti-reactor struggle into national politics.

Public interest in "Citizens Against the Wyhl Reactor" owed to good fortune, as well as shocking footage. Even before the Wyhl occupation began, WDR's television director, Werner Höfer, secured a coveted primetime slot for a *Vor Ort* special on the *Arbeitsgemeinschaft der öffentlich-rechtlichen Rundfunkanstalten der Bundesrepublik Deutschland* (ARD), West Germany's channel one.[65] The proposed special, which Schmitt titled "Demonstration," dealt with the ongoing Marckolsheim occupation. Höfer likely had an easier time securing airtime for "Demonstration" than he would have had for one of Schmitt's other films on Rhenish protest because it focused on a situation outside the FRG, and because even West German officials now openly opposed the proposed lead-processing plant in Alsace.[66] As fate had it, "Demonstration" was set to be broadcast on Wednesday, 26 February – three days after the reoccupation of the Wyhl construction site.[67] Schmitt, who had spent the previous week in Wyhl

---

[64] *Der Stille Weg.*   [65] Thomas Schmitt, interview with the author, via Skype, 14 February 2012.

[66] As late as 24 October 1974, Minister of Health Annemarie Griesinger said that lead emissions were not harmful. Nössler, "Das Genehmigungsverfahren," 58; see also: "Wyhl-Chronik von 1969 bis Januar 1982," *'s Eige zeige'* 29 (2015): 336. Just a few weeks later, Premier Hans Filbinger traveled to Paris in order to voice his government's concerns about the project. The press seemed to accept the about face. The *BZ*, for example, reported that environmentalists could only hope that Filbinger's intervention might block the project. "Tag und Nacht auf der Wacht am Rhein," *Badische Zeitung*, 26 October 1974.

[67] "Diese Woche im Fernsehen," *Der Spiegel*, 24 February 1975 43.

filming the initial occupation and the brutal police intervention that ended it, had other ideas of what to do with his hard-won airtime. While *Vor Ort*'s producer talked ARD officials into a slight program change, Schmitt hastily edited "Citizens Against the Wyhl Reactor."[68] The film primarily comprised material from previous *Vor Ort* episodes, but because it was broadcast nationally during primetime (and opposite an hour-long interview on financial matters with Austrian Chancellor Bruno Kreisky), it attracted far more viewers than Schmitt's previous films on Rhenish protest.[69]

Heart-wrenching footage of the 20 February police raid accounted for the film's immediate influence across the FRG. In an era when such lengthy on-location footage was a novelty, the *Vor Ort* program was a shocking introduction to the Wyhl protests. The widely viewed scene of police battering peaceful protesters with water cannons "created sympathy from Constance to Kiel" because of the David versus Goliath struggle it depicted.[70] Even for knowledgeable scientists and committed environmentalists, protesters' concerns about their livelihoods and government officials' shocking responses were more moving than rural activists' technical concerns about nuclear energy. A group of chemists from a Heidelberg research institute, for example, wrote that while they shared protesters' concerns about problems associated with radiation, they found it "particularly upsetting . . . that such projects are to be forced on you despite all of your protests and all the objections from across your Lebensraum."[71] Ralf Egel, of the Hamburg chapter of Friends of the Earth, "fully and completely support[ed] radical opposition to reactors and the further destruction of the environment," but found the "reactions of the political parties and the police to the clear declaration of opinion by the overwhelming majority of the population" far more upsetting. The officials' responses "made quite clear how little the

---

[68] In fact, as soon as the director of the *Südwestrundfunk* (SWR), CDU-member Helmut Hammerschmidt, caught wind of the possibility that a film on Wyhl might be aired on national television, he telephoned the WDR's programming director, Dieter Stolte, who was known to be supportive of the CDU. Hammerschmidt's questions about the proposed film were eventually fielded by Werner Höfer, the WDR's television director. He personally assured Hammerschmidt that "Citizens Against the Wyhl Reactor" was safe for the airwaves. "Fehl am Platze," *Der Spiegel*, 14 April 1975.

[69] The Kreisky interview aired on ZDF, West Germany's only other national broadcaster in 1975. "Diese Woche im Fernsehen," *Der Spiegel*, 24 February 1975.

[70] "Nach dem Wyhl-Report eine Telegrammflut," *Südwestpresse Schwäbische Donauzeitung Ulm a.D.*, 28 February 1975. As Karrin Hanshew has shown, even images of police attacking students received sympathy in the 1960s; live footage of brutal attacks against upstanding citizens took this outrage to a new level. Hanshew, *Terror and Democracy in West Germany* (Cambridge: Cambridge University Press, 2012), 94.

[71] Peter Trietech et al to Jürgen Nößler, 27 February 1975. ABEBI Haag Lore, 12HL12.

interests of the population are taken into account in the parliaments and what strong political changes are still necessary."[72] For these writers and many others besides, the overbearing police response and the government's intransigence evidenced a serious problem in the workings of West German democracy.

As outsiders focused on the clash between protesters and the government rather than specific environmental problems, the struggle's close ties to its provincial surroundings loosened – at least in the eyes of outside observers. Within days of the *Vor Ort* broadcast, the Berlin academic Roland Vogt wrote to Weisweil's Reverend Richter to ask how "outsiders" like himself and his colleague Professor Theodor Ebert "could make themselves useful in the Kaiserstühlers' cause." Rather than waiting for Richter's response, Vogt excitedly proposed the four-day Easter weekend as the ideal time for an event that would bring outsiders to Wyhl. "As old Easter Marchers," Ebert added, he and Vogt wanted to link the Wyhl struggle with an important West German activist tradition.[73] Though Vogt and Ebert hoped to influence the direction of Rhenish protests, they also realized the significance of the struggle's rootedness. They aimed to maintain its authenticity by convincing local people to call for an Easter March to Wyhl themselves.[74]

The back-and-forth over Vogt and Ebert's Easter March proposal revealed the discrepancy between the easily adaptable model protest that outsiders imagined was taking place at Wyhl and the distinctly local struggle that was actually underway. Because the Easter Marches of the 1960s had targeted nuclear weapons, Vogt claimed that "the idea of an Easter March could easily be associated with the topic of a nuclear reactor." Yet this proposed link, which seemed obvious in West Berlin, had little resonance in the Upper Rhine valley. Local activists were surely interested in garnering support from people elsewhere, but they did not wish to connect their struggle with the Easter Marches or tailor it to outsiders' political goals. In large part this was because, as Vogt himself admitted, the marches had been dismissed by many during the 1960s because they were considered to have been "infiltrated by Communists."[75]

---

[72] Ralf Egel (Freunde der Erde Hamburg) to Heinz Siefritz, 5 March 1975. ABEBI Haag Lore 12HL12.
[73] Theodor Ebert, "Als Berliner in Wyhl: Friedensforschung und Konfliktberatung vor Ort," *Gewaltfreie Aktion* Nr. 23, 24, 25 (1975): 37.
[74] On the meaning of "authenticity" for 1970s activists, see: Sven Reichardt, *Authentizität und Gemeinschaft. Linksalternatives Leben in den siebziger und frühen achtziger Jahren* (Berlin: Suhrkamp 2014), 57ff.
[75] Vogt to Richter, 9 March 1975. Holger Nehring has shown the extent to which Germans distanced themselves from the Easter Marches of the 1960s, particularly in rural areas, where marchers were

Instead of calling for an Easter March and intentionally linking their protest with one of West Germany's most venerable activist traditions, therefore, local activists remained true to the alternative style of protest they had deployed throughout their struggle by organizing an "International Easter Gathering of Anti-nuclear Activists at Wyhl." The fact that it took place on Easter Monday vaguely linked the Wyhl Gathering with the Easter March tradition, but the holiday was also selected because it came during a four-day weekend and was, therefore, a good day to organize a large action. As an "anti-nuclear rally, mini-Woodstock, family outing, and Volksfest" all rolled into one, the gathering was more reminiscent of earlier protests in the Upper Rhine valley than the somber and dignified Easter Marches.[76] The spectrum of people and groups involved was also similar to previous Rhine valley protests, but the Easter Gathering incorporated a diverse new cast of visitors from much further afield as well. Delegations from other proposed reactor sites in the FRG and Switzerland, including Mannheim, Schwörstadt, Schweinfurt, and Kaiseraugst, participated alongside groups from the Netherlands, Austria, Luxembourg, and France. Altogether, the rally drew between 10,000 and 20,000 participants.[77] "The mixture of age groups, which has been denounced as impossible, the city and country people, the hippies and the 'citizens' seems suddenly possible here," the *Dernières nouvelles d'Alsace* concluded.[78]

The crowd's diversity differentiated the Easter Gathering from traditional West German protest actions; it also evidenced the effectiveness of outsiders' attempts to universalize the Wyhl struggle. The BBU spearheaded these efforts by circulating a flyer proclaiming that:

> Wherever you live, whatever particular problems concern you, come to Wyhl this Easter ... Whatever happens in Wyhl will affect all future developments ... Our struggle is your struggle. "Wyhl" is all of our cause![79]

BBU Chairman Hans-Helmuth Wüstenhagen emphasized this interpretation of the struggle's adaptability and translocal significance at the rally. He

---

sometimes denied accommodations that had been promised before they set off. Nehring, *Politics of Security*, 201.

[76] "Kundgebung und Volksfest: Die neue Wacht am Rhein," *Dernières nouvelles d'Alsace*, 1 April 1975. HSAS EA 1/107 Bü 768.

[77] "10.000 beim Ostertreffen in Wyhl," *Kommunistische Volkszeitung*. The *Dernières nouvelles d'Alsace* noted the presence of delegations from the same countries. Neither report specified how large these groups were. "Kundgebung und Volksfest," *Dernières nouvelles d'Alsace*.

[78] "Kundgebung und Volksfest," *Dernières nouvelles d'Alsace*.

[79] Bundesverband Bürgerinitiativen Umweltschutz, "Oster-Treffen aller Atomkraftgegner in Wyhl." AGG PKA 3168.

titled his speech "Wyhl as an Example" and spoke of the occupation as "a page in the modern history of freedom."[80] Petra Kelly, then a young administrative worker at the Economic and Social Committee of the European Economic Community who finagled her way onto the podium at the last minute, also imagined broad – even transnational – resonance for the Wyhl struggle. An active member of the Young European Federalists, Kelly declared that advocates of European integration, "were waiting for Wyhl!"[81]

Despite such universalist rhetoric, local people's long experience organizing local resistance to nuclear reactor construction remained difficult for outsiders to access, limiting Wyhl's most important transnational effects to the region between Strasbourg and Kaiseraugst. "Only by sticking together," exclaimed Luc Aders of Nonviolent Action Kaiseraugst during his turn on the podium, "can the populations of Germany, France, Switzerland, even Europe and the whole world, prevent yet more misfortune on account of nuclear reactors."[82] To this end, Aders triumphantly ended his speech by declaring that an occupation of the nuclear reactor construction site in Kaiseraugst was to begin that very evening. "A coach [to the Kaiseraugst reactor site] was immediately organized," while "others went to find their tents and set off for Kaiseraugst [on their own]," Solange Fernex reported.[83] In total, "some 100 veteran occupiers from Alsace and Baden" left Wyhl for Kaiseraugst that evening.[84] When workmen arrived on the Swiss construction site the next day, they "found their machines had been immobilized by the demonstrators; tents had been pitched in front of them and women were sitting in the drivers' seats."[85] The scene bore an uncanny resemblance to the openings of the occupations at Marckolsheim and Wyhl.

Though outside sympathizers like Kelly were deeply moved by Rhenish solidarity, the bus that left Wyhl for Kaiseraugst was filled with local people, not visitors from outside the region. Even the Wyhl occupation's transnational salience was viewed quite differently within the region and beyond it. Just across the Rhine in Strasbourg, Mayor Pierre Pflimlin stated the protest's transnational significance bluntly. "If the nuclear plant at Wyhl is stopped," he reasoned, "it would be extremely difficult to put one

[80] Quoted in "Wieder ein Ostermarsch – Wyhl," *Infodienst.*
[81] Petra Kelly, Untitled Speech (Wyhl, 31 March 1975). AGG PKA 3166.   [82] Ibid.
[83] Solange Fernex, "Non-Violence Triumphant," *The Ecologist* 5, no. 10 (December 1975), 378.
[84] Michael Schroeren, "Vom legalen Protest zum Zivilen Ungehorsam. Bürger gegen das geplante Atomkraftwerk in Kaiseraugst (Schweiz)," *Gewaltfreie Aktion* 23, 24, 25 (1975): 50.
[85] Fernex, "Non-Violence Triumphant," 378.

in Alsace. If you can't do it here, where can you do it in France? I believe the entire French nuclear program rides with Wyhl."[86] Pfimlin's statement highlighted changes to the Rhenish anti-nuclear movement since the early 1970s, when opposition to the Fessenheim reactor had been muted. Pfimlin's thinking was influenced not only by Wyhl, but also the struggle over the Marckolsheim lead plant, which had been resolved a month earlier when Pfimlin himself received a letter from French Minister of Public Works Robert Galley announcing that the latter had intervened to block the project. The Mayor rightly suspected that the extent of Alsatians' concerns about nuclear energy as well as their confidence in their ability to influence politics were waxing.[87] After six months of occupation, Galley's decision to cancel the project amounted to an unlikely victory for rural activists. Yet, the protest's success was not trumpeted in France's mainstream press, which spoke of a "pyrrhic victory" that might harm the region in the long run.[88] The plant's opponents celebrated in proper grassroots fashion by "sowing four hectares of spring wheat" on the site.[89]

The broadcast of "Citizens Against the Wyhl Reactor" was the first step towards bridging the gap between grassroots action and national politics for many West Germans. Barely a month later, the International Easter Gathering brought people from all across Western Europe to the Rhine valley to express their solidarity with local protesters. As before, the struggle remained difficult to understand and open to a wide range of interpretations, but Rhenish protest took on new significance as it entered into the national political context. While many activists still hoped to fold the Wyhl struggle into their own projects, and some like Vogt and Ebert even sought to do so by reshaping the local movement to match preexisting protest traditions, familiarity with the dynamics of the struggle had begun to influence the way protesters reacted to it. For activists like Hans-Helmuth Wüstenhagen and Petra Kelly, the "example of Wyhl" was a powerful new political model. These excited outsiders began to attribute widespread ramifications to grassroots protest by emphasizing its influence on their own struggles and proclaiming their desire to follow up on what

---

[86] Quoted in John Vincourt, "Two Rhine Villages Succeed in Halting Industrial Invasion," *International Herald-Tribune*, 5 March 1975.

[87] "Die Wacht in Marckolsheim hat eine Ende," *Badische Zeitung*, 27 February 1975. "A propos de l'affaire de Marckolsheim: Victoire à la Pyrrhus?" *Le Monde*, 27 February 1975.

[88] There was no coverage in *L'Humanite* on 27 or 28 February. *Le Monde* called it a pyhrric victory. "A propos de l'affaire de Marckolsheim: Victoire à la Pyrrhus?" *Le Monde*, 27 February 1975.

[89] Fernex, "Non-Violence Triumphant," 376.

was going on at Wyhl with similar actions. The launch of the Kaiseraugst occupation in Switzerland and Pierre Pfimlin's deep concerns about the future of nuclear energy in Alsace revealed the Wyhl occupation's significant transnational ramifications within the Upper Rhine valley. These developments evidence the localized and personalized manner in which knowledge of the grassroots protest traveled. Knowledge transfer reached fever pitch as interested citizens and excited activists began visiting the rural construction site during the summer of 1975 in order to experience the occupation firsthand and find out about it for themselves.

"Wyhl Is Worth the Trip:" Living and Visiting the Occupation, Collapsing Contexts

The second occupation at Wyhl lasted from 23 February until 7 November 1975.[90] Over the course of the nearly nine months they were on the site, occupiers built up an impressive encampment that included housing, public meeting spaces, a field kitchen, and much more. As a result of their efforts, the clearing that construction workers had hewn in the remote Wyhl forest became a center of community life in the Upper Rhine valley and a magnet for visitors from outside the region. In stark contrast to the clashes with police that shocked West Germans at the occupation's outset, activists now furthered their anti-reactor goals by preparing meals or participating in scientific discussions at the Wyhl Forest Community College. The very banality of these actions made them difficult to fold into notions of militant resistance, particularly in light of the RAF's kidnapping of CDU politician Peter Lorenz and its armed seizure of the German Embassy in Stockholm, both of which occurred in early 1975, just as the occupation was beginning.[91] Even for those who read far beyond the headlines and introduced themselves to the details of the Wyhl protest, questions about the significance and meaning of the mundane activities protesters were carrying out on the site remained. Such confusion was compounded on 21 March when the Freiburg Administrative Court suspended the Badenwerk's license to build a reactor at Wyhl pending further

---

[90] Though the occupation officially ended on 7 November, when the Badensian and Alsatian Citizens' Initiatives entered into negotiations with the state government over the future of the reactor, a small watch over the site was maintained throughout the negotiations, which lasted until April 1976. Wolfgang Beer, *Lernen im Widerstand. Politisches Lernen und politische Sozialisation in Bürgerinitiativen* (Hamburg: Verlag Association, 1978), 81.

[91] Varon, *Bringing the War Home*, 196–197.

judicial review.[92] In an update on the project's status that it released in May, the Badenwerk noted the preliminary work that had been completed, and described the court ruling as the primary reason the project was delayed. The occupation was not mentioned at all.[93]

Even if the occupation was not solely responsible for preventing progress on the construction of the Wyhl reactor, visitors to the site gave it political significance by sharing their impressions of it with wide circles when they returned home. Though they diverged from pre-existing notions of protest, the occupation's most quotidian attributes proved particularly meaningful in the eyes of the many visitors who helped transmit Wyhl's signal far beyond the Rhine valley. "Packed buses" filled with "pupils, tourists, supporters and opponents" pulled up each day during the summer of 1975.[94] The occupiers often "had to re-tell the story of Wyhl three or four times in a single day" in order to welcome fifty to 100 curious guests.[95] But the protest's form and its most powerful ramifications were best understood experientially. For visitors who had learned everything they knew about Wyhl "from newspaper reports and television footage," an hour on the site corrected many misconceptions, and helped them to see the occupation as a powerful, and even militant, act of protest.

The quotidian nature of the Wyhl occupation was particularly evident to visitors. Many were taken aback by the spartan living conditions that protesters endured throughout the lengthy occupation, but all thoroughly enjoyed sitting around the campfire with the occupiers, "eating hot sausages and drinking good Silvaner."[96] The gustatory delights were just one aspect of the impressive "infrastructure of recreation" that the occupiers built on the site.[97] Drawing on their experiences at Marckolsheim, local activists worked quickly to make life on the Wyhl site as comfortable as

---

[92] Wolfgang Sternstein, *Mein Weg zwischen Gewalt und Gewaltfreiheit*, 176; also noted in Wolfgang Beer, *Lernen im Widerstand*, 76. After the Freiburg court's decision, Filbinger announced the site would not be cleared until the administrative court in Mannheim had made a final ruling on the case. That decision was overturned shortly before activists finally agreed to negotiate an end to the occupation in November, but construction did not resume once they left. "Der Ministerpräsident erklärt: Keine Räumung in Wyhl vor einem Urteil des Verwaltungsgerichts," *Badische Zeitung*, 3 May 1975.

[93] Kernkraftwerk Süd, *Projektinformation* 5 (May 1975). HSAS EA 1/107 Bü 769.

[94] Eine Platzbesetzerin, "Das Leben auf dem besetzten Platz," 147; and: "Wyhl ist eine Reise wert!" *Was Wir Wollen* 9 (28 July 1975).

[95] "Zur gegenwärtigen Situation," *Was Wir Wollen* 5 [n. d. presumably May 1975].

[96] Eine Platzbesetzerin, "Das Leben auf dem besetzten Platz," 147.

[97] As Anna Feigenbaum, Fabian Frenzel, and Patrick McCurdy have shown in their study of "protest camps," the "infrastructure of recreation" that activists construct shapes their ability to build new coalitions and to sustain their protests. Feigenbaum, Frenzel, and McCurdy, *Protest Camps* (London: Zed Books, 2013), 29–30 and 182–218.

possible. They immediately re-established institutions and practices that had developed in fits and starts across the Rhine. In Marckolsheim, for example, protesters slowly built a yurt to protect their central gathering spot from the wind and rain of fall, and eventually the cold of winter.[98] Almost as soon as the occupation began at Wyhl, Balthasar Ehret led a team of volunteers who built a much larger protective structure in less than two weeks. This "Friendship House" was a "large round construction, with space for several hundred people;" it did more than protect protesters from cold and rainy weather.[99] The sturdy structure symbolized the occupation's permanence and anchored the well-ordered effort to maintain it. The process of building the Friendship House, one occupier noted, brought the community together in new ways. "It's not how well one can speak that counts here," he explained, "but rather how one wields a tool."[100] Such sentiment explains why occupiers and visitors alike came to see life on the occupied site as more than a means of saying no to nuclear energy. Building up the occupation allowed citizens to use saws and hammers to physically construct the basis for an alternative society even as they worked against the reactor.

The infrastructure activists built on the site was powerful because it brought people together. Under normal circumstances, middle-aged vintners and Freiburg students rarely even spoke with one another; collaboration on a political project was out of the question. In the Wyhl forest, however, they were forced to work together just to keep the occupation going. Young people, many of whom were students or unemployed, remained on the site for weeks or even months at a time. These "permanent occupiers" pitched their tents around the Friendship House. Local farmers and vintners also played an essential role in the occupation. A rotating schedule called on members of individual rural citizens' initiatives to "appear regularly and in great numbers" on the site and remain there for twenty-four-hour shifts.[101] Such "orderliness and good planning," were considered keys to the occupation's success.[102] Planning also offered opportunities for young Freiburg activists and rural women to discuss Premier Filbinger's latest missteps or work together on craft projects to be sold at fundraisers.[103]

---

[98] Mossmann, interview, 8 March 2010; see also: Mossmann, "Die Bevölkerung ist Hellwach," 139.
[99] Baum, interview; see also: Beer, *Lernen im Widerstand*, 76.
[100] Marcel, "Möglichkeiten," *Was Wir Wollen* 1 (3 November 1974), 11.
[101] Die Bürgerinitiativen, "KKW Wyhl" (12 May 1975). ABEBI 2HL2.
[102] Die 30 Bürgerinitiativen, "Aufruf!" ASB "Wyhl—Die Anfänge," 3691.
[103] "Geschichten aus dem Wyhler Wald," *Was Wir Wollen* 5 [n. d. presumably May 1975], 3.

Even if it provided common ground and helped to stabilize the occupation, the process of building and maintaining infrastructure on the site could not overcome all of the tensions between the many different groups and individuals participating in the anti-reactor struggle. Visitors reported on the delicious food, and pictures of the occupied site showed smiling occupiers relaxing around the campfire, but the occupiers themselves carefully intoned that the occupation "is no picnic."[104] Their message was clear: interpreting the Wyhl occupation as an ongoing party where everyone got along famously would be a serious mistake. Some of the young, "permanent occupiers" chafed at rumors that they were either "lazy good-for-nothings" or – once they had proven they could get things done – "communists." They chalked the rumors' persistence up to a simple lack of contact.[105]

Roland Burkhart, a Jechtingen native studying at the University of Freiburg, personally embodied these tensions and missed connections. Burkhart had "neither become a pure, intellectual Freiburg student nor remained a true Kaiserstuhler." He was well aware of villagers' distrust of long-haired youths, whom they sometimes even suspected of belonging to the group of "radical students and manipulators" alleged by Premier Filbinger to have infiltrated the occupation. But Burkhart was also aware of Freiburgers' demeaning conception of rural people, whom they mocked on account of their dialect and chronic alcoholism. Though he had a foot in both worlds, it was difficult for Burkhart to overcome the divide. At first, he actively avoided acquaintances from his village because he "simply did not know what to talk about with them;" the feeling seemed mutual. Yet, the necessity of solving the problems facing the occupation promoted cooperation. After a Freiburg student called a site-wide meeting to order one morning and began to organize the occupiers to perform the day's duties "in typical university-jargon, as if this was an assembly of student radicals," a local vintner interrupted the speaker. In thick dialect, the vintner shouted out that he simply could not understand what was going on. Burkhart was called upon to connect the disparate worlds by serving as "translator."[106]

The infrastructure that served as the occupation's connective tissue went far beyond the structures, institutions, and personnel required to satisfy activists' basic needs. As a result, its effects extended well beyond basic contacts. Just as carrying out daily chores doubled as an opportunity for

---

[104] "Wir, die ständigen Platzbesetzer," *Was Wir Wollen* 4 (3 May 1975).
[105] "Zur gegenwärtigen Situation," *Was Wir Wollen* 5 [n. d. presumably May 1975].
[106] Roland Burkhart, "'G'hert dä aü zu däne do?,'" in *Wyhl* (see note 9), 260–262.

urban activists to get to know rural people, the "community college" that activists organized at Wyhl became an important center of collaboration and discussion. The Wyhl Forest Community College (WFCC) was initially proposed as a means of attracting people onto the site during cold winter evenings. It was to feature a rather pedestrian program including courses like "French for Germans" and "Plants of the Rhine forest," but this was quickly altered to better "represent the breadth of the movement."[107] The revised program offered evening lectures, discussions, travel reports, concerts, and sing-alongs.[108] Opportunities to discuss the region's rich history and sing folk songs did not just "add fresh vegetables

Figure 3.5 The Schedule for Meetings of the Wyhl Forest Community College is posted on the outside of the Friendship House. © Meinrad Schwörer.

[107] Beer, *Lernen im Widerstand*, 95; and: Baum, interview.
[108] Recurring lecture series were devoted to such themes as "History and culture of the Upper Rhine," and "The Alemannic people: over here and over there." Die Badisch-elsässischen Bürgerinitiativen, "Volkshochschule Wyhler Wald, 3. Vierwochenprogramm" (June 1975); Die Badisch-elsässischen Bürgerinitiativen, "Volkshochschule Wyhler Wald, 7. Vierwochenprogramm" (October 1975); Die Badisch-elsässischen Bürgerinitiativen, "Volkshochschule Wyhler Wald, 8. Vierwochenprogramm" (October/November 1975). In the possession of the author.

Figure 3.6 Walter Mossmann performs in the "Friendship House" on the occupied
site in Wyhl. © ABEBI.

to the reactor stew . . . they allowed for relaxation, entertainment, and even
contributed to solidarity."[109]

The WFCC's success in building community and promoting inclusion
was perhaps most evident in the way that technical topics were discussed
there. Beginning with the very first lecture, "How does a nuclear reactor
function?" difficult, scientific subjects retained pride of place on the
WFCC program. Every Tuesday night, scientists like the meteorologist
Hans von Rudloff, the physicist Hans Klumb, and even the director of the
Karlsruhe Nuclear Research Center, Hans Grupe, discussed their research
with occupiers.[110] Addressing farmers and vintners inside the Friendship
House was a big change for scientists, who typically spoke to fellow
academics at research institutes. Local people, on the other hand, were
right at home on the occupied site. The familiar faces and relaxed atmosphere put them at ease and fostered participation. Soon, Community

[109] Wolfgang Beer, "Volkshochschule Wyhler Wald," in *Wyhl* (see note 9), 266.
[110] "Grupe war da," *Was Wir Wollen* 8 (8 July 1975).

College events were drawing up to 400 people three or four nights each week.[111] To one visitor from Berlin, the lecture series' success was evident in that:

> everyone that you meet on the site, whether a permanent occupier or a visitor from the region, was well informed and remarkably well prepared to speak about all topics related to nuclear energy, from the workings of reactors, to their dangers, and even their economic and political components.[112]

Hans Schött, Endingen's village pharmacist, reported with perhaps a touch of hyperbole that after eight weeks of coursework, the people of the Kaiserstuhl knew more about nuclear energy production than did their representatives in Stuttgart.[113]

The sort of discussion and collaboration that institutions like the WFCC promoted expanded the community-building effects of the occupation beyond the site. The occupiers' newspaper, *Was Wir Wollen* (*WWW*) featured letters and reports from locals and visitors, relevant articles from the mainstream press, and photographs from the occupied site (many of which were likely developed in the encampment's darkroom). It was conceived as a counterweight to the mainstream media, which "reported daily on the need for nuclear energy and the safety of nuclear reactors," but also as a chance to inform neighbors about the goings-on at the site and to counteract vicious rumors. Though it was dominated by reports written by the young "permanent occupiers," *WWW* was clearly an attempt to build connections and foster inclusivity. By summer, reports detailed not only the latest developments in the anti-reactor struggle, but also the results of soccer matches organized between the occupiers and village clubs.[114]

Outsiders realized the site's potential as a networking center, too. Freiburg University's Environmental Action (Aktion Umweltschutz) organized a "Conference Against Nuclear Reactors" intended to bring scientists to the site so that they could "compare the state of knowledge and research that is being conducted in isolation at the universities and in the working groups." Some 300 scientists came to Wyhl for the conference, wildly exceeding organizers' estimates that eighty would participate. The scientists gladly coupled standard conference proceedings with firsthand

[111] Beer, *Lernen im Widerstand*, 115 and 129; see also: Beer, "Volkshochschule Wyhler Wald," 269.
[112] Beer, *Lernen im Widerstand*, 99.
[113] "Aufgebrachter Winzer sperren Wirtschaftsminister im Rathaus ein," *Badische Zeitung*, 18 June 1975.
[114] "Sport," *Was Wir Wollen* 7 (June 1975), 8.

experience of the occupation. After spending the day discussing their research, the visitors pitched tents on the site, huddled around the campfire with occupiers, and listened attentively to local farmers' presentations on nuclear energy.[115] Two weeks later, thirty-five young activists from West Germany, France, Switzerland, Belgium, and England came to Wyhl for a conference organized by the Young European Federalists entitled "Nuclear Energy – Risk or Advance for European Society?" Despite the JEF's reverence for grassroots activism, their gathering resolved that to be successful, anti-nuclear activists would have to bring "the resistance against nuclear reactors from the Kaiserstuhl to other parts of the Federal Republic." Furthermore, the problems of nuclear energy would have to be made a major issue at national elections and the upcoming direct elections to the European Parliament (EP). Advocating "trans-border electoral districts," and drawing attention to "the question of uncoordinated siting in [borderlands] like the Upper Rhine region," would help to connect grassroots anti-nuclear activism to European electoral politics, but these ideas marked a serious departure from a style of activism that had long been considered disconnected from parliament.[116]

By setting up infrastructure on the site, from basics like a field kitchen and the friendship house to organs of communication and learning like the WFCC and *WWW*, the occupiers made the Wyhl Forest into not just a meeting space for the local community, but also a center of collaboration and exchange for citizens, scientists, and activists from outside the region. Those who got to know the Wyhl occupation best saw it as a means of not only stopping development on the Wyhl reactor project, but also as an opportunity to build community and consider new approaches to politics. Spending time with friends on the site, cooking food in the field kitchen, and attending lectures at the Wyhl Forest Community College were all illegal activities; these mundane actions became powerful and daring contributions to the occupation. By making everyday activities the core of their movement, reactor opponents fashioned the occupation into a sustainable part of life in the Upper Rhine valley. Yet, the very fact that the institutions protesters developed in order to maintain their presence on the site forced participants to work together and to learn from one another

---

[115] They included "scientists from almost every university in the Federal Republic of Germany" as well as "delegations from Austria and Switzerland." "Statt 80 kamen 300 zum 'Kongress gegen Kernkraftwerke,'" *Stuttgarter Zeitung*, 30 June 1975.

[116] Josef Leinen, "Protokoll vom internationalen Seminar vom 11.–13. Juli in Freiburg," in Junge Europäische Föderalisten, *Presseecho auf die Bonner anti-Atomkraftwerke Aktion* (Bonn, 1975), 4–6. AdsD – 1976 JEF-Info Manuskripte, Belegexemplare.

explains the occupation's success. Even if life on the site was not always easy, protesters created a model for protest by establishing a cooperative atmosphere. While the excitement of the occupation attracted outsiders to Wyhl, its quotidian nature made it a constructive – not to mention transferable – political model, not just a means of stopping the construction of one particular reactor.

Conclusion

"In the first half of the 1970s," the sociologist Karl-Werner Brand has written, "next to no one could have predicted that in the following years a new, broad wave of protest movements would be sparked [*sic*] . . . by the problems of social reproduction." In making this claim, Brand surely had confusing protests like the Wyhl occupation in mind. It was difficult to interpret in part because anti-reactor protesters seemed focused on the post-material matter of preserving a provincial forest, they appeared "not [to be motivated] by the traditional problems of the capitalist order, which had so recently been repoliticized by the student movement."[117] Wyhl, after all, burst unexpectedly into West German national politics shortly after it attracted the attention of Stuttgart officials and Freiburg activists. Yet, the Rhenish anti-reactor struggle had developed haltingly at the grassroots level throughout the early 1970s. It built on protest strategies that came from France and were practiced in Switzerland. It was focused on particular local concerns, most of which had to do with material issues. Brand's startled prognosticators likely failed to locate the protest's deep roots because they weren't digging for them in rural Southern Baden, let alone searching beyond the Federal Republic's western and southern boundaries.

It is more surprising that the Wyhl occupation's roots proved difficult to identify within its local context, where it drew on a years' long history of anti-reactor protest. Though the local press occasionally referenced the Marckolsheim model in discussions of Wyhl, it struggled to explain what was going on when activists physically overran the reactor construction site. Reporters misunderstood activists' failure to adhere to traditional notions of protest as evidence of the movement's dysfunction. Government officials were also dumbfounded; they simply refused to

[117] Karl-Werner Brand, "Kontinuität und Diskontinuität in den neuen sozialen Bewegungen," in Brand, ed., *Neue soziale Bewegungen in Westeuropa und den USA. Ein internationaler Vergleich* (Frankfurt am Main: Campus Verlag, 1985), 30

believe that the occupation was a serious act of protest carried out by rural Badensians. It was only after police brutally removed reactor opponents from the site that the occupation briefly seemed more militant and therefore easier to understand. Following the brief burst of excitement incited by the police intervention, observers across the country were left to explain how attending a community college lecture or preparing breakfast in the field kitchen amounted to anti-nuclear activism. In essence, the Wyhl occupation was so difficult for observers to understand – and therefore so interesting – because it seemed so different from pre-existing notions of activism.

Despite observers' struggles to understand what was going on at Wyhl, the idea that protest itself was changing extended well beyond observations of the occupation. The differentiation between "protest" and "resistance" made by US activists during the late 1960s, and popularized in West Germany by RAF co-founder Ulrike Meinhof was one means of explaining this shift.[118] In her 1968 *Konkret* essay, "From Protest to Resistance," Meinhof famously defined the transition as going from "saying what I do not like" to "seeing to it that what I do not like does not happen."[119] By putting their bodies on the line, Rhenish activists were certainly seeing to it that the Wyhl reactor would not be built. In the Federal Republic of the 1960s and 1970s, however, Meinhof's formulation was a loaded one. In fact, Karin Bauer has argued, West Germans conceived of "resistance" in line with the resistance against the Nazi regime, "which could not be divorced from violent means."[120] In stark contrast to the practices of Meinhof's RAF, which suited such a martial definition of resistance, the Wyhl occupation lacked any of an armed struggle's trappings; some observers had a hard time distinguishing it from an ongoing picnic. Explaining Wyhl as an act of militant resistance

---

[118] As Karin Bauer has shown, though Meinhof referenced an anonymous speaker at the 1968 International Vietnam Congress in West Berlin (she was referring to SNCC-member Dale A. Smith), the phrase had deeper roots in US organizing. Bauer, "'From Protest to Resistance': Ulrike Meinhof and the Transatlantic Movement of Ideas," in Belinda Davis, Wilfried Mausbach, Martin Klimke, and Carla MacDougall, eds., *Changing the World, Changing Oneself: Political Protest and Collective Identities in West Germany and the U.S. in the 1960s and 1970s* (New York: Berghahn Books, 2010).

[119] Ulrike Meinhof, "Vom Protest zum Widerstand," *konkret* 5 (May 1968). In making this distinction, Meinhof drew directly on Dale A. Smith's differentiation between protest and resistance: "Protest is when I say I don't like this and that. Resistance is when I see to it that [the] thing I don't like no longer occurs." Quoted in Sibylle Plogstedt, ed., *Der Kampf des vietnamesischen Volkes und Globalstrategie des Imperialismus* (West Berlin: Internationales Nachrichten- und Forschungs-Institut, 1968), 139–140.

[120] Bauer, "From Protest to Resistance," 180.

despite its lack of "violent means" required looking outside the West German context. The French tradition of occupation strikes, and the recent protests on the Larzac plateau, which included the illegal construction of farmsteads on government-owned land, provided one transnational context within which occupation could be conceived as a powerful and militant form of protest. The Wyhl occupation's roots in France not only linked Wyhl to earlier French protests, they also obscured its meaning for West Germans.

The occupation's impact did not derive solely from its protagonists' importation of a foreign protest tactic into the FRG. It also relied on a significant shift in the way that activists themselves conceived what they were doing when they protested. In this respect, too, the idea of a shift from protest to resistance is apt. In a November 1967 essay, the American activist Staughton Lynd wrote that the adoption of "resistance" was best described as a transition from "lives devoted to activism" to "activist lives."[121] This transition was certainly reflected in Rhenish activists' quotidian participation in the Wyhl occupation, where daily life and protest converged, turning everyday activities into daring acts of protest and thus lives devoted to activism into activist lives. This new form of protest was also quotidian in that, despite their militancy, Rhenish activists sought primarily to supplement existing liberal democratic processes in order to challenge particular decisions they perceived as unjust; they had no interest in overthrowing the state. Though they seem moderate in comparison to the armed actions of the RAF or even the protest campaigns of dogmatic K-Groups, Rhenish protesters' efforts radically changed West Germans' approach to self-governance. By accepting both the framework of liberal democracy and extra-parliamentary activism Rhenish activists modeled a new style of democratic praxis that encouraged participation by making democracy more quotidian.

In challenging notions of protest and the relationship of protest to politics, the Wyhl occupation also shifted the political status of environmentalism. The second half of this book, which considers anti-nuclear protests beyond the Upper Rhine valley, investigates activists' attempts to build on Wyhl's powerful challenges to ideas of protest and politics and their effects. These ran the gamut from ill-fated mass occupation attempts to grassroots protests, to large rallies in capital cities, and even campaigns for political office. Whereas grassroots protest in the Upper Rhine valley had easily incorporated French, West German, and Swiss activists and

---

[121] Staughton Lynd, "Resistance: From Mood to Strategy," *Liberation* (November 1967): 40.

ideas, and found means of turning daily life into anti-nuclear action, attempts to build a larger movement cleaved more closely to national boundaries and more frequently respected traditional notions of protest. Paradoxically, the Wyhl occupation's notoriety was both a product of the way it challenged pre-existing notions of protest and of politics, and also a precursor to the nationalization and even the normalization of environmental protest in Europe.

CHAPTER 4

"Wyhl and Then What...?"* Between Grassroots Activism and Mass Protest

Activists scattered in every direction when the Easter Monday Rally ended at Wyhl. Locals organized transportation to Kaiseraugst, Switzerland in order to support the new occupation there. The thousands of protesters who had come from outside the region made their way home; many left in a state of awe. Petra Kelly and Jo Leinen, members of the pro-European integration Young European Federalists, left the Upper Rhine valley together. Discussing the mass demonstration they had just witnessed, they excitedly came to the conclusion that "nuclear energy would divide society." Like the locals who hastened to Kaiseraugst, Leinen and Kelly turned their thoughts to spreading anti-nuclear protest beyond Wyhl.

Despite their shared commitment to growing the anti-nuclear movement, the two young activists imagined its future differently. Leinen, who edited the JEF's *Forum E* magazine, described his bold plan for the movement in an April 1976 special issue.[1] Though the Wyhl occupation ended in November 1975, when the Alsatian and Badensian Citizens' Initiatives voted to leave the site and enter into negotiations with the state government and the Badenwerk, Leinen remained enraptured. Wyhl, he wrote, fostered "widespread public interest" in environmentalism and atomic energy, precipitated the development of a federal "network of Citizens initiatives," and garnered the attentione of the mainstream media as well as establishment political parties. But, his long term strategy for the movement pushed in a different direction. By calling on activists to create an "overarching environmental concept" in order to become "a long-term element of our political order," Leinen suggested that the movement

---

* Josef M. Leinen, "Wyhl und was dann...?" *Forum E* 3/4 (1976): 2.
[1] For more on the Young European Federalists' engagement in the anti-nuclear struggle, see: Stephen Milder, "Harnessing the Energy of the Anti-Nuclear Activist: How Young European Federalists Built on Rhine Valley Protest, 1974–1977." *Perspectives on Global Development and Technology* 9, no. 1–2 (Spring 2010): 119–133.

needed more centralized, top-down control.[2] Kelly, by contrast, called on Brussels-focused activists to learn from grassroots resistance across the continent and work to link local sites of anti-reactor protest together.[3] In a paper that she provocatively titled, "What is to be done???," she called the ongoing "chain reaction" of grassroots anti-reactor protest a learning process that could become the model for a new, bottom-up approach to high politics.[4]

Their visions were different, but Leinen and Kelly both smoothed Wyhl and the protests that followed it into a single narrative that made demonstrations on reactor sites the basis for a powerful social movement. A series of mass protests that took place at reactor construction sites in northern Germany matched the trajectory Leinen proposed because many participants considered these actions challenges to the federal nuclear program and even to government authority more generally.[5] Though only mass protests reliably made the national news, many more anti-reactor actions took place in Wyhl's wake. In France, little known, loosely linked, grassroots actions spread to disparate sites across the country, fitting Kelly's metaphor of a "chain reaction" of grassroots protest. Most of the French protests targeted individual reactors, some stopped particular projects and mobilized entire regions. This chapter juxtaposes the mass actions long considered evidence of nuclear energy's waxing political significance in West Germany – and thus counted as the basis for a powerful, unified environmental movement – with the widespread local protests in France that transformed local politics and individual lives but received less national attention, and continued to be seen as distant, provincial actions.

Despite numerous transnational links, the two movements have long been conceived as separate entities. The seemingly centralized West German movement has been deemed far more significant than its loosely coordinated French counterpart;[6] the fact that France continues to

---

[2] Leinen, "Wyhl und was dann...?"

[3] Petra Kelly, "WAS TUN??? Einige Aktionsmöglichkeiten für die Westeuropäischen Sozialisten!" (Letter, November 1975), 1. AGG PKA 534,2.

[4] Kelly and Vogt, "Ökologie und Frieden. Der Kampf gegen Atomkraftwerke aus der Sicht von Hiroshima," *Forum E*, 1–2 (1977), 18.

[5] The best known histories of the West German anti-nuclear movement have followed this trajectory. See, for example: Dieter Rucht, *Von Wyhl nach Gorleben. Bürger gegen Atomprogramm und nukleare Entsorgung* (Munich: C. H. Beck, 1980); and: Reimar Paul, *... und auch nicht anderswo! Die Geschichte der Anti-AKW-Bewegung* (Göttingen: Verlag die Werkstatt, 1997).

[6] In her comparison of the French and German ecology movements, for example, Céline Caro found that, while both countries saw significant environmental protests, Germany had a "more vital movement" and environmental concern has developed "more deeply and more broadly" there. Caro, "Le développement de la conscience environnementale et l'émergence de l'écologie politique

produce some 75 percent of its electricity at nuclear power stations while Germany has committed to a nuclear phase-out seems to prove this assertion. In the short-run, however, activists failed to stop the development of nuclear energy in either country, and even in Germany, the last reactor will only be switched off in 2022 – more than a half-century after the first protests on the Upper Rhine. So how different were the West German and French anti-nuclear movements really, and what are the consequences of placing so much emphasis on asserting hard and fast distinctions between activist projects in different countries? Differently put, what are the stakes of associating the progress and efficacy of a social movement with the construction of centralized, national structures and the formulation of overarching concepts? Seeking answers to these questions is a means of reconsidering narratives of the anti-nuclear movement's growth – and theories of the growth of social movements more generally.[7] Centralization and nationalization are unabashedly emphasized, for example, in the contention that only battles over nuclear waste processing facilities had the potential to "take on a key role" and serve as a "crystallization point for the federal protest against atomic energy," because they alone transcended the local dimensions of struggles over individual reactors.[8] And yet, grassroots anti-reactor protest transformed individual citizens and entire regions. After the occupation at Wyhl garnered press headlines and captured citizens' imaginations, locally-focused activists went so far as to argue that "one or two more 'Wyhls' would cause the atomic program of government and industry finally to collapse."[9] If local protests were half as powerful as their protagonists' rhetoric proposed, then centralization and the adoption of national structures and goals may not have been the only means of making the movement meaningful.

---

dans l'espace public en France et en Allemagne, 1960–1990" (PhD Dissertation Universite Sorbonne Nouvelle – Paris III and Technische Universität Dresden, 2009), 457–458. See also: Claus Leggewie, "Propheten ohne Macht. Die neuen sozialen Bewegungen in Frankreich zwischen Resignation und Fremdbestimmung," in Karl-Werner Brand, ed., *Neue soziale Bewegungen in Westeuropa und den USA. Ein internationaler Vergleich* (Frankfurt am Main: Campus, 1985), 114–115.

[7] Sidney Tarrow famously distinguishes between previous instances of "contentious politics" which had only "expressed the claims of ordinary people directly, locally, and narrowly, responding to immediate grievances" and the social movements of the nineteenth century, which deployed "modular repertoires, movement organizations, and broad collective action frames." Organization and centralization, in other words, are essential to Tarrow's definition of a social movement. Tarrow, *Power in Movement: Social Movements and Contentious Politics*, second edition (Cambridge: Cambridge University Press, 1998), 66.

[8] Rucht, *Von Wyhl nach Gorleben*, 210.

[9] A contention clearly influenced by Che Guevara's 1967 call to make "one, two . . . many Vietnams." Wolfgang Hertle, "Platzbesetzungen" in *graswurzelrevolution* 20–21 (June 1976): 21.

Tales from the Wyhl Forest

Outsiders like Jo Leinen and Petra Kelly were far from alone in their considerations of the Wyhl struggle's wider ramifications. Rhenish activists considered their actions' effects on anti-reactor protest elsewhere, too. Already in March 1975, Freia Hoffmann worried "that the example of Wyhl has led to resignation elsewhere." In other places, she explained, "they say, 'the people of the Kaiserstuhl, those are particularly courageous people, something like [the Wyhl occupation] would not be possible here.'" Even if Hoffmann was correct that the Wyhl occupation caused people elsewhere to resign themselves to failure, the courageous people of the Kaiserstuhl also inspired activists like Leinen and Kelly to promote anti-reactor protests all around the world. Moreover, the protagonists of the Wyhl struggle themselves worked to create the broadest possible resonance for their grassroots protests.

The primary problem these efforts faced, which Hoffmann had also foreseen, was that people beyond the Rhine valley spoke of the Wyhl occupation without referencing the history of anti-reactor protest that preceded it. Opponents and supporters alike cast the Wyhl occupation as a surprising and divergent development. One soul-searching article in the industry publication *atom-forum*, for example, failed to mention the way that anti-nuclear sentiment had developed slowly in the region and described "a population that had been systematically seduced" into participating in the occupation by radical outsiders.[10] On the other side of the political spectrum, a host of Left-wing groups in Freiburg suddenly supported anti-reactor protest after the brutal 20 February police intervention at Wyhl.[11] They overlooked years' of anti-reactor organizing in the region, and emphasized how shocked they were that rural people were struggling with the police in the Wyhl forest. In working to clarify the situation at Wyhl to people across the Federal Republic, Hoffmann sought to expose the occupation's roots. She was "forced to repeat time and again" that in the Upper Rhine valley "a few people began the painstaking work of pointing out the dangers of atomic power plants, the patient work of organizing countless informational meetings, passing out umpteen-thousand flyers, collecting signatures, etc." The occupation, Hoffmann told whomever would listen, was

---

[10] Klaus Montanus, "Die Wacht am Rhein," *atom-forum* 6/1975. Reprinted in *Was Wir Wollen* 8 (1975), 7.

[11] For more on the Freiburg Left's response to the Wyhl occupation, see Chapter 3.

not some inexplicable happening, but rather the best-known moment in a long-winded effort.[12]

Rhenish protesters worked alongside Hoffmann to fill the gaps in outsiders' knowledge of their struggle. Walter Mossmann "traveled with the story of Wyhl to every possible anti-nuclear citizens' initiative in West Germany and West Berlin, in Switzerland, in Austria, Luxembourg, Denmark, Holland, and time and again to Paris;" he was one of "hundreds who were fanning out to tell the story of Wyhl as an inspirational example."[13] Balthasar Ehret, the Weisweil Communist who owned the Fischerinsel pub, was particularly dedicated to spreading the idea that the Wyhl struggle was teachable and adaptable. In Freiburg, he gave a talk entitled "Lehrstück Wyhl," referencing Bertolt Brecht's "learning plays" in order to suggest that Freiburgers could draw valuable lessons from engaging themselves at Wyhl.[14] At Frankfurt's iconic Club Voltaire, he gladly discussed "the ways that experiences gained through the occupation of the site might prove useful for the [Frankfurt] squatters' movement." A representative of the Association of Electricity Suppliers (VDEW) who had been sent to observe the meeting, nervously reported that, "the citizens' initiatives in Wyhl are taking advantage of the local population's possibly inadequate understanding of nuclear reactors and their necessity in order to push for systemic change on the political level."[15] It was not so much the ins and outs of nuclear energy, but rather the bottom-up potential for making change, that made sharing the story of the Wyhl protests such a powerful undertaking. Person-to-person contacts allowed Rhenish activists to construe their achievements as evidence that the impossible was possible, but that realizing it required tireless work.

Rhenish activists' missionary work fostered grassroots protests taking place at the numerous nuclear sites proposed across France as part of the 1974 Messmer Plan. The Strasbourg student Jean de Barry was invited to discuss Rhenish protests in Normandy, where opposition to the reprocessing

---

[12] Freia Hoffmann, "Was bedeutet das Beispiel Wyhl?" (Freiburg: 21 March 1975). AGG PKA 2264. Erhard Schulz later spoke of the occupation as one small part of a long-winded effort that was approaching its fiftieth year by 2015. Schulz, "Ich hätte nicht gedacht, dass wir so einen langen Atem benötigen," *'s Eige zeige' Jahrbuch des Landkreises Emmendingen für Kultur und Geschichte* 29 (2015): 325–334.

[13] Walter Mossmann, *realistisch sein: das unmögliche verlangen. Wahrheitsgetreu gefälschte Erinerungen* (Berlin: der Freitag, 2009), 204–205.

[14] dkp-hochschulgruppe, "Lehrstück Wyhl" (1975). Universitätsarchiv Freiburg, Kernkraft – Kernforschung 3762.

[15] VDEW-Geschäftsstelle, "Vermerk. Betr.: Aktivitäten der 'Bürgerinitiative' gegen den geplanten Bau des Kernkraftwerkes Wyhl," 3. April 1975. HSAS EA 1/107 Bü 768.

center at La Hague and the proposed Flamanville reactor was growing.[16] Modell Wyhl influenced opponents of the Malville fast-breeder reactor, too. Screenings of footage from the Wyhl occupation were used as recruiting tools in neighboring villages.[17] The Lyon Committee against the Super-Phénix asked Inge and Jean-Jacques Rettig for a description of the Marckolsheim and Wyhl occupations. In a lengthy open letter that was eventually published in French and German alternative publications, the Rettigs explained in great detail just how Rhenish activists prepared for the occupations. The couple emphasized how important it was for occupiers to know one another even before the action began, and they insisted on the significance of occupiers' behavior on the site, which they believed was the reason a small group of protesters could prevent a police intervention. The Rettigs even provided a list of essential supplies, which ranged from "hammers, nails, hatchets, and matches" to "numerous megaphones (very important)" and "handkerchiefs dampened with the juice of half a lemon" to protect against tear gas. Careful, systematic preparation, the Rettigs inveighed, underpinned every successful occupation. But winning the support of the local population was perhaps the most important preparation. Even if "every French ecology group were to send a small delegation to Malville," the Rettigs warned their correspondents in Lyon, "the situation would be unsustainable in the long run" without local support.[18]

Rhenish activists also shared their story by taking their protests on the road. On 18 July 1975, three carloads of activists traveled down the Rhine from Wyhl to Bonn, where they planned to give government officials the opportunity to experience grassroots anti-nuclear protest firsthand. To "show that the [Badensian and Alsatian] Citizens' Initiatives were demonstrating against nuclear reactors," the activists brought signs and banners straight from the occupied site. Just in front of the Federal Ministry for Research, where reporters and officials were headed into a press conference on nuclear safety, they staged a funeral for West Germany's "radiant future," complete with tearful eulogies and a coffin borne by gas mask clad pallbearers.[19]

The small-scale re-enactment of a grassroots Rhenish anti-reactor protest elicited a notable response. Surprised passers-by flashed "condescending

---

[16] Jean de Barry, interview with the author, Strasbourg, 30 March 2010.
[17] "Malville," *La Gueule Ouverte* 110 (16 June 1976).
[18] The letter was published in French in *Combat non-violent* and translated into German by Wolfgang Hertle for publication in *graswurzelrevolution*. The quotes here use the German translation. Hertle, "Platzbesetzungen," *graswurzelrevolution* 20–21 (June 1976): 21.
[19] Christa aus Offenburg, "Unsere Demonstration in Bonn," *Was Wir Wollen* 10, (15 August) 1975; see also: Manuel Walther, "Bonn: Aktion gegen KKW" *graswurzelrevolution* 17 (1975).

smiles" or "simply took a flyer and moved on," but Minister of Research Matthöfer eventually agreed to meet with the protesters.[20] What is more, the action received coverage in fourteen West German newspapers, and was reported on five television and radio broadcasts across the Federal Republic.[21] The protest also set a new precedent for grassroots cooperation, since members of "the Offenburg Citizens' Initiative against Nuclear Reactors, the Tübingen Working Group for the Protection of Life, the Kalkar Citizens' Initiative, the Freiburg Working Group for Environmental Protection, and the Young European Federalists" all took part.[22] By targeting the Ministry for Research, these grassroots organizations positioned their small, bottom-up protest within the framework of national politics.

The travels of the movement's missionaries, the widely shared advice of Rhenish activists like the Rettigs, and model actions like the Bonn demonstration helped create activist networks and link together grassroots anti-reactor protesters. This sort of bottom-up organizing emphasized the adaptability of grassroots protest and the primacy of local activists – rather than a unitary, centralized movement, it created a patchwork of local sites of resistance. Though this patient networking enabled people all across Western Europe to apply Rhenish protesters' wisdom to their own projects, most observers were only familiar with the Wyhl occupation – they knew little of the movement building that preceded it or the negotiations and other protests that followed it. As a result, a few bombastic mass protests grabbed headlines and came to be perceived as the legacy of "Wyhl." These widely known protests, most of which revolved around confrontations between protesters and police, overshadowed the grassroots protest campaigns that proliferated in Wyhl's wake; even as Kelly's chain reaction of protests exploded across Western Europe, most citizens turned their attention elsewhere.

Following Modell Wyhl in the North[23]

Though they were in fact far less numerous than grassroots anti-reactor protests, mass reactor site occupation attempts seemed ubiquitous in the

[20] Walther, "Bonn: Aktion gegen KKW."
[21] Junge Europäische Föderalisten (JEF), "Presseecho auf die Bonner Antikernkraftwerke-Aktion," in *Bericht der Arbeitsgruppe III: "Umweltschutz als Gesellschaftspolitik"* (JEF: Bonn, September 1975).
[22] Bonner Redaktion of the *Stuttgarter Zeitung*, "Bürgerinitiativen protestieren in Bonn," *Stuttgarter Zeitung* [n.d. July 1975?], reprinted in JEF, "Presseecho."
[23] KKW Kommission, KB/Gruppe Hamburg, "'Modell' Wyhl," *Arbeiterkampf* 6, no. 96 (29 November 1976), 4.

late 1970s. In 1976 and 1977 alone, tens of thousands of demonstrators attempted occupations at reactor sites in Brokdorf and Grohnde in Northern Germany, at Malville in France, and even as far afield as Seabrook, New Hampshire.[24] Wyhl was these protests' protagonists' lodestar, but protesters elsewhere failed to gain control of the sites they targeted for a prolonged period. Most of the actions did not even get to the point of requiring the "hammers, nails, hatchets, and matches" that the Rettigs reminded would-be occupiers to have at the ready. Nor did they always receive strong support in the communities surrounding the reactors they targeted. Instead of tedious grassroots movement building, the mass occupation attempts of the late seventies drew on the most exciting moments of the Wyhl occupation – protesters' initial assertion of authority over an important construction site and the hard-nosed conflict with authorities that came immediately afterwards. Nonetheless, such actions quickly came to symbolize anti-nuclear protest, and thus came to be perceived as Wyhl's primary legacy.

The struggle at the Brokdorf reactor site in Northern Germany, which thousands of protesters twice attempted to occupy in fall 1976, came hot on the heels of Wyhl. Many were drawn to the Brokdorf protests because of what they knew of the Rhenish protest, even if that knowledge was limited. The Hamburg student Wolfgang Ehmke, for example, cited Nina Gladitz's popular documentary *Lieber heute aktiv als morgen radioaktiv* (Better Active Today than Radioactive Tomorrow), as his primary motivation for traveling to Brokdorf. Gladitz's footage of Badensian vintners comparing "real existing socialism" in Honecker's East Germany and Mao's China contributed to Ehmke's "glorification" of the Wyhl occupation and its protagonists. The farmers' consensus that Mao was a "practitioner" while the German Democratic Republic (GDR) was filled with useless theorists and bureaucrats, attracted the Maoist Ehmke to anti-nuclear protest. As he "travelled with friends in October 1976 to the first Brokdorf demonstration," Ehmke reflected on the film and thought "that's just how one has to do it."[25]

---

[24] On the international (including transatlantic) proliferation of the Wyhl struggle, see: Jan-Henrik Meyer and Astrid Kirchhof, eds., "Global Protest against Nuclear Power," *Historical Social Research* 39, no. 1 (2014); and: Andrew Tompkins, *Better Active than Radioactive! Anti-Nuclear Protest in 1970s France and West Germany* (Oxford: Oxford University Press, 2016).

[25] Wolfgang Ehmke, "Bewegte Zeiten: Von Wyhl bis zum Tag X," in Paul, *... und auch nicht anderswo!* (see note 5), 36. Gladitz's film seems to have had precisely the effect on Ehmke that the filmmaker had hoped. Walter Mossmann, for one, has criticized Gladitz for creating a particular image of the opponents of the Wyhl reactor that matched her own political views, thereby "sweeping away" people who do not fit her preconceptions. Mossmann, "Wo bitte geht's zum Ursprung? 12

The inhabitants of the Wilster Marsh region, which surrounded Brokdorf, also drew unabashedly on the Wyhl struggle. Dairy farmers and other residents of the "fertile marshland" near the mouth of the Elbe river had begun protesting before they were aware of Wyhl.[26] The mayor and several citizens of one neighboring town founded the Lower Elbe Citizens' Initiatives for Environmental Protection (BUU) just two weeks after the Brokdorf project was announced in the fall of 1973.[27] But as their struggle progressed, reactor opponents in the Wilster Marsch began taking cues from the Upper Rhine valley. After the beginning of the Wyhl occupation, they announced plans "to occupy the [Brokdorf] construction site if legal steps proved insufficient."[28] In December 1975, the BUU reaffirmed its commitment to occupy the Brokdorf site in a statement that mirrored the August 1974 "Declaration to the Alsatian and Badensian Population." This "Declaration of the North German Citizens' Initiatives and Organizations for the Protection of Life to the Population" used the same three sections, "because we know," "because we see," and "because we have learned" to articulate local opposition to the reactor project. Even the individual arguments used to justify the call for occupation were taken word for word from the Rhenish declaration.[29]

The start of construction at Brokdorf provided evidence that the officials managing the project had studied Modell Wyhl, too. Intent on preventing protesters from gaining the upper hand, the project's managers ordered work on the Brokdorf reactor to begin just after midnight on 26 October 1976. By the time the sun rose, the reactor site was surrounded by a tall and sturdy fence; construction crews could expect to work without interruption. As soon as they realized what had happened, outraged local people called for a mass demonstration to be held just days later, on Saturday, 30 October.[30] The threat of occupation loomed large, but as at Wyhl, protesters announced no formal plans to take over the site.

Anmerkungen zur Wyhlerzählung des Historikers Jens Ivo Engels," footnote 16. Unpublished manuscript, in the possession of the author.

[26] BUU, *Brokdorf. Der Bauplatz muß wieder zur Wiese werden!* (Hamburg: Verlag Association, 1977), 21.

[27] Stefan Aust, *Brokdorf. Symbol einer politischen Wende* (Hamburg: Hoffmann und Campe Verlag, 1981), 21. The BUU was founded on 26 November 1973. See: Gewaltfreie Aktion Sindelfingen (Olaf Paulsen), "Information zur Kernenergie – Am Beispiel Brokdorf – Eine Chronologie des Widerstands" (Sindelfingen: 1977). ASB 9.4.1.1 XVII.

[28] Aust, *Brokdorf*, 58.

[29] "Erklärung der Norddeutschen Bürgerinitiativen und Lebensschutzverbände an die Bevölkerung," December 1975. Reprinted in BUU, *Brokdorf*, 59–60.

[30] BUU, *Brokdorf*, 68.

The 30 October protest, which drew 8,000 reactor opponents, evidenced direct physical links between the anti-nuclear protest campaigns on the Rhine and the Elbe. Rhine valley activists highlighted the speakers' roster. Walter Mossmann used the example of Wyhl as evidence of the "legitimacy and necessity" of an occupation at Brokdorf.[31] But Wyhl's influence on the crowd went far deeper than the words of Rhenish activists. Throughout the speeches, "a group of young people chanted, 'Do it like Wyhl! Do it like Wyhl!'"[32] Immediately afterwards, protesters drifted towards the perimeter fence for what one activist referred to as the "obligatory 'stroll around the construction site.'" Familiar with the Wyhl occupation, police, too, knew to understand the call to stroll along the fence as code for an attempt to occupy the site. In addition to a barbed wire fence "à la Wyhl," a moat surrounded "Fort Brokdorf." As at Wyhl, however, wire and water proved insufficient to keep anti-nuclear activists out. Protesters forded the moat, toppled the fence, and made their way onto the site. Unable to stop the onslaught with "truncheons, chemical mace, and the reckless use of horses," the police changed their tactics and herded the protesters into a corner, which they enclosed with a new barbed wire fence.[33] As the twilight faded, activists pitched tents, lit campfires, and established a first aid station. Local farmers supplied a meal of soup, sausage, and bread. The protesters seemed to have successfully replicated Modell Wyhl.[34]

The Brokdorf occupation even ended just as the initial Wyhl occupation had – with an overpowering police intervention. At 8:30 pm, some 600 police officers surrounded the roughly equivalent number of occupiers and mounted an "unimaginably brutal ... counterattack."[35] After dispersing many of the protesters with smoke bombs, the police made liberal use of truncheons, mace, and tear gas. Those left standing were quickly arrested.[36] Meanwhile, "together with leftover items, including clothing, sleeping bags, and identity cards," the tents that protesters had hastily pitched were "gathered together by the police and immediately burned."[37] Along with this equipment, the Brokdorf occupation went up in smoke hours after it began.

Taking yet another cue from Wyhl, activists at Brokdorf quickly planned a second occupation attempt. But when they tried to reoccupy the site two weeks later, on 13 November 1976, violence erupted. Hundreds

---

[31] Ibid., 107.   [32] Mossmann, *realistisch sein*, 230.   [33] BUU, *Brokdorf*, 107–108.
[34] Matthias Moch, "Brokdorf. 1. Akt Platzbesetzung," *graswurzelrevolution* 25/26 (December 1977), 2.
[35] BUU, *Brokdorf*, 111.   [36] Aust, *Brokdorf*, 29.   [37] BUU, *Brokdorf*, 111.

of heavily armed police officers defended the site alongside Federal Border Control agents. A report on the demonstration in the popular weekly magazine *Stern* sounded more like the summary of a military engagement:

> Blinded by tear gas and soaked by water cannons, the citizens responded to the force behind the border fence – which not only looked like [the wall] in Berlin, but was equally ugly and equally impassable – with impotent rage. They threw clumps of mud at water cannons and police officers. Professional hooligans were also on hand; these small armed bands, which were repeatedly admonished by sober-minded demonstrators, threw rocks and poles. Water cannons were sometimes made inoperable, a police cruiser was set alight. Demonstrators cut holes in the fence at multiple locations. The police countered with stones of their own and with tear gas. As night fell, federal border troops made their first massive attack. They came by land and from the air. The ground troops cleared the streets around the site. Helicopters nose-dived towards demonstrators who had drifted away from the group. They dropped tear gas grenades amongst people who had already been thrown to the ground by the air pressure.[38]

The government's will to build the Brokdorf reactor and its awareness that at least some protesters would try to force their way onto the construction site motivated a response that dwarfed the defensive measures deployed successfully just two weeks earlier, let alone the February 1975 police intervention at Wyhl. Perhaps due to the sheer brutality of the police reaction, even the mainstream news media – as *Stern*'s willingness to differentiate between "hooligans" and "sober-minded demonstrators" suggested – was not without sympathy for the protesters.[39]

Though the struggle against the Wyhl reactor inspired the protagonists of the Brokdorf occupation attempts, the protests on the Elbe led to increased discussions of police brutality and construction site fortifications, not nuclear energy. The Hamburg student Ehmke remembered that he had "no time to come up for air" after experiencing the brutality of 30 October. He was thinking "first and foremost about technical details: the properties and height of the perimeter fence, which had been put up in quite a hurry, etc."[40] The cover page of the December 1976 edition of *graswurzelrevolution*, printed on special red newsprint, highlighted

---

[38] Quoted in Aust, *Brokdorf*, 29–30.

[39] Writing for the weekly newspaper *Die Zeit*, Horst Bieber noted that the police "sought out the most effective of all possible methods to turn the demonstrators against them," and agreed with the *Stern* article in his claim that of the 25,000 demonstrators present at Brokdorf only 1,000 were interested in pushing onto the site. Horst Bieber, "'Bürgerkrieg' in der Wilstermarsch," *Die Zeit*, 19 November 1976.

[40] Ehmke, "Bewegte Zeiten," 37.

activists' growing concerns about police brutality. The deployment of water cannons "before anyone had even begun [to protest]" and the attacks by "tear-gas bombs from low-flying helicopters" caused Marianne Horbelt to exclaim, "I have no idea what sort of country this is, where I live!" Horbelt had struggled to ensure the safety of her fellow protesters and wondered aloud whether she would still be permitted to work as a teacher after participating in the protest.[41] Fortifications and forceful police tactics stopped protesters from mounting a successful occupation at Brokdorf; they also drew attention away from the matter of nuclear energy and towards the repression and brutality required to defend the "atomic state." In the end, the failed Brokdorf demonstration highlighted the bombastic aspects of occupation that Freia Hoffmann and her Rhenish comrades had sought to de-emphasize by sharing the importance of their longer movement-building efforts.

Violent clashes with police – at Wyhl and at Brokdorf – did not just shift activists' attention from nuclear energy to violence. They also aided recruitment efforts, enabled a militant movement identity to emerge, and connected nuclear energy with debates about authoritarianism and democracy. "For many students, intellectuals, Leftists," one activist wrote after Brokdorf,

> experienceable or experienced injustice was the determinant factor in the decision to become active ... outrage about police actions and about construction sites that had been turned into fortresses ... often served as catalysts for the founding of anti-nuclear initiatives, which only later took up the matter of nuclear energy.[42]

The founding and development of the Göttingen Working Group against Nuclear Reactors exemplified this dynamic. The group was created in December 1976 because "even [in Göttingen] people were woken up by the demonstrations in Brokdorf." The group's initial focus on police brutality eventually merged together with interest in nuclear energy and its dangers, however. In May 1977, the Working Group created the monthly magazine *Atom-Express* to transmit "concrete information to as many people as possible about the dangers of reactors and reprocessing facilities," to promote the "discussion of alternative, environmentally friendly energy

---

[41] As of 1972, the "Radikalenerlass" or "Anti-Radical Decree" prevented those with radical political views from working in the civil service, including as teachers. Marianne Horbelt, "Brokdorf. Mitten in der Nacht. Montag nach Samstag," *graswurzelrevolution* 25/26 (December 1976), 1.

[42] Reimar Paul, "Die Anti-AKW-Bewegung: Wie sie wurde was sie ist," in *... und auch nicht anderswo!* (see note 5), 18–19.

sources," and to further calls for "an immediate stop for all reactor construction projects."[43] The centrality of "occupation" in this process, which connected concerns about police violence with the technical details of nuclear energy production, explains why mass occupation protests like the ones that took place at Brokdorf have long been considered the primary legacy of the Rhenish anti-nuclear struggle. The latter has been reduced, in turn, to the nine-month Wyhl occupation.

And yet, the Brokdorf protests hardly evinced the grassroots approach that Rhenish activists sought to spread from Wyhl. Instead of drawing attention to grassroots movement-building and the unusual protagonists of local anti-reactor protests, clashes with the police became ends in themselves. It was not the "single issue" of nuclear energy, but rather concerns about the nature of the West German nuclear state and its penchant for authoritarian repression that motivated the likes of Ehmke and Horbelt. Even mass protests like the failed Brokdorf occupations, however, clearly contributed to nuclear energy's linkage with wider political debates. As the subject became tied up with questions about government authority, free speech, and radicalism, nuclear energy became almost a cypher for politics as a whole in the Federal Republic. In France, by contrast, protests against nuclear energy retained particular focal points and strong regional identities.

Creating Regional Resistance

Well before the start of construction at Brokdorf was met with repeated mass occupation attempts, grassroots anti-reactor protests were taking place all over France. The publication in December 1974 of a list of thirty-four sites, from which the locations for a dozen new reactors were to be chosen, brought the nuclear issue to the doorsteps of many French. Grassroots protests at many of the potential sites caused Electricité de France to remove some from consideration.[44] Nonetheless, seen

---

[43] Die Redaktion, "In eigener Sache," *Atom-Express* 1 (May 1977), 2.
[44] René Pichavant writes that there were thirty-eight potential sites, *Les pierres de la liberté: Plogoff, 1975–1980: chronique* (Douarnenez: Editions Morgane, 1981), 17. A. Oudiz writes that a map of thirty-four potential sites was determined at an inter-ministerial meeting in June 1974, in Alexandre Nicolon, Francis Fagnani, and Marie Josephe Carrieu, *Nucléopolis: matériaux pour l'analyse d'une société nucléaire* (Grenoble: Presses universitaires de Grenoble, 1979), 170–171, 214. On the number of reactors to be built under the Messmer Plan, see: N. J. D. Lucas, *Energy in France: Planning, Politics, and Policy* (London: Europa Publications, 1979), 148–149. On the localization, see: Frank Nullmeier, Frauke Rubart, and Harald Schulz, *Umweltbewegungen und Parteiensystem: Umweltgruppen und Umweltparteien in Frankreich und Schweden* (Berlin: Quorum, 1983), 25.

from the national perspective, French anti-reactor protest seemed incredibly ineffective; some three dozen reactors went critical in France during the late 1970s and early 1980s alone. And yet, even as they succeeded in removing numerous sites from consideration, grassroots anti-reactor protesters fostered regional networks of anti-nuclear resistance that provided an alternative to national organizations. Accordingly, calculating these actions' effectiveness – or lack thereof – cannot be as simple as comparing the number of reactors that went online in France with the number that activists stopped from being built. Instead, understanding the efficacy of grassroots protests requires looking closely at the sorts of networks that developed both within and amongst individual regions in order to measure these collaborations' effects on nuclear policy debates and public participation more generally.

Though they were not always readily apparent, long-range links connected grassroots protesters all over Western Europe.[45] They comprised the ongoing "chain reaction" that Petra Kelly considered the basis for a new politics. The largest single protest against a reactor proposed for Braud-et-St. Louis in the Gironde, for example, attracted only 4,000 participants, but in addition to local reactor opponents, it drew significant numbers of activists from the Upper Rhine valley and from Brittany.[46] Coverage in alternative publications like *La Gueule Ouverte, Super-Pholix,* and *Was Wir Wollen* contributed to the trans-local resonance of grassroots actions in such out-of-the-way places, even if they were "concealed by the [mainstream] French press."[47] Unorthodox anti-reactor protests, including beach campouts near proposed reactor sites at Bretignolle-sur-Mer on the Atlantic coast and Port-la-Nouvelle in the Languedoc were particularly well-suited to coverage in the alternative press; the satirical *Charlie-Hebdo* reminded its readers not to miss the

---

Michael Bess notes that the plan was not debated in the National Assembly until May 1975. Bess, *The Light Green Society: Ecology and Technological Modernity in France, 1960–2000* (Chicago: University of Chicago Press, 2003), 95. A study conducted by SOFRES showed the extent to which living near a reactor or proposed reactor site influenced neighbors' opinions of nuclear energy. See: Nicolon et al., *Nucléopolis*, 332–333.

[45] For more on the nature of these links, see: Andrew Tompkins, "Grassroots Transnationalism(s): Franco-German Opposition to Nuclear Energy in the 1970s," *Contemporary European History* 25, no. 1 (February 2016): 117–142.

[46] Elisabeth, "In Braud et St. Louis geht der Kampf weiter!" *Was Wir Wollen* 6 (1975), 9–10. For more on the opposition at Braud-et-St Louis, see: Alexandre Nicolon, "Analyse d'une opposition à un site nucléaire," in Nicolon, et al., *Nucléopolis* (see note 44), 223–315. On Bretons' participation, see: Gilles Simon, *Plogoff: l'apprentissage de la mobilisation sociale* (Rennes: Presses universitaires de Rennes, 2010), 57–58.

[47] One article in *Was Wir Wollen*, for example, linked together protests at Gravelines, Paluel, and Paris among others. "Frankreich: Die Bewegung verbreitet sich," *Was Wir Wollen* 5 (1975), 5.

opportunity to get their tans at the latter protest.[48] Perhaps most importantly, *La Gueule Ouverte*'s weekly directory of grassroots protests taking place across France, published under the rubric "In the Field," promoted the sense that the multitude of small-scale, disparate actions taking place all over the country were part of a shared struggle against nuclear energy.

A series of anti-reactor campaigns in Brittany exemplified grassroots anti-reactor protest's local efficacy, its potential for wider ramifications, but also its ambiguous short-term results. The Breton peninsula's ample supply of cooling water and relatively low population density, not to mention its lack of pre-existing power stations, caused rumors about plans to build reactors in Brittany to begin making the rounds soon after the announcement of the Messmer Plan in March 1974. When the list of potential reactor sites was announced the following December, maps showing four proposed sites in Brittany made the front page of regional newspapers.[49] Though four sites had been selected, EDF and local officials were agreed that only one reactor was to be built in Brittany in the short term. From the beginning, therefore, Breton reactor opponents conceived of the four potential reactor sites as a single, regional problem.

Because Brittany was first targeted for nuclearization relatively late, Breton reactor opponents benefited from technical know-how and protest experience garnered elsewhere.[50] After attending an informational meeting in Paris in November 1974, the doctor Michel Le Corvec and the café-owner Serge Daniel, both residents of the Breton town of Etel, organized a public meeting to share what they had learned about the dangers of nuclear technology. Just a few weeks later, neighboring Erdeven was announced as a potential reactor site. Le Corvec and Daniel quickly scheduled a second meeting to which they recruited 80 concerned local people. Their group dubbed itself the Regional Nuclear Information Committee (CRIN), and began spreading awareness of the nuclear threat throughout Brittany.[51] For the next two months, the CRIN organized information sessions in

---

[48] "Campings anti-nucléaires," *Charlie-Hebdo* 242 (1975), 10.

[49] See: "L'Ouest a l'heure nucléaire," *Ouest France* (3 December 1974), 1; and: Simon, *Plogoff*, 26. Brittany had not previously been a center for discussions of nuclear energy, however. Prior to the announcement of the four potential Messmer Plan sites, the region was home only to the Brennilis research reactor, which had gone critical in 1967, well before the debate about nuclear energy was widespread.

[50] Gérard Borvon, *Plogoff: un combat pour demain* (Saint Thonan: éditions Cloître, 2004), 96.

[51] Simon, *Plogoff*, 51, 57–58.

villages near the proposed Erdeven reactor site.[52] At the same time, the group helped found sixty new Local Nuclear Information Committees (CLINs) in towns and villages throughout the region – a strategy that fostered anti-nuclear sentiment all over Brittany.[53]

The CRIN used protests against the proposed Erdeven reactor, which began before concrete plans for the facility even existed, to strengthen its nascent grassroots anti-nuclear network. The protests at Erdeven had much more in common with the festive protests in the Upper Rhine valley than with the combative attempts to stop construction at Brokdorf. The first mass rally at Erdeven, which was held over Easter weekend in March 1975 and attended by 15,000 reactor opponents, exemplified the festive approach to anti-nuclear protest.[54] Activists packed a 2,500-seat big-top tent where performances by Breton folk-singers were interspersed with speeches by leading French and Belgian activists. Meanwhile, on a fair-like midway, demonstrators participated in games and activities, visited anti-nuclear organizations' booths, and made anti-reactor art. A statue of a green hand, meant to symbolize the region's resistance, was installed on the site. But no site occupation was attempted, nor were strong criticisms of the state voiced. Though the festival attracted enough participants to create traffic jams on par with those of the "great summer weekends," it received little coverage in the national news, was left off the cover page of regional newspapers, and hardly even made waves in the publications of the anti-nuclear movement.[55]

Regardless of its muted echo in the press, the CRIN used the well-attended Festival as a springboard to organize an anti-reactor activists' conference at Spézet. A new journal called *A tous crins* maintained the local groups' contacts with one another. On the basis of this infrastructure, reactor opponents protested at all of the proposed Breton reactor sites long before any of the projects got off the drawing board. Already

---

[52] According to local press reports, many of these meetings drew hundreds of participants. See: CRIN, *Erdeven 1975* (film) (www.vimeo.com/122459396, last accessed, 15 December 2015).

[53] More than half of them were located near Erdeven along Brittany's southern coast. Most CLINs had 10–50 members. Borvon, *Plogoff,* 94.

[54] The Erdeven rally took place the same weekend as the Wyhl Easter Monday Rally; though people in the Upper Rhine valley had been working against reactors for a half-decade, and resistance had only been organized for several months in Erdeven, both festivals attracted around 15,000 protesters. "Kundgebung und Volksfest: Die neue Wacht am Rhein," *Dernières nouvelles d'Alsace,* 1 April 1975.

[55] On the Easter Festival, see: "15.000 personnes à la 'fête antinucléaire' d'Erdeven," *Ouest France* 1 April 1975. See also: CRIN, *Erdeven 1975* (film).

in November 1974, for example, the group For the Life of the Cape (in the local dialect, it was known as: Evit Buhez ar C'hap) was formed on Cape Sizun, where the village of Plogoff – another potential reactor site – was located.[56] That group began hosting information sessions in January 1975, and organized a summer festival with "discussions, musical groups, [and] singers" that brought 5,000 to Cape Sizun on 13 July 1975.[57]

Displays of local resistance near the various Breton sites initiated a sort of cat-and-mouse game between grassroots activists and EDF, which in turn evidenced the strength of the regional network fostered by the CRIN. The utility responded to the anti-reactor festivals at Erdeven and Plogoff by proposing two new sites outside the village of Ploumoguer, near Brest. There, young farmers came together with scientists from the Oceanographic Center of Brittany and dockworkers from the port town of Conquet to form a CLIN. By early 1976, the councils of four neighboring villages joined the opposition and warned that if either reactor were built, their villages would become communes mortes (dead towns), provocatively linking the municipalities to six villages that "died for France" when they lost their entire populations in the battle of Verdun.[58] A leaked EDF memo, published in the environmentalist journal *La Gueule Ouverte*, revealed that the utility had underestimated the breadth of the local resistance, which it described as widespread amongst citizens and likely to expand amongst notables soon.[59] Finally realizing the strength of the resistance at Ploumoguer, EDF shifted its focus back to Plogoff. Studies showed that the Plogoff site, located far out in the Atlantic on the Point du Raz, was technically superior to other Breton sites due among other things to favorable currents that would disperse cooling water into the open ocean.[60] By the time EDF sent technicians to begin exploratory work at Plogoff in June 1976, however, local activists were well connected with reactor opponents throughout Brittany, and prepared to protest against plans to build a reactor in their village. Protesters, whose ranks included the town's mayor as well as "grandparents with babies and entire families," blockaded the main

---

[56] Borvon, *Plogoff*, 63.
[57] Ibid.; see also: "La fête anti-nucléaire de Plogoff," *Ouest France*, 15 July 1975.
[58] Sophie Michiels in Jocelyn Wolff, ed., *Le patrimoine des communes de la Meuse* (Paris: Flohic Editions, 1999), 26.
[59] Borvon, *Plogoff*, 12.
[60] Centre océanologique de Bretagne, *Synthese des études écologiques d'avant-projet des sites Bretons de Beg an Fry, Ploumoguer, Plogoff, Saint-Vio et Erdeven* (Brest: Centre océanologique de Bretagne, 1978).

routes into town and prevented EDF technicians from carrying out their tests.[61] Though it could not proceed with its preparations on account of the strong local resistance, the utility refused to renounce its plans for Plogoff, making the results of the struggle there ambiguous. Nonetheless, the CRIN-network prevented the utility from beginning construction at site after site throughout Brittany and prepared activists for the prolonged struggle at Plogoff.

Strasbourg Mayor Pierre Pflimlin's quip that, "If you can't put [a reactor] in Alsace, where can you do it in France?" expressed the strength of regional resistance in places like Alsace and Brittany. Breton protesters showed their awareness of the dynamic to which Pflimlin alluded when they explained that they were focused on blocking the proposed Ploumoguer reactor "because it is the site most targeted by EDF anywhere in the West." These attitudes suggest that anti-reactor activism in places like Alsace and Brittany was part of the "struggles of the new regionalism of the 1970s," which Herman Lebovics argues redefined the relationship between Paris and the provinces on the basis of debates over decolonization.[62] Turning regions like Brittany and Alsace into bastions of resistance, where siting new reactors became all but impossible in the mid-1970s, was not the same as blocking reactor construction throughout France since reactor projects went ahead elsewhere. Nonetheless, there can be little doubt that grassroots anti-reactor protests empowered local people to act against a centrally steered national policy and fostered the creation of an alternative to the Fifth Republic's famous centralization in the process. Compared to larger, more confrontational demonstrations, which briefly dominated the headlines and excited many outside observers, small-scale grassroots demonstrations made less of a splash. But they did foster the development of long-term anti-nuclear consciousness and of grassroots political engagement. In fact, since the Messmer Plan was not even debated in the National Assembly until May 1975, grassroots struggles over individual reactor projects became the primary places where nuclear energy was actually discussed in France amidst the early 1970s reactor building boom.[63]

[61] Borvon, *Plogoff,* 62.
[62] Herman Lebovics, *Bringing the Empire Back Home: France in the Global Age* (Durham, NC: Duke University Press, 2004), 14.
[63] Bess, *The Light Green Society,* 95. The debate in the National Assembly resulted only in an affirmation of the program and a request for more safeguards. Claus Leggewie and Roland de Miller, *Der Wahlfisch. Ökologiebewegungen in Frankreich* (Berlin: Merve-Verlag, 1978), 45.

Of Mass Struggles and Struggles to Cooperate: The 19 February 1977 Occupation Attempts at Brokdorf and Grohnde

As opposition to the centrally dictated Messmer Plan developed in provincial pockets, Brokdorf became the single most important rallying point for German reactor opponents. But national unity proved too grand an ambition for the anti-Brokdorf reactor coalition, which fractured in the run-up to a day of protest planned for 19 February 1977. Nonetheless, both of the resulting factions continued to see Brokdorf as a focal point for West German anti-reactor protest. Arguing that a protest at the site itself was necessary in order to prove the seriousness of the anti-Brokdorf project, the smaller faction planned a protest at the construction site despite a protest ban enacted after the November occupation attempt. Meanwhile, the larger faction organized an anti-Brokdorf demonstration at the town of Itzehoe, nearly twenty kilometers away from the reactor site.[64] Because it would take place off the site, the Itzehoe action seemed to lack the militancy of the protest at the construction site. Its organizers believed, however, that it would send a more inclusive message of opposition against the project. Though they had very different ideas about just how it would happen, the organizers of both protests remained convinced that a single action targeting a particular reactor could appeal to activists across the country.

The protest at the Brokdorf site was clearly organized around the principle that challenging authority – as Rhenish activists had done when they first occupied the Wyhl site – enabled protests targeting particular reactors to address broader issues. That action was spearheaded by the Communist League, which had only involved itself in the anti-nuclear struggle after the initial Brokdorf occupation attempts of October and November 1976, which, its leadership found, evidenced anti-nuclear activism's potential to become "a political mass movement." Seeking to instrumentalize this growing struggle towards its own anti-capitalist ends, KB members were directed by the Executive Committee (Leitendes Gremium) to enter the anti-nuclear movement en masse, and take up positions of influence.[65] At Brokdorf

---

[64] Accurate estimates of how many protesters attended each of the two demonstrations are very hard to come by. Organizers of each demonstration estimated that it was far larger than the other. All estimates seem to suggest, however that between 30,000 and 40,000 activists were in the Wilster Marsh on 19 February 1977. See, for example: BUU, *Brokdorf*, 116; Petra Kelly and John Lambert to Hans-Helmuth Wüstenhagen and Freimut Duve, 23 February, 1977. AGG PKA 2879.

[65] Michael Steffen, *Geschichten vom Trüffelschwein. Politik und Organisation des Kommunistischen Bundes, 1971 bis 1991* (Berlin: Assoziation A, 2002), 179.

in February, the KB hoped to attack the capitalist West German state by forcing the "police apparatus" to "massively concentrate its forces at the construction site fence (with the associated costs in terms of personnel and the associated political consequences)."[66] The KB's lack of interest in actually stopping construction on 19 February was apparent in the rationalization, published its *Arbeiterkampf* newspaper, that once the occupation attempt forced the police to take such a costly action, the protesters' mission would be accomplished, and it would be time to beat an "orderly retreat."[67] For the KB, in other words the protest was a wedge that could be hammered into a sensitive pressure point. It was supposed to shatter police authority and provoke bigger political consequences, not to halt construction forcibly.

Those who protested at Itzehoe were also aware of the national dimensions of their struggle. Rather than seeking to transform the political order

Figure 4.1 Police prepare to defend the reactor construction site at Brokdorf against anti-reactor demonstrators, 19 February 1977. © Günter Zint.

[66] Paul, ... *und auch nicht anderswo*, 54.
[67] "Schafft zwei, drei, viele Brokdorf," *Arbeiterkampf* 7, no. 96 (10 January 1977), 3.

with a single powerful action, they believed they would win the long conflict at Brokdorf through community-based movement-building. Accordingly, their day of action featured a cultural program, roundtable discussions, free childcare, and even a "marketplace of ideas" where locals could share their thoughts with anti-nuclear activists from the Upper Rhine valley, Lower Saxony, and Denmark.[68] Though many outside groups participated in the rally, its lead organizers were the local activists who comprised the BUU. They explained their decision to protest at Itzehoe as the result of cool-headed political calculus:

> a demonstration at the construction site is not supported by the local population at the present moment. This is because a violent confrontation at this moment, which simply cannot be avoided, would give the state government the opportunity to turn away from the discussion of atomic energy and to focus instead on violence. We do not want that![69]

Clearly, the BUU saw Itzehoe as part of a long-winded struggle, not a one-off protest.

Though neither action delayed construction at Brokdorf, both sets of organizers described their protests as remarkable successes given the broader goals to which they aspired. The KB, which had avoided real violence by refraining from a site occupation attempt, proudly proclaimed an "enormous victory for the militant anti-nuclear movement." In a series of polemical *Arbeiterkampf* articles, the organization discredited every other Leftist group engaged in anti-nuclear protest.[70] Meanwhile, two local farmers whose property abutted the Brokdorf site expressed their pleasure with the outcome of the rally at Itzehoe. "We proved that we're not crazy," they explained, "Nonviolence was the most important result, in order to bring the debate back to the future."[71] Neither the KB's

---

[68] "Aktionstag in Itzehoe (19.02.77)." ASB 9.4.1.1 XVII.

[69] BUU, "Demonstration und Kundgebung am 19.2.1977 in Itzehoe." ASB 9.4.1.1 XVII. The close vote can be explained in part by changes to the BUU that took place after the 13 November protest. At that time, a wide range of Hamburg groups, as well as citizens' initiatives from as far afield as Flensburg, Kiel, and even the North Sea islands of Sylt and Föhr had become part of the BUU. As a result, the groups from the Wilster Marsh, now grouped within the organization as the "Marschen Konferenz," no longer had complete control over the larger BUU. See "Organisationsstruktur der BUU nach dem 13.11," reprinted in BUU, *Brokdorf*, 192.

[70] "30.000 im Wilster Marsch," *Arbeiterkampf* 7, no. 99 (21 February 1977), 1. On the KB's discrediting of other Leftist groups, see: "SB ganz 'undogmatisch'?;" "KBW dreht durch;" "Der Absprung der GIM;" "Wie man eine(n) ID(ee) kaputtmacht;" "'KPD/ML' bestätigt Provokateurs-Rolle;" "Die DKP: Auf der anderen Seite der Barrikade;" "EAP-Provokateure für Atomprogramm!" *Arbeiterkampf* 7, no. 99 (21 February 1977). "Das ist unser nächstes Ziel: Grohnde 19.3," *Arbeiterkampf* 7, no. 100 (7 March 1977), 1.

[71] Margit Gerste und Horst Bieber, "Ein Scheibchen Sieg für jeden," *Die Zeit*, 4 March 1977.

declaration that its march to the perimeter fence had changed everything nor the farmers' prognosis that they had won the future at Itzehoe was particularly easy to corroborate. What was evident, however, was that proponents of each action considered their own protest particularly successful because it was not the other protest form; the fracturing of the campaign against the Brokdorf reactor happened precisely because of organizers' attempts to raise their struggle's national profile and broaden its political ramifications.

The fierce division between the two camps even caused the nonviolent action groups (or "*graswurzel*-groups") affiliated with the journal *graswurzelrevolution* to organize a third protest on 19 February. Rather than protesting along the Lower Elbe, they protested nearly 300 km to the south at the town of Grohnde on the Weser river, where yet another reactor was under construction. The *graswurzel*-groups, too, sought to organize an ideal protest that would showcase their vision of effective anti-nuclear action by combining the militancy of the Brokdorf protest with the nonviolence and joyfulness of the Itzehoe rally. Though they billed their own action as an inclusive middle-way, the *graswurzel*-groups actually provided yet another competing model of anti-reactor protest.[72] The 1,000 nonviolent protesters at Grohnde were the only group of anti-nuclear activists to make their way onto a West German reactor construction site on 19 February 1977. After cutting a hole through the perimeter fence, however, the nonviolent activists refused to scuffle with police. Instead, they agreed to end their occupation peacefully as soon as the police ordered them to vacate the site. The cover story in the next edition of *graswurzelrevolution* described the protest at Grohnde as "a successful example of our action form next to Wyhl, Larzac, etc." Only slightly less pointedly than the articles in *Arbeiterkampf* attacked critics of the Brokdorf protest, the *graswurzelrevolution* article criticized the rest of the Left-leaning alternative press for mentioning Grohnde "only as an ornamental attachment to the main articles about Brokdorf and Itzehoe."[73]

Though the organizers of all three protests claimed Wyhl as an inspiration, and spoke of uniting anti-reactor protesters of many stripes, those familiar with the Rhenish struggle considered the separate protests far less

---

[72] These groups, associated with the publication *graswurzelrevolution*, had been closely following the struggle on the Upper Rhine since before the Wyhl occupation and had worked to promote cooperative, nonviolent anti-nuclear actions in the southwest; clearly their Grohnde action on 19 February did not further cooperation with other opponents of nuclear energy.

[73] Jean, "Mauerblümchen Grohnde," *graswurzelrevolution* 27/28 (Winter 1977): 1–3.

effective than the inclusive Wyhl occupation.[74] A meeting of 100 reactor opponents sponsored by Freiburg University's Environmental Action sent two delegates to the Wilster Marsh shortly before the February protests in order to express Rhenish activists' concerns about the future of anti-nuclear protest and voice support for the right to protest at reactor construction sites.[75] Petra Kelly, the young JEF activist who had been so deeply inspired by the Wyhl struggle's transnational nature, lambasted the organizers of the Itzehoe rally for not thinking in big enough terms. Though protesters from several countries were present, Kelly was disappointed by the demonstration's lack of a purposefully deployed "international or transnational element." In failing to report on "Wyhl court proceedings, Danish activities, the seminar in Malville, or about the EEC proceedings regarding the issue of site selection," she complained, the organizers of the Itzehoe rally had allowed "40,000 prepared anti-nuclear activists to come for nothing."[76]

Even as the grassroots protests proliferating throughout France subtly complemented one another, the groups battling the Brokdorf project went out of their way to differentiate their protests and to criticize competing actions. The links anti-nuclear activists sensed between the nuclear debate, violent police interventions, and political expression itself caused each group to imagine its own actions as essential to a much larger plan to change society – and thus to see other protests as misguided, ineffective, or provincial. Differently put, the inclusive vision that enabled Balthasar Ehret to connect Rhenish anti-reactor protest with the Frankfurt squatters' movement was absent on 19 February. Though each protest mobilized numerous activists and received coverage in its particular niche within the alternative press, none of the protests shifted the broader political debate or became the basis for a unified, national anti-nuclear movement. In this sense, at least, targeted grassroots protests proved easier to imagine as pieces of a larger whole than as mass protests with big goals.

The End of the "Anti-Nuclear Current"?

The difference between targeted grassroots actions and mass protests became particularly evident at Malville, where anti-nuclear activists

---

[74] Petra Kelly and John Lambert to Hans-Helmuth Wüstenhagen and Freimut Duve, 23 February, 1977. AGG PKA 2879.

[75] Arbeitskreis Umweltschutz an der Universität Freiburg, "Freiburger KKW-Gegner!" ASB 9.4.1.1 XVII.

[76] Petra Kelly and John Lambert to Hans-Helmuth Wüstenhagen and Freimut Duve, 23 February 1977. AGG PKA 2879.

worked against EDF's proposed fast-breeder reactor. Capable of turning uranium into plutonium at accelerated rates even as it produced electricity for the grid, the Super-Phénix was expected to play a special role in the French nuclear program. Before the plant's soon-to-be closest neighbors opposed it, activists from Lyon and Grenoble, the nearest major cities, sought to build grassroots resistance in order to stop the fast-breeder project in its tracks. Their regional focus did not last long. A consortium of French, Italian, and German firms supported the project, causing activists across Western Europe to consider the fast-breeder a natural focal point for their protests. Eager activists from West Germany and Switzerland, in particular, sought to involve themselves in the anti-Malville movement, making the differences between the grassroots campaign envisioned by activists in Lyon and Grenoble and the two internationally organized, mass protests that took place at Malville in 1976 and 1977 particularly evident.

The first protest at Malville was supposed to be a grassroots action similar to other French anti-reactor protests. Early in 1976, George Didier, a member of the Lyon Committee against the Malville Super-Phénix, sought advice from the Alsatian activists Inge and Jean-Jacques Rettig on how to build a movement against the fast-breeder.[77] With the Rettigs' emphasis on winning the support of the plant's neighbors in mind, the Lyon Committee envisioned a small-scale protest for July 1976 that would allow activists from nearby cities to get to know one another and to recruit the plant's neighbors to the anti-reactor cause before further action was even considered. In reality, however, somewhere between 5,000 and 20,000 demonstrators came from across France, as well as Germany and Switzerland to participate. Nonetheless, the action was different from the mass occupation attempts that would take place at Brokdorf in October and November.[78] Instead of pushing relentlessly towards the construction site, and squaring off immediately with police, the visitors camped in farmers' fields, played music, and danced.

After several days in the community, activists did finally cut through the fence on 4 July 1976. They made their way onto a corner of the site, where they ploughed a small plot of land and planted beans. Though they were now effectively occupying the site, the protesters stuck to their non-confrontational approach that seemed focused on the long-term. They

---

[77] A letter of advice that the Rettigs sent to Didier was published in *Combat non-violent* as George Didier, no title ("Cher Amis") in *Combat non-violent* 93 (April 1976), 10–11.

[78] Estimates on the number of activists vary from the 5,000 announced by police and reported in the local press, to the organizers' own estimate of 20,000. Collectif d'Enquete, *Aujourd'hui Malville, demain la France!* (Claix: La Pensée Sauvage, 1978), 8.

organized information sessions on nuclear energy for local farmers and even challenged the Republican Security Companies (CRS) tasked with defending the site to a soccer match. Fraternization did not cause the CRS-men to hesitate when the order to clear the site was given, however. Over a three-day period, they twice deployed overpowering force against the unarmed demonstrators. First, they cleared the site by dropping tear gas grenades from low-flying helicopters onto sun-bathing occupiers. Two days later, CRS agents used billy clubs and lobbed gas grenades to drive the demonstrators off a new campsite two kilometers from the reactor construction site. The brutality of these interventions "stupefied" local farmers, helping the protesters to achieve their goal of connecting with local people and attracting their support.[79]

The brutal crackdown also deepened international interest in the project. In the winter of 1976–1977, West German anti-nuclear activists, fresh off their own combative site occupation attempts at Brokdorf, eagerly anticipated a new mass protest at Malville. As rumors about plans for the protest circulated, leading anti-nuclear publications across the FRG urged their readership to take part.[80] Amidst growing interest, the French network of Malville Committees called for a February 1977 conference at the town of Morestel, ten kilometers from the fast-breeder site. They planned to use the meeting in order to lay the groundwork for another protest, expected to take place the following July.[81] In the event, organizers estimated that between 2,500 and 3,000 activists, representing dozens of groups from all over Western Europe, participated in the conference.[82] The "overwhelming influx of newcomers," who spoke several languages, and whose ranks included Maoists and autonomists, as well as reactor opponents of every other imaginable political persuasion, meant that participants struggled to hash out concrete plans for a new protest.

Since few definitive decisions were taken at Morestel, the primary harvest of all this wrangling was confusion. The Malville Committees'

---

[79] Eventually, local people even organized two days of hearings on the fast-breeder project. Andrew Tompkins, "Transnationality as a Liability? The Anti-Nuclear Movement at Malville," *Revue belge de philologie et d'histoire* 89, no. 3 (2011): 1360–1370; and Lucas, *Energy in France*, 197–198.

[80] Tompkins, "Transnationality," 1368–1369.

[81] The Comités Malville had their roots in the Lyon region, but had become a national network by the spring of 1977. They followed on the model of the Comités Larzac, which existed all over France and even abroad, and aided the Larzac farmers by "organizing support groups, explaining the issues to their friends and co-workers, sending money, welcoming marchers, and returning to the plateau for demonstrations." Lebovics, *Bringing the Empire Back Home*, 54.

[82] Collectif d'enquête, *Aujourd'hui Malville*, 17.

Super-Pholix magazine served as the forum for continued discussions throughout the Spring of 1977.[83] Even the editors' efforts to promote a coordinated "nonviolent march" on 30 July 1977 were questioned in the magazine's pages by a group of Grenoble anarchists, who argued that less coordination and more individual initiative was necessary to take on the "electrofascists" behind the fast-breeder project.[84] That a clear, comprehensive plan for the July 1977 Malville protest could not be formulated in advance is hardly as surprising as it might sound. Activists at Brokdorf argued for months before finally deciding to go their separate ways just before their February 1977 protests. Even the highly successful Wyhl occupation, which was planned by people who had been working together against reactor projects for half a decade, was only vaguely planned by the time construction began in February 1975.[85] At Malville, by contrast, thousands of activists hailing from northern Germany, to Italy, to the Atlantic coast of France sought to plan a common action. Regardless of local organizers' intentions, the Malville protest was made into an ambitious attempt to link together diverse national anti-nuclear movements that were not even internally coherent.

Unlike at Marckolsheim and Wyhl, where years of close cooperation preceded the occupation attempt and activists from Alsace and Baden actually grew closer by protesting together, the Malville demonstration was a disaster for transnational cooperation, as Andrew Tompkins has shown.[86] More than 60,000 anti-nuclear activists gathered in the rural Isère Department on the northwestern fringes of the Alps for the protest in late July 1976. French protesters filled three separate campsites, and foreign activists were directed to make camp near Morestel. Significant numbers of activists came from Italy, Switzerland, Belgium, and the Netherlands, but the "foreigners' camp" was dominated by thousands of West Germans, who bemoaned their insufficient contact with French protesters and complained that they were excluded from the decision-making process.[87] French officials, in turn, claimed that the German invaders spearheaded the protest and held their unwelcome guests responsible for other problems throughout the region. After a scuffle near the town hall in Morestel, for

---

[83] Tompkins, "Transnationality," 1370.

[84] Membres de la coordination anarchiste de Grenoble, "Retraitement des dechets de la coordination anti-nucléaire" *Super-Pholix* 13 [undated, July 1977?], 3.

[85] See Chapter 3.   [86] See: Tompkins, "Transnationality."

[87] On the separate camps, see: Lucas, *Energy in France*, 201. For an example of a West German activist's complaints about Malville, see: Hajo Karbach, "Malville," *graswurzelrevolution* 32 (October 1977): 11. The incomplete live translation from French into German of the protesters' plenary meeting was among the Germans' main complaints.

example, the Prefect declared that, "for the second time Morestel is occupied by the Germans."[88] Denunciations of foreign activists were only the beginning of French officials' plan to both defend the Malville site and discredit the protesters. The 5,000 men assigned to protect the Super-Phénix, whose ranks included paratroopers, were armed with concussion grenades and tear gas. They also had helicopters and amphibious vehicles at their disposal. Regardless of this overwhelming force, antinuclear activists laid siege to the site. Amidst a "heavy glacial rain," a showdown occurred between protesters "wearing helmets and masks and armed with iron bars, clubs, slings, and Molotov cocktails" and the site's defenders with their military-grade weapons and machinery. Amidst the fighting, the 31-year-old teacher Vital Michalon was killed, nearly a dozen protesters lost limbs, and hundreds more were injured.[89]

On both sides of the Rhine, the deadly violence at Malville dampened the allure of site occupation as a means of anti-nuclear protest. The attempt to occupy the Super-Phénix site was widely considered the "end of a certain style of environmental activism in France."[90] Perhaps most famously, the sociologist Alain Touraine concluded that the violent and deeply flawed demonstration evidenced "the inability of the anti-nuclear current to organize itself into a political force."[91] Despite such obituaries, however, the era of mass site occupations never really even began in France. French anti-reactor protests before Malville had been small in scale. The activists who comprised Touraine's "anti-nuclear current" had long since organized themselves into a political force, albeit one comprising loose grassroots networks that operated simultaneously in a decentralized fashion at reactor sites all across the country. Their work transformed individuals and reshaped entire regions, but their grassroots efforts were still overshadowed by headline-grabbing protests like the Malville showdown, which pitted

---

[88] Accounts of this incident differ. The British energy policy analyst N. J. D. Lucas claimed that the Germans actually prevented damage that would have been caused by a group of French activists. Lucas, *Energy in France*, 202.

[89] Walter Mossmann, *realistisch sein*, 245; see also: Tompkins, "Transnationality."

[90] Michael Bess, *The Light Green Society*, 104. Vital Michalon's death and the hundreds of casualties inflicted on protesters by heavily armed police played a major part in the turn away from this tactic in France. Herbet Kitschelt, "Political Opportunity Structures and Political Protest: Anti-Nuclear Movements in Four Democracies," *British Journal of Political Science* 16 (1984): 75. See also: Daniel P. Aldrich, *Site Fights: Divisive Facilities and Civil Society in Japan and the West* (Ithaca, NY: Cornell University Press, 2008), 152–153.

[91] Alain Touraine, *Anti-nuclear protest: The opposition to nuclear energy in France* (Cambridge: Cambridge University Press, 1983), 28. Touraine linked the Malville debacle with ecologist candidates' failure to win seats in the National Assembly in 1978. See Chapter 5 for more on the ecologists' 1978 campaign.

combative protesters against well-armed police. Even if neither approach proved capable of stopping European governments' ambitious plans for nuclear development, narratives of the rise of anti-nuclear protest typically suppose some sort of Whiggish progression from grassroots protests to ever larger mass actions, followed at last by an inevitable fall. Lost by the wayside are the transformative effects of slow-moving, but long-winded locally focused anti-reactor protests.

"Environmental Destruction Was All Around Us"

If the anti-reactor protesters of the mid-1970s could not stop their governments' nuclear programs, it is fair to ask what they did achieve. Because they frequently failed to make national headlines, the effects of grassroots anti-reactor actions seem negligible. Measured locally and over time, however, these protests' cumulative effects were unmistakable.[92] In the Upper Rhine valley, for example, activists mastered occupation as a protest tactic and used it to prevent additional reactors from being built throughout the region. Their protests also led to a deeper transformation of the region's inhabitants, who became dedicated not only to the anti-nuclear cause, but also to a broader environmental vision.

Occupations at Upper Rhine valley reactor sites in Kaiseraugst, Switzerland and Gerstheim, France, both of which took place in the second half of the decade, exemplified local protesters' mastery of the tactic, but also the long-term effects of grassroots anti-reactor protest on individuals and social relationships.[93] The occupation in Kaiseraugst, which began the day after the Wyhl Easter Monday Rally, was particularly well organized so as to build community and thus to strengthen the anti-reactor movement. At the same time as Luc Aders was sent to announce the new occupation from the podium at Wyhl, activists were sounding the

---

[92] Helen Poulos shows that "NIMBY" protests are far more likely to produce "innovation" if they last longer than 1.5 years. Poulos, "How do Grassroots Environmental Protests Incite Innovation?" in Carol Hager and Mary Alice Haddad, eds., *NIMBY Is Beautiful: Cases of Local and Environmental Innovation around the World* (New York: Berghahn, 2015), 15.

[93] The Gerstheim project never really even got off the ground. See: Gerhard Peringer, "Gerstheim eine Bilderbuchplatzbesetzung," in Christoph Büchele, Irmgard Schneider, and Bernd Nössler, *Wyhl. Der Widerstand geht weiter. Das Bürgerprotest gegen das Kernkraftwerk von 1976 bis zum Mannheimer Prozeß* (Freiburg: Dreisam-Verlag, 1982), 83. The Kaiseraugst reactor was the subject of a protracted struggle of which the occupation was only a small part. Patrick Kupper, *Atomenergie und Gespaltene Gesellschaft. Die Geschichte des gescheiterten Projektes Kernkraftwerk Kaiseraugst* (Zurich: Chronos, 2003); and: Michael Schroeren, *z.B. Kaiseraugst. Die gewaltfreie Widerstand gegen dem Atomkraftwerk, vom legalen Protest zum zivilen Ungehorsam* (Zurich: Schweizerischer Friedensrat, 1977).

"atomic alarm" in Swiss villages and setting up "tents and banners" on the site, which had been left vacant over the holiday weekend. When construction crews returned on Tuesday morning to resume their work, they found 500 occupiers in complete control of the site. By the end of its first week, local farmers were ready to show their support by delivering "hay, wood, and provisions" to the occupiers, and 15,000 local people rallied amidst snow flurries to prove that the community supported the occupation. In its coverage of the demonstration, Basel's *National-Zeitung* spoke of a "people's movement" comprising "voters of every party and every age-group."[94]

Work required to sustain the occupation reinforced feelings of widespread cooperation within the people's movement. In less than a month, the occupiers transformed the site into a "proper village of huts and barracks, surrounded by raised beds of flowers and vegetables." Following the Marckolsheim and Wyhl models, they erected a central Friendship House and added a daycare center, a café, and a guardhouse. In addition to this impressive physical infrastructure, the occupiers organized committees to manage everything from propaganda and community life to construction and cookery. The "occupiers' village" also became "the crystallization point for an entire network of social relationships and organizational connections."[95]

Each day that the occupation endured was a "victory" in the sense that it prevented work on the reactor and fostered community-building processes. Nonetheless, activists were not interested in prolonging the occupation for its own sake, because:

> the participants were also well aware that the occupation could not last forever ... it had to cause negotiations over the abandonment of the Kaiseraugst project, which had not been achieved through years of legal protest.[96]

At Pentecost, just eleven weeks after they took over the site, a mass meeting of more than 3,000 reactor opponents voted overwhelmingly to end the occupation so as to enter into negotiations with the authorities.[97] In a special message published in *Was Wir Wollen*, opponents of the Kaiseraugst project explained that their decision marked a step towards their goal of stopping the reactor, and painstakingly separated it from the ongoing Wyhl occupation, for which they voiced continued support.

[94] Schroeren, *z.B. Kaiseraugst*, 67–71. The quote from the *National-Zeitung* is on page 71.
[95] Ibid., 73–74.   [96] Ibid., 92.   [97] Ibid., 105.

Attempts to play the two occupations against one another, they argued, were meant only to "split the European movement!"[98] Not only did the methodical decision to end the occupation reveal the skill with which Rhenish activists wielded their best known "tool," it also offered a glimpse of their bottom-up vision of an international anti-nuclear movement comprising local people fighting individual reactor projects on their own terms.

In fact, despite the skill with which they had wielded it, occupation's significance seemed to be waning in the region by the end of 1975, when opponents of the Wyhl reactor followed the Kaiseraugst protesters off the site in order to enter into negotiations on the project's future. The only "occupation" then taking place in the Upper Rhine valley was the ongoing watch over the Wyhl site, which endured until April 1976 as the negotiations continued. To outside observers, it appeared as though the Rhenish movement was over. Even a local activist later admitted that "the fire of resistance was weak" after the Wyhl occupation ended – though he hastened to add that "the embers of resistance were still glowing."[99] Those embers could spark new fires quickly. More than 15,000 local people attended a rally marking the first anniversary of the Wyhl occupation on 22 February 1976. Annemarie Sacherer, a vintner from Oberrotweil, defiantly told the crowd that though the government believed it had won "a peaceful Kaiserstuhl" by entering into negotiations on the Wyhl project, "we won't be peaceful and we won't be quiet until the reactor won't be built!"[100] Activists elsewhere had turned their interest to Brokdorf or Malville, but Wyhl remained a seminal subject in the region. Reactor opponents fiercely debated the terms offered them by the state government, seeking further assurances that construction would not resume. Even after the "Offenburg Agreement" between the state government and the Badensian and Alsatian Citizens' Initiatives was finally signed in April, activists busied themselves getting its provisions enforced.[101]

The long-lingering effects of the region's occupation protests also made recruiting local people to anti-reactor protests much easier since they

---

[98] "Resolution der Gegner des AW Kaiseraugst an die badisch-elsässischen Bürgerinitiativen und die öffentlichen Medien der BRD," *Was Wir Wollen* 7 (June 1975), 17.

[99] Bernd Nössler, "Verhandlungen – eine neue Phase beginnt," in Bernd Nössler and Margret de Witt, *Wyhl. Kein Kernkraftwerk in Wyhl und auch sonst nirgends. Betroffene Bürger berichten* (Freiburg: Dreisam-Verlag, 1976), 154.

[100] Annemarie Sacherer "369 Tage Platzbesetzung," in *Wyhl* (see note 99), 161.

[101] Activists had to work until July to get the state attorney's office to drop charges against some of the former occupiers, for example, even though dropping all of the charges against all of the former occupiers had been a provision of the agreement.

responded quickly to every rumor of a new reactor. Perhaps the best example of this readiness came in January 1977, when EDF erected a sevesnty-meter-tall meteorological measuring tower near the Alsatian village of Gerstheim. After forcing the utility to admit that the tower was actually intended to collect meteorological data for a planned 180-hectare nuclear park that might include reprocessing facilities, local people launched a "textbook occupation." On 26 January 1977, just as activists in Northern Germany were fiercely debating their competing plans for the 19 February protests at Brokdorf and Itzehoe, 150 activists gathered around the Gerstheim measurement tower, forcing EDF technicians to disperse. Much like the Marckolsheim occupation two years earlier, the nascent Gerstheim occupation quickly garnered the support of local officials. Village councilors and even the mayors of Gerstheim and nearby Erbheim came to the occupied site and called for a mass demonstration. Four days after the occupation began, on 30 January 1977, more than 5,000 activists, including "many Alemannic people from the right bank of the Rhine" rallied against the project.[102]

The occupiers dug in for the long haul after a defiant EDF spokesman declared that the "measurement tower will not be taken down. Not in a half year, not in two years."[103] The "Friendship House" that they built on the site "was always full during the obligatory Sunday events." New citizens' initiatives formed in nearby villages in order to organize participation. Finally, in August 1977, the Prefect of the Lower Rhine Department announced that the weather station was going to be removed, and plans for the nuclear park would not proceed. Despite the "textbook" occupation's success, which must have been particularly evident in comparison to the failed July 1977 protest at Malville, one veteran of the Rhenish movement summarized his conversations with Hamburg anti-nuclear activists: "Marckolsheim, Wyhl, Kaiseraugst, yes! Gerstheim? I've never heard of it!"[104] In France, news of the Gerstheim occupation was shared through ecological publications like *La Gueule Ouverte*. In contrast to the Malville demonstration, which was seen as a national – or even international – event, the Gerstheim occupation was described as part of a larger effort to "defend the Alsatian soil" from industrial development.[105] Such treatment

---

[102] Peringer, "Gerstheim – eine Bilderbuchplatzbesetzung," 81.
[103] Ibid., 83. See also: "Neues aus Wyhl, Fessenheim & Gerstheim," *graswurzelrevolution* 27/28 (Winter 1977), 13.
[104] Peringer, "Gerstheim – eine Bilderbuchplatzbesetzung."
[105] Catherine Decouan, "Plan d'Occupation de sol Alsacien," *La Gueule Ouverte* 145 (16 February 1977), 11.

helped spread the good news from the Upper Rhine valley, and acknowledged the many other significant protests that had taken place there. At the same time, however, it also supported Freia Hoffmann's concern that successful Rhenish protests might be read as the work of "particularly courageous people," and thus set aside from other activist projects.

The way Gerstheim was received beyond the Upper Rhine valley sheds light on two important aspects of the division between often violent mass site occupation attempts and nonviolent grassroots protests. It helps to explain why grassroots protests mattered in the long run. To a certain extent, Hoffmann was correct: the Gerstheim occupation was successful because people in the region were special. They were ready to protest as soon as the first hints of a nuclear project appeared, and they were well-versed in the tactics of site occupation. Significantly, however, Alsatians had not always been this way; they had become better at protesting by practicing – first at Fessenheim, then at Marckolsheim, and later at Wyhl and Kaiseraugst. It was not only the protesters who were unique: the occupation certainly would not have lasted long if hundreds of heavily armed police officers, not to mention border patrol units and attack helicopters, had been ordered to end it. Thus, its very success underscored the problem that anti-nuclear activists at Malville and in Northern Germany confronted in 1977. Occupation worked well in the Upper Rhine valley because protesters were willing to confront government officials well before reactor plans were formally announced, because police proved reticent to react forcefully to protests comprised primarily of middle-aged locals, and because seven years of grassroots activism had created a broad base of support for such protests throughout the region.

The personal and social transformations that occurred in the Upper Rhine valley on account of anti-nuclear protest could hardly have been more fundamental. As the vintner Annemarie Sacherer later put it, "the discussion about atomic energy," caused her and her family "to open up their eyes." All at once, they saw environmental destruction all around them. They now grouped together restructuring of local vineyards, which they had once celebrated as a boon for local viticulture, with other wasteful and destructive practices like "exaggerated road construction, pollution of the Rhine, and the reckless use of pesticides." Her newfound consciousness of environmental threats led Sacherer to begin baking whole-grain bread, to adopt organic gardening methods, and to utilize medicinal plants that she had previously considered weeds. It was, in other words, on the basis of experience speaking out against the Wyhl reactor project that the Sacherers' family values shifted.[106]

Such transformations occurred in villages all over the region, where farmers and vintners began to think of themselves as environmentalists and to act on that conviction. Maria Köllhofer, the mother of five who was arrested during the police raid at Wyhl, said decades later that "all of our children were shaped by [the anti-nuclear protests]." They had become "people who don't say 'yes' to everything."[107] Others were inspired by the protests to install solar water heaters built by the "young, crazy avant-gardist" and local tinkerer, Werner Mildebrath.[108] Early adoption of solar technology led directly to the region's first Solar Energy Expo, which was held in Mildebrath's hometown of Sasbach. More than 12,000 people attended this event though it was held in a small village far from Freiburg.[109] The political scientist Carol Hager has argued that the expo comprised the taproot of Germany's early twenty-first century transition to renewable energy.[110] Though finding them required examining individual biographies and regional transformations, the effects of local anti-reactor protests were unmistakable.

Conclusion

By the summer of 1977, two distinct types of anti-nuclear protest had emerged. On the one hand, small-scale grassroots anti-reactor protests continued in places like Brittany and the Upper Rhine valley. On the other hand, mass occupations were attempted at Brokdorf and Malville. Rhenish reactor opponents' willingness to quickly occupy sites and to turn these liberated areas into outdoor community centers made their grassroots protests an effective means of stopping reactors. Over time, the occupations themselves altered people's lives and changed their values. Long after the Wyhl occupation ended, inhabitants of the Upper Rhine valley remained committed to anti-nuclear protest and continued to incorporate

---

[106] Annemarie Sacherer, "Zehn Jahre danach," 38. Sacherer won election to the village council. Walter Mossmann saw her as one of the most important anti-nuclear activists of his age group (i.e. around thirty years old in the mid-1970s). Walter Mossmann, *realistisch sein*, 186.

[107] Christel Hülter-Hassler, "Angst vor der Übermacht," *Badische Zeitung*, 30 April 2013.

[108] Mossmann, *realistisch sein*, 187–188.

[109] Carola Bury, "Sonnentage in Sasbach. Wir wollen Sonne – keine Kühlturmnebel," in *Wyhl* (see note 93), 63.

[110] Carol Hager, "From NIMBY to Networks: Protest and Innovation in German Energy Politics," in Hager and Haddad, eds., *NIMBY is Beautiful* (see note 92).

activism and environmentalism into their daily lives. Likewise, Breton activists built a strong anti-reactor network that stymied EDF's efforts throughout the region and furthered an insurgent regional identity. Though they rarely receive pride of place in histories of the anti-nuclear movement, small-scale grassroots anti-reactor protests contributed to a larger universe of regional struggles that implicitly challenged centralized power – and thus the French Fifth Republic itself.[111]

The divergence between grassroots initiatives and mass protest invites us to reflect on Todd Gitlin's famous declaration that the post-1968 US Left wasted its time battling for the English Department while the Right won the battle for the White House.[112] It is easy to propose that the battles of Brokdorf and Malville, which attracted the attention of the national press, represented the anti-nuclear movement's potential for real political relevance while rarely discussed occupations in places like Gerstheim, for example, showed the insignificance of anti-nuclear protest. But the sorts of deep personal transformations that occurred in the Upper Rhine valley, and the challenges to the Fifth Republic implicit in the regionalist movements of which local anti-reactor struggles were part, suggest that grassroots protest was not simply a rejection of meaningful high politics in favor of small, self-interested campaigns. Rhenish protesters' attitudes in the wake of Wyhl, in fact, show that grassroots protest had the potential – over time, at least – to initiate profound cultural changes, which might eventually alter citizens' political outlook. Annemarie Sacherer, the vintner who so clearly articulated how her family's values changed in the mid-1970s, understood – as a result of her activism – that "that the values of health, life, and peace are not to be taken for granted" and "may not even be guaranteed by democratically elected governments." She sought to address this newfound concern by running for office herself. In 1976, she was elected to the village council in Oberrotweil, where she hoped to change the system from the grassroots up.[113] Her example was followed by others across the region, and similar regional transformations motivated new candidates to run for office elsewhere as well.

But charting such regional transformations and measuring their significance remained difficult. After the Malville debacle, when activists in both France and Germany attempted yet again to create the sort of national

---

[111] Lebovics, *Bringing the Empire Back Home*, 179–190.
[112] Todd Gitlin, *The Twilight of Common Dreams* (New York: Metropolitan Books, 1995), 126.
[113] Annemarie Sacherer, "Zehn Jahre danach," in *Wyhl* (see note 93), 38.

environmental current for which the likes of Leinen and Touraine yearned, prominent activists downplayed localized protests in an attempt to make their movement appear less provincial and more deeply enmeshed in national politics. Continued appeals for the creation of tighter networks and stronger structures facilitated the selfsame focus on mass protests and national politics that has obscured grassroots action's reshaping of the political by decentralizing governance and empowering individuals.

CHAPTER 5

Political Questions, Grassroots Answers: Shaping
an Environmental Approach to Electoral Politics

During the summer of 1977, negative press reports, government officials' denunciations, and harsh police crackdowns seemed to derail the anti-nuclear movement. The troubles became serious in July with the disastrous Malville demonstration. French newspapers blamed protesters' injuries – and even Vital Michalon's death – on "violent elements (and especially Germans)."[1] West German officials, meanwhile, used a string of attacks by the Red Army Faction to justify indictments of combative anti-reactor protests, which they considered further evidence of the "civil war-like conditions" obtaining in the Federal Republic.[2] Following these rhetorical attacks and police crackdowns, a representative of the French Atomic Energy Commission could "calmly claim" that "it is a fact that in France the anti-nuclear movement has been losing its audience and its efficiency over the last year."[3] West German activists agreed with this analysis, noting that in the FRG their movement was "in a difficult position" because "the

[1] In fact, Michalon died of cardiac arrest after a police assault. "Malville: Le sang après la boue," *L'Aurore* (1 August 1977). Reprinted in Collectif d'Enquete, *Aujourd'hui Malville, demain la France!* (Claix: La Pensée Sauvage, 1978), 158. Yves Frémion notes the press's fixation on German militants' role in the protest. Frémion, *Histoire de la révolution écologiste* (Paris: Hoëbeke, 2007), 143.
[2] The "German Autumn" was highlighted by the RAF's murder of Hanns Martin Schleyer and hijacking of a Lufthansa airliner. Jeremy Varon, *Bringing the War Home: The Weather Underground, the Red Army Faction, and Revolutionary Violence in the Sixties and Seventies* (Berkeley: University of California Press, 2004); and: Karrin Hanshew, *Terror and Democracy in West Germany* (Cambridge: Cambridge University Press, 2012). Politicians' attempts to classify anti-nuclear protest as a part of a civil war included the promotion of legislation to prohibit activists from wearing "passive armament" such as "facemasks, helmets, and gasmasks" at demonstrations by Hesse's Minister of Justice. "Demonstrieren ohne Helm und Maske," *Der Spiegel*, 16 May 1977. Communist splinter groups' growing participation in site occupation attempts served officials as a justification of their strategy. Michael Steffen, *Geschichten vom Trüffelschwein. Politik und Organisation des Kommunistischen Bundes 1971 bis 1991* (Berlin: Assoziation A, 2002), 187.
[3] Quoted in Frank Nullmeier, Frauke Rubart, and Harald Schulz, *Umweltbewegungen und Parteiensystem: Umweltgruppen und Umweltparteien in Frankreich und Schweden* (Berlin: Quorum, 1983), 30.

federal government has done everything in its power to brand the citizens' initiatives as criminal organizations."[4]

Activists' attempts to escape from their difficult position initiated a deep intramovement debate. In West Germany, this internal struggle has been interpreted as an iteration of "the [undying] debate about violence" that consumed the Left after 1968.[5] Scholars have claimed that the debate itself crippled the anti-nuclear movement, dividing anti-nuclear activists into two factions, and causing observers to perceive direct-action occupation protests as locked into a downward trajectory that "culminated in violence."[6] In fact, as Karrin Hanshew has observed, the West German Left's violence debate was not so straightforward. At stake was how resistance and violence could be decoupled from one another in order to promote a workable opposition politics in a young democracy attempting to stabilize itself and establish security amidst the political violence perpetrated by the RAF.[7] For many activists, then, the violence debate was also a debate about how citizens could make their concerns heard within a democratic order where there was little room for maneuver between acceptable parliamentary opposition and unacceptable challenges to the system. Efficacy, therefore, was of the utmost importance to anti-nuclear activists. Walter Mossmann, himself no advocate of violence, criticized "demos at the perimeter fences" not because of their protagonists' lacking commitment to the principle of nonviolence but because they had become "ritualized and futile" and thus no longer effected change.[8] The Communist League, which claimed still

---

[4] Die Redaktion, "In eigener Sache," *Atom Express* (May 1977), 2.

[5] See, also: A. Dirk Moses and Elliot Neaman, "West German Generations and the *Gewaltfrage*: The Conflict of the Sixty-Eighters and the Forty-Fivers," in Warren Breckman, Peter E. Gordon, A. Dirk Moses, Samuel Moyn, and Elliot Neaman, eds., *The Modernist Imagination: Intellectual History and Critical Theory* (Berghahn, 2009).

[6] On the movement's "culmination in violence," see: Dorothy Nelkin and Michael Pollak, *The Atom Besieged: Extraparliamentary Dissent in France and Germany* (Cambridge, MA: MIT Press, 1981), 3. An argument similar to the one that has frequently been used to discredit the West German student movement (i.e. that it ended in the rise of the RAF). See, for example: Götz Aly, *Unser Kampf. 1968 – ein irritierter Blick zurück* (Frankfurt am Main: Fischer, 2008). On the division of the anti-nuclear movement into two factions, see: Christian Joppke, *Mobilizing Against Nuclear Energy: A Comparison of Germany and the United States* (Berkeley: University of California Press, 1993), 105 and 128.

[7] Roger Karapin's findings in the specific case of the anti-nuclear movement are aligned with Hanshew's more broadly drawn conclusions, since he argues that "[anti-nuclear] protest leaders deliberately blurred the distinction between violent and nonviolent actions." Karapin, *Protest Politics in Germany: Movements on the Left and Right since the 1960s* (University Park, PA: Pennsylvania State University Press, 2007), 151.

[8] Walter Mossmann, *realistisch sein: das unmögliche verlangen. Wahrheitsgetreu gefälschte Erinnerungen* (Berlin: edition der Freitag, 2009), 245. Karrin Hanshew also analyzes Walter Mossman's self-critical intervention into the violence debate. Hanshew, *Terror and Democracy*, 180–182.

to support occupation as a tactic, implicitly agreed with Mossmann when it admitted that how activists should "responsibly organize further occupation attempts" was a "political question" – that is, a question of whether such protests would effect change – not a question about the legitimacy of the protest form itself.[9]

Though the violence debate had theoretical and moral underpinnings, reactor opponents sought to resolve it in the realm of action. Because press harangues, official condemnation, and police crackdowns made high profile protests ineffective as challenges to national nuclear policy and government authority, advocates of site occupation slowly dedicated themselves to finding a better practical answer to the political question confronting them.[10] The ensuing debate opened a way forward for alternative modes of anti-nuclear activism; many of which had already been in practice before the summer of 1977, but received far less attention than headline-grabbing mass site occupation attempts. Different factions promoted solutions that ranged from bottom-up recruiting drives, to national organizing meetings, to peaceful mass rallies. Surprisingly, in their attempts to distance their own local anti-reactor campaigns from the discredited mass actions, grassroots activists provided the most effective answer to the political question. By challenging pro-nuclear elected officials at the ballot box they used the tools of liberal democracy itself in order to bring the weight of the extra-parliamentary opposition to bear on parliamentary decision-making. This chapter will consider the search for a more effective means of protesting the proliferation of nuclear reactors and the emergence of an alternative electoral politics, developments that proceeded amidst the violence debate and the anti-nuclear movement's crisis of summer 1977. This new, more explicitly politicized environmentalism initiated a transformation of the liberal democratic order by giving personal concerns and immediately local issues pride of place in an area of policy that had been dominated by the decisions of central governments and national parliaments.

Violence, Resistance, and Efficacy

Between October 1976 and February 1977, three attempts to occupy the reactor construction site at Brokdorf failed to stop the project. Nonetheless, a series of decisions by the Lunenburg Administrative

[9] "Brokdorf-Grohnde-Malville-Der Kampf geht weiter," *Arbeiterkampf* 7, no. 110 (8 August 1977), 5.
[10] To some extent, grassroots occupations in places like Gerstheim were disconnected from these wider debates because they were considered too provincial to be political. See Chapter 4.

Court halted construction from early 1977 until 1981.[11] Instead of jeopardizing the West German nuclear program, and calling the repressive nature of the "atomic state" into question, however, the turn of events raised questions about occupation's potential to stop even a single reactor project, and suggested that another means of challenging the proliferation of nuclear energy might be more effective. By the time the campaign against the Brokdorf reactor shattered into three factions amidst the tumultuous protests of 19 February 1977, few activists remained committed to occupation as a political strategy. Occupation's waning importance mooted a series of open-ended questions about anti-nuclear activists' immediate and longer-term goals, and how they might best be achieved. In seeking to answer these questions, activists stopped describing their actions as particular anti-reactor protests and began to conceive of a larger, comprehensive anti-nuclear rhetoric as the key to enhancing their movement's efficacy.

Even organizations like the Communist League, which had strongly supported the occupation attempts at Brokdorf, slowly shifted their views of occupation. The KB's evolving viewpoint exemplified the way in which activists gave up on confrontational occupation attempts at particular sites and sought instead to build a more broadly conceived anti-nuclear movement throughout the country.[12] The KB's attitude changed only slowly. The divided and ineffective protests of February 1977 did not outwardly shake its belief in the power of occupation as a mode of protest. In late February, as discussion of the Malville demonstration percolated through the pages of *Super-Pholix*, an article in the KB's *Arbeiterkampf* newspaper mischievously noted that the reactor construction site at Grohnde was being "built up into a fortress." In contrast to the sort of long-winded community-building effort that the *graswurzel* groups had pursued in their 19 February protest at Grohnde, the KB called for an all-out attack on the construction site that would "smash the federal atomic program" in one powerful blow. Some 20,000 activists heeded the battle cry and came to Grohnde on 19 March 1977 intent on creating a "second Brokdorf" on the River Weser.[13]

The action at Grohnde was an important turning point in the KB's relationship with occupation. Despite the large turnout and the Communists' intention to use a powerful protest at Grohnde to obliterate

---

[11] Despite the four-year delay in construction, the project continued. The completed reactor began to deliver energy to the grid in October 1986.
[12] For an in-depth account of the KB's involvement in anti-nuclear protest, see: Steffen, *Geschichten vom Trüffelschwein*.
[13] "Das ist unser nächstes Ziel," *Arbeiterkampf* 7, no. 100 (7 March 1977), 1–2.

the entire German atomic program, even the action's protagonists later agreed that "a demonstration did not occur [that day]." Rather than holding a rally or issuing demands, "the activists immediately attacked the fence with the necessary tools."[14] The combative action seemed well-aligned with the KB's understanding of occupation, which it described as a means of "storming the atomic fortresses."[15] *Arbeiterkampf* crowed that at the battle's "highpoint" reactor opponents "ripped an approximately ten-meter breach in the fortifications." Because it was accomplished "inclusively" by 300 activists pulling together on a 100-meter rope, the breach came to symbolize the struggle's collective nature.[16] But by toppling a section of fence, activists did not bring down the federal nuclear program. Protesters were immediately repelled from the construction site by well-armed police, and the protest itself ended quickly without slowing progress on the reactor, which went critical in September 1984.

Though the KB celebrated the Grohnde attack as "a step forward in the struggle against the nuclear program," the failed occupation attempt was one of the last combative site occupation attempts it promoted.[17] And its self-congratulatory attitude provided perfect cover for reconsiderations of whether such protests were really the best way forward. In a shocking departure, an overwhelmingly positive cover story in *Arbeiterkampf* ended with a call for a "reprieve" from confrontational actions so that protesters could "strengthen themselves" and "'massify' the struggle by bringing political agitation and propaganda into the villages, towns, and cities."[18] Though the KB never backed down from triumphant descriptions of its past exploits, it tacitly accepted strategic reconsiderations intended to grow the movement beyond a hard core of activists hell-bent on clashing with police at construction site fences. By expanding the movement, it clearly hoped to increase the political efficacy of anti-nuclear protests in the longer term.

Other organizations interested in fostering widespread anti-nuclear sentiment agreed that protesting more effectively would require stepping back from reactor sites and recruiting new activists. The June/July 1977 issue of the Göttingen Working Group against Nuclear Reactors' new

---

[14] *Autonomie. Materialien gegen die Fabrikgesellschaft* 4–5 (1980), 7. Quoted in: Joppke, *Mobilizing Against Nuclear Energy*, 106.

[15] "Grohnde am 19.3.: Ein Schritt voran im Kampf gegen das Atomprogramm," *Arbeiterkampf* 7, no. 101 (21 March 1977), 1; see also: Joppke, *Mobilizing Against Nuclear Energy*, 106.

[16] Steffen, *Geschichten vom Trüffelschwein*, 186.

[17] "Grohnde am 19.3," *Arbeiterkampf* 7, no. 101 (21 March 1977), 1.   [18] Ibid., 3.

magazine *Atom-Express* called on protesters to stop dwelling on how they could overcome defensive tactics that "the state had learned from the events at Wyhl." Instead, in a statement that echoed *Arbeiterkampf*'s directive to bring the recruiting effort to the "villages, towns, and cities," *Atom-Express*'s editorial team advocated "strengthening the [organizing] efforts at workplaces, neighborhoods, schools, and universities."[19] Both groups re-envisioned the anti-reactor struggle as a long-term undertaking that would advance as coalitions were slowly built where people lived and worked. In essence, they sought to shift their focus from demonstrative mass actions to grassroots "movement building." But managing the growth of a broad and effective national movement was a different challenge than targeting a particular reactor and recruiting a diverse group of people to carry out the concrete tasks required to maintain an occupation.

In effect, anti-nuclear activists tasked themselves with forming an united movement and redefining their purpose. To this end, three north German anti-nuclear groups – the Citizens' Initiative Hameln, which comprised the primary local opposition to the Grohnde project, the Citizens' Initiative Hanover, and the anti-Brokdorf Lower Elbe Citizens' Initiatives for Environmental Protection – organized a Federal Congress of Reactor Opponents in May 1977.[20] Representatives of 256 anti-nuclear groups participated. Of the more than 800 voting delegates present, however, the KB comprised the largest organized bloc with some eighty members; other national organizations like the Communist League of West Germany (Kommunistische Bund Westdeutschland – KBW), the *graswurzel*-groups, and even the SPD each had ten or more delegates.[21] The organized Left's outsized role prevented the meeting from uniting the full spectrum of anti-nuclear groups as a national movement. Members of many southern German citizens' initiatives affiliated with the Federal Association of Citizens' Initiatives for Environmental Protection boycotted the conference altogether because, although they were willing to work against particular reactor projects as part of a diverse coalition, they were reticent to make

---

[19] "Thesen zur Stand der Bewegung gegen AKWs und zur Weiterarbeit," *Atom-Express* 2 (June/July 1977), 30–31. On the founding of the Göttingen Working Group against Nuclear Reactors, see Chapter 4.

[20] Z. Red., "Der KB Nord, die Bürgerinitiativen und das Atom," *Kommunistische Volkszeitung* 5, no. 19 (12 May 1977), 15.

[21] "Bundeskonferenz, 14. 15. Mai 77," *Atom-Express* 2 (June/July 1977), 23; see also: *... und nicht anderswo*, 59–60; and: Steffen, *Geschichten vom Trüffelschwein*, 189.

common cause with Communists at a national congress. Defining the movement's direction also proved rather difficult. Much of the meeting was consumed with heated procedural debates between delegates of the KB and the KBW.[22] When the delegates finally began discussing their ideas for the movement's future, the Communist splinter groups again dominated the discussion, putting forward resolutions that other activists found too theoretical.[23] A reporter for *Atom-Express* concluded, therefore, that "there would be no sense in detailing the many resolutions, since they will have no effect on the further struggle against reactors ... this Federal Congress was no step forward."[24]

In the Spring and Summer of 1977, West German anti-nuclear activists failed to establish a national organization or to stop the proliferation of nuclear energy at Brokdorf, Grohnde, and Hanover. But these stumbling blocks did not end their hopes of uniting and empowering their movement at the national level. Shortly after the denunciations of the Federal Congress of Reactor Opponents ended – and well before the dust settled at Malville – a wide range of anti-nuclear groups threw themselves into the planning of a protest at Kalkar on the Lower Rhine, where German officials were overseeing the construction of a fast-breeder reactor akin to Malville's Super-Phénix. Though planners initially conceived of the Kalkar protest's goal as yet another site occupation, the RAF's kidnapping of Hanns Martin Schleyer led the government to ban the demonstration altogether.[25] Instead of continuing to work towards an occupation, the organizers called on "all opponents of nuclear reactors" to participate in an "unified demonstration at Kalkar and to overcome divisions." By bringing together the full spectrum of opponents of nuclear energy the organizers hoped to show that the "population is absolutely opposed to the construction of the fast-breeder."[26] As soon as the KB joined the effort, *Arbeiterkampf* began trumpeting the inclusive sentiment with its hallmark polemics. The newspaper proudly listed the many citizens' initiatives participating in planning meetings,

[22] "Bundeskongreß der Bürgerinitiativen," *Arbeiterkampf* 7, no. 104 (16 May 1977); see also: Steffen, *Geschichten vom Trüffelschwein*, 189.

[23] "Nach der Bundeskonferenz: Es brodelt in der Gerüchte-Küche," *Arbeiterkampf* 7, no. 105 (31 May 1977).

[24] "Bundeskonferenz, 14. 15. Mai 77," *Atom-Express* 2 (June/July 1977), 23.

[25] On this decision, and on the influence of state responses to terrorism on anti-reactor protest in 1977, see Jutta Ditfurth, *Krieg, Atom, Armut. Was sie reden, was sie tun: Die Grünen* (Berlin: Rotbuch-Verlag, 2011), 57. As Walter Mossmann put it, "one could have come to the conclusion [in 1977] that there was a competition between the anti-nuclear movement and the RAF for viewership ratings." Mossmann, *realistisch sein*, 243.

[26] "Am 24. September nach Kalkar!" *Arbeiterkampf* 7, no. 112 (5 September 1977), 10.

noting with great satisfaction their geographic distribution and ideological diversity.[27] As far as size and diversity were concerned, the protest lived up to its organizers' goals. *Arbeiterkampf* immediately deemed the demonstration, in which at least 50,000 took part, the largest in the history of the West German anti-nuclear movement.[28]

The Kalkar protest's efficacy was another matter entirely. Plans for the site's defense were informed by officials' perception that the West German government was fighting a civil war against forces that wished to topple the state. Between 15,000 and 20,000 policemen – the largest deployment in West German history – confronted the protesters. Roadblocks and train cancellations stopped as many as 20,000 activists from getting anywhere near Kalkar. Even those protesters who made their way to the meeting point hardly dared to challenge the authority of the police, who utilized military hardware including tanks and helicopters to defend the site. Late in the afternoon, the 50,000 or 60,000 activists who had finally made it through the checkpoints and roadblocks rallied briefly near the construction site and marched towards the fence before turning around and heading home. Most participants remembered the overbearing police presence and the long journey to Kalkar far better than the brief protest itself.[29] Moreover, in the wake of the battle at Malville, and amidst a wave of violent RAF actions now known as the "German Autumn," the peaceful rally was a non-event in the national press.

The demonstration's lack of resonance was not lost on its proponents. In an introspective column, the editors of *Atom-Express* wondered whether the Kalkar demonstration was a step "forward or backward." On the one hand, the protest could be considered the anti-nuclear movement's "latest high point" because it had reunited the diverse currents of activists who had protested separately at three different sites on 19 February. Kalkar also contrasted starkly with the more recent occupation attempts at Grohnde and Malville, which had discredited activists and jeopardized what remained of the movement's cohesion. In so far as it represented a new model for action, the demonstration could even be considered an improvement over the recent Federal Congress of Reactor Opponents in Hanover, where activists had failed to lay out a vision for the movement's future. On the other hand, however, the demonstration marked a step backwards if it meant that anti-nuclear activism was moving towards the sort of

[27] "27./28.8.: Vorbereitungstreffen für die Kalkar Aktion" *Arbeiterkampf* 7, no. 110 (8 August 1977), 7; and: "Kalkar: Breites Bündnis," *Arbeiterkampf* 7, no. 112 (5 September 1977), 1.
[28] "Trotz Polizeistaats-Manöver 50 000 in Kalkar," *Arbeiterkampf* 7, no. 114 (3 October 1977).
[29] See, for example: "Kalkar," *graswurzelrevolution* 32 (October 1977), 15.

"bourgeois civility that won't allow for reactor construction sites to be turned back into meadows."[30] Amidst the extreme violence of the German Autumn, anti-nuclear activists were thinking long and hard about the tactics they ought to use in order to stop the proliferation of nuclear energy. Because traditional protest tactics paled in comparison to site occupations – let alone the RAF's hijackings, kidnappings, and assassinations – well-heeled anti-nuclear protests ran the risk of failing to garner attention and thus becoming ineffective. Thus, though the Kalkar demonstration proved more inclusive than other West German anti-reactor protests, it also raised more political questions about anti-nuclear protest's future than it answered.

In Kalkar's wake, the editors of *Atom-Express* suggested that the future of occupation – and therefore of efforts to grow the anti-nuclear movement – would become known only after the court order stopping construction at Brokdorf was lifted.[31] Then, they explained, activists would finally be forced to decide whether or not to confront the police in order to attempt a new occupation at what had become the best known West German reactor. Yet, the very fact that the movement's future remained in limbo until the courts reopened the debate over occupation indicated the challenges activists faced as they sought to restore anti-nuclear activism's efficacy amidst the German Autumn and government crackdowns on protest. By replacing occupation with an unremarkable rally, Kalkar brought anti-nuclear activists together, but left them without their "most important tool." As a result, the Kalkar demonstration was hard to conceive as the appropriate model for a politically effective anti-nuclear movement.

Political Questions, Grassroots Answers

The high-profile intra-movement debates taking place at national gatherings and in the pages of alternative publications influenced local discussions about the future of anti-nuclear protest. In the eyes of many grassroots activists, restoring lost respectability was essential to their protests' efficacy. Because "big police interventions" frequently ended them, protests at construction sites were "discrediting" the movement and enabling government officials to lump even small-scale protests together with the political violence of the RAF.[32] Federal congresses and mass

---

[30] "Randbemerkung," *Atom-Express* 4 (October 1977), 3.   [31] Ibid.

[32] Police interventions were believed to discredit the movement not only because press coverage emphasized fighting and aggressiveness, but also because – as Michael Hughes has shown – the idea of being punished for participation in protest was widely rejected by German activists as well as

demonstrations were appealing alternatives for members of national organizations eager to garner headlines and affect high politics by forming a more legible national structure for anti-nuclear protest, but many concerned citizens continued to view the nuclear threat from their front porches.[33] Though they were well aware that nuclear energy was not only a local issue, grassroots activists saw stopping local projects as the first step towards ending the proliferation of nuclear energy. They were much less concerned about portraying themselves as a national movement with strictly delineated, "political" goals.

When anti-nuclear activism came under fire in the summer of 1977, inhabitants of Lower Saxony were directly confronted with a unique conglomeration of nearby nuclear projects. In their state and in neighboring Schleswig-Holstein alone, two reactors had just gone critical and four more were under construction. At the same time, federal planners' realization that they had nowhere to store rapidly accumulating nuclear waste introduced Lower Saxonians to another aspect of the nuclear debate. Stable underground salt formations considered amenable to safe, long-term storage "predestined" the state to become the site of West Germany's first nuclear waste storage and reprocessing facility.[34] After federal officials proposed three potential sites for the facility in 1976, most inhabitants of Lower Saxony suddenly lived near a functioning reactor, a reactor construction site, or a proposed nuclear dump.[35] Moreover, with Grohnde in the center of the state and Brokdorf directly on its northeastern border, Lower Saxonians had front row seats for the failed occupation attempts of Fall 1976 and Spring 1977.

Carl Beddermann, a 35-year-old attorney who worked in the state's finance department and lived near the Lichtenmoor, a sparsely populated marshland that had been named a potential site for the nuclear waste facility, took a leading role in the search for an effective, localized alternative to site occupation.[36] Beddermann had not been opposed to mass demonstrations when he first became concerned about nuclear energy; he even took part in the occupation attempts at Brokdorf and

---

the German public. Hence, protests that led to arrests were looked down upon. Hughes, "Civil Disobedience in Transnational Perspective: American and West German Anti-Nuclear-Power Protesters, 1975–1982," *Historical Social Research* 39, no. 1 (2014).

[33] Foley, *Front Porch Politics*; see also Chapter 1.   [34] Rucht, *Von Wyhl nach Gorleben*, 100.

[35] "Gorleben: Das Zeitalter der Angst?" *Der Spiegel* 26 March 1979.

[36] Carl Beddermann, "Die 'Grüne Liste Umweltschutz' in Niedersachsen," in Rudolf Brun, ed., *Der Grüne Protest. Herausforderung durch die Umweltparteien* (Frankfurt: Fischer Taschenbuch, 1978), 107. On Lichtenmoor as a potential site for the nuclear waste facility, see: Rucht, *Von Wyhl nach Gorleben*, 104–105.

Grohnde. But after being attacked by a helicopter on his way home from Brokdorf and "chased across the fields" at Grohnde, he had had enough. The high profile failures were enabling politicians to demean anti-nuclear activism and "take advantage" of the citizens' initiatives.[37]

To win respect and credibility, Beddermann proposed a campaign for office that could "turn [activists'] ballots into object lessons" for obdurate officials. The formal organization required of an electoral campaign would enable responsible individuals – Beddermann had himself in mind – to manage participation.[38] Differently put, an anti-nuclear electoral campaign would use the framework of electoral politics to bolster the movement's respectability and force elected officials to take extra-parliamentary activists and their concerns more seriously. On 11 May 1977, just days before the Federal Congress of Reactor Opponents began in nearby Hanover, Beddermann founded the Environmental Protection Party (USP) in his hometown of Schwarmstedt with twenty other opponents of the proposed Lichtenmoor facility. Though the USP's founders were active in the struggle at Lichtenmoor, they did not stop at engaging their neighbors in a local electoral campaign. Instead, cognizant that they would need a statewide list of candidates in order to enter the June 1978 elections to the state parliament and thus turn their ballots into lessons for the state government, activists from Lichtenmoor attempted to organize USP chapters throughout Lower Saxony.[39] Armed with a six-point program which focused exclusively on ecological matters, Beddermann and his colleagues visited nature protection groups across the state.[40] In the spring and summer of 1977 alone, they convinced activists in twelve towns to found chapters of their new party.

---

[37] Beddermann quoted in: "Zelle in der Heide," *Der Spiegel,* 30 January 1978; see also: Anna Hallensleben, *Von der Grünen Liste zur Grünen Partei? Die Entwicklung der Grünen Liste Umweltschutz von ihrer Entstehung in Niedersachsen 1977 bis zur Gründung der Partei DIE GRÜNEN 1980* (Göttingen: Muster-Schmidt Verlag, 1984), 50.

[38] Beddermann, "Die 'Grüne Liste Umweltschutz'," 106. Activists in the Upper Rhine valley began running campaigns for local office already in the mid-1970s, when Annemarie Sacherer ran for village council; Hans Erich Schött even joined the F.D.P. in order to run for the Landtag (Sacherer and Schött both won the seats for which they ran).

[39] Beddermann himself became increasingly devoted to the partisan project, working hard to establish green electoral lists linked to his own party in other West German states. See: Lilian Klotzsch and Richard Stöss, "Die Grünen," in Richard Stöss, ed., *Parteien-Handbuch. Die Parteien der Bundesrepublik Deutschland, 1945–1980* (Opladen: Westdeutscher Verlag, 1984), 1525.

[40] Beddermann, "Die 'Grüne Liste Umweltschutz'," 107. The party's short, six-point platform focused almost entirely on ecological matters. It called for an end to the atomic program, a reduction of water pollution, the protection of endangered species, the preservation of farmland, small towns, and cities from overdevelopment, and a stop to mass projects of all kinds. "Programm der Umweltschutzpartei Niedersachsen," reprinted in Beddermann, "Die 'Grüne Liste Umweltschutz,'" 115–116.

Independently of Beddermann's organizing efforts, activists in the town of Hildesheim put together their own slate of candidates for the October 1977 local council elections.[41] The major difference between the USP and the Hildesheim slate, which called itself the Green List for Environmental Protection (GLU), lay in the fact that the GLU's lead organizer, Georg Otto, had long been involved in minor party politics; he had even run for the Bundestag as a candidate of the Free Social Union (FSU) in 1969.[42] As such Otto had come to environmental politics for rather different reasons than had Beddermann. A fierce advocate of Silvio Gesell's "natural economic order," Otto emphasized the environmental qualities of Gesell's monetarist program so as to broaden its appeal.[43] Aware of Beddermann's success organizing USP chapters across the state, Otto's group campaigned as an USP affiliate until Beddermann excluded it from the party for overemphasizing monetarism. Since Beddermann had founded his new party because of environmental concerns, but Otto had latched onto environmentalism as a means of popularizing his obscure program, the two perspectives seemed irreconcilable.

Nonetheless, a modicum of success brought them together rather quickly: after a lone member of Otto's slate was elected to the Hildesheim town council, Beddermann negotiated a merger between the two parties so that his group could exploit the GLU's name recognition at the upcoming June 1978 election to the state parliament.[44] This first statewide candidates' list in the FRG to use the word "Green" in its name, therefore, had originally intended the color to represent Gesell's monetarism rather than environmental issues.[45] It was an interesting cooperation of an initiative intended to force politicians to address environmental issues, and an effort to use the currency of environmental rhetoric to interest citizens in other issues. Despite these two rather

---

[41] The October 1977 elections were only held in parts of the state where recent reforms had changed municipal districts, necessitating new elections.

[42] In addition to Beddermann's group, and the Hildesheim group, an anti-nuclear slate that called itself the Wählergemeinschaft Atomkraft – Nein Danke (Voters' Association Nuclear Energy, No Thanks!), was formed in Hameln by local opponents of the Grohnde reactor. It differed from the USP in that it perceived of its electoral campaign even more instrumentally – describing it as a means of supporting ongoing extra-parliamentary activism, not a form of action in and of itself. Klotzsch and Stöss, "Die Grünen," 1516.

[43] Ibid., 1515.

[44] The lists scored 1.2 percent and 2.3 percent in Hildesheim and Hameln respectively, electing one activist to each local council.

[45] Klotzsch and Stöss, "Die Grünen," 1515.

different meanings, using the adjective "green" proved a powerful means of papering over such differences and "branding" the new party as something different from the red Social Democratic Left or the black Christian Democratic Right.[46] Seeking to build on the GLU's initial success in Hildesheim, and open to further cooperation, anti-nuclear activists visited towns with active citizens' initiatives throughout Lower Saxony and asked citizens' initiative members to contribute their concerns to the party's election platform. Where no citizens' initiative existed, GLU organizers sought out "bird protectors, sport fishermen, gardeners, beekeepers, hunters, or chapters of the German Forest Protection Society."[47] By tailoring the program to local concerns, organizers enabled new branches to "shoot up like mushrooms" all over the state. In April 1978, the GLU's first statewide congress was attended by 100 delegates representing 800 members organized into forty-two local chapters.[48]

Though it was organized statewide, the GLU's campaign emphasized distinct, local issues throughout the state. Party activists collected the 100 signatures required to get a candidate on the ballot in ninety-eight of Lower Saxony's ninety-seven legislative districts.[49] The candidates themselves worked together with volunteers to stuff envelopes and deliver leaflets, and deployed the sorts of creative, alternative approaches that anti-nuclear activists had long used at the grassroots level. Just what these efforts entailed differed from district to district. In the city of Brunswick, GLU campaigners distributed homemade multigrain rolls and delivered manure to fertilize urban gardens. The GLU candidate in the port of Cuxhaven showcased the effects of waterborne pollution by dumping oil, a tin can, and a dead fish into a bathtub full of seawater that he had hauled into the city's central shopping district.[50]

---

[46] Andrei Markovits and Joseph Klaver, "Thirty Years of Bundestag Presence: A Tally of the Greens' Impact on the Federal Republic of Germany's Political Life and Public Culture," *AICGS German-American Issues* 14 (2012). In fact, this conception was already evident to Greens in Baden-Württemberg in 1979, when they argued that "Green" had established itself as a brand following the European election. Kreis Lörrach, "Fragebogen zur Ermittlung der Relation zwischen Aufwand und Erfolg, um die vor uns liegende Wahlkämpfe aufgrund gemachter Erfahrungen planen zu können," (20 June 1979). AGG Ba-Wü 109

[47] "Immer Mitgegeistert," *Der Spiegel*, 12 June 1978.

[48] Hallensleben, *Von der Grünen Liste*, 73 and 84.

[49] Beddermann, "Die 'Grüne Liste Umweltschutz,'" 108. According to Hallensleben, Beddermann himself claimed that one district had no candidate because the candidate failed to submit paperwork on time. Hallensleben, *Von der Grünen Liste*, 97.

[50] "Immer Mitgegeistert," *Der Spiegel*, 12 June 1978.

Figure 5.1 Poster used by the Green List for Environmental Protection in its 1978 campaign in Lower Saxony. The headline reads, "Don't make yourself black with anger, vote green!" © AGG. PL-04033.

Measured in votes cast for the GLU, this unique combination of traditional campaign work and locally focused direct action proved particularly successful in areas surrounding nuclear sites and in districts where party chapters had been organized in 1977. In Lüchow-Dannenberg, for example, where the village of Gorleben had recently been selected as the site for the nuclear waste facility, the GLU received a remarkable 17.8 percent of the vote. The List's statewide result of 3.9 percent far outstripped the eight other minor parties standing for election, which together garnered only 1.2 percent of the vote. Moreover, the GLU's result nearly matched the long-established Free Democratic Party's (F.D.P.) 4.2 percent, and was widely perceived to have contributed to the Free Democrats' failure to jump the 5 percent hurdle and retain their representation in parliament. The GLU's near-breakthrough "was briefly the subject of widespread public interest and evaluated largely positively by the press."[51] The conservative daily Die Welt, placed enormous emphasis on the result, speculating that after nearly three decades of a political system with only three parties, "it could easily come to a fourth, fifth, and sixth party." Meanwhile, "political scientists everywhere called the result 'alarming' ... commentators called it 'sensational' ... and the Free Democrats said it was 'catastrophic.'"[52]

The GLU campaign's resonance was particularly surprising because previous environmentally focused electoral campaigns in the FRG had received almost no coverage and garnered a miniscule share of the vote. Minor parties like the FSU and the Action Community of Independent Germans (AUD), for example, had emphasized environmental issues since the late 1960s with little to show for it.[53] In the 1969 Bundestag campaign in which Georg Otto served as a candidate, for example, the FSU joined forces with the World Federation for the Protection of Life and dedicated its efforts to the "protection of life." Nevertheless, the national campaign received only 16,371 votes. As grassroots ecological activism took off in the early 1970s, the FSU and WSL

[51] Hallensleben, Von der Grünen Liste, 97 and 135.
[52] "Keine Schwarzen, keine Roten, einfach Grüne," Der Spiegel, 12 June 1978.
[53] On the environmental strategies of the FSU and AUD, see: Stöss, Parteien Handbuch; and: Richard Stöss, Vom Nationalismus zum Umweltschutz. Die Deutsche Gemeinschaft/ Aktionsgemeinschaft Unabhängiger Deutscher im Parteiensystem der Bundesrepublik (Opladen: Westdeutscher Verlag, 1980). The liberal F.D.P. also tried to rebrand itself as Germany's environmental party by releasing an environmental program as early as 1971. See, for example: Peter Menke-Glückert, "Der Umweltpolitiker Genscher," in Klaus Kinkel, ed., In der Verantwortung. Hans Dietrich Genscher zum Siebzigsten (Berlin: Siedler, 1997): 155–168.

could not get their proposed Life Protection Party off the ground.[54] As late as 1976, the AUD ran an ineffective environmentally focused Bundestag campaign. Organizers claimed they had cooperated with 600 citizens' initiatives, and focused their campaigning on regions where reactors were planned or being built. Nevertheless, AUD candidates garnered only 22,202 votes throughout the Federal Republic, the campaign received no notable press coverage, and the party fared no better in districts where it recruited citizens' initiative members to run for office than it did elsewhere.[55]

The GLU surpassed these failed environmental campaigns by prioritizing the immediate interests of grassroots activists and building on organizing work carried out locally by citizens' initiative members.[56] Even if most citizens' initiatives did not simply join the GLU en masse, the Green List honored their work by presenting itself as a new sort of party that matched their localized, "apolitical" outlook. Challenging elected officials in order to gain their respect and to force them to act on specific, urgent environmental matters, was its raison d'être; governing Lower Saxony was not on its agenda. By naming it a "list" rather than a "party," the GLU's organizers emphasized its informal nature and distance from the establishment. The List's platform, according to Beddermann, was "just political enough" to serve as an election program. Rather than adhering to an all-encompassing ideology, it comprised a hodgepodge of local groups' particular interests, which ranged from individual nuclear reactors and sewage treatment plants to a British tank unit's training maneuvers.[57] The difficult position in which anti-nuclear activists found themselves in 1977

[54] On the 1969 campaign, see: Stöss, *Parteienhandbuch*, 1413–1415. On the FSU and WSL's proposed Life Protection Party, see: Stöss, *Vom Nationalismus*, 246.

[55] Stöss, *Vom Nationalismus*, 255–256. For election returns, see: Bundeswahlleiter, "Wahl zum 8. Deutschen Bundestag am 3. Oktober 1976," (www.bundeswahlleiter.de/de/bundestagswahlen/frue here_bundestagswahlen/btw1976.html, last accessed 14 July 2015). Despite the fact that the AUD had failed to field candidates in Lower Saxony for its 1976 Bundestag campaign, its operatives promoted themselves as the best positioned organizers in Lower Saxony and urged the GLU to allow them to manage the 1978 state parliament campaign. When the GLU refused the AUD's entreaties, the AUD went ahead with its own campaign, which failed to cross even the vaunted "0.0% hurdle." Stöss, *Vom Nationalismus*, 261. For election returns, see: Bundeswahlleiter, "Ergebnisse frühere Landtagswahlen" (Wiesbaden: March 2015), 56.

[56] Markovits and Gorski note that citizens' initiatives did not typically join the GLU en masse, but they certainly tilled the soil upon which it grew. Markovits and Gorski, *The German Left: Red, Green, and Beyond* (Oxford: Oxford University Press, 1993), 193. The campaign was much more effective in building on the previous efforts of local citizens' initiatives because it allowed them to help write the program and share in the party's creation – an important difference in comparison with the AUD and the FSU/WSL.

[57] "Immer Mitgegeistert," *Der Spiegel*, 12 June 1978. The organizers of Hamburg's BuLi took this openness even further, opening their "rainbow list" to non-ecological issues, too.

motivated Beddermann to found his ecologically focused party and recruit grassroots activists to electoral politics; the local election breakthrough in Hildesheim began with Otto's efforts to use environmental rhetoric to popularize monetarism. But the GLU's success in the 1978 election was a departure from previous minor parties' attempts to run environmental campaigns for office because it drew on longstanding grassroots organizing efforts, and focused on local conditions and particular concerns rather than itself.

The (Bottom-Up) Birth of Political Environmentalism

The idea that ecologists ought to engage themselves directly in electoral politics predated the crisis of 1977, and extended well beyond the unspectacular efforts of West German fringe parties like the AUD and the FSU to make their way in national politics. The first truly noteworthy ecological campaign in Europe, René Dumont's campaign for the French Presidency, took place already in 1974. Though he scored only 1.32 percent of the national vote and placed fifth out of twelve presidential candidates, the outcome of Dumont's campaign set ecologists across France into a frenzy.[58] Alain Herve, editor of the environmental magazine *Le Sauvage*, proclaimed the campaign's outcome the "birth of political ecology."[59] The newborn, he wrote, had gestated over a three-year period that had seen tremendous changes to the Earth and to human society, ranging from NASA astronauts' exhilarating first trip to the moon to horrible famines in sub-Saharan Africa and South Asia. Awareness of environmental threats all over the globe had also risen during this period, evidenced in 1972 by the UN's Stockholm Conference on the Human Environment and the publication of the Club of Rome's *Limits to Growth*. Closer to home, the period had seen anti-reactor marches at Bugey, Fessenheim, Paluel, and Gravelines as well as ecological protests on the Larzac and in Paris.[60] Herve's account of political ecology's nativity emphasized both international developments and local protests; national influences were absent. Perhaps there was a good reason Herve overlooked national politics. Despite the excitement the Dumont campaign created, political ecology's growth after 1974 was stunted, inconsistent, and discoordinated – particularly when viewed from

---

[58] See Chapter 2 for more on the Dumont campaign in Alsace.
[59] Claude-Marie Vadrot, *L'Écologie, histoire d'une subversion* (Paris: Syros, 1978), 41.
[60] Alain Hervé, "Naissance de l'écologie politique," in René Dumont, ed., *La campagne de René Dumont et du mouvement Écologique. Naissance de l'Écologie Politique* (Paris: Jean-Jacques Pauvert, 1974): 25–28.

Figure 5.2 René Dumont in Brittany during his 1974
Presidential campaign. © Magnum Photos.

the top-down. It flourished in a few regions – Alsace in particular – but languished across vast swathes of France. Nonetheless, locally focused political ecology took on increasing importance in French politics and European public opinion by the late 1970s.

French ecologists' failure to coordinate their electoral efforts across the country evidenced the movement's many internal tensions and the ecologists' uneasy engagement with high politics. Though ecologists opposed politics-as-usual and sought to differentiate themselves from the parties of the establishment, the most obvious strategy for coordinating ecologists' efforts in electoral politics was building a national party; the first serious attempts to do so came immediately after the Dumont campaign. In June 1974, 3,000 activists met in Montargis to debrief the presidential campaign and plan their next steps, but their meeting disintegrated into bitter infighting, in part simply because many of those present were opposed to the idea that a single national organization could – or even should – represent the diverse ecological movement. Nonetheless, one of the factions that emerged from the meeting, a group comprising forty grassroots initiatives, held a series of further meetings, named itself the Ecological Movement (ME), and billed itself as France's "first ecological 'party.'" The local groups involved in the ME, however, were concentrated in Eastern France. As a result, vast swathes of the country were not included in the new party.[61] Just before the March 1976 cantonal elections, where the ME campaigned for the first time, the group decided to focus on local and regional actions, since both its own capacity and the public's awareness were too small for national campaign work.[62] Unsurprisingly, then, it fielded candidates for only fifteen of the nearly 2,000 general council seats up for election in 1976; nine of its candidates ran in Alsace. Regardless of the "brilliant" results in Alsace, where two candidates even jumped the 10-percent hurdle required to participate in the election's second round, the ME's participation in the cantonal elections did not change the balance of power in the region, and it could hardly be billed as a matter of national political significance.[63]

Given its commitment to local and regional action, defining itself vis-à-vis national politics continued to cause problems for the ME, even though it had been created as a "national collective" for the ecology movement.[64] Finally, at a national meeting in June 1976, the group adopted a bold statement that it would "not participate in the struggle for central power on account of its pursuit of decentralization and self-management." Instead, the ME dedicated itself to "grassroots struggles for power," where "the possibilities for action matched those of ecology, of self-management, and of direct democracy." To this end, the group announced its plans to participate in the March 1977 municipal elections.[65] At a national meeting held in Mulhouse from 30 October until 1 November 1976, the ME drafted a common program for the municipal elections that took a localist approach by attacking centralization and advocating the self-sufficiency of municipalities, shorter distances between residential and business districts, a halt to urban

---

[61] Frémion, *Histoire de la révolution écologiste*, 127–128.

[62] "Le 'Mouvement Ecologique' adopte une stratégie non-violente," *La Gueule Ouverte* 93 (18 February 1976), 14.

[63] "Percée écologique aux cantonales," *La Gueule Ouverte* 97 (17 March 1976), 14. In Mulhouse, Henri Jenn scored 10.64 percent of the vote and Antoine Waechter received 11.92 percent. Frémion, *Histoire de la révolution écologiste*, 134; Gregoire Gauchet, "Implantation Politique et Associative des Ecologistes en Alsace," (Master's Thesis, Université Robert Schuman de Strassbourg, 1991), 20; and: Jenn, email to author, 28 July 2015. Jenn and Waechter were told by the Mayor of Mulhouse that they should give up their campaigns in the second round, since that was the time for "serious politics";both candidates received higher percentages of the vote in the second round than they had in the first round. Jenn, interview with the author, Mulhouse, 21 March 2016.

[64] "Informations Diverses," *Ionix* 8 (August 1974), 28.

[65] "L'écologie aux municipales," *La Gueule Ouverte* 111 (23 June 1976), 15.

growth, and the revitalization of rural life.[66] By November, the group had recruited some 300 candidates in Alsace, but it still struggled to recruit candidates elsewhere or even to map out the cities across France where it hoped to field candidates, and thus to expand its grassroots struggle beyond a single region.[67]

Later that same month, another decidedly local happening helped expand the 1977 campaign across much of France. When the leader of the French section of Friends of the Earth, Brice Lalonde, scored an impressive 3.5 percent in a special parliamentary election held in his Paris district, FoE and ME realized their shared interest in a national strategy for the municipal elections. At a December meeting in the town of Saint Omer, near Pas-de-Calais, representatives of FoE, ME, and other environmental groups considered the municipal elections once again. Though it formed no new permanent organization, the meeting expanded on ME's platform in a programmatic text called the "Charter of Saint Omer." The Charter incorporated many of the ME program's planks word-for-word, but it also expanded on them by taking a localist approach to issues from inequality to third world affairs. Thus, the Charter called, for example, for a municipal housing office that could fulfill the functions of private lawyers and banks, for public telephones for the elderly and handicapped, and for 1 percent of municipal budgets to be spent in the third world, possibly to "finance material improvements."[68] Still, since the entire text fit on a single sheet of newsprint, it was hardly a comprehensive program. In effect, the Charter of Saint Omer overcame the many differences of opinion between French ecological groups, not to mention their dismissive attitude towards high politics, and enabled national coordination by focusing on local politics and leaving space for the initiative of individual groups. The result was a coalition of national and local groups that ran 1,300 candidates for the municipal councils in 100 different cities. Thirty of the group's candidates were elected.[69]

[66] B. F., "Mulhouse: Le mouvement écologique et les limites du pouvoir communal," *Dernières Nouvelles d'Alsace,* 31 October 1976; and: "Le Mouvement écologique et les municipales: 'Il faut rendre la commune à ses habitants,'" *L'Alsace,* 2 November 1976.

[67] "L'écologie municipale du 'Mouvement écologique,'" *La Gueule Ouverte* 131 (10 November 1976). See also: "Il faut instaurer une participation beaucoup plus active de la population à la gestion de la commune," *Dernières Nouvelles d'Alsace,* 2 November 1976.

[68] "La charte de Saint Omer," *La Baleine – Municipales Special Paris-Ecologie* Supplement to no. 25 (February-March 1977), 3.

[69] Frémion, *Histoire de la révolution écologiste,* 138. Vadrot shows that the areas with the strongest results frequently corresponded with sites of anti-reactor protest. Vadrot, *L'Écologie,* 147ff.

In Alsace, the municipal elections fit perfectly into Solange Fernex's "multi-strategy," which called for "action everywhere ... outside of parliament, within parliament (within the established parties *and* as environmental groups)."[70] Alsatians were acting everywhere in 1977. The occupation of the Gerstheim reactor site, which began in January, continued until August. Fernex herself, who was running for the village council in Biederthal, spent twenty-four days in February and March on a hunger strike demanding "basic guarantees" about the safety of the communities surrounding the Fessenheim reactor, which was scheduled to begin generating electricity in early 1977. The hunger strikers' demands included the creation of a public control commission with members from the anti-nuclear citizens' initiatives, and the publication of the disaster plan.[71] The hunger strike, which Fernex undertook with her son and five other students from the University of Strasbourg, attracted broad attention in the press. Solidarity actions took place all over Alsace, and across France.[72] Functionaries from the major parties and unions, as well as Catholic and Protestant churchmen, government officials, and reporters came to visit the fasting activists. After more than three weeks, each participant had lost between ten and thirteen kilograms of weight, and the strikers' health was clearly in jeopardy. When the departmental government agreed to appoint a control commission for the Fessenheim plant, but not to fulfill any of their other demands, the fasters finally stopped their hunger strike.[73] On the final day of the fast, just one week before the first round of the municipal elections, 5,000 Alsatians marched in Colmar and 4,000 more in Strasbourg in support of the strikers' demand that the government guarantee the safety of the communities surrounding Fessenheim. Given the constant stream of anti-nuclear activism in Alsace early in 1977, it was not much of a surprise that ecological candidates, including Fernex in Biederthal, were elected to eight village councils in Alsace in March 1977.[74]

Though the ME's strong showing in Alsace depended on the long history of local organizing and the numerous other actions taking place there amidst the election campaign, it could be seen in a national context on

---

[70] Solange Fernex, "Konzept der Multistrategie," *BBU-Aktuell* 9 (May-June 1979), 32–33. Emphasis from the original.

[71] "À Fessenheim, sept écologistes entament un jeûne illimité," *L'Alsace*, 11 February 1977.

[72] See, for example: "Le jeûne pour Fessenheim: A Saint-Louis aussi, action de solidaité," *Dernières Nouvelles d'Alsace*, 20/21 February 1977; and: "Jeûne anti-nucléaire à Guebwiller," *L'Alsace*, 18 February 1977.

[73] Solange Fernex, "Hungerstreik von Umweltschützern in Roggenhouse." SFP – Jeûne à Roggenhouse.

[74] "Alsace: Les écologistes dans 8 conseils municipaux," *Libération*, 22 March 1977. Fernex held her local council seat from 1977 until 2001.

account of the national cooperation articulated in the Charter of Saint Omer and ME's dozens of other victories across France. Impressive results across the country caught the attention of anti-nuclear activists and environmentalists all over Western Europe, not to mention the major parties and the mainstream press. Already, two weeks before the municipal election's first round, President Giscard read the writing on the wall and published a 68-page book describing his environmental positions and the record of environmental progress under his administration.[75] Shortly thereafter, the perennial socialist presidential candidate François Mitterrand jumped on the bandwagon, proposing a national referendum on the future of nuclear energy in France. The *New York Times* proclaimed the emergence of a "potent force" in French politics, and the ecologists themselves sought to use the local electoral campaign as a springboard into national politics.[76] Immediately after the first round of the municipal election, Brice Lalonde declared on behalf of FoE that the ecologists intended to develop a national program and run candidates in the 1978 legislative elections.[77] Their next step, he quipped, would be "to take over parliament."[78] Extrapolating from the results of the municipal elections, a report in *Le Matin de Paris* did not share all of Lalonde's optimism, but it did foresee the potential for ecological candidates to receive more votes from socialist than communist voters in 1978, thus shifting the balance between the two major parties of the Left in a way that would "benefit the Communist Party."[79] Though they relied on an unsteady political constellation and were only able to agree on a minimal, locally focused program that specifically neglected national politics and depended on specific local circumstances for success, the ecologists' 1977 municipal election campaign was widely considered to have a striking effect on national politics in France and public opinion across Europe.

Localism as Strategy: Reconsidering Left and Right in City and Countryside

Leading politicians' responses to ME's 1977 entry into the municipal elections suggested that, despite their local focus, ecologists' campaigns for

---

[75] "Pour un environnement à la française," *Le Monde*, 1 March 1977.
[76] "Ecologists Emerge As a Potent Force In French Election," *New York Times*, 20 March 1977.
[77] Marc Ambroise-Rendu, "M. Brice Lalonde: nous présenterons un programme et des candidats aux législatives," *Le Monde*, 19 March 1977, 10.
[78] "Ecologists Emerge," *New York Times*, 20 March 1977.
[79] "Un vote qui préfigure les législatives de 1978," *Le Matin de Paris*, 14 March 1977.

political office were taken much more seriously than grassroots protests. In fact, ME's campaign garnered attention across the Rhine, too. The French ecologists' strong result intrigued West German activists and contributed to Carl Beddermann's decision to organize the new environmental party that became the Green List for Environmental Protection. Likewise, after ecologists won seats in two Lower Saxon town councils during that state's October 1977 municipal elections, the excitement carried across the border to Hamburg. Elections for Hamburg's citywide parliament, the Bürgerschaft, as well as the city-state's district parliaments were scheduled for the same day as Lower Saxony's June 1978 state parliament election. Anti-nuclear activists helped establish the Rainbow List – Defend Yourselves (BuLi) to compete in the Hamburg elections. Political scientists have been keen to distinguish the Leftist BuLi from Lower Saxony's centrist or even conservative GLU.[80] But comparing the processes by which the two Lists were founded offers a different perspective on their place in the political spectrum. Both emphasized grassroots activism and differed more from established political parties and even the organizations of the alternative Left than they did from one another.

The discussions that led to the founding of the BuLi began in Hamburg's neighborhoods and brought together a diverse group of activists. These initial conversations centered around the same questions of efficacy that had motivated Beddermann and his colleagues in Lower Saxony. Hamburg activists were uninterested in parliament, which they saw as a distraction. They also claimed to have no illusions about the potential of parliamentary work. They were convinced, however, that they could "use the election to improve [their] grassroots work."[81] In the northern districts of Eimsbüttel and Steilshoop, local associations including anti-nuclear citizens' initiatives, women's groups, and autonomists met regularly throughout the fall of 1977 in order to discuss a potential electoral campaign. Participating in the election, they concluded, offered an opportunity to open new conversations and build broader coalitions in the districts where they were active.[82] After the October 1977 municipal

---

[80] Markovits and Gorski, for example, contrast the two groups. Markovits and Gorski, *The German Left*, 194.

[81] "Vorwort," in BUU, ed., *Die Bürgerschaftswahlen ...* [undated, November 1977]. Materialien zur Analyse von Opposition (www.mao-projekt.de/BRD/NOR/HBG/Hamburg_AKW_BUU_Buergers chaftswahl.shtml, last accessed 2 July 2016).

[82] "Aktivitäten der BUU/Hamburg zu den Bürgerschaftswahlen (Stand 25.11.77)," in BUU, *Die Bürgerschaftswahlen* (see note 81), 1; see also: Steffen, *Geschichten vom Trüffelschwein*, 229.

elections in Lower Saxony, which "showed that the chances [for electoral participation] were not so bad," neighborhood-level discussions quickly reached a city-wide meeting of the BUU.[83] At a late October meeting, thirty-five individual initiative groups representing 750 members spoke up in favor of active engagement in the elections on the basis of a "wide coalition with other grassroots initiatives;" only two groups were opposed to the idea.[84]

One faction of BUU members suggested that such a broad grassroots coalition be organized under the rubric, "Defend Yourselves!" Their proposal for the campaign began by explaining the roots of the BUU, and the wider citizens' initiative movement of which it was part. Having realized that the parties were no longer "in the position to represent the people's interest," and having become "more aware that we cannot expect anything from parliament," renters, women, children, trainees, homosexuals and migrants had decided to "take their own interests in hand" and organize their own associations. Almost paradoxically, proponents of a "Defend Yourselves!" list argued that it was time to take these self-protection groups into parliament – but only as a means of attacking the establishment parties and the broken parliamentary system, since "every vote for us is a vote for grassroots work and against parliamentarianism."[85] But the idea that the system could be used against itself was not so easily accepted. Critical members of Hamburg citizens' initiatives worried that simply by engaging in the electoral process, they would give the impression that their own direct action protests were illegitimate. Moreover, since they were certain to obtain a miniscule percentage of the total vote for the state parliament, the campaign might also be counted by the political establishment as "a referendum decided in favor of nuclear energy."[86] Up for debate, in other words, were the very same political questions about efficacy that had influenced activists' responses to failed site occupation attempts and informed Lower Saxon and Alsatian grassroots activists' decisions to form electoral lists.

After several months of study and discussion, the BUU voted on 19 January 1978 to form a wide coalition "with all other initiatives, groups, and organization who were also fighting against the disrespect of their

---

[83] BI Rotherbaum, "Liste: 'Atomkraft – Nein Danke,'" in BUU, *Die Bürgerschaftswahlen* (see note 81), 5–6.
[84] "Aktivitäten der BUU/Hamburg zu den Bürgerschaftswahlen (Stand 25.11.77)."
[85] "Vorschlag: 'Wehrt Euch' – Liste," in BUU, *Die Bürgerschaftswahlen* (see note 81), 3.
[86] "AK – politische Ökologie," in BUU, *Die Bürgerschaftswahlen* (see note 81), 14.

interests and the restriction of democratic rights."[87] The decision allowed Leftist groups, including the KB, to join the campaign. It also reinforced the campaign's bottom-up emphasis on individual rights and community interests that distinguished Lower Saxony's GLU and France's ME from traditional bourgeois parties as well as the organized Left. The diversity of groups working to "defend themselves" from the mainstream parties and the parliament was readily apparent at the March 1978 founding meeting of this group, which became the BuLi. It brought together 200 representatives from a wide range of organizations including:

> renters' initiatives, women's, pupils' and apprentices' groups, reactor opponents, environmentalists, groups of colleagues, homosexuals, cultural and teachers' groups, health professionals' groups, clergy, draft resistors, prisoners' groups, media groups, progressive filmmakers, antifascist action groups, the citizens' initiative to save free broadcasting, [and] communist groups.

The emphasis on cooperation and grassroots power continued once the campaign began in earnest in Spring 1978. BuLi activists organized "street theater presentations and open air concerts, parties and happenings." On a single Saturday, the BuLi held "more than a dozen" individual neighborhood festivals, each of which attracted thousands of participants, allowing it to emphasize its local approach even within the compact city-state.[88]

Since the BuLi's basis in grassroots groups, its inclusive approach, and even its alternative political style all mirrored the GLU, it seems fitting to ask why the two groups are typically perceived to be so different. The most frequently mentioned reason has to do with the individuals at the head of the two groups. The GLU was organized by the conservative bureaucrat Beddermann while the BuLi's lead candidates were the KB cadre Rainer Trampert and the well-known anti-nuclear activist Holger Strohm, who had recently resigned from the SPD. The founding of a competing Hamburg Green List for Environmental Protection (GLU-HH) also bolstered the BuLi's Left-wing image, since two of the GLU-HH's leaders reportedly had ties to the far Right United People's Movement (SVB). Though the founding of the GLU-HH suggested that the BuLi was at loggerheads with the GLU-Lower Saxony, too, the relationship between the BuLi and the two GLUs was anything but straightforward. GLU-Lower Saxony chairman Carl Beddermann personally supported the

[87] Klotzsch and Stöss, "Die Grünen," 1519.
[88] Holger Strohm, "Waurm die Bunten bunt sind," in *Der Grüne Protest* (see note 36), 129.

GLU-HH, and allowed it to use the GLU moniker because unlike the BuLi, it promised to exclude Left-wing K-groups.[89] But the rest of Beddermann's party was not so bullish on its Hamburg namesake. In an attempt to head-off a competition between two ecologically minded lists in the Hamburg elections, the GLU-Lower Saxony officially inveighed the GLU-HH to give up its campaign for the Bürgerschaft, because "the unity of all anti-nuclear forces is a necessity, even in questions of electoral candidacies and parliamentary work."[90] Since a few key players' positions on the Left or the Right seemed to animate the conflict between BuLi and GLU, the idea that anti-nuclear activism could stand outside the Left-Right divide was challenged, but not upended, by the exchange.

During the campaign, in fact, distinctions between Left and Right seemed to fade into insignificance. The GLU-Lower Saxony was supported by groups from both Left and Right, who lauded the Green List on account of its differences from other parties. As the campaign gained strength in the spring of 1978, for example, the KB commended the GLU-Lower Saxony as an "alternative to the major parties" and expressed a willingness to support GLU candidates.[91] Three weeks before the election, the explicitly non-partisan (and implicitly conservative) BBU used a similar logic to justify its own support for the GLU. "The three major parties," a BBU press release explained, "have failed to address concerns about nuclear energy articulated by the affected population, the environmental, nature, and life protection organizations as well as qualified scientists."[92] The ecological focus and non-traditional campaign style that earned the GLU Lower Saxony praise from Left and Right were attributes that it shared with Hamburg's BuLi, regardless of where each group's prominent members' political biographies fit on the Left/Right spectrum.

In fact, the GLU-Lower Saxony depended on its diverse supporters' agreement that it really was different from the established parties, and that it transcended the divide between Left and Right, for its strong showing in the 1978 state parliament election. Support from both Left and Right enabled Lower Saxony's Green List to quash the founding of a rival "Rainbow List," supposedly modeled on Hamburg's BuLi. The GLU-Lower Saxony's executive committee successfully united anti-nuclear activists around itself and took support away from the proposed rainbow list by releasing a statement calling for agreement on "objective statements"

---

[89] Beddermann quoted in Hallensleben, *Von der Grünen Liste*, 88.
[90] Hallensleben, *Von der Grünen Liste*, 86.   [91] Cited in Ibid., 92.   [92] Cited in Ibid., 95.

about goals rather than "positions towards individual groups." In so doing, the GLU made room for individual activists from both Left and Right to participate so long as they checked their previous party affiliation at the door.[93] As a result, the proposed Lower Saxony Rainbow List never got off the ground and many of its would-be supporters joined the GLU campaign instead, helping it to score 3.9 percent of the vote.

Like its counterpart in Lower Saxony, the locally focused campaign in Hamburg was surprisingly successful. The BuLi scored 3.5 percent of the city-wide vote and elected two councilors to the district parliament in Eimsbüttel, where local initiatives had begun organizing for the election already in the early fall of 1977.[94] As did the GLU in Lower Saxony, the BuLi outscored the other minor parties handily and came close to the F.D.P.'s result of 4.8 percent. It nearly doubled the total share of the vote received by several Communist splinter groups, or K-Groups, in the 1970 and 1974 elections to the Bürgerschaft, which had hovered around 2 percent. As its many parallels with the simultaneous GLU campaign in Lower Saxony suggested, the BuLi was not a logical outgrowth of Left-wing parties' earlier organizing efforts; it was a departure from them.

As if to prove the importance of the electoral campaigns themselves for the fleeting moment of unity that made such a novel approach possible, high profile resignations hit both the BuLi and the GLU shortly after the June 1978 elections. Holger Strohm, one of the BuLi's two lead candidates, resigned shortly after the election because he disliked the way in which the KB was "using its dominance more visibly and blocking everything that doesn't fit its political concept."[95] Strohm was careful to note, however, that the KB "had shown model behavior before the election." It was only afterwards that KB activists became keen to take over BuLi committees and to divert campaign reimbursement funds towards pet projects. Carl Beddermann, the GLU founder, also resigned shortly after the election. In a statement explaining his resignation, Beddermann wrote that he had sought to keep the organization

> a new party free of sectarianism, of quixotic do-gooders, and of Marxist-influenced social romantics, [a party] that could offer every citizen who has read the writing on the wall an opportunity to use his or her ballot as a weapon against life-threatening environmental destruction.

---

[93] Ibid., 83–84.
[94] On the BuLi campaign, see: Steffen, *Geschichten vom Trüffelschwein*, 229–231.
[95] Strohm, "Offener Brief an den Kommunistischen Bund," quoted in Steffen, *Geschichten vom Trüffelschwein*, 230.

Beddermann was particularly critical of his party's growing emphasis on "radical democratic experiments" and its "transformed party concept." Though they disappointed the GLU's founder, these unorthodox characteristics had grown out of the local focus he had deployed to recruit members and candidates across Lower Saxony and to help the List to enter state politics in the first place.[96] In effect, therefore, Beddermann's attitude after the elections stood in sharp contrast to his earlier willingness to organize from the bottom-up. Since they had made the new List possible and even enabled a short-lived Left–Right cooperation, however, the alternative party concept and the experiments in grassroots democracy that Beddermann denounced were among the most significant legacies of West Germany's first green and alternative campaigns. In this sense, political environmentalism, couched in a language of self-defense and the protection of democratic rights, symbolized a wholly new approach that transcended what Beddermann himself referred to as the "Left/Right schema" by building from the ground up and foregrounding local issues.[97]

Between Local Approaches and National Elections: The Struggle to Organize Political Environmentalism Across Space

The resignations of Beddermann and Strohm did not unravel the BuLi or the GLU. They did suggest, however, that it would be difficult for internally diverse political initiatives to endure beyond particular campaigns. While a focus on local issues enabled broad coalitions to form and the constant challenges of an ongoing electoral campaign left little time for abstract ideological debates, aspirations to work trans-locally and to form permanent organizations turned traditional political structures and the Left–Right divide into sticking points. To avoid these contentious issues, French ecologists first organized themselves across the country on a strictly local basis. The Charter of Saint Omer, which underpinned their national cooperation in the 1977 municipal elections, made even issues like aid for

---

[96] Carl Beddermann to Liebe Freunde, 12 September 1978. Reprinted in Hallensleben, *Von der Grünen Liste*, A 72–73.

[97] As Markovits and Gorski put it, "Ecology was not . . . the sole or even dominant intellectual theme or political preoccupation of the Greens. Rather, it served as the conceptual underpinning of green policies and, above all, as the ideological legitimation for a reconstitution of radical politics." Markovits and Gorski, *The German Left*, 152. Silke Mende similarly argues that redefining political terminology (she is referring primarily to the terms Left and Right), seemed a "way out of an ideological cul-de-sac" for all the groups involved in the founding of the Greens. Mende, *"Nicht rechts, nicht links, sondern vorn." Eine Geschichte der Gründungsgrünen* (Munich: Oldenbourg Wissenschaftsverlag, 2011), 428.

the third world into local matters. Taking a localized approach to the 1978 legislative elections proved more difficult, however, since there could be no downplaying parliament's role in national politics. Falling somewhere between municipal and national elections, state elections in West Germany appeared to be a useful forum for the development of political environmentalism beyond the local level. The important role that state officials played in reactor siting processes helped anti-nuclear activists to emphasize local concerns when they campaigned for seats in state parliaments. Moreover, though they were open to local concerns, state elections had a relatively high profile in West German politics, not least because they were considered bellwethers for upcoming federal elections. Coincidences in the electoral calendars of France and West Germany made the late 1970s an ideal trial period for various types of trans-local campaigns in both countries. While French ecologists organized themselves for the 1978 legislative elections, their West German counterparts prepared to "push their luck" by running state parliament campaigns in Bavaria, Hesse, West Berlin, and Schleswig-Holstein.[98] In both countries, the activists' ambition to effect change collided with their wariness towards politics-as-usual.

Local organizing was the first step towards coordinated action across space in both countries; the March 1977 municipal elections in France provided a particularly salient model for such cooperation. Even before the Municipal elections' decisive second round, ME planned a meeting at Lons-le-Saunier to capitalize on the campaign's momentum. The meeting was dominated by activists from the ME's strongholds in Alsace and Rhône-Alpes, who quickly agreed to target the 1978 legislative elections as the next step in the development of a trans-local organization. The decision caused "Arthur," a dismayed reporter from the environmentalist publication *La Gueule Ouverte*, to complain that a campaign in 1978 was all but inevitable, since the mainstream press had reported that the ecologists would participate in the elections.[99] Arthur's criticism of the way activists from just part of the country seemed to act on behalf of ecologists everywhere presaged the problem that French ecologists faced as they considered a campaign for the National Assembly in 1978 – namely, there was no national ecology party in France, nor were ecologists across the country in agreement that one should exist.

Beginning with the 1974 Dumont Presidential campaign, several attempts to establish a national ecology party in France had been either

[98] "Keine Schwarzen, keine Roten," *Der Spiegel*.
[99] "Arthur," "Les Taupes Vertes aux 'Legislatives'?" *La Gueule Ouverte* 151 (30 March 1977), 2.

short-lived or insufficiently national. The most significant attempts to build national organizations were ME and Brice Lalonde's effort to transform the Paris-based Friends of the Earth into a national "Network." Both eschewed formal national coordination. While the ME saw itself as an alliance of local groups, Lalonde conceived of the FoE Network as a "movement in the milieu of the parties" that would maintain strong, largely autonomous regional chapters.[100] This sort of loose network model, which had worked well in the 1977 municipal elections, became the basis for the ecologists' national campaign for the 1978 legislative elections. Formal planning for the 1978 campaign began at a meeting in the fall of 1977 at Froberville, where French ecologists founded a new organization called Ecologie 78. The creation of yet another new grouping exemplified what the historian Michael Bess has referred to as French ecologists' preference for "biodegradable" campaign organizations.[101] In an election flyer, the group boasted that:

> After the elections, no one has the right to speak in the name of Ecologie 78 . . . the ecological struggle, reinforced, will continue as ever, on the basis of broader objectives that will develop at the local level . . . Ecologie 78 will cease to exist [the day after election day].[102]

Not only did Ecologie 78 come with an expiration date, it was also decentralized and driven by bottom-up initiatives. In each region, local organizations controlled the selection of candidates and supported their campaigns. Thus, in Alsace, where eleven candidates ran for the National Assembly, the candidates were chosen by Ecology and Survival, which served as Ecologie 78's affiliate in the region.Given the wide differences in the way the campaign was organized in different regions of France, it is unsurprising that the results revealed deep variations in local support for political ecology. In Alsace, Ecology and Survival's candidates scored an average of 6.06 percent of the vote in the first round, significantly higher than Ecologie 78 candidates' national average of 4.7 percent.[103] The *Dernières Nouvelles d'Alsace* described the results, which amounted to "four times the vote the ecologists had received in the 1973 legislative elections," as "encouraging" even though all of the candidates were knocked out in the

---

[100] Frémion, *Histoire de la révolution écologiste*, 136.
[101] Michael Bess, *The Light Green Society: Ecology and Technology in France, 1960–2000* (Chicago: University of California Press, 2003), 105.
[102] Ecologie 78, "Comment participer aux elections" [undated campaign flyer, likely early 1978]. CIRE H4 EELV 1978.
[103] Gauchet, "Implantation Politique," 18–19.

election's first round.[104] Thinking locally, Antoine Waechter described the campaign as a "happy consequence for the future of our land," because "45,259 Alsatian voters had chosen life." His localized reading of the results shaped his hopes for the future. Rather than following French tradition and offering his supporters advice about how they should vote in the election's decisive second round, from which he had been excluded by his low first-round vote total, Waechter called on them to "get active in their neighborhoods or their towns for ecological progress . . . and for the alteration of our conditions of life."[105]

Unsurprisingly, the campaign's results were more difficult to interpret optimistically from a national perspective. Having failed to send even a single candidate into the election's decisive second round, the ecologists certainly would not participate in debates within the National Assembly. President Giscard's decision to enhance the authority of the Ministry of the Environment, which was cited by observers as a reaction to Ecologie 78's campaign, was also considered of relatively little consequence by the ecologists themselves, since "in reality it was just a renaming of the Ministry of Infrastructure that put all the [environmental] services under the thumbs of the least protective officials."[106] Thus, the sociologist Alain Touraine famously described the 1977 Malville demonstration and the 1978 legislative campaign as twin failures that evidenced "the inability of the anti-nuclear current to organize itself into a political force."[107]

And yet, ecologists found some modicum of success in their election results. The 621,100 votes they received across France "stimulated interest in electoral politics for the more organized wing of the environmental movement."[108] In Alsace, and elsewhere, campaigners were egged on by increasing election returns to continue working towards the establishment of an enduring political party. But standard electoral procedures and permanent parties remained taboo for many ecologists, who essentially refused to commit themselves to any strategy that was explicitly geared towards success in national politics. Even Henri Jenn, who had run for the National Assembly as an ecological candidate in 1973 and continued to participate in local electoral campaigns into the 1980s, distanced himself

[104] "Des résultats encourageants pour les écologistes," *Dernières Nouvelles d'Alsace*, 14 March 1978.
[105] "En vue de 2e tour . . .," *Derniéres Nouvelles d'Alsace* 14 March 1978.
[106] Frémion, *Histoire de la révolution écologiste*, 146.
[107] Alain Touraine, *Anti-Nuclear Protest: The Opposition to Nuclear Energy in France* (Cambridge: Cambridge University Press, 1983), 28.
[108] Brendan Prendiville, *Environmental Politics in France* (Boulder: Westview Press, 1994), 23.

from attempts to form a national party since he considered himself "no party man."[109] On account of such attitudes, building a national ecology party that would send ecologists to parliament in order to legislate changes to French nuclear policy seemed just as unlikely as using site occupation to stop the entire French nuclear program.

In West Germany, the types of elections scheduled for the late 1970s seemed to offer better opportunities for opponents of nuclear energy. Beginning with the June 1978 elections in Lower Saxony and Hamburg, seven of the FRG's ten states were scheduled to elect new parliaments in the next eighteen months. The string of elections excited anti-nuclear activists, since they had done well in Lower Saxony and Hamburg where they had taken advantage of state elections' proximity to local issues and hence their attractiveness for grassroots campaigners. Despite activists' high hopes, the series of state elections quickly became a forum for a divisive internal struggle between activists with competing visions for the future of political environmentalism. The election to Hesse's state parliament, scheduled to take place just sixteen weeks after the Lower Saxony and Hamburg elections, exemplified the problems of coordination across space since it inspired the formation of two self-described green candidates' lists, not to mention a green party. The Hessian Green List (GLH), which announced its candidacy immediately after the Lower Saxony and Hamburg elections, comprised a wide range of grassroots activists' groups.[110] It was challenged in short order by a new, centralized party with explicit national ambitions, Green Action Future (GAZ), founded by the ex-CDU parliamentarian Herbert Gruhl. A third group, the GLU-Hesse, which was organized under the guidance of Lower Saxony GLU-founder Carl Beddermann, tore itself in two by seeking to make common cause first with the GLH and then with the GAZ. The struggle in Hesse, therefore, eventually pitted the bottom-up GLH against the top-down GAZ.

The cleavages amongst – and within – Hesse's green lists and parties divided activists interested in grassroots approaches from those with explicit national ambitions, but they are frequently classified instead as divisions between "Left" and "Right." Such a classification is not without

---

[109] Jenn, email to the author, 28 July 2015.
[110] The GLH was originally founded as the Grüne Liste/Wählerinitiative für Umweltschutz (Green List/Voters' Initiative for Environmental Protection), but renamed itself the Hessian Green List after a 10–11 June meeting with members of the GLU-Hesse. Since the organization campaigned as "GLH," I have used the acronym GLH throughout in order to simplify the alphabet-soup of organizations. See: Klotzsch and Stöss, "Die Grünen," 1523.

cause. GLH supporters like Jutta Ditfurth proudly referred to their organization as "Left-alternative." Scholars cited the involvement of prominent Frankfurt Spontis, the Socialist League/Socialist Office (SB), and most importantly, the KB in order to justify their classifications of the GLH as a Leftist group.[111] But the GLH also comprised groups that had little to do with the organized Left, including "various environmental initiatives and Hesse's small state chapter of the AUD."[112] Perhaps more significantly, some groups with Left-wing pedigrees had decided to join the green list in order to distinguish themselves from pre-existing parties and to help build a new approach to politics. The Spontis, for example, made no secret of the fact that they were interested in the GLH because they conceived it as a medium for issues-focused discussions that transcended traditional Leftist politics.[113] Shortly after the famous Sponti Daniel Cohn-Bendit was chosen for the seventh position on the GLH's candidates' list, he withdrew from the race calling his candidacy itself "a provocation, which therefore has already achieved its goal."[114]

Similarly, the GAZ was classified as "Right-conservative" because Herbert Gruhl had resigned from the CDU in order to found it.[115] More important for the party's sense of itself and its approach to politics, however, was Gruhl's statement that he now intended to "do ecological politics at the federal level . . . with a big stick and a federal party."[116] Plans to compete against the established parties on their own terms attracted prominent Hessian environmentalists, such as the astronomer Heinz Kaminski and the Frankfurt Zoo Director Bernhard Grzimek. As a result, the GAZ became a tightly controlled association of elite environmentalists rather than a wide-open umbrella organization like the GLH.[117] Ultimately, therefore, the most important difference between the political approaches of the GAZ and the GLH was that while the GAZ's founder proposed that a new environmental party ought to compete with the established parties on their own terms, the GLH model supposed

[111] KB members comprised one fifth of the GLH's 1,000 members by September 1978. Joachim Raschke, *Die Grünen: Wie sie wurden, was sie sind* (Cologne: Bund-Verlag, 1993), 328–329.
[112] Stöss, *Vom Nationalismus zum Umweltschutz*, 262.
[113] Laura, "weg von der liste," *Pflasterstrand* 36 (26 August–8 September, 1978), 29.
[114] Daniel [Cohn-Bendit], "runter von der liste," *Pflasterstrand* 36 (26 August–8 September, 1978), 26.
[115] Klotzsch and Stöss, "Die Grünen," 1525.   [116] Hallensleben, *Von der Grünen Liste*, 140.
[117] Kaminski called the GAZ the only green alternative "for ecologists committed to the Basic Law— that is, responsible to the free-democratic rule of law." Kaminski, quoted in Klotzsch and Stöss, "Die Grünen," 1550. Gruhl's first action after the party's founding was to rent a headquarters for GAZ within sight of the CDU's headquarters in Bonn. Mende, *"Nicht rechts, nicht links,"* 87.

that environmentalism necessitated an entirely different approach to electoral politics. In essence, the GLH's bottom-up approach was aligned with French critics of national electoral participation, who argued that there was no point in battling the established parties with "a less powerful version of the same weapon."[118] In the end, neither group did well in Hesse: the GLH received a disappointing 1.1 percent of the vote while the GAZ received an even more paltry 0.9 percent. The poor showing had much to do with the disputes caused by Hessian activists' move away from the sort of bottom-up organizing style that had enabled the campaigners in Lower Saxony and Hamburg to work together. In particular, Carl Beddermann's attempt to found new branches of his GLU in other states regardless of lackluster grassroots support, and Herbert Gruhl's attempt to build a nationwide party from his office in Bonn, marked major departures from the bottom-up approaches that had maintained green campaigners' focus on local issues and benefited their attempts at widespread cooperation.[119] In both France and West Germany, then, attempts to move beyond a strictly local approach to political campaigning were weighed down by heated disputes over environmentalism's relationship to establishment politics. While some ecologists were eager simply to compete with the established parties at any cost, others found their organizations' approach to politics most important. They understood political environmentalism as a wholesale challenge to politics-as-usual.

Conclusion

Studies of political environmentalism's emergence have emphasized its "newness" but sought also to classify the phenomenon according to the traditional Left/Right spectrum. Most scholars place the new environmental lists and parties that began to emerge in the late 1970s squarely on the political Left, explaining them as "the logical outcome of historical developments relating to the extra-parliamentary opposition and the New Left."[120] Such conclusions are supported by the best known case studies of the emergence of local green parties, which tend to focus on the first

---

[118] "Arthur," "Les Taupes Vertes aux 'Legislatives'?" *La Gueule Ouverte* 151 (30 March 1977), 2.

[119] Klotzsch and Stöss, "Die Grünen," 1525.

[120] Keith Alexander, "From Red to Green in the Island City: The Alternative Liste West Berlin and the evolution of the West German Left, 1945–1990," PhD Dissertation (University of Maryland, 2003), 42. Though they note the place of conservative activists in the founding of Die Grünen, Markovits and Gorski see the Greens as part of the New Left. Markovits and Gorski, *The German Left.* Herbet Kitschelt has grouped ecological parties together with New Left parties and labeled them as "Left-Libertarian" on account of their "libertarian commitments to individual autonomy and popular

alternative campaigns for city parliaments in large, progressive cities like West Berlin, Hamburg, and Frankfurt.[121] These studies support the argument that the Greens came from the Left by emphasizing the contributions of young Leftists and dogmatic communist splinter parties. In the West German case, they give "Rainbow" or "Alternative" lists pride of place as Die Grünen's most important precursors. A set of competing explanations classifies the German Greens as a barely unified "catch-all party that included not only different sectors of the new movements, but also Left and Right."[122] French environmentalists' inability to establish a permanent national political party during the 1970s has been explained by joining together these two interpretations and arguing that French political environmentalism depended on a catch-all approach but that the proponents of electoral campaigning failed to make common cause with the Left.[123] By focusing on internal differences and relying on labels that early political ecologists themselves rejected, all of these explanations overemphasize the role of the organized Left and obscure the fact that there was a shared basis to political ecologists' early ideology that transcended the Left/Right divide and was more than just a marriage of convenience.

The engagement of anti-nuclear activists in the green campaigns of the late 1970s and their localized approach to electoral politics underpins an alternative narrative of political environmentalism's emergence. Anti-nuclear activists' early efforts to enter electoral politics were premised on their desires to avoid politics-as-usual, and to transcend the violence debate

---

participation [and] Leftist concern for equality." Kitschelt, "Left-Libertarian Parties: Explaining Innovation in Competitive Party Systems," *World Politics* 40, no. 2 (January 1988): 195. Andreas Pettenkoffer explains environmentalism as an outgrowth of Left-wing politics. Pettenkoffer, *Die Entstehung der grünen Politik. Kultursoziologie der westdeutschen Umweltbewegung* (Frankfurt: Campus, 2014).

[121] On West Berlin, see: Alexander, "From Red to Green in the Island City." On Hamburg, see: Steffen, *Geschichten vom Trüffelschwein*. Paul Hockenos's biography of Joschka Fischer links the founding of the Frankfurt Greens with the prominent New Leftists, Fischer and Daniel Cohn-Bendit. See: Hockenos, *Joschka Fischer and the Making of the Berlin Republic: An Alternative History of Postwar Germany* (Oxford: Oxford University Press, 2008). Important exceptions are Hallensleben's study of the GLU in Lower Saxony and Frank Schnieder's study of the founding of the Greens in the towns of Bonn, Hannover, and Osnabrück. Schnieder argues that the alternative lists only ever mattered in big cities and began to lose their significance for green politics already at the end of 1979, when they joined the federal Green Party. Schnieder, *Von der sozialen Bewegung zur Institution? Die Entstehung der Partei DIE GRÜNEN in den Jahren 1978 bis 1980* (Münster: LIT Verlag, 1998), 80.

[122] Raschke, *Die Grünen*, 50. Silke Mende's excellent new study of the "founding Greens" also supports this image of the Greens as a sort of catch-all party, since it focuses on the many different groups that came together to found the party in the late 1970s and early 1980s. Mende, *"Nicht rechts, nicht links, sondern vorn."*

[123] Prendiville, *Environmental Politics in France*, 26 and 41.

that had made recent direct-action anti-reactor protests ineffective. They did so by focusing on the sorts of immediate local issues around which diverse anti-reactor coalitions had formed earlier in the decade. Thus, green politics was "new" in the sense that it expressly rejected typical political classifications and sought to disassociate itself from the form and style of traditional political parties, even as it asserted the place of immediate, personal concerns in high politics. The same strategy was deployed earlier by ecologists in France. In their preparations for the March 1977 municipal elections, French ecologists made a point of organizing their cooperation around local issues; the Charter of Saint Omer, which enabled their first effective national collaboration, stressed local action and deliberately avoided national politics. Thus, the first green lists were neither part and parcel of the Left, nor simple catch-all parties. Instead, they were grassroots-focused organizations joined together in a common purpose. They sought efficacy by distancing themselves from brutal clashes between protesters and police, and using the rhetoric of localized "self defense" – an idea with clear roots in grassroots anti-reactor struggles. By circumventing national politics and the Left/Right divide, and by focusing on local issues, political environmentalism offered a means of speaking up for oneself that was at once militant, democratic, and at least somewhat effective in garnering attention – yet still distant from high politics, and hardly able to effect immediate changes in government policy.

Thus, if the "question of violence subsided [after 1977] as much of the sixty-eighter milieu found a political vehicle in the new Green party," it was not because the Greens were a project of the Left.[124] Instead, it was because the Left engaged itself in a new means of protesting – and even resisting – that was based on grassroots' activists attempts to go beyond the Left/Right divide and to evade the constraints of high politics. The problem was that this strategy emphasized local issues in a way that implicitly rejected national politics as a meaningful realm of action. As awareness of the threat posed by nuclear energy expanded at the end of the decade – with the steady progress on the Malville fast-breeder reactor, German officials' plans for a nuclear waste-reprocessing site, and the near meltdown at Three Mile Island in Pennsylvania – anti-nuclear activists became increasingly dissatisfied with the sort of localism that made green lists possible and sought yet again to find a more effective means of addressing the nuclear issue across space.

---

[124] Moses and Neaman, "West German Generations," 288.

CHAPTER 6

Organizing a "Decisive Battle Against Nuclear Power Plants": Europe and the Nationalization of Green Politics in West Germany

Writing in 1976 in the Young European Federalists' *Forum E* magazine, Petra Kelly and Roland Vogt rallied support for a "decisive battle against nuclear reactors." On its face, their call to action was hardly surprising. In the wake of the Wyhl occupation, opponents of nuclear energy were eager to expand their struggle in order to stop nuclear energy everywhere. But the place that the pair suggested for the anti-nuclear showdown, direct elections to the European Parliament, was something of a shock.[1] Not only did Kelly and Vogt suggest that an as yet unannounced election to an impotent parliament was an essential theater for the anti-nuclear struggle, they also turned the environmental movement's well-known motto, "think globally, act locally!" on its head.[2] That phrase had been an apt description of previous anti-nuclear protests: local action had been essential to neighbors' efforts to fight together against particular reactor projects. Global thinking – in the form of ideas, scientific research, and protest models from elsewhere, but also trans-border coalitions – had underpinned those struggles. But Kelly and Vogt proposed that local people "bring their experience in the resistance" into a single political campaign that would span the nine member states of the European Economic Community. Grassroots activists could demand trans-border election districts and use their "new sense of belonging as a pathbreaking force for a nonviolent European community, a Europe from below."[3]

In the first half of 1979, Kelly and Vogt's dream of a locally rooted anti-nuclear movement that acted across broad spaces seemed plausible. Protests against a nuclear waste processing and storage facility planned for the village of Gorleben provided an opportunity to unite anti-nuclear activists across the FRG. The nuclear accident at Three

---

[1] Petra Kelly and Roland Vogt, "Ökologie und Frieden," *Forum E* 1–2 (1977), 18.
[2] Brendan Prendiville, *Environmental Politics in France* (Boulder: Westview Press, 1994), 91–3.
[3] Kelly and Vogt, "Ökologie und Frieden," 18.

Mile Island (TMI) in the United States had the potential to link together disparate anti-nuclear struggles since it reminded Europeans that an accident could occur even in the developed West. And just as Kelly and Vogt had predicted, the first direct election to the European Parliament was a chance for opponents of nuclear energy to come together across the EEC's internal borders. Rather than expanding the movement's links across Europe, however, these events contributed to the nationalization of anti-nuclear protest in the Federal Republic of Germany.

This nationalization was fostered first and foremost by activism that took place above or below the national level. The TMI accident, which occurred across the Atlantic, and ecologists' campaign for the European Parliament contributed more to the nationalization of West Germany's anti-nuclear movement than even the debate over the Gorleben facility, which pitted local and national perspectives against one another. A year earlier, the June 1978 state elections in Lower Saxony and Hamburg had caused establishment politicians to begin thinking of anti-nuclear protest in terms of high politics. Considering the Green and Rainbow Lists' respective shares of 3.9 percent and 3.5 percent of the statewide vote in Lower Saxony and Hamburg, CDU Chairman Helmut Kohl warned that the "greens' forward march ... certainly would not stop." The prominent Social Democrat Erhard Eppler was likewise convinced that German ecologists would enter the Bundestag in 1980 with just "a little luck."[4] Based solely on the results of two state elections, such comments marked a sharp departure from earlier marginalizations of anti-reactor protests as provincial affairs with limited ramifications.

How did anti-nuclear activists' experience in local protests and their desire to engage in political frameworks beyond the nation-state propel them into national politics at the end of the 1970s? And what does the anti-nuclear movement's rise to high political significance tell us about the relationship between grassroots anti-reactor protest and green politics? Despite politicians' dire warnings about the greens' relentless forward march into parliament, after all, anti-nuclear activists – even those interested in electoral politics – had long kept their distance from anything that could be perceived as national or explicitly political. Nonetheless, West Germany's green party, Die Grünen, came to be perceived as the national embodiment of grassroots anti-nuclear protest campaigns – and many other so-called New Social Movements

---

[4] "Keine Schwarzen, keine Roten, einfach Grüne," *Der Spiegel*, 12 June 1978.

besides.[5] In France, by contrast, the failure of a single, united ecological party to emerge by the end of the 1970s was treated by scholars as evidence of the anti-nuclear movement's failure.[6]

It is fitting, then, that the nationalization of the anti-nuclear movement in West Germany was hardly a linear process through which local initiatives united into a single nationwide movement. Instead, transnational frameworks – and Europe in particular – served as essential stages in the anti-nuclear movement's meandering path towards nationalization. Though it seemed to be an international event, was treated as a sideshow by establishment politicians, and disregarded by many voters, the EEC-wide direct election to the European Parliament was perhaps the most important moment in the crystallization of the Greens as a national political party in West Germany. The EP election also played an essential part, therefore, in the establishment of nuclear energy as a seminal issue in the Federal Republic's national political life. In contrast to their French counterparts, who continued to focus on local issues and prioritized regional structures even during their campaign for the European Parliament, West German activists used transnational frameworks to move their nuclear concerns beyond the local level in 1979. Amidst the new opportunities and challenges presented to the movement by the TMI disaster and the Gorleben project, "Europe" became the unlikely forum for experiments in political cooperation and nationally coordinated electoral campaigning. Leading anti-nuclear activists' willingness to think across borders, and their excitement about the European vote made the EP election not just a "window of opportunity" but a transformative moment for West Germany's anti-nuclear movement.[7] Paradoxically, transnationalism itself, and the notion that the EEC-wide election stood outside the framework of national politics, was the basis for Die Grünen's emergence as a single entity across the Federal Republic. At the same time, the EP campaign's outcome and Die Grünen's founding in January 1980 reshaped

---

[5] See, for example: Paul Hockenos, *Joschka Fischer and the Making of the Berlin Republic: An Alternative History of Postwar Germany* (Oxford: Oxford University Press, 2008), 150; and: Andrei Markovits and Philip Gorski, *The German Left: Red, Green, and Beyond* (Oxford: Oxford University Press, 1993), 99ff.

[6] This judgment was made most famously by Alain Touraine. Touraine, *Anti-Nuclear Protest: The Opposition to Nuclear Energy in France* (Cambridge: Cambridge University Press, 1983), 28. Michael Bess describes the late 1970s as the French greens' "political nadir," in part because they were "wracked by internal divisions." Bess, *The Light-Green Society: Ecology and Technology in France, 1960–2000* (Chicago: University of Chicago Press, 2003), 104.

[7] Silke Mende, *"Nicht rechts, nicht links, sondern vorn." Eine Geschichte der Gründungsgrünen* (Munich: Oldenbourg Wissenschaftsverlag, 2011), 486.

the participatory potential of political environmentalism by displacing grassroots action as the essential symbol of anti-nuclear protest and giving citizens' nuclear concerns pride of place in high politics.

European Dreaming

Even as grassroots anti-nuclear activists organized campaigns to challenge local officials at the ballot box in the mid-1970s, other reactor opponents looked far beyond the local level – to Europe – for opportunities to build a more cooperative, more effective movement against nuclear energy. Europe had become a more attractive framework for environmentalists following the entrance of the United Kingdom, Denmark, and Ireland into the European Economic Community in 1973. Already in 1974, several long-established environmental NGOs formed the European Environmental Bureau (EEB) in Brussels in order to lobby European policymakers.[8] Two years later, in June 1976, five well-to-do environmentalists, including the Lancôme cosmetics heir Armand Petitjean, met in the South of France to plan a new organization that they called ECOROPA.[9] Inspired by the Club of Rome, ECOROPA's founders sought to build an Europe-wide network of elite environmentalists. Their idea was not unlike the ex-CDU parliamentarian Herbert Gruhl's proposal to create a national environmental party from the top-down under the guidance of well-known ecologists like the Frankfurt zoo director Bernhard Grzimek. Thus, in September 1977, at the same time as Carl Beddermann was organizing local chapters of the Green List for Environmental Protection in Lower Saxony, ECOROPA held its "founding colloquium" in Metz.[10] Leading members of several West German regional green lists and parties attended the colloquium and became co-founders of the new European group.[11]

---

[8] Jan-Henrik Meyer, "Challenging the Atomic Community: The European Environmental Bureau and the Europeanization of Anti-Nuclear Protest," in Wolfram Kaiser and Jan-Henrik Meyer, eds., *Social Actors in European Integration: Polity-Building and Policy-Making, 1958–1992* (Houndmills: Palgrave Macmillan, 2013), 202.

[9] ECOROPA, "History," www.ecoropa.info/history (last accessed 16 December 2015).

[10] On Beddermann, see: Anna Hallensleben, *Von der Grünen Liste zur Grünen Partei? Die Entwicklung der Grünen Liste Umweltschutz von ihrer Entstehung in Niedersachsen 1977 bis zur Gründung der Partei DIE GRÜNEN 1980* (Göttingen: Muster-Schmidt Verlag, 1984); see also Chapter 5.

[11] Christoph Becker-Schaum, "Die Grünen als Anti-Parteien Partei," paper presented at *Die Ökologie im rechten und linken Spektrum: Konvergenzen und Divergenzen zwischen Deutschland und Frankreich von den 1970er Jahren bis heute*, Universität des Saarlandes, Saarbrücken, 19 November 2015.

Environmentalists turned their attention to Europe at the same time as talk of better engaging citizens was gaining steam amongst Brussels "Eurocrats." The long-mooted idea of direct elections to the European Parliament interested both groups as a means of increasing European citizens' sense of inclusion in the distant EEC. Though the anti-nuclear activist and EEC official Petra Kelly had complained that plans for direct elections to the EP were "yellowing in Brussels desk drawers" as recently as 1975, those proposals were being discussed in earnest by 1977.[12] Within a year, EEC officials had come to an agreement to hold a direct election to the parliament by the end of the decade. Sensing an important opportunity to unite ecologists and change the EEC's direction, ECOROPA quickly advocated a Community-wide ecological campaign for seats in the European Parliament. The German physicist Manfred Siebker, who had become critical of nuclear energy through his work at Euratom in Brussels, was tasked with drafting the group's election manifesto.

Though the details of the EP election were still being ironed out in Brussels, ECOROPA was hardly alone in its eagerness to describe the poll as an important opportunity for European environmentalists. Leaders of West Germany's Federal Association of Citizens' Initiatives for Environmental Protection, which had long asserted its non-partisan status as an umbrella group for grassroots environmental initiatives, also promoted participation in the EP election in 1977. At a meeting in Bergisch-Gladbach, BBU Chairman Hans Günter Schumacher implored activists from ten countries that:

> It must be our task, indeed our duty, to draft an environmental program for the elections to the European parliament, to present it to the public, and to debate these issues . . . We must be there when it is time to build the Europe of the future.[13]

Schumacher's pronouncement painted the European election as something different – perhaps something more – than a traditional partisan political contest. He described the EP vote as a matchless opportunity to foster a more ecological Europe. Kelly and Vogt's declaration that the EP vote was an opportunity to stage "a decisive battle against nuclear power plants" showed that they, too, viewed the EP election as an unique

---

[12] Petra Kelly, "Europe . . . It is a little mainland of the south-east coast of Northern Ireland . . ." speech at the University of Coleraine (7 May 1975), 7. AGG PKA 533,4.

[13] Hans Günter Schumacher, "Verhältnis des Bundesverbandes Bürgerinitiativen Umweltschutz zu den Umweltparteien," in Rudolf Brun, ed., *Der Grüne Protest. Herausfoderung durch die Umweltparteien* (Frankfurt am Main: Fischer, 1978), 60.

opportunity with possibilities far beyond those of a normal, national electoral campaign. Even grassroots environmental groups became interested in the election to the distant European parliament. At a special April 1978 meeting in Kassel entitled "Citizens' Initiatives face the Elections," West German ecologists focused on the EP election, regardless of impending state elections in Hamburg, Lower Saxony, Bavaria, Hesse, West Berlin, and Schleswig-Holstein.[14]

The Democratic Movement for the Protection of Life (DLB), an obscure group created by the Action Community of Independent Germans in 1974 as part of that small, independent party's efforts to organize an environmental campaign for the Bundestag, went furthest in its efforts to promote the EP election. The DLB sought to use the upcoming election as an opportunity to unite the disparate green lists and parties competing in state elections into a single green electoral movement – within which it hoped to play a leadership role.[15] To this end, the DLB scheduled a "German Environmental Meeting" for June 1978, in the town of Troisdorf, fifteen kilometers outside of Bonn. Timed fortuitously to reap the excitement sown by the surprising results of the Lower Saxony and Hamburg campaigns but also to address the growing discord emanating from Hesse, where green lists and parties were competing against one another in the state election, the meeting was described by its organizers as an opportunity to "leave everything that divides us at home." Their goal was nothing less than the "'Copernican' change necessary to ensure the future of life on earth." But it was the organizers' call for an assembly of "the ecological movements of EUROPE," which they suggested would ensure that "they will see us and hear us in Bonn," that shaped their effort's short-term course.[16] In fact, the decision to describe the meeting as an "European" undertaking intended for the consumption of Bonn politicians suited the DLB's attempts to build common cause and form a more influential organization. "Europe" was an end-run around domestic politics that transcend squabbles amongst

---

[14] Some environmentalists, including many members of the BBU, ardently opposed the idea of a Green Party, regardless of what sort of elections it might contest. They feared for grassroots activists' independence and worried that as a political party, their ability to deconstruct power structures would be diminished. Mende, *"Nicht rechts, nicht links,"* 56–57.

[15] For more on the AUD's 1974 Bundestag campaign, see: Richard Stöss, *Vom Nationalismus zum Umweltschutz. Die Deutsche Gemeinschaft/Aktionsgemeinschaft Unabhängiger Deutscher im Parteiensystem der Bundesrepublik* (Opladen: Westdeutscher Verlag, 1980).

[16] Deutsches Umwelttreffen 1978, "Einladung. Die Stunde ist reif für ein großes Umwelttreffen!" [n.d. Spring 1978]. AGG Kerschgens 6. Emphasis from original.

competing green factions in states like Hesse, but also a potent weapon that could be aimed at Bonn politicians.

Despite the organizers' transnational framing of their "German Environmental Meeting," only a handful of activists from abroad came to Troisdorf. The gathering's European profile was provided primarily by ECOROPA members, including the Viennese Social Democrat Paul Blau and the Brussels-based activist Kelly. Though she was a West German citizen, Kelly had lived outside the FRG since she was twelve years old and thus become involved in West German politics from abroad.[17] From her perspective within the Brussels bureaucracy, which she believed was in need of urgent reform, Kelly eagerly argued that an insurgent EP campaign could reshape Europe. Her primary interest in Europe differed somewhat from DLB activists' plans to bring together West Germany's numerous green lists and parties into a single national organization by working first on the European level. Regardless of their divergent long-term goals, however, the activists assembled at Troisdorf agreed to set their course towards participation in the EP election. They elected a coordinating committee, laid plans to select a slate of West German candidates, and even initiated what proved to be a rather ineffectual search for partner organizations elsewhere in Western Europe.[18]

Bringing together all of the groups and individuals participating in green and alternative campaigns at the state level proved a difficult task, especially since some of them were campaigning against one another. Questions about the unusual European campaign caused additional challenges. The Communist League and the Socialist League/Socialist Office, which had contributed to the recent BuLi and GLU campaigns in Hamburg and Hesse respectively, were reticent to participate in the EP election.[19] Their lack of interest seemed to "separate" along ideological lines, "the bourgeois and conservative camp," which purportedly spearheaded the European project, from

---

[17] After attending high school and college in the United States during the 1960s, Kelly began a job with the EC in Brussels in 1971. Saskia Richter has written the first authoritative scholarly biography on Kelly. Richter, *Die Aktivistin. Das Leben der Petra Kelly* (Munich: Deutsche Verlags-Anstalt, 2010). On Kelly's transnational approach to politics, see also: Milder, "Thinking Globally, Acting (Trans-) Locally: Petra Kelly and the Transnational Roots of West German Green Politics," *Central European History* 43, no. 2 (June 2010): 301–326.

[18] Stephen Milder, "Between Grassroots Activism and Transnational Aspirations: Anti-Nuclear Protest from the Rhine Valley to the Bundestag, 1974–1983," *Historical Social Research* 39, no. 1 (2014): 201.

[19] Mende, "*Nicht rechts, nicht links,*" 52, 189.

Leftists who steered clear of it.[20] As in the Hessian election, however, the divide also pitted activists against one another on the basis of their visions of the electoral insurgency, and the importance they attributed to the formation of a single, centrally organized political party. Widely different ideas about Europe played a role, too. A press release by Hamburg's BuLi explained that its decision not to participate in the EP campaign was guided by the conviction that preparations for the 1980 Bundestag election were far more important.[21] Jutta Ditfurth, a self-described anti-EP Leftist, rejected the campaign for another reason. She argued that while "Europe" was of interest, "a European Parliament? . . . that was too distant and too mixed up in super-power thinking."[22] Though he supported green participation in the EP vote, the transnationally minded Hamburg activist Albert Taeger echoed Ditfurth's concerns, explaining that "the global basis for life can only be secured at the global level, not at the national and also not at the European level." He concluded that, "'Europe' is a dead end street unless it is conceived as an incubator, open on all sides, from the very beginning."[23]

Despite his misgivings about politics on a European scale, Taeger was convinced that "the European election [was] made to order" for the task of uniting the various Green lists and parties, which he believed, "cannot be melted together quickly enough." In contrast to a national election, the EP election had more flexible electoral rules and, Taeger argued, it would be acceptable to use a "still incomplete" program statement.[24] The looser frameworks Taeger emphasized proved essential for cooperation within the new organization. After a series of coordinating committee meetings throughout 1978 and early 1979, representatives of regional green lists, like the GLU-Lower Saxony and the Schleswig-Holstein Green List (GLSH), as well as Gruhl's Green Action Future, the longstanding AUD,

---

[20] Jutta Ditfurth, *Krieg, Atom, Armut. Was sie reden, was sie tun: Die Grünen* (Berlin: Rotbuch Verlag, 2011), 62.

[21] Bunte Liste-Wehrt Euch Hamburg, "Presserklärung: Ergebnis der Europa-Wahlen," 14 June 1979. AGG PKA 2553.

[22] Ditfurth, *Krieg, Atom, Armut*, 62.

[23] Albert Taeger, "Denkschrift" (25 January 1979). AGG Kerschgens 6.

[24] As part of the compromise that allowed for the direct election to the EP, each country was allowed to set its own rules for the contest. Both the French and West German governments set out electoral rules that differed from their rules for elections to their national parliaments. Roger Morgan and David Allen "The European Parliament: Direct Elections in National and Community Perspective," *The World Today* 34, no. 8: 396–302; and: Albert Taeger, "Denkschrift" (25 January 1979). AGG Kerschgens 6.

and members of ECOROPA, agreed to found the Alternative Political Association: The Greens (SPV) at a congress in Sindelfingen in March 1979.[25] The organization's "alternative" form took advantage of an exception to Germany's normal electoral law that allowed loose confederations to participate in the EP election alongside standard political parties.[26] Never intended to replace the regional lists and minor parties that comprised it, the SPV truly was an "alternative political association" – it had no formal structure beyond a federal board comprising representatives of the minor parties like AUD, GLU, and GAZ and organizations like ECOROPA that had come together to found it.[27]

Despite their debates over the meaning of the European elections, when it came to action the SPV's organizers were focused on domestic cooperation; they hardly looked beyond West Germany's borders. Nonetheless, ecological EP campaigns were also organized by Britain's Ecology Party and by the Flemish Agalev and the Walloon Ecolo in Belgium. The ECOROPA network, whose members had taken an active role in organizing a West German list, also helped to launch an ecological EP campaign in France. Like its German counterpart, the organization that French ecologists created in order to run for the European parliament was temporary and crafted with the specific requirements of the EP election in mind. As in West Germany, participating in the EP election required French activists to organize a national candidates' list. Since the French government had decided that the EP election would seats MEPs by proportional representation, campaigning for seats in the EP actually required more central coordination than typical French legislative elections, which were contested on a district-by-district basis.[28] To foster the necessary national coordination, French ecologists formed a new organization called Europe Ecologie (EE), which was comprised of regional groups like Nord Ecologie, Paris Ecologie, and Alsace's Ecology and Survival. At a coordinating meeting in Saint-Germain en Laye on 5 and 6 January 1979,

---

[25] In order to differentiate the Alternative Political Association – The Greens from the Green Party (which was founded a year later), I refer to it here simply as "the SPV."

[26] "Gesetz über die Wahl der Abgeordneten des Europäischen Parlaments aus der Bundesrepublik Deutschland (Europawahlgesetz—EuWG) von 16. Juni 1978," *Bundesgesetzblatt* 1978, Pt I: 709–717.

[27] Becker-Schaum, "Die Grünen als Anti-Parteien Partei."

[28] For the European election, the French government decided to use proportional representation rather than its usual single member district system. It also chose to enact a 5 percent threshhold for representation, like the one used in West German elections. "Loi no. 77–729 du 7 juillet 1977 relative à l'élection des représentants à l'Assemblée des communautés européennes," *Journal Officiel de la Republique Française* 3579 (8 July 1977).

representatives from the regional groups comprising EE agreed to draw up the required list of eighty-one candidates and endorsed a thirteen-point common platform. Despite this national coordination, which continued from a Paris office through the June election, pre-existing groups remained key players in the campaign. They ran the campaign in practice by nominating candidates to the national list, publicizing the campaign, and ensuring that local candidates' share of the 100,000 Franc deposit required by French electoral law was paid to a central account.[29]

In the mid-1970s, the idea of a direct election to the EP motivated a handful of activists to consider the potential of Europe as a framework for anti-nuclear and environmental action. At the end of the decade, once the election had been formally organized, the stakes changed significantly. Though the handful of activists engaged in ECOROPA continued to work across borders, most activists focused on the task at hand: organizing the sort of cooperation necessary to actually mount a campaign for the European Parliament. Because the election was actually nine separate national elections, each with its own unique set of rules, such coordination had to be carried out at the national level. Hence, even if transnationalism and dreams of creating a more environmentally friendly Europe, or stopping the proliferation of nuclear energy throughout the EEC motivated the first advocates of an ecological campaign for the European Parliament, the first step towards their goal was national organization. The "grassroots transnationalism(s)" that had proven so useful for the opponents of particular reactors proved incompatible with the sort of formal national organization required of participants in the elections to the European Parliament.[30] Nonetheless, when advocates of the EP campaign organized their candidates' lists and began to solicit the voters' support early in 1979, the beginning of preliminary work on the Gorleben nuclear waste facility in Lower Saxony and the partial reactor meltdown at Three Mile Island in Pennsylvania forced further reconsiderations of the appropriate scale for anti-nuclear protest and the sort of cooperation that activists should seek over wide spaces and across borders.

---

[29] Europe Écologie, "Compte-rendu de la réunion des 21 et 22 mai à Paris." SFP EE 1979.

[30] Andrew Tompkins, "Grassroots Transnationalism(s): Franco-German Opposition to Nuclear Energy in the 1970s," *Contemporary European History* 25, no. 1 (2016): 117–142. For further discussion of the workings of transnationalism in the Upper Rhine valley, see Chapter 2.

Questions of Scale: Towards National Significance
at Gorleben, Harrisburg, and Bonn

Rumors began circulating in 1976 that Gorleben, a village of some five-hundred inhabitants situated on a "peninsula" of Lower Saxon territory surrounded on three sides by East Germany, would be the site of the FRG's first facility for nuclear waste reprocessing and long-term storage.[31] The start of exploratory drilling on 14 March 1979, intended to make a final determination about an underground salt formation's suitability for long-term nuclear waste storage, reinvigorated questions about the relationship between grassroots activism, transnational thinking, and national politics. Over time, discussions about how to protest against the Gorleben facility caused significant changes in the way West German anti-nuclear activists framed their struggle. In the short run, exploratory drilling initiated local "demonstrations, church occupations, blockades, and other direct action protests."[32] Because the Gorleben facility would process and store the nuclear waste produced by reactors all over the FRG, however, the project came to be seen as a "a key term on which the future construction of nuclear reactors depends;" its political significance extended far beyond the rural district in which it was to be built.[33] Nonetheless, finding strategies fit for the national stage and defining the struggle over the remote Gorleben facility as a central matter of national politics proved difficult.

Because they emphasized the Gorleben facility's centrality to the West German nuclear program, activists' attempts to broaden the Gorleben struggle differed from the local transnationalism they had deployed on the Upper Rhine earlier in the decade. There was no question that any sort of radioactive emissions from the Gorleben facility, which was to be situated less than twenty kilometers from East German territory, would affect people living across the border. But collaborating with the affected population across the iron curtain was far more difficult than working with the "hereditary enemy" across the Rhine, since opportunities to cross the German–German border were all but non-existent in the late

---

[31] Lower Saxony's Premier, Ernst Albrecht, suggested in a November 1976 speech that a location in Lüchow-Dannenberg county (where Gorleben is located) was under consideration as the site of a nuclear facility. "SPD-Ortsverein Lüchow will Antwort von Albrecht," *Elbe-Jeetzel-Zeitung* (11 January 1977). Reprinted in Wolfgang Düver, ed., *Fünf Jahre Gorleben 1977–1981. Von der Standort-Benennung bis zum Zwischenlager* (Lüchow: Selbstverlag, 1983); see also: Dieter Rucht, *Von Wyhl nach Gorleben: Bürger gegen Atomprogramm und nukleare Entsorgung* (Munich: C. H. Beck, 1980), 99ff.

[32] Reimar Paul, . . . *und auch nicht anderswo! Die Geschichte der Antiatombewegung* (Göttingen: Verlag Die Werkstatt, 1997), 70.

[33] "Gorleben – ein Bericht aus dem Landkreis," *die tageszeitung*, Null-Nr. 1 (22 September 1978), 10.

1970s.[34] At the same time, as the sole West German facility that would process and store waste generated by nuclear power stations across the entire FRG, Gorleben had a different sort of translocal significance than did a particular nuclear reactor.

Despite the Gorleben facility's national profile, its opponents soon realized how difficult it would be to bring their struggle into the context of national politics. One problem was local opponents' strong desire to maintain control of protests taking place in their own backyard. After the failure of high-profile site occupation attempts at Brokdorf, Grohnde, and Malville in 1977, the Gorleben project's local opponents worried that an influx of "outside" protesters would jeopardize the grassroots movement that they had carefully nurtured since the first rumors about the waste processing facility arose in autumn 1976.[35] Though activists in the sparsely populated area around Gorleben, known as the Wendland, had grown their movement from 25 to 250 members within a single year, they remained hard pressed to win the active engagement of many local people in 1979 when the preliminary work began. Concerns about cooperation with outside groups, particularly those believed to be interested in "militant resistance" were paramount in discussions about joining the local anti-Gorleben campaign.[36]

Efforts to coordinate the Gorleben struggle across a wider space took place at meetings of the Federal Congress of Reactor Opponents, the same group which had struggled to reach national consensus on protests at Brokdorf in 1977. Delegates to the Federal Congress's February 1979 meeting in Brunswick agreed to organize a week-long tractor caravan from the rural construction site to Lower Saxony's capital, Hanover. Local activists accepted the solution because they felt it would coordinate local and national opposition to the project without bringing outsiders to Gorleben.[37] The 160-kilometer trek was timed to end as public hearings on the project began in Hanover, thus enabling protesters from Gorleben to attend the hearings.[38] In addition to the Federal Congress of Reactor

---

[34] Andrew Tompkins has nonetheless shown how West German protesters found ways of "playing with the border" near Gorleben, by protesting on the narrow strip of East German territory beyond the border fortifications, for example. Tompkins, "Grassroots Transnationalism(s)," 133. Astrid Eckert's forthcoming book, *West Germany and the Iron Curtain* also takes up Gorleben's relationship to the German–German border.

[35] In fact, the local campaign against the facility, which began as soon as the first rumors that Gorleben would be chosen, had its roots in an earlier citizens' initiative, which had been organized already in 1973 amidst rumors that a nuclear reactor might be sited outside the nearby village of Langendorf. Rucht, *Von Wyhl nach Gorleben*, 115.

[36] Ibid., 118.   [37] Zint, "Und auch nicht anderswo," 70.

[38] "Sternmarsch nach Hannover," *die tageszeitung*, 8 March 1979.

Opponents, the trek received national support from the nascent SPV Die Grünen, which called on "all of our members and all sympathetic organizations" to take part.[39] Nonetheless, the 5,000 participants in the Trek's opening rally at the village of Gedelitz near Gorleben came from the Wendland, not across the country.[40] Supporters from elsewhere were expected to join the trek along the way and to take part in a mass rally in Hanover, but it remained to be seen how effectively the action could bridge the divide between local and national action.

The trek's national political significance changed dramatically halfway between Gorleben and Hanover. On 28 March 1979, three days after the trekkers had left Gorleben, Reactor Two at the Three Mile Island nuclear facility near Harrisburg, Pennsylvania underwent a partial meltdown.[41] The TMI disaster, which immediately made headlines across Western Europe, forced Europeans to consider the fact that a nuclear disaster was possible in the West.[42] Petra Kelly understood the accident as a warning that "an explosion in the planned integrated reprocessing center in Gorleben would mean the evacuation of all of Central Europe."[43] In additional to stoking Europeans' nuclear fears, TMI gave activists new ways of describing the transnational nature of the nuclear danger, which had the potential to cause "changes to economic, political, and military strategy on a global scale," and thus to influence European states' nuclear programs.[44] The concerns raised by TMI translated directly into support for the Gorleben trek. By the time the procession reached Hanover on Sunday, 31 March, its ranks had swelled to include more than 100,000

---

[39] Die Grünen – Alternative für Europe, "Presseerklärung zum Treck [sic] nach Hannover," 26 March 1979. AGG PKA 2555.

[40] Paul, "Und auch nicht anderswo," 70.

[41] On the accident and its causes, see: J. Samuel Walker, *Three Mile Island: A Nuclear Crisis in Historical Perspective* (Berkeley: University of California Press, 2004), 71–101.

[42] Reports that the accident led to the discharge of radioactive steam as well as tens of thousands of liters of water "with a radioactivity eight times the deadly level" was the lead story in the next morning's news. Daniela Zetti, "Three Mile Island und Kaiseraugst. Die Auswirkungen des Störfalls im US-Kernkraftwerk Harrisburg 1979 auf das geplante KKW Kaiseraugst," in *Preprints zur Kulturgeschichte der Technik* 13 (2001): 5. The accident was the cover story of the next issue of *Der Spiegel*. "Alptraum Atomkraft. Nach der Reaktorunfall von Harrisburg," *Der Spiegel*, 9 April 1979. On the TMI accident's echo in the world press and its effects in several European countries (including the FRG), see: Frank Bösch, "Taming Nuclear Power: The Accident near Harrisburg and the Change in West German and International Nuclear Policy in the 1970s and early 1980s," forthcoming in *German History* 35, no. 2 (2017).

[43] Petra Kelly, "Harrisburg oder die Evakuierung Mitteleuropas" (Press release), 3 April 1979. AGG PKA 2555.

[44] "Harrisburg USA!" *die tageszeitung*, 2 April 1979. Bösch charts the ways that TMI did, indeed, shift nuclear policy in the FRG in particular in the realm of safety regulations for nuclear plants. Bösch, "Taming Nuclear Power."

concerned West Germans.[45] With "opponents of nuclear power arriving from every direction by bus, train, and automobile," the alternative newspaper *die tageszeitung* (*taz*) reported that Hanover was about to "burst at the seams." The main column of the demonstration, which was now ten kilometers in length, was so long that the last activists, waiting outside of the city, "had not even begun to march" by the time the head of the march had arrived at the site of the final demonstration in central Hanover.[46] Overnight, the far-off TMI accident dramatically broadened the significance of the locally rooted anti-Gorleben protest as concerns related to the American nuclear disaster motivated West Germans to participate.

Nonetheless, the disaster at TMI did not reframe the Gorleben struggle as a global protest campaign. Ardent transnationalists had advocated "European" participation in the Gorleben Hearings even before TMI in order to emphasize the nuclear threat's transcendence of national borders. But others, focused on national political issues, began to see the introduction of "Europe" into such focused proceedings as "as only a distraction."[47] Far from bolstering the transnationalists' position, the TMI accident boosted efforts to nationalize the anti-nuclear movement. Barely a month after the disaster, in early May 1979, the Federal Congress of Reactor Opponents sought to capitalize on the "favorable situation in Harrisburg" by quickly organizing another mass protest. Local opponents of the Gorleben project, who were eager to keep outside activists away from the Wendland proposed that such a mass protest be held in a political center. Having already paid a "visit to [Premier] Albrecht in Hanover," they convinced the delegates that "it was time to call on [Chancellor] Schmidt in Bonn."[48] In their push to keep outsiders away, local activists even asked that a planned anti-nuclear "summer camp," be moved from Gorleben to the center of Hamburg because "it's better to show alternative ways of life in a big city."[49]

[45] Wolfgang Ehmke, "Der Gorlebenkonflikt: Geschichte wird gemacht," in Paul, . . . *und auch nicht anderswo* (see note 32), 185. The *taz* deemed the demonstration the largest in West Germany since the anti-rearmament protests of the 1950s. "140.000," *die tageszeitung*, 2 April 1979.

[46] "140.000," *die tageszeitung*, 2 April 1979.

[47] Helmut Lippelt to Petra Kelly and Manfred Siebker, 12 February 1979. AGG PKA 2552.

[48] "Wir wollen alles jetzt und anderswo," *die tageszeitung*, 8 May 1979.

[49] "Gorleben—wie geht der Widerstand weiter?" *die tageszeitung*, 4 May 1979. The Congress also voted to hold a mass protest in Gorleben immediately after construction began, but that decision was taken over the objections of local anti-Gorleben groups, whose chairwoman walked out of the meeting in protest. The contested decision evidenced reactor opponents' continuing inability to easily incorporate grassroots protest into a unified, translocal movement. Paul, . . . *und auch nicht anderswo*, 74. "Wir wollen alles jetzt und anderswo" *die tageszeitung*, 8 May 1979.

The Bonn anti-nuclear protest was scheduled for October 1979. The demonstration evidenced an important change in the way reactor opponents portrayed the nuclear issue's place in national politics, since it focused activists' efforts onto the seat of West Germany's government, not a provincial nuclear site. Relocating from the provinces to the FRG's political power center allowed anti-nuclear activists to emphasize national policy rather than individual power stations, and thus to portray nuclear energy as a more ubiquitous, if less concrete, threat. At the same time as it targeted government officials, the Bonn protest took on a distinctly West German identity.[50] In contrast to major West German cities like Hamburg, West Berlin, or Frankfurt, which had gained international notoriety as sites of protest during the student movement, Bonn remained a sleepy university town whose provincial image was well-suited to the myth that the FRG was a "political dwarf."[51] With 150,000 participants, the October 1979 anti-nuclear demonstration was easily the largest protest yet to occur in West Germany's "provisional" capital.[52]

Because it fit so nicely into national frameworks, global action simply did not come across as the primary focus of the Bonn demonstration. "Large groups" of activists from France, Austria, Switzerland, Holland, and England were treated by the press as curiosities rather than evidence of the protest's legitimacy. American perspectives were provided by Kathy McCaughin of Harrisburg, who spoke about the TMI disaster, and Herb Petchford, "an Indian from the USA" who told of native people's

---

[50] Holger Nehring has argued that Bonn was a contested site of protest in the early days of the FRG, since protesting there implicitly acknowledged German division. Nehring, *The Politics of Security: British and West German Peace Movements and the Early Cold War, 1945–1970* (Oxford: Oxford University Press, 2013), 201 and 203. The FRG's "provisional capital" really only began to gain pride of place as a site of activism with the May 1968 demonstration against the emergency laws.

[51] On this idea and its problems by 1979, see: "An interview with *The Economist*," in Wolfram F. Hanrieder, ed., *Helmut Schmidt: Perspectives on Politics* (Boulder: Westview Press, 1982), 209.

[52] The anti-nuclear energy protest became the model for a series of anti-nuclear weapons demonstrations that took place in Bonn during the early 1980s. Some earlier antiwar protests (including a 1 September 1979, World Peace Day, protest entitled "Secure Peace, end the nuclear arms race!") were held in Bonn. But despite growing discussions of the missile gap between Eastern and Western Europe, even the 1979 World Peace Day protest attracted only 40,000 participants, making the October 1979 anti-nuclear energy protest the first Bonn demonstration to be counted amongst the largest demonstrations in West German history. Rüdiger Schmitt, *Die Friedensbewegung in der Bundesrepublik Deutschland. Ursachen und Bedingungen der Mobilisierung einer neuen sozialen Bewegung* (Opladen: Westdeutscher Verlag, 1990), 14. On the relationship between the movement against nuclear energy and the peace movement, see: Silke Mende and Birgit Metzger, "Ökopax. Die Umweltbewegung als Erfahrungsraum der Friedensbewegung," in Christoph Becker-Schaum, ed., *Entrüstet Euch! Nuklearkrise, NATO Doppelbeschluss und Friedensbewegung* (Paderborn: Schöningh, 2012).

"resistance against uranium mining." The Americans' speeches were a reminder that the far-off TMI accident had prompted the protest in the first place. But all of the other speakers focused on the protest's central demand, that Chancellor Schmidt stop the West German nuclear program. That demand had very little to do with the people living in Harrisburg and everything to do with the sense that TMI meant such an accident could occur in the FRG – and that only Chancellor Schmidt's government could prevent such an accident from occurring. As the Bonn demonstration evidenced, the far-off accident had provided common ground for West German activists and helped transcended the distinctions between national politics and local concern. For similar reasons, the transnationally imagined green campaign for the European parliament, which also hit its stride in the spring of 1979, advanced the nationalization of anti-nuclear protest in the FRG further still.

European Elections, Local Issues, Domestic Goals

Pro-European rhetoric and meetings amongst candidates from across the EEC suggested that ecologists' campaign for the European Parliament was a transnational enterprise, but in reality the effort comprised a group of distinct campaigns, each one organized on the national level. ECOROPA members like Petra Kelly and Solange Fernex, who became the campaign's figureheads in West Germany and France respectively, saw the EP campaign as a prefigurative effort that could create a more ecologically friendly Europe. These activists controlled the campaign's rhetoric, but other activists shaped it on the ground. In France, regional organizations like Paris Ecologie and Ecology and Survival carried out the campaign work in the cities and villages. They tailored the campaign to particular local issues. Yet, in West Germany, where veteran minor party activists were motivated by their desire to create a new, national umbrella organization comprising their own parties, the ecological candidates' lists, members of the citizens' initiatives, and even "the ecological minorities in the establishment parties," a national focus developed.[53] The competing approaches in France and West Germany, but also the internal competition that pitted the transnationally minded lead candidates against the bulk of the campaigners in both countries, raised an important question about the relationship between local, national, and European politics: was it in

---

[53] "Protokoll der 2. Sitzung des Bundeskoordinierungsausschusses (BKA) des Umwelttreffens in Troisdorf" (undated). AGG PKA 2551.

fact possible to carry out a transnational electoral campaign on the basis of local engagement, within national political frameworks, and before the backdrop of debates over Europe's future as a site of ecological politics?

The lead campaigners, Kelly and Fernex, saw the campaign as an opportunity to prefigure a new, more ecologically friendly Europe. When she was elected to head SPV Die Grünen's list of candidates, Kelly informed friends and colleagues across the EEC that she was running in order to "speak up for a decentralized, non-nuclear, non-military and gentle Europe – a Europe of the Regions and of the People." She pledged, furthermore, to do so "without the usual party machinery . . . even without motor cars."[54] Fernex, Kelly's counterpart in France, went on an indefinite hunger strike to protest unfair electoral rules and the insufficient public discussion of the TMI disaster.[55] Within days, Kelly had put together a press release from the SPV's Bonn office, declaring her organization's solidarity with Fernex and seeking funds in West Germany in order to help EE raise the 100,000 Franc deposit required to secure their place on the ballot.[56] Thinking outside the national framework, and open to challenging common approaches to electoral campaigning, Kelly and Fernex sought to model a new Europe that would be a motor for environmental protection and progressive change.

Kelly and Fernex's familiarity with activists from all over Western Europe, enabled them to conceive a "nonviolent Europe . . . of the people, the regions, and the minorities" as a realistic goal, not an empty phrase.[57] In early April, the duo met in Brussels for a press conference with other candidates from the SPV and Europe Ecologie, as well as candidates from Belgium's Agalev, the Italian and Dutch radical parties, and the chairman of the British Ecology Party.[58] Two additional press conferences brought together female candidates from all of these parties, who

[54] Petra Kelly to Dear Friends and Comrades, 24 March 1979. AGG PKA 540,6.
[55] Solange Fernex, "Declaration." AGG PKA 953. The fast was one of the few elements of the French ecologists' campaign that German activists noticed. See, for example: Helmbrecht von Mengershausen (GAZ Bayern) to Liebe Freunde, 13 June 1979. AGG PKA 2553.
[56] Petra Kelly, Roland Vogt, Eva Quistorp, "An alle, die es angeht!" 10 May 1979. AGG PKA 2555.
[57] Elisabeth Schulthess, *Solange l'insoumise: écologie, féminisme, non-violence* (Barret-sur-Méouge: Y. Michel, 2004), 111. Eva Quistorp, a West German anti-nuclear activist and feminist whom Kelly had recruited to the SPV's List, felt that the campaign built on connections she had developed with Fernex and other French ecologists earlier in the decade. Ute, "Ein grünes, lila, buntes Europa," *die tageszeitung*, 4 May 1979.
[58] The press conference was hosted by ECOROPA, and included eight German Green candidates in addition to candidates and party officials from elsewhere in Europe. ECOROPA to Sehr geehrte Damen und Herren, 28 March 1979. AGG PKA 954. See also: "Die Kandidaten zur Europawahl 1979," picture taken 3 April 1979. AGG FO-01331-02-cp. The Dutch and Italian radicals had pledged to caucus together with the Greens if elected to parliament.

Figure 6.1 Green candidates for the European Parliament from across the EEC convene for a press conference in Brussels. Petra Kelly, standing fourth from left. Solange Fernex, seated third from left. © AGG. FO-01331-02-cp.

announced an ecological women's program. With women serving as lead candidates in France, West Germany, and the United Kingdom, the ecological campaign for the EP did seem – from a bird's eye perspective, at least – aligned with Kelly's vision of an effort to transform the "crisis-producing" EEC by flooding the European Parliament with "counter-forces" including "women, feminists, regionalists, anti-nuclear activists and draft resisters, members of citizens' initiatives, eco-socialists, [and] federalists."[59]

Despite Kelly and Fernex's European dreams, the EP campaign was not waged solely as an effort to overwhelm the Strasbourg parliament and remake Europe. While Kelly and Fernex criss-crossed the EEC, advocating an alternative Europe and marshaling the continent's "counter-forces,"

[59] Petra Kelly to "Liebe Freundinnen und Freunde," 27 April 1979. AGG PKA 954. On the prevalence of female lead candidates, see: Yves Frémion, *Histoire de la révolution écologiste* (Paris: Hoëbeke, 2007), 147.

others coordinated the various national campaigns and organized the grassroots activists who hung election posters, staffed information stands, and passed out pamphlets in their hometowns. Despite even the lead campaigners' influence in the national offices of EE and SPV Die Grünen, therefore, the two women did not hold a monopoly of power in either organization.[60] Instead, they shared control of the campaigns with activists interested primarily in local issues and the fate of pre-existing organizations. In the end, competing approaches and goals affected the campaigns' direction even more fundamentally than did the lead candidates' grandiose pro-European rhetoric and prefigurative conduct on the campaign trail.

Since local concerns were the connective tissue that brought together various regional environmental organizations as Europe Ecologie, the French ecologists' "European" campaign emphasized local distinctions. Even the campaign literature differed from region to region. Though many locally distributed flyers used the same centrally produced text, they did so in a way that seemed locally influenced. In each region or department, campaign flyers were printed on the letterhead of a particular local group. In describing the list of candidates, the flyers highlighted local activists over nationally known environmentalists. Prominent references to "our region," made the text seem locally distinct even though it had been mass-produced.[61] In some regions, Europe Ecologie's supporters went further and wrote their own texts in order to focus exclusively on local issues. In Franche-Comté, for example, the Anti-Canal Committee (Comité de Liaison Anti-Canal) was EE's local affiliate. It circulated flyers explaining the environmental impact of the Rhine–Rhône canal's ongoing expansion, and called on its supporters to vote for Europe Ecologie as a form of resistance against the project.[62] Though EE's strong regional accents made its demands for a Europe of the regions credible, they also downplayed the importance of Europe itself, since it remained unclear why

---

[60] Along with her friend and fellow Young European Federalist Roland Vogt, who held the second place on the West German list, Kelly made more than fifty stump speeches, managed the SPV's Bonn office, and served as the campaign's press secretary. Roland Vogt, "Bericht zur Bundesgeschäftsstelle" [undated; presumably June/July 1979]. AGG PKA 2553. Saskia Richter writes that "Petra Kelly was lead candidate, personal assistant and secretary all in one." Richter, *Die Aktivistin*, 182. Likewise, in addition to her role as lead candidate, Fernex served as EE's secretary. See: SFP EE.

[61] See, for example: Écologie et Survie, "Ce que tout le monde voit," (undated election flyer). CIRE K6 EELV Box 2.

[62] Comité de Liaison Anti-Canal, "L'Europe actuelle est celle qui cherche a imposer le Grand Canal a la Franche-Comté. Europe Écologie combat pour une autre Europe" (undated election flyer). CIRE K6 EELV Box 2.

problems caused by the Paris government, and particular to Franche-Comté, ought to be resolved by the weak EP.

In West Germany, in contrast, local campaigners emphasized the national significance of their work. The campaign in Baden-Württemberg's Breisgau district, where resistance to the Wyhl reactor had first developed, exemplified the way in which activists used their efforts to push for national unity. Nine activists ran the SPV's campaign in the Breisgau. None of them had been deeply engaged in the struggle at Wyhl, but eight had previously been members of minor parties, like the AUD. Their history of party-political activism informed their approach to the campaign, but also allowed them to access material support. Georg Otto, who was in charge of disbursing the GLU-Lower Saxony's 1978 campaign reimbursements to activists throughout the FRG, sent 100,000 DM worth of posters and other campaign materials to individuals in the AUD's Baden-Württemberg membership directory.[63]

Emphasis on forming an united national party was hardly limited to Baden-Württemberg. In Hesse, Karl Kerschgens, an AUD activist and member of SPV Die Grünen's federal board, consoled anxious campaigners by asking them to think ahead to the 1980 Bundestag election rather than focusing on the European Parliament.[64] "Many of us," he wrote to colleagues who were organizing the EP campaign in towns across the state, "needed to give ourselves a little push in order to get going despite the general disinclination towards the European elections." Yet, he reasoned, "if we want to have a meaningful campaign in the next Bundestag election, we need to get every possible vote this time around."[65] Similarly, one Hamburg activist described the process of drafting a program for the European election as an invaluable opportunity to hash out the party's federal election program an entire year before the next Bundestag election.[66] Perhaps the biggest inducement for domestically focused activists was the West German government's campaign reimbursement scheme, which would pay each party 3.50 DM per vote received – money that would likely far exceed the SPV's expected outlays for the EP campaign

---

[63] Georg Otto to Die Bundesverband DIE GRÜNEN und die Landeswahlausschüsse, 4 April 1979. AGG Ba-Wü 109. For more on Otto and his role in the founding of Lower Saxony's GLU, see: Chapter 5.

[64] Richard Stöss, *Vom Nationalismus zum Umweltschutz*, 277.

[65] Karl Kerschgens to Freundinnen und Freunde aus der grünen und alternativen Bewegung, 6 May 1979. AGG Kerschgens 10.

[66] Helmut Lippelt to Mitglieder des Programmausschusses, 9 January 1979. AGG Kerschgens 10.

Figure 6.2 Supporters of SPV Die Grünen campaign for the European Parliament
in the Bavarian city of Passau. © AGG. FO-01653-04-cp.

and could thus become a war chest for future campaigns, including the
fast-approaching 1980 Bundestag campaign.[67]

The distinct ways in which each group cast the EP campaign – whether as a
means of building a new Europe, a chance to further particular local or regional
interests, or an opportunity to garner reimbursement funds and build national
party infrastructure – was embodied in their proposals for the campaign's
platform. In France, the balance between the interests of pre-existing local
groups and national coordination was struck relatively early. Locally organized
groups conducted the campaign autonomously in each region. Europe
Ecologie's eighty-one candidates were only required to agree to a thirteen-
point platform that contained concise goals, like the "abandonment of civil and
military nuclear technology." Because specific laws or political frameworks
were not mentioned in the common platform, the goals it advocated could just

[67] "Gesetz über die Wahl der Abgeordneten des Europäischen Parlaments aus der Bundesrepublik
Deutschland (Europawahlgesetz—EuWG) von 16. Juni 1978," *Bundesgesetzblatt* 1978, Pt I: 709–717.

as easily be tailored to local struggles as they could be articulated as European objectives. The national level, however, was downplayed since the program called for the "progressive abandonment of the prerogatives of the nation-state in favor of the citizen, the community, and the region."[68]

In contrast to EE's loose thirteen-point platform, which fit on a single page, SPV Die Grünen drafted a detailed fourteen-page election manifesto. The German Greens' program certainly differed from the establishment parties' programs in that it opened with a statement proclaiming that the future of Europe "must be shaped by ecology rather than economy" and concluded with an appeal for a "nonviolent and peaceful Europe." Nonetheless, its primary focus was on technical demands, such as a call for farmers' subsistence to be guaranteed via "a direct income payment independent of production, with a related system of premiums if the principles of ecological agricultural are followed."[69] In contrast to Europe Ecologie's general and malleable demands, SPV Die Grünen's precise program appeared to be almost a rough draft of a parliamentary election manifesto, just as the Hamburg activist who advocated participation in the European campaign had earlier proposed.

Both programs contrasted starkly with the radical, pro-European program advocated by the SPV's lead candidate, Petra Kelly. When the SPV's board met to begin discussions of the platform, Kelly was in the midst of a campaign swing through "Kiel, Gorleben, Nijmegen, Nuremburg, Brussels, Deggendorf, Passau, etc." Unable to attend the meeting, the perturbed lead candidate called on the board to adopt as the core of its program six theses that she and her friend Roland Vogt had discussed with ecologists elsewhere in Europe. Strongly influenced by ECOROPA's Manifesto for an Ecological Europe, Kelly and Vogt's six points concluded with a call to "progressively abolish" Europe's nation-states and replace the EEC with an "ecological democracy."[70] In Kelly's eyes, adopting the six-point program would prove the campaign's radical vision and the campaigners' commitment to EEC-wide cooperation. After all, Kelly informed the platform's would-be framers:

> At the international level we simply must have platform points that everyone can accept. The ones Roland and I have worked out are in agreement with those of the French, the Dutch, and the Italians.[71]

[68] Europe Écologie, "Plate forme des candidats," (undated campaign flyer). CIRE K6 EELV Box 4.
[69] Die Grünen, "Die Grünen: Alternative für Europa," undated [1979].
[70] No author [likely Petra Kelly or Petra Kelly and Roland Vogt], "Programmthesen der Gemeinsamen europäischen Plattform für eine ökologische Demokratie," undated [Spring 1979]. AGG PKA 954.
[71] Petra Kelly to Vorstand "Der Grünen" (undated). AGG PKA 2552.

Since the SPV's board was also seeking to forge a compromise between many actors, Kelly's angry letter raised a pertinent question about which "everyone" the SPV ought to take into account. While Kelly was in conversation with colleagues elsewhere in Europe, the SPV's leadership was struggling to maintain fragile compromises between the various minor parties that comprised it.

The need to forge compromises within the national organizations clearly won the day. In fact, the French and German programs contained within them the seeds of the distinctive, but nationally organized, French and German Green parties of the 1980s. While the French emphasized local and regional distinctions and relied on temporary cooperation, the Germans quickly outlined an united national party that proved capable of holding together in the 1980 and 1983 Bundestag campaigns. The neglected radical six-point program advocated by Kelly, in contrast, represented the continuation of 1970s ecologists' transnational thinking and even dreams for an alternative Europe. Since it proved impossible to think in European terms, act locally, and organize at the national level, the first direct elections to the European parliament both provided the opportunity for national cooperation and caused the bold ideas represented by Kelly's program to fall into neglect.

Europe and the Varieties of National Party Organization

Commentators were underwhelmed by the results of the June 1979 EP election, which seemed not to have excited Europeans. Though 86 percent of eligible voters went to the polls in Italy, turnout was only 66 percent in West Germany and 62 percent in France. In some parts of the EEC, barely 30 percent of eligible voters cast ballots.[72] The journalist Indro Montanelli explained in *Der Spiegel* that the EEC's "soft underbelly," had outperformed the rest of the Community in voter turnout because his countrymen, the "lazy Italians," were concerned about the unsteady state of their democracy and saw every election, including the EP vote, as a potential fundamental crisis.[73] In other member-states, the election was perceived as anything but fundamental; it seemed instead to be a superfluous poll of the major parties' support between national elections. Precisely because it was taken so lightly by the voters, West Germany's new alternative newspaper *die tageszeitung* complained that the vote would have serious consequences

---

[72] "Ergebnis der Europa-Wahlen," *die tageszeitung* (12 June 1979).
[73] "Die Anarchie kennt keine Regeln," *Der Spiegel* (18 June 1979).

in national politics. Specifically, the election's results would pour a combined 145 million Marks of campaign reimbursement funds into the depleted coffers of the CDU, the SPD, and the F.D.P. – just 18 months before the 1980 Bundestag election.[74]

The results were particularly disappointing for EE and the SPV. Already in April, polls had predicted that Europe Ecologie would receive more than 5 percent of the vote and thus win seats in parliament.[75] SPV Die Grünen was also hopeful that it would jump the 5 percent hurdle. Campaigners prepared to celebrate the conclusion of the long campaign with an "unconventional sleepover" at their Bonn headquarters.[76] But the voters gave neither EE nor the SPV much to celebrate on election night. The problems of low voter turnout and the bonanza the election provided for the major parties were compounded by the ecologists' own results of 3.2 percent for the SPV in West Germany and 4.4 percent for EE in France. Activists could boast of having won nearly 1 million votes in each country, but since electoral laws in both countries required a list to receive 5 percent of the vote in order to be represented in parliament, no green candidates won seats in Strasbourg. The campaigners, and especially the lead candidates, were bitterly disappointed.

Though they seemed lackluster to the frustrated campaigners, the results of the European election marked a major turning point in the development of green politics. Because neither the SPV nor Europe Ecologie had won any seats in Strasbourg, Roland Vogt could only imagine the pan-European green parliamentary delegation of "certainly more than ten representatives" that he believed ought to be on its way to parliament.[77] In fact, a total of nine MEPs had been elected from insurgent groups like

[74] "Ergebnis der Europa-Wahlen," *die tageszeitung*, 12 June 1979. The three established parties, all of which had been struggling with their finances earlier in the decade, benefited enormously from the campaign, since each had spent much less on the campaign than the amount they were reimbursed. Thomas Drysch, *Parteienfinanzierung. Österreich, Schweiz, Bundesrepublik Deutschland* (Wiesbaden: Springer, 1998), 126.

[75] According to a Eurobarometer poll conducted in early April, Europe Ecologie would receive 5.9 percent of the vote, and SPV Die Grünen 1.4 percent. Eurobarometer 11 (April 1979), "Year of the Child in Europe."

[76] Petra Kelly and Dorothea Wieczorek to Liebe Freunde, "Einladung an die Vorstandsmitglieder und Kandidaten der GRÜNEN," 6 June 1979. AGG Kerschgens 10.

[77] "Stellungnahme von Roland Vogt zum Wahlergebnis," *die tageszeitung*, 12 June 1979. The delegation finally materialized in 1984, when Die Grünen won seven seats, the Dutch Green Progressive Accord won two, and the two Belgian parties, Ecolo and Agalev, each won a single seat. Elizabeth E. Bomberg, *Green Parties and Politics in the European Union* (New York: Routledge, 1998), 86. The German Constitutional Court declared a hurdle to representation "unconstitutional" for the European elections in 2014. "Dreiprozenthürde bei Europawahl ist verfassungswidrig," *Die Zeit*, 26 February 2014.

Italy's Partido Radical, the Netherlands' Democracy '66, and Denmark's anti-EEC party, all of whom had announced willingness to cooperate with the EE and the SPV before the elections. But only the Italian Radicals prioritized cooperation with the excluded ecologists after the vote. In a sign of international solidarity, three newly elected Radical MEPs marched through Strasbourg alongside 500 supporters of the SPV and Europe Ecologie when the parliament opened on 16 July 1979.[78] But the transnational coalition was tested by the election's results; it seemed to fray at the entrance to the parliament's plenary hall in the Palace of Europe. After the Radicals, who were about to participate in the parliament's constitutive session, reneged on their pledge to form a human chain with the unelected French and German "legitimate deputies" and block the plenary hall's entrance, two French and two German candidates sullenly made their way to seats the Italians had reserved for them in the press balcony.[79] While the Radicals voiced opposition to the electoral procedures that had excluded EE and the SPV from the floor, the French and German activists unfurled a banner protesting their exclusion from the parliament on account of the "undemocratic and anti-European five percent hurdle." The Parliament proved impervious to the counter-forces' assault. The Italians' complaints went unanswered and the French and Germans' banner was promptly confiscated.[80]

Ecologists' inability to make themselves heard in the plenary hall sapped the EP's potency as a forum for promoting the new, ecological Europe the campaigners had set out to achieve. As a result, the transnationalists' influence over their parties began to fade. The Italians remained committed to cooperation with their French and German colleagues, but their privileged position as parliamentarians made the relationship difficult. Despite their surprisingly similar results in terms of votes received, even the SPV and EE were divided by the election's results. The Germans' 893,683 votes entitled them to 4.8 million DM in campaign reimbursement funds.[81] Far from entitling the French ecologists to funding, EE's 888,134 votes actually forced the group to forfeit its 100,000 Franc deposit, since

---

[78] The street protest foreshadowed Die Grünen's triumphant procession into the Bundestag four years later. On Kelly's love of symbolic action, see: Richter, *Die Aktivistin*, 245–247 and 253.

[79] Roland Vogt, interview with Christoph Becker-Schaum and Robert Camp, 29–30 March 2012, 58.

[80] Solange Fernex to Cher Amis, 26 July 1979. SFP EE 1979; see also: J. P. Vesper, Colmar, Photograph. AGG FO-01702-01-rp.

[81] Detlef Murphy, "Politischer Protest und strukturelle Korruption – Die GRÜNEN und die staatliche Parteienfinanzierung," in Göttrik Wewer, ed., *Parteifinanzierung und politischer Wettbewerb. Rechtsnormen – Realanalysen – Reformvorschläge* (Opladen: Westdeutscher Verlag, 1990), 298.

Figure 6.3 Petra Kelly and Solange Fernex protest in the gallery of the European Parliament's Plenary Hall in Strasbourg during the Parliament's constitutive session on 16 July 1979. AGG. FO-01702-02-cp

Figure 6.4 The conclusion of the Gorleben Trek in central Hanover. © Günther Zint.

only lists scoring more than 5 percent of the vote were entitled to their deposit's return.[82] Kelly and Vogt helped alleviate EE's sudden financial crisis by convincing the SPV's federal board to donate 100,000 Franc to the EE's debt retirement campaign, but the transfer was among the two Germans' last transnational successes, and did not fully erase EE's debt, which also included the actual costs of running the campaign. The SPV federal board's decision to open an European office in Strasbourg, taken at the same meeting and also at Kelly and Vogt's behest, actually finalized the transnationalists' isolation.[83] By October 1979, Vogt was managing the new Strasbourg office and Kelly had left for Brussels, where she had returned to her day job at the EEC and continued organizing European contacts for the German SPV.[84] A steady stream of correspondence came to the SPV's Bonn headquarters from Kelly's desk, and Vogt distributed frequent, lengthy reports on his activities in Strasbourg to the party's federal board; but the two transnationalists' withdrawal across the Rhine distanced them from the regular deliberations of the SPV's federal board – the ongoing importance of which had been insured by its control of the campaign reimbursement funds.[85]

For both EE and the SPV, in fact, the results of the election paved a path away from European dreams and towards national politics. Paying off the remainder of its debt and changing the electoral rules that prevented it from being seated in Brussels became Europe Ecologie's raison d'être. Already on the eve of the election, EE's leadership began concluding its fundraising letters with the phrase: "Europe Ecologie is you," in an apparent attempt to increase ecologists' identification with the temporary national organization and not just the local and regional groupings it comprised.[86] As part of their prolonged efforts to change the electoral

[82] "Loi no. 77–729 du 7 juillet 1977 relative à l'élection des représentants à l'Assemblée des communautés européennes" *Journal Officiel de la Republique Française* 3579 (8 July 1977).

[83] Petra K. Kelly, "Vorschlag für ein europäisches Aktions/Informationsbüro in Strassburg oder Brüssel," [undated, likely 3 July 1979]. AGG Ba-Wü 109. The next edition of the party newsletter, which trumpeted the German Greens' support for their French allies and devoted significant attention to the transnational protest of 17 July 1979, evidenced the success of Kelly and Vogt's efforts. Lukas Beckmann and Otto Fanger, "Rundbrief," August 1979. AGG Kerschgens 10. The board's decisions to support the European office and the French Greens were taken at its 14–15 July 1979 meeting in Bonn. "Protokoll der Bundesvorstandsitzung der Grünen am 14–15.7.1979 in Bonn." AGG PKA 2553.

[84] Roland Vogt, "Bericht zur europäischen Geschäftsstelle der Grünen," October 1979. AGG PKA 2553.

[85] Some of Kelly's letters from Brussels can be found in AGG Ba-Wü 109. Leinen's reports from Strasbourg are in AGG PKA 2553. On Kelly's isolation despite her frequent letters to the SPV, see: Becker-Schaum, "Die Grünen als Anti-Parteien Partei."

[86] Europe Écologie, "Souscription nationale pour les elections au parlement européen," [undated, likely May/June 1979]. AGG PKA 935.

law, members of Europe Ecologie hired legal representation, lobbied other French parties to introduce the desired changes in the National Assembly, and even arranged a meeting with President Giscard.[87] Such efforts to reform French law helped integrate EE's supporters into the political mainstream, distancing them from radical visions of withered nation-states and a decentralized Europe of the regions, even if they had little impact on French electoral law.

Solange Fernex, who played a leading part in the effort to retire EE's debt, continued to speak in an unabashedly transnational way. But her immediate goals proved well-suited to the development of a national political organization. The EP elections, she wrote to her fellow ecologists, had provided evidence that "despite the numerous obstacles, an ecological current exists within the population in France, Germany, Belgium, etc., etc." In the election's aftermath, it was time for that current "to affirm its identity." The proper venue for such an affirmation, she suggested, was a meeting to be held in Dijon in November 1979. Fernex emphasized the Dijon meeting's transnational bona fides. She trumpeted the presence of "other 'European Greens'" and emphasized the fact that the organizational form "political environmentalism" would take remained open.[88] But even if Roland Vogt was scheduled to talk about the West German Greens' experience, and the relative merits of regional and departmental organization were to be discussed at Dijon, the meeting's participants had their sights set on national politics, particularly the fast-approaching 1981 Presidential election.[89] Little space was left for European concerns.

In order to "permanently occupy the political field" the delegates to the Dijon meeting voted to found yet another new party, the Political Ecology Movement (MEP), but the new organization struggled to articulate its identity.[90] An EE campaigner from the tony Paris suburb of Bièvres – where EE had scored more than 9 percent of the vote – articulated the MEP's schizophrenia in a letter to Fernex.[91] All at once, he encouraged local action, national coordination, and lamented the loss of the "more pleasant" and "attractive" name "Europe Ecologie."[92] The MEP's bylaws only added to the ambiguity.

[87] "Compte-rendu de la réunion des 6 et 7 octobre 1979 à Saint-Germain en Laye." SFP EE 1979.
[88] Solange Fernex, "Invitation au Congres National, Dijon les 24 et 25 novembre 1979." CIRE K6 EELV 1979 Box 3.
[89] Sara Parkin, *Green Parties: An International Guide* (London: Heretic Books, 1989), 98.
[90] Mouvement d'Ecologie Politique, "Les elections européenes ont montré l'audience grandissante des préoccupation écologiques" [undated, likely January 1980]. SFP EE 1979.
[91] François Carrive to Jean-Claude Delarue, 26 December 1979. SFP EE 1979.
[92] François Carrive to Solange Fernex, 26 December 1979. SFP EE 1979.

Ecologists' desire to create "a recognizable, national pole within the political system" was reflected in the MEP's more permanent national structures, which included a national executive and council.[93] And yet, regional and local groups were to continue to "have the broadest possible autonomy."[94] Despite the fact that the establishment of the MEP marked a clear turn towards national politics, local initiative and an affinity for Europe played important roles within it. Tensions between local, national, and transnational activism were present within the MEP and other French ecological organizations well into the 1980s.

If French ecologists attempted to create a more permanent and more national organization on account of EE's organizational shortcomings, SPV Die Grünen's permanence and its ongoing importance for West German ecologists was reinforced by the 4.8 million DM in campaign reimbursements it received after the EP election. The reimbursement funds placed SPV Die Grünen's federal board at the center of efforts to organize a national green party in West Germany as the various minor parties that comprised the SPV clamored for their share of the funds. The Bremen Green List (BGL) was in particularly dire need of support since the next election to the city-state's parliament, which eager campaigners described as an opportunity for greens across the country, was scheduled for October.[95] Noting that the European campaign had received its best statewide result in the Hanseatic city-state, Georg Otto, who had been hired by the SPV's board to coordinate preparations for the 1980 Bundestag campaign, acknowledged the Bremen election's "trendsetting function," and called for "federal solidarity with the BGL." Otto buttressed his position by arguing that a strong result in Bremen would allow the greens to "help ourselves for the Bundestag election."[96] His logic mirrored Karl Kerschgens's earlier rationalizations of participation in the EP vote for reluctant campaigners, since both emphasized a non-national election's significance primarily as a step towards the upcoming Bundestag election. By replacing inchoate Europe with tiny and clearly bounded Bremen, however, Otto implicitly dismissed the idea that electoral campaigning was a means of thinking beyond borders and realizing a radically different ecological society. The sudden pivot from Europe back

[93]   Prendiville, *Environmental Politics in France*, 25.
[94]   Mouvement d'Écologie Politique, "Statuts." SFP EE 1979.
[95]   Bremer Grüne Liste to Bundesvorstand "DIE GRÜNEN," 27 August 1979. AGG PKA 2553.
[96]   Georg Otto, "An alle Landes- und Kreisorganisationen der Trägergruppen der Vereinigung DIE GRÜNEN," [undated, July or August 1979]. AGG PKA 2553.

to state-level elections initiated the embedding of green politics into the FRG's liberal democratic structures.

The BGL was hardly alone in viewing the results of the EP vote as evidence that a green approach to electoral politics was viable. In Baden-Württemberg, where SPV Die Grünen had received an impressive 4.5 percent of the vote, members of the minor parties that comprised it chomped at the bit to continue campaigning, wipe away their new organization's status as a "special political association," and formally establish themselves as "The Greens." Though the next state parliament election in Baden-Württemberg was not due for nearly a year, activists in Karlsruhe immediately demanded "more info stands with lots of materials," more posters, and "more and better balloons!"[97] In spite of their failure to win seats in Strasbourg, they apparently intended to campaign, non-stop, for the next year. In Southern Baden, campaigners pushed for "the utter disappearance of the old party names (GLU, AUD, etc.)" since "'Die Grünen' had established itself as a brand."[98] In the Breisgau, meanwhile, it was "the unanimous opinion of all the activists" that "the merger of the 'greens' into a unified party . . . must happen as quickly as possible."[99] In July 1979, activists around Freiburg took the first practical step in that direction by establishing themselves as a local chapter of Die Grünen – an organization which did not yet exist at the state or national level.[100] Since the SPV had been comprised of pre-existing smaller parties and groups and thus had no local chapters of its own, the founding of a local chapter of Die Grünen in Freiburg marked a significant step towards the creation of a single, clearly structured national green party rather than a conglomeration of statewide lists and regional parties.[101] Across the country, in fact, the new party was organized from the bottom up by local party chapters, which had

---

[97] Roland Kiesel to Die Grünen, 26 June 1979. AGG Ba-Wü 109. "Fragebogen, Kreis: KA Stadt und Land," 22 June 1979. AGG Ba-Wü 109.

[98] "Fragebogen, Kreis: Lörrach," 20 June 1979. AGG Ba-Wü 109. Andrei Markovits and Joseph Klaver make the concept of a well-known "Green brand" the centerpiece of the Green success story in their essay on the Greens' first thirty years in parliament. Markovits and Klaver, "Thirty Years of Bundestag Presence: A Tally of the Greens' impact on the Federal Republic of Germany's Political Life and Public Culture." *AICGS German-American Issues* 14 (2012).

[99] Werner Joost, "Fragebogen, Kreis: Breisgau-Hochschwarzwald," 20 June 1979. AGG Ba Wü 109.

[100] Die Grünen Kreisverband Freiburg, Breisgau-Hochschwarzwald, und Emmendingen c/o Günter Tomberg to Franz Neumann, Landesgeschäftstelle der Grünen, 11 September 1979. AGG Ba-Wü 171 (2).

[101] As Silke Mende has shown, the strong support for Die Grünen in Baden-Württemberg led directly to the decision to hold the party's founding congess in the city of Karlsruhe in 1980. Silke Mende, "Reinhdd Weber, ed., Asterix in Musterländle? Zur Entstehung und Geschichte der baden-württembergischen Grünen," in Reinhold Weber, ed., *Aufbruch, Protest und Provokation. Die bewegten 70er- und 80er-Jahre in Baden-Württemberg* (Stuttgart: Theiss, 2013), 60.

first identified themselves as greens in the EP campaign and now sent delegates to state-level founding meetings.[102] Rather than the various state lists and minor parties that had comprised the SPV, delegates from these local chapters came together at Karlsruhe in January 1980 in order to found Die Grünen as a national political party.[103]

Europe fell by the wayside as activists in the two countries formed national parties and prepared to engage in West Germany's 1980 Bundestag election and France's 1981 Presidential election. The EP election had changed the potential for national cooperation on both sides of the Rhine, but French and German ecologists' different approaches to coordination afterwards pushed green politics onto different trajectories in the two countries. The resources the SPV had received as a result of the EP election, but also minor party activists' newfound commitment to the green project contributed to the rapid creation of a single, unified green party in West Germany. In France, the EP campaign contributed greatly to the formation of the MEP, but it did not shift French ecologists' overwhelming interest in temporary national cooperation on the basis of their regional organizations. Because it marked such a departure from earlier organizing efforts, the quick rise to prominence of West Germany's new green party, Die Grünen, shifted the course of the ongoing debate about the anti-nuclear movement's place in national politics.

High Politics, Grassroots Activism, and Die Grünen

The West German Green Party, Die Grünen, was founded at Karlsruhe three months after Bremen's Green List entered the city-state's Bürgerschaft with 5.1 percent of the vote. Between the October 1979 election in Bremen, and Die Grünen's January 1980 founding congress, membership in the SPV shot up from just 2,830 to more than 10,000.[104] Two months later, in March 1980, Die Grünen entered Baden-Württemberg's state parliament

---

[102]   See, for example: "Gründung eines Kreisverbandes" [Osnabrück, 19 September 1979]. Reprinted in Frank Schnieder, *Von der sozialen Bewegung zur Institution? Die Entstehung der Partei DIE GRÜNEN in den Jahren 1978 bis 1980* (Münster: Lit Verlag, 1998), 171.

[103]   In contrast to the SPV, in other words, Die Grünen was founded from the bottom up by its own members. It was not a coalition of various pre-existing parties. Lilian Klotzsch and Richard Stöss, "Die Grünen," in Richard Stöss, ed., *Parteien-Handbuch. Die Parteien der Bundesrepublik Deutschland, 1945–1980* (Opladen: Westdeutscher Verlag, 1984), 1533–1534.

[104]   Klotzsch and Stöss, "Die Grünen," 1534. The new Green Party was a traditional party in the sense that it was comprised of local chapters and state branches (i.e. it was not a Special Political Association that comprised various minor parties). Members of these local groups became members of SPV Die Grünen until the new party, Die Grünen, was created in January 1980.

with 5.3 percent of the vote. By 1982, Greens had been elected to the state parliaments of West Berlin, Lower Saxony, Hamburg, and Hesse.[105] Despite this remarkable trajectory of membership growth and electoral success, support for Green electoral campaigns was far from universal amongst anti-nuclear activists. The grassroots activists who had been the first to protest against particular reactors, and who had thus initiated the anti-nuclear movement, were among the most reticent to participate actively in the new Green Party. Some even went out of their way to disassociate their activism from Die Grünen, despite the party's clear anti-nuclear program, its alternative political style, and its internal diversity. Thus, if the Greens' emergence represented the Federal Republic's successful chan-neling of the "new social movements back into regular politics," that process was hardly smooth or self-evident in the eyes of the anti-reactor activists themselves.[106]

Neither the SPV's campaign for the European Parliament nor the founding of Die Grünen in 1980 was brought about by the leading protagonists of earlier anti-nuclear struggles, though both fed on the anti-nuclear sentiment that grassroots activists had created through their protests. Wishing to preserve the primacy of "non-partisan" extra-parlia-mentary activism, some grassroots activists actually spoke out against the founding of the Greens.[107] The criticism began with BBU Chairman Hans Günter Schumacher, who called for a boycott of the EP vote in 1979 despite his own prior glorification of an ecological EP campaign.[108] Margot Harloff, the Freiburg activist who had helped organize the first anti-reactor protests at Fessenheim and Breisach, went even further, stating that the citizens' initiatives "saw no need for a Green party in the foresee-able future."[109] Walter Mossmann, the Freiburg singer-songwriter who had become one of the best known representatives of the grassroots struggle against the Wyhl reactor, even used his bully pulpit as emcee of the October 1979 Bonn anti-nuclear rally to talk down green politics. Though Mossmann seemed to echo Solange Fernex's "multi-strategy" when he called for "resistance on every level" from the stage at Bonn, he explicitly discounted the sort of resistance possible from within an

[105] Markovits and Gorski, *The German Left*, 291.
[106] Konrad Jarausch, *After Hitler: Recivilizing Germans, 1945–1995*, trans. by Brandon Hunziker (Oxford: Oxford University Press, 2006), 178; see also: Markovits and Gorski, *The German Left*, 30; and: Hockenos, *Joschka Fischer and the Making of the Berlin Republic*, 324.
[107] Schnieder, *Von der sozialen Bewegung zur Institution?*, 173.
[108] Herbert Gruhl to Petra Kelly, 11 July 1979. AGG PKA 2553.
[109] "Rot ohne Grün ist nicht bunt," *Badische Zeitung*, 22/23 July 1978.

alternative political party.[110] In front of 150,000 activists, Mossmann announced his concerns that as a "party of a new sort" the Greens might obliterate the citizens' initiatives' non-partisan model and also fail to achieve anything within parliament.[111] The stalwart of Rhenish anti-reactor protest effectively proposed that an insurgent political party was neither the best way to achieve the anti-nuclear movement's goals, nor was it a means of incorporating grassroots activists more closely into parliamentary democracy.

Mossmann's belief that the alternative, participatory citizens' initiative model would not be effective within parliamentary politics, did not stop the "founding Greens" from staking a claim to grassroots reactor opponents' signature cooperation of local action and global thinking.[112] In so doing, the Greens of the late 1970s and early 1980s hoped to style themselves as an alternative to the existing parties and to command the support of grassroots reactor opponents. Jutta Ditfurth's account of Die Grünen's founding congress was reminiscent of reactor opponents' descriptions of life on an occupied site, since it featured unlikely interactions between "farmers from the Kaiserstuhl, feminists from Cologne, militant anti-Brokdorf demonstrators from Hamburg and Hesse, Christian pacifists from Bavaria, bird protectors from Lower Saxony."[113] Similarly, Petra Kelly lionized anti-reactor protests in her campaign speeches and proclaimed such grassroots activism as the model for the new party's conduct, much to the chagrin of movement veterans like Mossmann.[114] Taking a more systematic approach, Herbert Gruhl emphasized the similarities between the SPV's program for the 1979 EP election and the BBU's "Eco-Concept." He berated citizens' initiative members for their lackluster support of the new party by likening the BBU's boycott of the EP vote to "a statement by the Chancellor that the party that shared his program ought not to be elected."[115] Regardless of their own weak connections to local anti-reactor protests, founding Greens like Ditfurth, Kelly, and Gruhl were keen to emphasize their solidarity with grassroots activists, celebrated

[110] Walter Mossmann, *realistisch sein: das unmögliche verlangen. Wahrheitsgetreu gefälschte Erinnerungen* (Berlin: edition der Freitag, 2009), 248. On Fernex's multi-strategy, see Chapter 2.

[111] Mossmann, *realistisch sein*, 246.

[112] Silke Mende coined the phrase "founding greens" in her comprehensive study of the Greens' emergence. She uses it to describe those who "participated in the green electoral movement in the final third of the 1970s." Mende, *"Nicht rechts, nicht links,"* 6.

[113] Ditfurth, *Krieg, Atom, Armut*, 64–65. See Chapter 4 for more on the diversity of the meetings that took place at the Wyhl reactor site.

[114] Walter Mossmann, interview with the author, Freiburg, 20 February and 3 March 2010.

[115] Gruhl to Kelly, 11 July 1979. AGG PKA 2553.

grassroots strategies and deployed the colorful imagery of anti-reactor protest.

Despite some prominent anti-reactor activists' outright rejection of the greens as a threat to non-partisan, grassroots action, many reactor opponents were less concerned about whether the new party had been incorrect to appropriate their alternative identity; they were more interested in Die Grünen's political goals and its chances of implementing them. On the Kaiserstuhl, grassroots activists became deeply engaged in local politics, but they were so dismayed by state government officials' actions that they had difficulty exciting themselves about partisan state and national elections.[116] Mossmann, who bitterly criticized the new Green Party's pretension to be a radically different sort of political party, claimed he would have had no problem with an "ordinary" party devoted to ecological matters. Such a party, he explained, would send "green representatives to parliament who would be so good and so professional as the citizens' initiatives' lawyers were in court."[117] His interest lay in the Greens' ability to get things done, not their alternative habitus. In 1980, in spite of his stance "against all the parties" and his "disagreements with the Greens' program," Mossmann even held his nose and voted for the Greens in Baden-Württemberg's state parliament election. In a public statement that he wrote together with four other veterans of the anti-reactor protests on the Upper Rhine, Mossmann explained that he would vote Green in spite of his misgivings because doing so was "the only possibility to clearly articulate protest against the nuclear industry."[118]

The results of this stand-offishness were readily apparent. On the one hand, few Green candidates or party functionaries came directly from the citizens' initiatives. Those grassroots activists who did gravitate towards the Greens typically came from the fringes of the movements. The first Green representative elected from southern Baden to the state parliament in Stuttgart, for example, was a bookish biologist who had struggled to relate to others on the occupied site at Wyhl; other Badensian activists "were glad to see him kept busy in Stuttgart."[119] On the other hand, however, despite grassroots activists' uneasiness with the Greens, the Kaiserstuhl – once

---

[116] For more on Kaiserstuhl activists' engagement in local politics, see Chapter 5.

[117] Mossmann, *realistish sein*, 247.

[118] Roland Burghard [sic], Nina Gladitz, Heidi Knott, Peter Krieg, and Walter Mossmann, "Vorschlag für eine Protestwahl in Baden-Württemberg" [undated, sometime before the March 1980 election]. AGG PKA 2559.

[119] Irmgard Beckert, discussion at *Die Ökologie im rechten und linken Spektrum: Konvergenzen und Divergenzen zwischen Deutschland und Frankreich von den 1970er Jahren bis heute*, Universität des Saarlandes, Saarbrücken, 19 November 2015.

amongst the CDU's foremost strongholds in Baden-Württemberg, if not in the entire FRG – became a center of support for the Greens well into the twenty-first century.[120] It was in this limited sense of voting for Green candidates on election day that the main protagonists of the anti-reactor protests of the 1970s supported the Green Party. Even if the Greens were, as Mossmann proposed, the only means of using their votes in the struggle against nuclear energy, grassroots activists had become well aware that there were many other weapons available to them. They did not shy away from availing themselves of them. Local protests continued in West Germany at the Gorleben waste facility construction site, and took off at Wackersdorf in Bavaria, where a new nuclear waste reprocessing facility was planned in the 1980s.[121] Site occupation also got a new lease on life as part of the struggle over the new runway planned for the Frankfurt am Main airport.[122] Meanwhile, local perspectives were used to recruit hundreds of thousands of West Germans to participate in both localized and national demonstrations against NATO's "Dual Track" decision, which would lead to the stationing of new nuclear missiles on West German territory.[123]

The notion that a green party and grassroots activism could co-exist, and thus that normal engagement in parliamentary democracy worked in concert with grassroots protest, stood at the core of the anti-nuclear movement's renewal of democratic praxis in the Federal Republic. The idea marked a significant change not least because the combination of parliamentary and extra-parliamentary protest was far more controversial than it seems. The closer the Greens came to a national election, the more their alternative style or endorsement of extra-parliamentary action was described by the mainstream press and by establishment politicians as a threat to liberal democracy.

---

[120] When the Greens won Baden-Württemberg's 2011 state parliament elections, they received 30.4 percent of the vote in the Emmendingen district, which included most of the Kaiserstuhl villages. This was the Greens' ninth highest percentage anywhere in the state (and their highest in any rural district). The Emmendingen result trailed behind only three urban districts in Stuttgart, and the university towns of Freiburg, Heidelberg, Constance, and Tübingen. Statistisches Landesamt Baden-Württemberg, *Wahl zum 15. Landtag von Baden-Württemberg am 27. März 2011* (Stuttgart: Statistisches Landesamt Baden-Württemberg, 2011), 21.

[121] On Gorleben, see: Paul, *und auch nicht anderswo . . .*; On Wackersdorf, see: Janine Gaumer, "WAAhnsin in der bayerischen Provinz. Der Konflikt um die atomare Wiederaufarbeitunsanlage in Wackersforf, 1980–1990" (PhD Dissertation, Friedrich-Schiller Universität Jena, forthcoming).

[122] Hartmut Johnsen, *Der Startbahn-West-Konflikt. Ein politisches Lehrstück? Zeitzeugen ziehen Bilanz* (Frankfurt am Main: Societäts-Verlag, 1996).

[123] On the importance of localism for 1980s peace protesters, see: Susanne Schregel, *Der Atomkrieg vor der Wohnungstür. Eine Politikgeschichte der neuen Friedensbewegung in der Bundesrepublik, 1970–1985* (Frankfurt am Main: Campus, 2011). On the links between the anti-nuclear energy movement and the 1980s peace movement, see: Mende and Metzger, "Ökopax."

Whereas *Der Spiegel* celebrated the diversity of parties participating in the EP election, which ranged from Trotskyists to neo-fascists, and the *taz* scoffed at rock bottom voter turnout across much of the EEC, the 1980 Bundestag election was taken very seriously by the press, the parties, and the voters.[124] Widespread concern about the possibility that the arch-conservative Franz-Josef Strauß might win the chancellorship if the Greens' siphoned votes away from the SPD prompted negative responses to the Greens' plans to participate. According to a *Der Spiegel* cover story, in fact, the Greens were actually "The last hope for Strauß."[125] Believing that they had the most to lose from the Greens' entrance into the election, Social Democratic politicians took an even more negative view of the Greens. The SPD's secretary-general Egon Bahr referred to the new party as a "threat to democracy," while his colleague Erhard Eppler compared the Greens to the "marching columns of the SA."[126] Even the feminist magazine *Emma* was critical of the Greens' campaign, which it accused of neglecting women (just like the major parties) at the same time as it would likely split the anti-Strauß vote and thus bring the Bavarian Premier to power in Bonn.[127]

In the event, Strauß was solidly defeated; the governing coalition of SPD and F.D.P. was re-elected with an increased share of the vote. The Greens, who scored only 1.5 percent of the vote proved themselves irrelevant. Rather than treating their result as a debacle or slinking away from analysis of the election in the press, the Greens' celebrated the vote's outcome. Petra Kelly, who served once again as the Greens' lead candidate, took the opportunity yet again to propose a wide significance for the Greens' electoral campaign. "We [Greens] aren't sad at all," she exclaimed, "we are very happy that there's no Chancellor Strauß!"[128] Not only did the Greens downplay their miserable result by proclaiming their solidarity with Strauß's opponents and "flaunting their happiness," they also dismissed their inability to send representatives to parliament and influence politics there. Instead, in a press release circulated shortly after the election, Die Grünen trumpeted the extra-parliamentary strategies of the anti-nuclear movement, calling for its supporters to undertake "open, nonviolent resistance against the life threatening policies of the institutions of power in this country."[129] Even

---

[124] "Deine Stimme für dein Europa," *Der Spiegel*, 1 January 1979.
[125] "Die Grünen. Letzte Hoffnung für Strauß?" *Der Spiegel*, 24 March 1980.
[126] Quoted in: Ditfurth, *Krieg, Atom, Armut*, 65.
[127] Alice Schwarzer, "Haben Frauen noch die Wahl?" *Emma* Sonderband 1 (1980): 6.
[128] "Menge gebracht," *Der Spiegel*, 13 October 1980.
[129] "Presseerklärung des Bundesvorstandes der GRÜNEN nach dem Wahlausgang," Bonn, 7 October 1980. AGG Ba-Wü 185 (2).

once it was amply clear that Strauß would not become Chancellor, these sorts of statements could be construed by anxious establishment politicians as evidence that the Greens opposed parliamentary democracy.

Yet, the very co-existence of the Greens and the extra-parliamentary movement proved both the resilience of liberal democracy and citizens' increasing openness to a conception of democratic praxis that incorporated not only the Bundestag but also their daily lives. As even Die Grünen's most fervent advocates acknowledged, voting green was only one part of anti-nuclear activists' far more expansive efforts to contest the development of nuclear energy and create an alternative society. Nonetheless, by claiming to represent grassroots activists and deploying their rhetoric in electoral campaigns, the Greens widened liberal democracy, forcing the press and politicians alike to accept their participation, giving even disgruntled anti-nuclear voters a choice in the elections, but also proving that there was more to self-government than voting, and more to elections than electing a government. The combination was neither perfect nor free of risk, since the repurposing of the electoral process had the potential to turn citizens off from voting altogether or perhaps even to upend the FRG's fragile liberal democratic order. But the co-existence of Green politics and extra-parliamentary anti-nuclear protest showed that overlaps between parliament and grassroots activism were possible, and embodied the sort of "common work" in "agenda-setting, deliberation, legislation and policy implementation" between institutions and civil society that Benjamin Barber described as the prerequisite for "strong democracy."[130] In short, the idea that both liberal democratic procedures and citizens' own interests and lived experiences could play a part in the way Germans governed themselves was the basis for the transformation of democratic praxis that the anti-nuclear movement inspired in the FRG.

Conclusion

Since the emergence of the West German Greens established nuclear energy as a matter of high politics and finally provided the contemporary press and latter-day scholars with an identifiable national entity to embody the movement, it might be read as an unmitigated success story. Despite the Greens' claim to national representation, not to mention their early successes, however, many anti-nuclear activists were not deeply involved in the Greens. From their perspective, in fact, much of the anti-nuclear

---

[130] Benjamin Barber, *Strong Democracy* (Berkeley: University of California Press, 1984), 151.

movement's potential was lost in the formation of a national political party. While grassroots anti-nuclear action persisted, it was often over-shadowed by the Greens' actions. Founding a national party also went hand in hand with the de-emphasis of the transnational perspectives that had shaped green politics, and provided the framework for the Greens' convergence. In fact, the year after the 1980 election, the Greens felt the necessity to close down their Strasbourg office and lay off Vogt just to survive financially until the next Bundestag election, which was not expected until 1984.[131] The closure marked the end of the belief that thinking globally and organizing across transnational spaces might be a means of reshaping society from the bottom up. It also evidenced the disparate national trajectories taken by anti-nuclear activists in France and West Germany. Perhaps most unfortunately, overemphasis on the Greens has erased the significance and the potential of the extra-parliamentary protest of the 1970s, reducing it to a sort of sideshow or training ground for future green leaders. In fact, such protests were the sites where citizens became more engaged in democratic processes – often by acting beyond the bounds of liberal democracy. The importance of this experimentation, and the challenge to the political establishment it embodied, cannot be adequately addressed in studies that focus on the Greens alone, or in analyses that understand the movements of the 1970s solely as the Greens' predecessors. Though the emergence of Die Grünen created the sense that West Germany's anti-nuclear movement had become a well-organized and potent force in national politics, it was neither so all-encompassing nor such an obvious step forward as Whiggish narratives of West German democratization might lead us to think.

---

[131] Helmust Lippelt to Roland Vogt, 24 August 1981. AGG PKA 2559. In fact, the election was held in 1983 after the Liberal Democrats decided to end their support for the Schmidt government in 1982.

Conclusion: Protesting Nuclear Energy, Greening Democracy

In 2001, Chancellor Gerhard Schröder's government of Social Democrats and Greens signed an agreement with Germany's utilities operators to phase out nuclear power. The agreement, which came three decades after the first protests on the Upper Rhine, allowed existing reactors to operate until the end of their 32-year lifespans. Rather than celebrating a major victory, reactor opponents were angered that even Die Grünen, with its roots in the anti-nuclear protests of the 1970s, had failed to secure an immediate stop to nuclear energy production. Ilka Schröder, herself a Green Member of the European Parliament, denounced the agreement as having "successfully blocked the nuclear phase-out," and quit the party shortly thereafter.[1] Since Chancellor Angela Merkel's government revised the phase-out in 2009, prolonging the lifespans of Germany's reactors, the 2001 phase-out was not successful. But Merkel herself reversed course rapidly after the 2011 disaster at Fukushima, Japan, immediately closing all reactors built before 1980 and enacting a new plan to shut down Germany's remaining reactors by 2022. The end of nuclear energy in Germany was barely a decade away. Switzerland, too, committed to a phase-out after Fukushima, planning to shut down its last reactor by 2034. This was not the case in France, where President Nicolas Sarkozy committed one billion Euros to fourth-generation reactor research immediately after the accident.

In light of activists' goal of immediately stopping nuclear energy production throughout Western Europe, it is difficult to count the anti-nuclear movement of the 1970s as a clear success. Even in Germany, reactors will continue running until 2022 and the problem of nuclear waste remains unsolved. In France, a nuclear phase-out was never even seriously debated. At the time of this writing, the country still receives

---

[1] Ilka Schröder, "Den Atomausstieg erfolgreich verhindert," *Sonderdenkpause* 2 (28 September 2001), www.ilka.org/material/denkpause/sonderdenkpause2c.html (last accessed 30 December 2015).

75 percent of its energy from nuclear power, and a new 1,750 MW reactor is under construction at Flamanville.[2] Nonetheless, over the course of a half-century, anti-nuclear activists' efforts will shut down many of Europe's reactors. The Wyhl reactor project, which played such an enormous part in motivating the movement, never even made it off the drawing board. The Plogoff reactor project, a focal point of anti-nuclear protest in France, was also cancelled before construction began. The Kalkar fast-breeder reactor, completed in 1985, was never turned on. Rather than delivering electricity to the grid, the site became an amusement park. The Malville Super-Phénix, meanwhile, was decommissioned in 1997 to after only a decade of service.

If it is necessary to look into the future in order to see the fulfillment of anti-nuclear protesters' primary goal, even in Germany and Switzerland, the emergence of Europe's green parties made the anti-nuclear movement's contribution to the renewal of democracy visible already in the late seventies and early 1980s. Daniel Brélaz became the first Green in a national parliament when he was elected to Switzerland's National Council in 1979. Four years later, the German Greens "jumped the 5 percent hurdle" and won twenty-seven seats in the Bundestag.[3] The newly elected Green MPs' "ritual procession" to parliament, in which they were accompanied by activists from across the FRG, has served as the opening motif for many histories of Die Grünen.[4] The march must have been a moving sight – one that evidenced the significance of both global thinking and environmental matters for the new party's approach to parliament. One group of activists pushed an enormous rubber globe through the streets of Bonn. The newly elected Green MP Marieluise Beck "appeared with a pine tree pockmarked by acid rain," and her colleague Petra Kelly marched beside her, holding "a large bouquet of fresh flowers."[5]

---

[2] On the current status of the French nuclear program, see: World Nuclear Association, "Country Profile: France," last modified November 2015, www.world-nuclear.org/info/Country-Profiles/Cou ntries-A-F/France/ (last accessed 30 December 2015).

[3] The Greens also won a non-voting seat in West Berlin; some publications, therefore, list the total number of seats won by the Greens in 1983 as twenty-eight.

[4] This is especially true of histories intended for non-German readers. See, for example: Charlene Spretnak and Fritjof Capra, *Green Politics: The Global Promise* (New York: E. P. Dutton, 1984), xiii; or: Brian Tokar, *The Green Alternative: Creating an Ecological Future* (San Pedro, CA: R&E Miles, 1987).

[5] Andrei S. Markovits and Joseph Klaver, "Thirty Years of Bundestag Presence: A Tally of the Greens' Impact on the Federal Republic of Germany's Political Life and Public Culture," *AICGS German-American Issues* 14 (2012), 7.

The march's triumphant conclusion at the Bundeshaus, which only the parliamentarians could enter, marked the separation of West Germany's Green Party from the transnational grassroots movements that conceived political environmentalism during the late 1970s. The scene at the Bonn parliament's door mirrored the split between the Italian Radicals on the one hand and the French and German Greens on the other, at the door to the European Parliament four years earlier; though the groups continued to cooperate with one another after the parliamentarians were seated in the plenary hall, their relationship had changed. The 1983 break between parliamentarians and grassroots activists in Bonn was not complete, but it was more significant than the Greens' self-description as the parliamentary arm of the movements made it out to be.[6] Whereas 1970s activists had fashioned an extra-parliamentary approach to democracy, building broad coalitions by working across borders, eschewing partisan politics, and focusing on local issues, Green MPs' engagement in parliament, despite even the protests they mounted in the plenary hall or their many speeches at demonstrations outside parliament, took place in adherence to the rules and regulations of liberal democracy. Despite their insistence on being "neither Left, nor Right, but ahead," the Greens did not claim that their parliamentary work was "apolitical."

The differences between grassroots anti-reactor protest and Green politics become particularly evident when their respective relationships to liberal democracy are taken into account. Hessian Premier Holger Börner, a recalcitrant Social Democrat who once said that the only way to communicate with a protester seeking to occupy a construction site was "with a two-by-four," ably described the different positions of anti-nuclear protesters and Green politicians vis-à-vis the political establishment. Whereas Börner quite clearly had little patience for extra-parliamentary protest, he was willing to acknowledge the integrative function of Green politics, proclaiming in 1985 (as he sought to make Die Grünen the junior partner in his government) that the Greens would "bind a new generation to parliamentary democracy."[7] Börner's comments supported the well-established idea that the German Greens' entrance into the Bundestag marked a major step forward along a Whiggish trajectory that brought errant "extra-parliamentary protest" into parliament, effectively

---

[6] Silke Mende, "'Enemies at the Gate:' The West German Greens and Their Arrival at the Bundestag—Between Old Ideals and New Challenges," *German Politics and Society* 33, no. 4 (Winter 2015): 72.

[7] Andrei Markovits and Philip Gorski, *The German Left: Red, Green, and Beyond* (Oxford: Oxford University Press, 1993), 207.

incorporating militant sixty-eighters into the liberal democratic fold and proving the resilience of the Federal Republic's democratic institutions.[8] The reality was more complicated.

Studies of the German Greens' early years in parliament are replete with evidence of the ways that the new party altered the staid traditions of Bonn politics, renewing parliamentary democracy in spite of the Greens' miniscule presence in the Bundestag. For one thing, the Greens pushed parliamentary procedure to its limits: Green MPs used their prerogative to force Chancellor Helmut Kohl's government to answer 820 written questions between 1983 and 1987.[9] The Greens' entrance into parliament also helped previously unrepresented Germans to feel enfranchised. Opponents of nuclear energy who had been ignored by officials from the mainstream parties now knew there was an unabashedly anti-nuclear party in parliament; in fact, the Greens' place in the opposition during the 1980s actually bolstered their radical anti-nuclear credentials since they were never forced to actually solve the problems posed by nuclear energy production, but could continue criticizing government policies without abandon. Women, too, were finally represented by at least one of the parliament's four parties at a rate close to their share of the West German population.[10] By taking new approaches to parliamentary work and changing the Bundestag's demographics, the Greens shifted the ways in which important topics were discussed in parliament even if the small opposition party shepherded no legislation through the Bundestag in the 1980s.[11]

---

[8] Konrad Jarausch, *After Hitler: Recivilizing Germans 1945–1995* trans. Brandon Hunziker (Oxford: Oxford University Press, 2006), 178. See also: Markovits and Gorski, *The German Left*, 30; and: Paul Hockenos, *Joschka Fischer and the Making of the Berlin Republic: An Alternative History of Postwar Germany* (Oxford: Oxford University Press, 2008), 324.

[9] The small Green delegation asked nearly six times as many written questions or Kleine Anfragen as did the much larger SPD delegation, which sat with the Greens in the opposition. E. Gene Frankland and Donald Schoonmaker, *Between Protest and Power: The Green Party in Germany* (Boulder: Westview Press, 1992), 161. In total, the Greens, who comprised just 5 percent of the parliament, posed 80 percent of all the Kleine Anfragen from 1983 until 1987. Josef Boyer and Helge Heidemeyer, eds., *Die Grünen im Bundestag. Sitzungsprotokolle und Anlagen, 1983–1987* (Düsseldorf: Droste Verlag, 2008), XXXIV.

[10] The first Green delegation, which served from 1983–1987, initially had ten female members out of twenty-eight total members. After most of the MPs followed party rules and "rotated" out of office in Spring 1985, there were only seven women in the twenty-eight-member delegation. However, the second delegation, which served from 1987–1990, had twenty-five women out of forty-four members. For more on the ways the Green delegation changed women's place in parliament, see: Claudia Pinl, "Green Feminism in Parliamentary Politics," in Margit Mayer and John Ely, eds., *The German Greens: Paradox Between Movement and Party* (Philadelphia: Temple University Press, 1998): 128–140; see also: Sarah Summers, "'Thinking Green!' (and Feminist): Female Activism and the Greens from Wyhl to Bonn," *German Politics and Society* 33, no. 4 (Winter 2015): 40–52.

[11] As Frankland and Schoonmaker put it in 1992, "On the national level, the Greens can point to no one piece of legislation upon which they left their stamp of particularity, but they can show their

This renewal of parliamentary praxis, significant though it was, was only one aspect of the greening of democracy initiated by grassroots anti-nuclear protesters during the mid-1970s. In causing individuals to realize the political salience of their own particular concerns, grassroots anti-nuclear activism fostered "individual self-respect" and "collective self-confidence" amongst people who had previously refrained from challenging elected officials or questioning decisions made within the liberal democratic order.[12] These realizations enabled anti-nuclear activists not only to assert themselves, but also to find common cause – if only fleetingly – with people from many different backgrounds. Differently put, in the process of speaking up for their own interests and being ignored by democratically elected government officials, individuals began to engage more actively in self-governance – both within the boundaries of the liberal democratic order and beyond them. While the emergence of new parties was the most readily apparent symptom of democracy's greening, individuals' changing attitudes about political engagement and their formation of democratic subjectivities extended far beyond their choices at the polling booth.

Assessing the significance of these new democratic subjectivities means looking beyond the realm of formalized organizations and institutions to changes within individuals and the society they comprise. In a recent essay on the concept of "democratization" as a shared master narrative for histories of Germany and the United States in the postwar period, Charles Maier observed that "society can intervene to shatter ossified forms, but civil society is not a sufficient institution for governance."[13] The informal communities created at sites of anti-reactor protest, and even the longer-lasting structures of movement organizations are difficult to take seriously as long-term efforts at governance; nor were they ever intended as such by the activists who created them. But jumping too quickly ahead to considerations of governance overlooks the ways in which citizens rethought their ideas of what democracy – and, for that matter, democratization – looked like on account of their engagement in

---

'fingerprints' on a wide range of legislation in their role as competitive and constructive opposition." Frankland and Schoonmaker, *Between Protest and Power*, 190. Silke Mende has shown, for example, that the Greens changed the debate on the social integration of migrants, by advocating a "multicultural society" long before the term was en vogue. Mende, "Enemies at the Gate," 74.

[12] Lawrence Goodwyn, *The Populist Moment: A Short History of the Agrarian Revolt in America* (Oxford: Oxford University Press, 1976), xix.

[13] Charles Maier, "History Lived and History Written: Germany and the United States, 1945/55–2015," *Bulletin of the German Historical Institute* 57 (Fall 2015): 21–22.

anti-nuclear protest and their newfound ability to bring together the social and the democratic.

This change is particularly important since by one set of measurements at least, the people who protested against nuclear reactors were already committed democrats in the 1950s and 1960s. Voter turn-out in Southern Baden and Alsace was consistently high in the postwar period.[14] Alsatians' incorporation into postwar France, Badensians' support for the ruling Christian Democrats, and even the stunning postwar boom itself suggested that voters along the Upper Rhine identified with their governments.[15] Beneath the surface, however, voters were becoming increasingly critical of government officials' attitudes. In postwar Alsace, centralized rule from Paris was intended to quash regional identity and limit ordinary Alsatians' part in crucial decision-making processes.[16] As their assumptions about the linkages between the prosperity of the "thirty glorious years" and postwar democracy were tested, grassroots reactor opponents began to think about how they could make sure their own interests were served. They advocated for themselves by speaking up at licensing hearings, gathering petition signatures, and eventually by coming together to protest on reactor construction sites.

This increased involvement went hand in hand with the changes to citizens' attitudes towards democracy. In the FRG, citizens sought to continue the sort of participation modeled by grassroots anti-reactor protest by supporting the Green Party or participating in mass protests in Bonn, first against nuclear reactors in 1979 and then against NATO's "Euromissiles" in the early 1980s.[17] In the centralized Fifth Republic, meanwhile, grassroots movements for regional autonomy and independence from Paris retained special importance.[18]

---

[14] On Baden, see: "Endgültige Ergebnisse der Wahl zum Landtag von Baden-Württemberg am 23. April 1972," *Statistische Berichte des Statistischen Landesamts Baden-Württemberg* B VII 2 (9 May 1972); and on Alsace, see: Marc Burg, *Les Gauches face aux Droites dans le Bas Rhin sous la Ve Republique, 1958–1988* (PhD Dissertation, Université Robert Schuman, Strasbourg, 1988).

[15] Baden-Württemberg's yearly economic growth was second only to Bavaria in the FRG. Udo Vullhorst, "Strukturwandel und Wirtschaftsentwicklung," *Statistisches Monatsheft Baden-Württemberg* 65, no. 4 (April 2012): 54; see also: "Im Südwesten ein achtes Weltwunder," *Der Spiegel* (17 April 1972): 35–49.

[16] See, for example: "Jean," *Elsaß. Kolonie in Europa* (Berlin: Wagenbach, 1976).

[17] On the links between protest against nuclear energy and peace protests, see: Silke Mende and Birgit Metzger, "Ökopax. Die Umweltbewegung als Erfahrungsraum der Friedensbewegung," in Christoph Becker-Schaum, ed., *Entrüstet Euch! Nuklearkrise, NATO-Doppelbeschluss und Friedensbewegung* (Paderborn: Schöningh, 2012); and: Susanne Schregel, *Der Atomkrieg vor der Wohnungstür. Eine Politikgeschichte der neuen Friedensbewegung in der Bundesrepublik, 1970–1985* (Frankfurt am Main: Campus, 2011).

[18] Herman Lebovics, *Bringing the Empire Back Home: France in the Global Age* (Durham, NC: Duke University Press, 2004), 183ff.

Though citizens' changing ideas about democratic participation caused West Germans to take their immediate concerns to Bonn and gave local struggles a special sort of national significance in France, personal transformations are left out of the sweeping narratives of democracy's advance across Western Europe in the postwar period. These tend to describe a process that occurred to states and their institutions, not one by which individuals changed themselves and created democratic subjectivities.[19] On account of its Nazi past, democratization has become a particularly prominent trope in histories of postwar Germany. Nonetheless, aside from leading politicians, the only individuals likely to be given pride of place in histories of Germany's democratization are "the sixty-eighters." That generation is portrayed as a singular force, much different from its parents (and its children), that marched through the institutions, leaving democratized states in its wake.[20] With the exception of this unique, particularly engaged generation, questions about whether or not Germans themselves came to see their role in self-governance differently, and of how and why they shifted their conceptions of themselves as democrats during the postwar period, are rarely addressed.[21] It is simply assumed that the older generations rejected the participatory approach of the sixty-eighters while younger generations silently benefitted from it. Yet, the anti-nuclear movement engaged Germans of different generations, including many who had survived the Second World War and accepted democracy's return without

---

[19] This is particularly true of histories of the FRG. See, for example: Edgar Wolfrum, *Die geglückte Demokratie: Geschichte der Bundesrepublik Deutschland von ihren Anfängen bis zur Gegenwart* (Stuttgart: Klett-Cotta, 2006); Heinrich-August Winkler, *Der Lange Weg nach Westen* (Munich: Beck, 2000); or: Ulrich Herbert, *Geschichte Deutschlands im 20. Jahrhundert* (Munich: Beck, 2014). The history of the Fifth Republic has also been written as a history institutions gaining legitimacy. Robert Gildea, for example, has written of the formation of the "Republic of the Centre." Gildea, *France since 1945* (Oxford: Oxford University Press, 2002).

[20] Paul Hockenos argues particularly forcefully that the "long march through the institutions" undertaken by West Germany's "disenchanted postwar generations ... contributed decisively to Germany's remarkable transformation from an occupied post-Nazi state into a healthy, democratic country." Hockenos, *Joschka Fischer*, 5. But this same argument is also made in many other histories of postwar Germany. Edgar Wolfrum writes, for example, that. "Joschka Fischer in particular embodies the integrative achievement of the Federal Republic's democracy." Wolfrum, *Die geglückte Demokratie*, 479. Several recent studies of 1968 that deploy oral histories have opened the black box of the sixty-eighters' identity by emphasizing the ways that the sixty-eighters themselves changed on account of their political engagement. See, for example: Robert Gildea, James Mark, and Anette Warring, eds., *Europe's 1968: Voices of Revolt* (Oxford: Oxford University Press, 2013); and: Belinda Davis, *The Internal Life of Politics: The New Left in West Germany, 1962–1983* (forthcoming).

[21] Heinrich August Winkler, for example, sets "the 68ers" against "the democratic system," when he argues that, "the extra-parliamentary opposition proved what it sought to disprove: the reformability of the democratic system." Winkler, *Der Lange Weg nach Westen* (Munich: Beck, 2000), Vol. II, 252.

much comment and many others who first came of political age in the 1970s.

To the extent they are included at all, these "extra-parliamentary" activists of the 1970s play a much different part in the narrative of postwar democratization. Rather than being seen as democratizers, they are held responsible for fracturing pre-existing social ties and pushing democratic institutions to their breaking points. But the broad resonance of particular anti-reactor protests, evident in the coalitions that came together on occupied reactor sites and in efforts to recreate such protests in many parts of Western Europe – and even across the Atlantic – suggests a different interpretation of grassroots anti-reactor protest. According to this revised interpretation, anti-nuclear protest had the potential to bring together individuals from a wide range of backgrounds who previously had little in common. Far from contributing to the fracturing of society, anti-nuclear protest stitched it together in new ways.

Grassroots protests were attractive to so many people in part because of their purportedly "apolitical" nature. By staking a claim to be "outside the liberal democratic order," local anti-nuclear protests fostered participation and contributed to a reinvigoration of social activism and democratic engagement. In the early 1970s, Solange Fernex and her colleagues in Ecology and Survival were already considering ways to merge together this inclusive, grassroots approach with participation in electoral politics. In 1979, Fernex and Petra Kelly spearheaded an unprecedented effort to deploy grassroots models in the first direct elections to the European Parliament. They sought to build on anti-reactor protesters' trans-border cooperation and to prefigure a new transnational democracy that transcended previous conceptions of party politics. Paradoxically, though the EP campaign fell far short of these leading activists' goals of forging a wholly new polity on the basis of grassroots anti-nuclear protests, it ably demonstrated Green candidates' ability to earn votes. In seeking to improve on the results of the EP vote, Europe's nascent green parties moved ever closer to the political establishment. The abolition of national states and the creation of the new bottom-up political order envisioned by advocates of radical ecology were heavily reliant on a transnational frame-work – they required Europe for their success. The road that green parties did not take left the nation-state and its liberal democratic institutions behind and led to a new European ecological society. In a globalizing world, this blend of grassroots engagement and transnational perspective represented a truly radical alternative to the top-down Europe of the nations developing in Brussels' bureaucratic orbit. Thus, the

Greens' emergence as a national party downplayed the radical potential of grassroots activism to create a new, more participatory form of democracy that transcended the nation-state.

Re-focusing on the citizens who were transformed by their experiences in the anti-nuclear movement helps us to see the links between personal transformations and changes to democracy itself. The anti-nuclear movement fostered these links by allowing individuals to see themselves, their concerns, and their particular interests reflected in high politics.[22] In this way, it expanded the meaning of democracy for many citizens. That the ends of that process of democratic expansion and renewal were different in France and West Germany, and that neither country dissolved into a Europe of the regions or replaced its liberal democracy with some sort of radical ecological alternative, does not decrease the importance of the new possibilities for democratic engagement opened up by grassroots anti-nuclear protesters in the 1970s. Instead, the new understanding of one's own place in the democratic order, which both motivated increased engagement and offered access to these sweeping democratic vistas, was itself the greening of democracy's most meaningful result.

---

[22] Lawrence Goodwyn describes this as the people "seeing themselves experimenting in democratic forms." Goodwyn, *The Populist Moment*, 295–296.

Bibliography

ARCHIVES VISITED

Archiv-Aktiv, Hamburg
Archiv der Badisch-Elsässsiche Bürgerinitiativen, Weisweil (ABEBI)
Archiv des Deutschen Museums, Munich
Archiv für Christlich-Demokratische Politik, Bonn (ACDP)
Archiv zur Geschichte der Kernenergie in der Schweiz, Zürich
Archiv Grünes Gedächtnis, Berlin (AGG)
Archiv Soziale Bewegungen, Freiburg (ASB)
Archiv der sozialen Demokratie, Bonn (ASD)
Archiv für Zeitgeschichte, Zürich (AfZ)
Bundesarchiv, Berlin
Bundesarchiv, Koblenz
Bundesverband Bürgerinitiativen Umweltschutz Archiv, Bonn
Centre international de recherches sur l'écologie, Grignon (CIRE)
Generallandesarchiv, Karlsruhe (GLA)
Hamburger Institut für Sozialforschung (HIS)
Hauptstaatsarchiv, Stuttgart (HSAS)
Institut für Zeitgeschichte, Munich (IfZ)
Landesarchiv Nordrhein Westfalen, Detmold
Siemens Benutzerarchiv, Munich
Solange Fernex Papers (Private Collection), Biederthal (SFP)
Stadtarchiv, Endingen (StA-EN)
Staatsarchiv Freiburg (SAFR)
Universitätsarchiv, Freiburg

NEWSPAPERS, MAGAZINES, AND OTHER PERIODICALS CONSULTED

AGENOR
Amtliches Mitteilungsblatt, Gemeinde Wyhl a. K.
Anti-AKW Telegramm
Arbeiterkampf
Atom-Express

Atomwirtschaft
Badische Zeitung
BBU-Aktuell
Cahiers de la Reconciliation
Charlie-Hebdo
Combat non-violent
Dernières nouvelles d'Alsace
The Ecologist
Forum E
Frankfurter Allgemeine Zeitung
Frankfurter Rundschau
Freiburger Wochenbericht
Gewaltfreie Aktion
Das Gewissen: Zeitschrift für Lebensschutz
Graswurzelrevolution
La Gueule Ouverte
L'Humanité
Infodienst für gewaltfreie Organisatoren
Informations-Dienst zur Verbreitung unterbliebener Nachrichten
International Herald-Tribune
Ionix
Klassenkampf
Kommunistische Volkszeitung
Kommunismus und Klassenkampf
Konkret
Kursbuch
Lahrer Zeitung
Le Monde
New York Times
Ouest france
Pflasterstrand
Rhein-Neckar-Zeitung
Rote Fahne Informationsdienst
Der Spiegel
Staatsanzeiger für Baden-Württemberg
Stadtzeitung für Freiburg
Der Stille Weg
Stuttgarter Nachrichten
Stuttgarter Zeitung
Südwestpresse Schwäbische Donauzeitung Ulm a.D.
Survivre
die tageszeitung
Was Wir Wollen
Die Welt
Wyhl-Arbeit
Die Zeit

INTERVIEWS

Auer, Gerd. Emmendingen, 22 February 2010.
de Barry, Beate. Strasbourg, 3 March 2010.
de Barry, Jean. Strasbourg, 3 March 2010.
Baum, Frank. Staufen, 19 February 2010.
Beer, Wolfgang. Telephone, 26 February 2011.
Berstecher, Dieter. Oberrotweil, 18 February 2010.
Burkhart, Roland. Freiburg, 24 February 2010.
Ehrler, Heinz. Weisweil, 23 February 2010.
Fernex, Michel. Biederthal, 18 and 20 March 2016.
Göpper, Siegfried. Weisweil, 16 February 2010.
Haug, Marie-Reine. Freiburg, 8 March 2010 and Ferette, 19 March 2016.
Hoffmann, Freia. Bremen, 17 June 2010.
Jenn, Henri. Mulhouse, 21 March 2016.
Kehler, Randy. Brattleboro, 23 March 2011.
Knobloch, Wilhelm. Karlsruhe, 24 April 2010.
Mayer, Axel. Freiburg, 17 February 2010.
Mossmann, Walter. Freiburg, 20 February and 3 March 2010.
Nössler, Bernd. Freiburg, 26 February 2010.
Quistorp, Eva. Berlin, 16 June 2010.
Peter-Davis, Esther. Strasbourg, 8 May 2014.
Rettig, Jean-Jacques. Freiburg, 8 March 2010.
Sacherer, Günter. Oberrotweil, 18 February 2010.
Schirmer, Raymond. Ferette, 19 March 2016.
Schleunig, Peter. Bremen, 17 June 2010.
Schmitt, Thomas. Skype, 14 February 2012.
Schulthess, Elisabeth. Ferette, 19 March 2016.
Schulz, Erhard. Freiburg, 29 July 2010.
Schwörer, Meinrad. Wyhl, 3 March 2010.
Sternstein, Wolfgang. Stuttgart, 27 October 2009.

AUDIO RECORDINGS

Die 31 badisch-elsässischen Bürgerinitiativen. *Lieder im'Frendschaft's Huss'/ Chansons dans la 'Maison de l'Amité.'* 9 February 1975.
Badisch-Elsässische Bürgerinitiativen. *Neue Lieder und Gedichte aus Dreyeckland.* Munich: Trikont-Verlag. 1977.
KKW-NEIN! Freiburg. *Die Wacht am Rhein.* Munich: Trikont Verlag. n.d. [1975].

VIDEOS

Green Mountain Post Films. *Lovejoy's Nuclear War.* 1975.
Green Mountain Post Films. *Nuclear Reaction in Wyhl.* 1976.

Medienwerkstatt Freiburg. *S'Wespenäscht – Die Chronik von Wyhl, 1970–1982.* 1982.

Westdeutscher Rundfunk. *Vor Ort. Bürger gegen Atomkraftwerk in Wyhl.* Directed by Thomas Schmitt. 1975.

PUBLISHED SOURCES

Abendroth, Wolfgang. "Das KPD-Verbotsurteil des Bundesverfassungsgerichts. Ein Beitrag zum Problem der richterlichen Interpretation von Rechtsgrundsätzen der Verfassung im demokratischen Staat." *Zeitschrift für Politik* 3, no. 3 (1956): 305–327.

Aldrich, Daniel. *Site Fights: Divisive Facilities and Civil Society in Japan and the West.* Ithaca: Cornell University Press, 2008.

Alexander, Keith. "From Red to Green in the Island City: The Alternative Liste West Berlin and the Evolution of the West German Left, 1945–1990." PhD Dissertation, University of Maryland, 2003.

Anderson, Benedict. *Imagined Communities: Reflections on the Origin and Spread of Nationalism.* London: Verso, 1983.

Anger, Didier. *Chronique d'une Lutte: Le combat antinucléaire à Flamanville et dans La Hague.* Paris: Simoën, 1978.

Applegate, Celia. *A Nation of Provincials: The German Idea of Heimat.* Berkeley: University of California Press, 1990.

Association contre le nucléaire et son monde. *Histoire lacunaire de l'opposition à l'énergie nucléaire en France.* Paris: La Lenteur, 2007.

Auer, Gerhard A. "Siebenunddreißig Wyhl-Geschichten." *'s Eige zeige' Jahrbuch des Landkreises Emmendingen für Kultur und Geschichte* 29 (2015): 1–347.

Auer, Gerhard A. and Jochen Reich. "Gebrannte Kinder. Vorgeschichten vom Kampf gegen das Atomkraftwerk Wyhl." *'s Eige zeige' Jahrbuch des Landkreises Emmendingen für Kultur und Geschichte* 15 (2001): 87–112.

Aust, Stefan. *Brokdorf. Symbol einer politschen Wende.* Hamburg: Hoffmann und Campe Verlag, 1981.

Barber, Benjamin. *Strong Democracy.* Berkeley: University of California Press, 1984.

Bastian, Till. *Die Finsternis der Herzen. Nachdenken über eine Gewalttat.* Cologne: PapyRossa, 1994.

Bausinger, Hermann. "Die 'Alemannsiche Internationale.' Realität und Mythos." *Recherches Germaniques* 8 (1978): 143–157.

Becker-Schaum, Christoph. "The Origins of the German Greens." In *Green Parties: Reflections on the First Three Decades.* Frank Zelko and Carolin Brinkmann, editors. Washington, DC: Heinrich Böll Stiftung North America, 2006.

Becker-Schaum, Christoph, editor. *"Entrüstet Euch!" Nuklearkrise, NATO-Doppelbeschluss und Friedensbewegung.* Paderborn: Schöningh, 2012.

Beckmann, Lukas. "'Beginne dort, wo Du bist.' Das Leben der Petra K. Kelly." In *Petra Kelly: Eine Erinnerung.* Berlin: Heinrich-Böll-Stiftung, 2007.

"Zum 60. Geburtstag von Petra Kelly: Wer den Beginn nicht kennt, hat für Veränderungen keinen Maßstab." Lecture, Heinrich-Böll-Stiftung, Berlin, November 28, 2007.

Beckmann, Lukas and Lew Kopelew, editors. *Gedenken heißt erinnern. Petra K. Kelly, Gert Bastian.* Göttingen: Lamuv, 1993.

Beer, Wolfgang. *Lernen im Widerstand. Politisches Lernen und politische Sozialisation in Bürgerinitiativen.* Hamburg: Verlag Association, 1978.

Bennahmias, Jean-Luc and Agnes Roche. *Des Verts de toutes les couleurs: Histoire et sociologie du mouvement écolo.* Paris: Albin Michel, 1992.

Benz, Wolfgang, editor. *Die Bundesrepublik Deutschland: Geschichte in drei Bänden.* Frankfurt am Main: Fischer, 1983.

Bess, Michael. *The Light-Green Society: Ecology and Technology in France, 1960–2000.* Chicago: University of Chicago Press, 2003.

Bevan, Ruth. "Petra Kelly: The *Other* Green." *New Political Science* 23 (2001): 181–202.

Birkland, Thomas A. "Focusing Events, Mobilization, and Agenda Setting." *Journal of Public Policy* 18, no. 1 (January–April 1998): 53–74.

Blackbourn, David. *The Conquest of Nature: Water, Landscape, and the Making of Modern Germany.* London: Jonathan Cape, 2006.

Bomberg, Elizabeth. *Green Parties and Politics in the European Union.* London: Routledge, 1998.

Borvon, Gérard. *Plogoff: un combat pour demain.* Saint-Thonan: Éd. Cloître, 2004.

Bösch, Frank. *Macht und Machtverlust. Die Geschichte der CDU.* Stuttgart: Deutsche Verlags-Anstalt, 2002.

"Taming Nuclear Power: The Accident near Harrisburg and the Change of West German and International Nuclear Policy in the 1970s and early 1980s." *German History* 35, no. 2 (2017).

Bourg, Julian. *From Revolution to Ethics: May 1968 and Contemporary French Thought.* Montreal: McGill-Queen's University Press, 2007.

Boy, Daniel. "Les écologistes en France." *French Politics and Society* 10, no. 3 (Summer 1992): 1–25.

Boyer, Josef and Helge Heidemeyer, editors. *Die Grünen im Bundestag. Sitzungsprotokolle und Anlagen, 1983–1987.* Düsseldorf: Droste Verlag, 2008.

Bracher, Karl-Dietrich. "Die Kanzlerdemokratie." In *Die Zweite Republik. 25 Jahre Bundesrepublik Deutschland. Eine Bilanz.* Richard Löwenthal and Hans-Peter Schwarz, editors. Stuttgart: Seewald Verlag, 1974.

Brand, Karl-Werner, editor. *Neue soziale Bewegungen in Westeuropa und den USA. Ein internationaler Vergleich.* Frankfurt am Main: Campus Verlag, 1985.

Brechin, Steven R. and Willett Kempton. "Global Environmentalism: A Challenge to the Postmaterialism Thesis?" *Social Science Quarterly* 75, no. 2 (June 1994): 245–269.

Bridgford, Jeff. "The Ecologist Movement and the French General Election 1978." *Parliamentary Affairs* 31, no. 3 (1978): 314–323.

Brophy, James. "The Rhine Crisis of 1840 and German Nationalism: Chauvinism, Skepticism, and Regional Reception." *Journal of Modern History* 85, no. 1 (March 2013): 1–35.

Brown, Kate. *Plutopia: Nuclear Families, Atomic Cities, and the Great Soviet and American Plutonium Disasters.* Oxford: Oxford University Press, 2013.

Brown, Timothy Scott. *West Germany and the Global Sixties: The Anti-Authoritarian Revolt, 1962–1978.* Cambridge: Cambridge University Press, 2013.

Brüggemeier, Franz-Josef. *Tschernobyl, 26. April 1986. Die ökologische Herausforderung.* Munich: Deutsche Taschenbuch-Verlag, 1998.

Brühöfener, Friederike. "Politics of Emtions: Journalistic Reflections on the Emotionality of the West German Peace Movement, 1979–1984." *German Politics and Society* 33, no. 4 (Winter 2015).

Brun, Rudolf, editor. *Der Grüne Protest. Herausforderung durch die Umweltparteien.* Frankfurt: Fischer, 1978.

Büchele, Christoph, Irmgard Schneider, and Bernd Nössler editors. *Wyhl. Der Widerstand geht weiter. Der Bürgerprotest gegen das Kernkraftwerk von 1976 bis zum Mannheimer Prozeß.* Freiburg: Dreisam-Verlag, 1982.

Buchholtz, Hans-Christoph, Lutz Mez, and Thomas von Zabern. *Widerstand gegen Atomkraftwerke. Informationen für Atomkraftwerkgegner und solche, die es werden wollen.* Wuppertal: Peter Hammer Verlag, 1978.

Bürgerinitiative Umweltschutz Unterelbe, *Brokdorf. Der Bauplatz muß wieder zur Wiese werden!* Hamburg: Verlag Association, 1977.

Burg, Marc. "Les Gauches face aux Droites dans le Bas Rhin sous la Ve Republique, 1958–1988." PhD Dissertation, Strasbourg: Université Robert Schuman, 1988.

Burns, Rob and Wilfried van der Will. *Protest and Democracy in West Germany: Extra-Parliamentary Opposition and the Democratic Agenda.* London: Macmillan Press, 1988.

Calhoun, Craig. "'New Social Movements' of the Early Nineteenth Century." *Social Science History* 17, no. 3 (Fall 1993): 385–427.

Camp, Robert. "'Für ein Europa der Regionen. Für eine ökologische europäische Gemeinschaft.' Über die Europapolitikerin Petra Kelly." In *Die Grünen in Europa. Ein Handbuch.* Münster: Heinrich-Böll-Stiftung, 2004.

Capra, Fritjof and Charlene Spretnak. *Green Politics.* New York: Dutton, 1984.

Caro, Céline. "Le développement de la conscience environnemental et l'émergence de l'écologie politique dans l'espace public en France et en Allemagne, 1960–1990." PhD Dissertation, Technische Universität Dresden and Université Sorbonne Nouvelle – Paris III, 2009.

Centre océanologique de Bretagne. *Synthese des études écologiques d'avant-projet des sites Bretons de Beg an Fry, Ploumoguer, Plogoff, Saint-Vio et Erdeven.* Brest: Centre océanologique de Bretagne, 1978.

Chaney, Sandra. *Nature of the Miracle Years: Conservation in West Germany, 1945–1975.* New York: Berghahn Books, 2008.

Cioc, Marc. *Pax Atomica: The Nuclear Debate in West Germany During the Adenauer Era.* New York: Columbia University Press, 1988.

The Rhine: An Eco-biography, 1815–2000. Seattle: University of Washington Press, 2002.

Cohn, Steve. *Too Cheap to Meter: An Economic and Philosophical Analysis of the Nuclear Dream*. Albany: State University of New York Press, 1997.

Collectif d'Enquete. *Aujourd'hui Malville, demain la France: Livre noir*. N.p.: La pensée sauvauge, 1978.

Confino, Alon. *The Nation as Local Metaphor: Württemberg, Imperial Germany, and National Memory, 1871–1918*. Chapel Hill: University of North Carolina Press, 1997.

Crouch, Colin. *Post-Democracy*. Malden: Polity, 2004.

Cruikshank, Barbara. *The Will to Empower*. Ithaca: Cornell University Press, 1999.

Dalton, Russel J. *The Green Rainbow: Environmental Groups in Western Europe*. New Haven: Yale University Press, 1994.

Daubner, Heinrich and Etienne Verne, editors. *Freiheit zum Lernen*. Reinbek bei Hamburg: Rowohlt, 1976.

Davis, Belinda. "A Brief Cosmogeny of the Green Party." *German Politics and Society* 33, no. 4 (Winter 2015).

The Internal Life of Politics: The New Left in West Germany, 1962–1983. Forthcoming.

"What's Left? Popular Political Participation in Postwar Europe." *American Historical Review* 113, no. 2 (April 2008): 363–390.

Davis, Belinda, Wilfried Mausbach, Martin Klimke, and Carla MacDougall, editors. *Changing the World, Changing Oneself: Political Protest and Collective Identities in West Germany and the U.S. in the 1960s and 1970s*. New York: Berghahn Books, 2010.

Deleage, Jean-Paul. *Une histoire de l'écologie*. Paris: La Découverte, 1991.

Dinan, Desmond, editor. *Origins and Evolution of the European Union*. Oxford: Oxford University Press, 2006.

Ditfurth, Jutta. *Krieg, Atom, Armut. Was Sie Reden, Was Sie Tun: Die Grünen*. Berlin: Rotbuch Verlag, 2011.

Dittmer, John. *Local People: The Struggle for Civil Rights in Mississippi*. Urbana: University of Illinois Press, 1995.

Dominick, Raymond. *The Environmental Movement in Germany: Prophets & Pioneers, 1871 – 1971*. Bloomington: Indiana University Press, 1992.

Drysch, Thomas. *Parteienfinanzierung. Österreich, Schweiz, Bundesrepublik Deutschland*. Wiesbaden: Springer, 1998.

Dumont, René, editor. *La campagne de René Dumont et du mouvement Écologique. Naissance de l'Écologie Politique*. Paris: Jean-Jacques Pauvert, 1974.

Dutschke-Klotz, Gretchen. *Wir hatten ein barbarisches, schönes Leben. Rudi Dutschke. Eine Biographie*. Cologne: Kiepenheuer & Witsch, 1996.

Ebert, Theodor, Wolfgang Sternstein, and Roland Vogt. *Ökologie Bewegung und ziviler Widerstand. Wyhler Erfahrungen*. Stuttgart: Umweltwissenschaftliches Institut, 1977.

Eley, Geoff. *Forging Democracy: The History of the Left in Europe, 1850–2000*. Oxford: Oxford University Press, 2002.

Engels, Jens Ivo. "Gender Roles and German Anti-Nuclear Protest. The Women of Wyhl." In *Le demon moderne: la pollution dans les sociétés urbaines et industrielles d'Europe.* Christoph Bernhardt, editor. Clermont-Ferrand: Presses universitaires Blaise Pascal, 2002: 407–424.

"'In Stadt und Land:' Differences & Convergences Between Urban and Local Environmentalism in West Germany, 1950–1980." In *Resources of the City: Contributions to an Environmental History of Modern Europe.* Dieter Schott, Bill Luckin, and Geneviève Massard-Guilbaud, editors. London: Ashgate, 2005.

Naturpolitik in der Bundesrepublik: Ideenwelt und politische Verhaltensstile in Naturschutz und Umweltbewegung, 1950–1980. Paderborn: Schöningh, 2006.

Epstein, Barbara. *Political Protest and Cultural Revolution: Nonviolent Direct Action in the 1970s and 1980s.* Berkeley: University of California Press, 1991.

Essig, Michael. *Das Elsaß auf der Suche nach seiner Identität.* Munich: Eberhard, 1994.

Fagnani, Francis, and Alexandre Nicolon, editors. *Nucléopolis: Materiaux pour l'analyse d'une societe nucléaire.* Grenoble: Presses Universitaires de Grenoble, 1979.

Farmer, Sarah. *Martyred Village: Commemorating the 1944 Massacre at Oradour-sur-Glane.* Berkeley: University of California Press, 1999.

Feigenbaum, Anna, Fabian Frenzel, and Patrick McCurdy. *Protest Camps.* London: Zed Books, 2013.

Fenske, Hans. *Der liberale Südwesten. Freiheitliche und demokratische Traditionen in Baden und Württemberg, 1790–1933.* Stuttgart: Kohlhammer, 1981.

Ferguson, Niall, Charles S. Maier, Erez Manela, and Daniel J. Sargent, editors. *The Shock of the Global: The 1970s in Perspective.* Cambridge, MA: Harvard University Press, 2010.

Fink, Jessica and Johnny Peter. *Geschichte der Grünen in Niedersachsen.* Hannover: Die Grünen Niedersachsen, 2002 (updated 2013).

Fischer, Christopher. *Alsace to the Alsatians? Visions and Divisions of Alsatian Regionalism, 1870–1939.* New York: Berghahn Books, 2010.

Flam, Helena, editor. *The State and Anti-Nuclear Movements.* Edinburgh: Edinburgh University Press, 1994.

Foley, Michael. *Front Porch Politics: The Forgotten Heyday of American Activism in the 1970s and 1980s.* New York: Hill and Wang, 2013.

François, Etienne and Hagen Schulze, editors. *Deutsche Errinerungsorte.* Munich: Beck, 2001.

Frankland, E. Gene and Donald Schoonmaker. *Between Protest and Power: The Green Party in Germany.* Boulder: Westview Press, 1992.

Fraser, Clara. *Which Road Towards Women's Liberation: A Radical Vanguard or a Single-Issue Coalition?* Seattle: Radical Woman Publications, 2003 (first printed 1970).

Frei, Norbert. *1968. Jugendrevolte und Globaler Protest.* Munich: Deutscher Taschenbuch Verlag, 2008.

Frémion, Yves. *Histoire de la révolution écologiste.* Paris: Hoëbeke, 2007.

Frenzel, Fabian, Anna Feigenbaum, and Patrick McCurdy. "Protest camps: an emerging field of social movement research." *The Sociological Review* 62 (2013): 457–474.

Füglister, Stefan. *Darum werden wir Kaiseraugst verhindern.* Zürich: Orte-Verlag, 1984.

Gatzka, Claudia. "Demokratie als lokale Praxis. Bürger, Politik und urbane Wahlkampfkultur in Italien und der Bundesrepublik, 1945–1976." PhD Dissertation, Humboldt Universität zu Berlin, 2015.

"Des Wahlvolks großer Auftritt. Wahlritual und demokratische Kultur in Italien und Westdeutschland nach 1945." *Comparativ* 23, no. 1 (2013): 64–88.

Gauchet, Gregoire. "Implantation Politique et Associative des Ecologistes en Alsace." Master's Thesis, Université Robert Schuman de Strasbourg, 1991.

Gaumer, Janine. "WAAhnsin in der bayerischen Provinz. Der Konflikt um die atomare Wiederaufarbeitunsanlage in Wackersforf, 1980–1990." PhD Dissertation, Friedrich-Schiller Universität Jena, forthcoming.

Gildea, Robert. *France since 1945.* Oxford: Oxford University Press, 2002.

Gildea, Robert and Andrew Tompkins. "The Transnational in the Local: The Larzac Plateau as a Site of Transnational Activism since 1970." *Journal of Contemporary History* 50, no. 3 (July 2015): 581–605.

Gildea, Robert, James Mark, and Anette Warring, editors. *Europe's 1968: Voices of Revolt.* Oxford: Oxford University Press, 2013.

Gitlin, Todd. *The Twilight of Common Dreams.* New York: Metropolitan Books, 1995.

Goodwyn, Lawrence. *Breaking the Barrier: The Rise of Solidarity in Poland.* Oxford: Oxford University Press, 1991.

Democratic Promise: The Populist Moment in America. Oxford: Oxford University Press, 1976.

The Populist Moment. A Short History of the Agrarian Revolt in America. Oxford: Oxford University Press, 1978.

Goldsmith, M. *Frederic Joliot-Curie: A Biography.* London: Lawrence and Wishart, 1976.

Görtemaker, Manfred. *Geschichte der Bundesrepublik Deutschland. Von der Gründung bis zur Gegenwart.* Munich: Beck, 1999.

Gladitz, Nina, editor. *Lieber heute aktiv als morgen radioaktiv. Wyhl, Bauern erzählen. Warum Kerkraftwerke schädlich sind. Wie man eine Bürgeriniative macht und wie man sich dabei verändert.* Berlin: Wagenbach, 1976.

Gräber, Gerhard. "Von Wyhl in die Villa Reitzenstein: Die wundersame Reise der Grünen in Baden-Württemberg." *Grünes Gedächtnis* (2011): 18–34.

Greenberg, Udi. *The Weimar Century: German Émigrés and the Ideological Foundations of the Cold War.* Princeton: Princeton University Press, 2014.

Guedeney, Colette and Gérard Mendel. *L'angoisse atomique et les centrales nucléaires.* Paris: Payot, 1973.

Habermas, Jürgen. *The Structural Transformation of the Public Sphere.* Translated by Thomas Burger. Cambridge, MA: MIT Press, 1991.

Hager, Carol. "Germany's Green Energy Revolution: Challenging the Theory and Practice of Institutional Change." *German Politics and Society* 33, no. 3 (Autumn 2015): 1–27.

Technological Democracy: Bureaucracy and Citizenry in the German Energy Debate. Ann Arbor: University of Michigan Press, 1995.

Hager, Carol and Mary Alice Haddad, editors. *NIMBY is Beautiful: Cases of Local Activism and Environmental Innovation Around the World.* New York: Berghahn, 2015.

Hallensleben, Anna. *Von der Grünen Liste zur Grünen Partei? Die Entwicklung der Grünen Liste Umweltschutz von ihrer Entstehung in Niedersachsen 1977 bis zur Gründung der Partei DIE GRÜNEN 1980.* Göttingen: Muster-Schmidt Verlag, 1984.

Hanrieder, Wolfram F., editor. *Helmut Schmidt: Perspectives on Politics.* Boulder: Westview Press, 1982.

Hansen, Jan, Christian Helm, and Frank Reichherzer, editors. *Making Sense of the Americas: How Protest Related to America in the 1980s and Beyond.* Frankfurt am Main: Campus, 2015.

Hanshew, Karrin. "Daring More Democracy? Internal Security and the Social Democratic Fight against West German Terrorism." *Central European History* 43, no. 1 (2010): 117–147.

"'Sympathy for the Devil?' The West German Left and the Challenge of Terrorism." *Contemporary European History* 21 (2012): 511–532.

Terror and Democracy in West Germany. Cambridge: Cambridge University Press, 2012.

Harvey, Kyle. *American Anti-Nuclear Activism, 1975–1990.* Houndmills, Basingstoke: Palgrave Macmillan, 2014.

Hecht, Gabrielle. *The Radiance of France: Nuclear Power and National Identity after World War II.* Cambridge, MA: MIT Press, 1998.

Heck, Bruno. *Hans Filbinger. Der "Fall" und die Fakten.* Mainz: V. Hase & Koehler Verlag, 1980.

Heiko, Haumann, editor. *Vom Hotzenwald bis Wyhl. Demokratische Traditionen in Baden.* Cologne: Pahl-Rugenstein Verlag, 1977.

Herbert, Ulrich. *Geschichte Deutschlands im 20. Jahrhundert.* Munich: Beck, 2014.

Hermann, Winne and Wolfgang Schwegler-Rohmeis, editors. *Grüner Weg durch schwarzes Land. 10 Jahre Grüne in Baden-Württemberg.* Stuttgart: Edition Erdmann, 1989.

Hertle, Wolfgang. *Larzac, 1971–1981. Der gewaltfreie Widerstand gegen die Erweiterung eines Truppenübungsplatzes in Süd-Frankreich.* Kassel: Weber, Zucht & Co., 1982.

"Larzac, Wyhl, Brokdorf, Seabrook, Gorleben ... Grenzüberschreitender Lernprozeß Zivil Ungehorsams." In *Ziviler Ungehorsam. Traditionen, Konzepte, Erfahrungen, Perspektiven.* Wolf-Dieter Narr, Roland Roth, Klaus Vack, editors. Sensbachtal: Das Komitee, 1992.

Hobsbawm, Eric. *The Age of Extremes: A History of the World, 1914–1991.* New York: Vintage, 1994.

Hockenos, Paul. *Joschka Fischer and the Making of the Berlin Republic: An Alternative History of Postwar Germany*. Oxford: Oxford University Press, 2008.

Hohensee, Jens. *Der erste Ölpreisschock 1973–74. Die politischen und gesellschaftlichen Auswirkungen der arabischen Erdölpolitik auf die Bundesrepublik Deutschland und Westeuropa*. Stuttgart: Steiner Verlag, 1996.

Hughes, Michael. "Civil Disobedience in Transnational Perspective: American and West German Anti-Nuclear-Power Protesters." *Historical Social Research* 39, no. 1 (2014): 236–253.

Hünemörder, Kai F. *Die Frühgeschichte der deutschen Umweltpolitik (1950–1973)*. Stuttgart: F. Steiner, 2004.

Inglehart, Ronald. *The Silent Revolution: Changing Values and Political Styles Among Western Publics*. Princeton: Princeton University Press, 1977.

"The Silent Revolution in Europe: Intergenerational Change in Post-Industrial Societies." *The American Political Science Review* 65, no. 4: (1971): 991–1017.

Jachnow, Joachim. "What's Become of the German Greens?" *New Left Review* 81 (May–June 2013): 95–117.

Jacob, Jean. *Histoire de l'écologie politique*. Paris: A. Michel, 1999.

Jasper, James. *Nuclear Politics: Energy and the State in the United States, Sweden, and France*. Princeton: Princeton University Press, 1990.

Jarausch, Konrad. *After Hitler: Recivilizing Germans, 1945–1995*. Translated by Brandon Hunziker. Oxford: Oxford University Press, 2006.

Jarausch, Konrad, editor. *Das Ende der Zuversicht? Die siebziger Jahre als Geschichte*. Göttingen: Vandenhoek und Ruprecht, 2008.

Out of Ashes: A New History of Europe in the Twentieth Century. Princeton: Princeton University Press, 2015.

Jarausch, Konrad and Michael Geyer. *Shattered Past: Reconstructing German Histories*. Princeton: Princeton University Press, 2003.

"Jean." *Elsass: Kolonie in Europa*. Wagenbach: Berlin, 1976.

Johnsen, Hartmut. *Der Startbahn-West-Konflikt. Ein politisches Lehrstück? Zeitzeugen ziehen Bilanz*. Frankfurt am Main: Societäts-Verlag, 1996.

Johnson, Robert Underwood. *Remembered Yesterdays*. Boston: Little, Brown, and Co., 1923.

Joppke, Christian. *Mobilizing Against Nuclear Energy: A Comparison of Germany and the United States*. Berkeley: University of California Press, 1993.

Judt, Tony. *Postwar: A History of Europe since 1945*. New York: Penguin, 2005.

Judt, Tony with Timothy Snyder. *Thinking the Twentieth Century*. New York: Penguin, 2012.

Juillard, Étienne. *L'Europe Rhénane. Géographie d'un grand espace*. Paris: Libraire Armand Colin, 1968.

Jund, Thierry. *Le nucléaire contre l'Alsace*. Paris: Syros, 1977.

Jungk, Robert. *Der Atomstaat. Vom Fortschritt in die Unmenschlichkeit*. Munich: Kindler, 1977.

Kalb, Martin. "'Rather Active Today than Radioactive Tomorrow!' Environmental Justice and the Anti-Nuclear Movement in 1970s Wyhl, West Germany." *Global Environment* 10 (2012): 156–183.

Kalmbach, Karena. *Tschernobyl und Frankreich. Die Debatte um die Auswirkungen des Reaktorunfalls im Kontext der französischen Atompolitik und Elitenkultur.* Frankfurt am Main: Peter Lang, 2011.

Karapin, Roger. *Protest Politics in Germany: Movements on the Left and Right Since the 1960s.* University Park: Pennsylvania State University Press, 2007.

Kirchhof, Astrid Mignon, and Jan-Henrik Meyer, editors. "Global Protest Against Nuclear Power. Transfer and Transnational Exchange in the 1970s and 1980s." *Focus* in *Historical Social Research* 39, no. 1 (2014).

Kitschelt, Herbert. *The Logics of Party Formation: Ecological Politics in Belgium and West Germany.* Ithaca, NY: Cornell University Press, 1989.

"Left-Libertarian Parties: Explaining Innovation in Competitive Party Systems." *World Politics* 40, no. 2 (January 1988): 194–234.

"Political Opportunity Structures and Political Protest: Anti-Nuclear Movements in Four Democracies." *British Journal of Political Science* 16, no. 1 (1986): 57–85.

Politik und Energie: Energie-Technologiepolitiken in den USA, der Bundesrepublik Deutschland, Frankreich und Schweden. Frankfurt am Main: Campus, 1983.

"Social Movements, Political Parties, and Democratic Theory." *Annals of the American Academy of Political and Social Science* 528 (July 1993): 13–29.

Klimke, Martin. *The Other Alliance: Student Protest in West Germany and the United States in the Global Sixties.* Princeton: Princeton University Press, 2010.

Koenen, Gerd. *Das rote Jahrzehnt. Unsere kleine deutsche Kulturrevolution, 1967–1977.* Cologne: Kiepenheuer & Witsch, 2001.

Kommers, Donald P. *The Constitutional Jurisprudence of the Federal Republic of Germany.* Durham: Duke University Press, 1997.

Koshar, Rudy. *Social Life, Local Politics, and Nazism: Marburg: 1880–1935.* Chapel Hill: University of North Carolina Press, 1986.

Kraushaar, Wolfgang. *Die Protest-Chronik 1949–1959. Eine illustrierte Geschichte von Bewegung, Widerstand, und Utopie.* Hamburg: Rogner & Bernhard, 1996.

Kraushaar, Wolfgang, editor. *Was sollen die Grünen im Parlament?* Frankfurt am Main: Verlag Neue Kritik, 1983.

Kufer, Astrid, Isabelle Guinaudeau, and Christophe Premat, editors. *Handwörterbuch der deutsch-französischen Beziehungen.* Baden-Baden: Nomos, 2009.

Kupper, Patrick. *Atomenergie und gespaltene Gesellschaft. Die Geschichte des gescheiterten Projekts Kernkraftwerk Kaiseraugst.* Zürich: Chronos, 2003.

Landesarchivdirektion Baden-Württemberg and Landkreis Emmendingen. *Der Landkreis Emmendingen.* Stuttgart: Jan Thorbecke Verlag, 1999.

Landry, Marc. "Europe's Battery: The Making of the Alpine Energy Landscape, 1870–1955." PhD Dissertation, Georgetown University: 2013.

Lasky, Melvin. "The Pacifist and the General." *The National Interest* 34 (Winter 1993): 66–78.

Lebovics, Herman. *Bringing the Empire Back Home: France in the Global Age.* Durham: Duke University Press, 2004.

Leggewie, Claus and Roland de Miller. *Der Wahlfisch: Ökologiebewegungen in Frankreich.* Berlin: Merve-Verlag, 1978.

Lekan, Thomas. *Imagining the Nation in Nature: Landscape Preservation and German Identity, 1885–1945.* Cambridge, Massachusetts: Harvard University Press, 2004.

Lieber heute aktiv als morgen radioaktiv. Hamburg: Laika-Verlag, 2011.

Linse, Ulrich, Reinhard Falter, Dieter Rucht, and Winfried Kretschmer. *Von der Bittschrift zur Platzbesetzung. Konflikte um technische Großprojekte.* Berlin: Verlag J. H. W. Dietz Nachf., 1988.

Löser, Georg. *Grenzüberschreitende Kooperation am Oberrhein. Die Badisch-Elsässischen Bürgerinitiativen.* Stuttgart: Landesarchivdirektion Baden-Württemberg, 2003.

Lucas, N. J. D. *Energy in France: Planning, Politics, and Policy.* London: Europa, 1979.

Lynch, Timothy P. *Strike Songs of the Depression.* Jackson: University of Mississippi Press, 2001.

Lyons, Matthew. "The Grassroots Movement in Germany, 1972–1985." In *Nonviolent Social Movements: A Geographical Perspective.* Stephen Zunes, Lester R. Kurtz, and Sarah Beth Asher, editors. Malden, MA: Blackwell Publishers, 1999.

Maier, Charles. "History Lived and History Written: Germany and the United States, 1945/55–2015." *Bulletin of the German Historical Institute* 57 (Fall 2015): 7–23.

Markovits, Andrei S. and Katherine N. Crosby. *From Property to Family: American Dog Rescue and the Discourse of Compassion.* Ann Arbor: University of Michigan Press, 2014.

Markovits, Andrei S. and Philip S. Gorski. *The German Left: Red, Green, and Beyond.* Oxford: Oxford University Press, 1993.

Markovits, Andrei S. and Stephen Silvia. "Green Trumps Red? Political identity and left-wing politics in united Germany." In *Transformation of the German Political Party System.* C. S. Allen, editor. New York: Berghahn Books, 1999.

Markovits, Andrei S. and Joseph Klaver. "Thirty Years of Bundestag Presence: A Tally of the Greens' Impact on the Federal Republic of Germany's Political Life and Public Culture." *AICGS German-American Issues* 14 (2012).

Marwick, Arthur. *The Sixties: Cultural Revolution in Britain, France, Italy, and the United States, 1958–1974.* Oxford: Oxford University Press, 1998.

Massey, Andrew. *Technocrats and Nuclear Politics: The Influence of Professional Experts in Policy-Making.* Aldershot: Avebury, 1988.

Mayer, Axel. "Politisches Lernen und politische Sozialisation dargestellt am Bespiel der Badisch-Elsässischen Bürgerinitiativen." Diploma Thesis, Fachhochschule für Sozialwesen Freiburg, 1982.

Mayer, Margit and John Ely, editors. *The German Greens: Paradox Between Movement and Party.* Philadelphia: Temple University Press, 1998.

Mayer-Tasch, Peter Cornelius. *Die Bürgerinitiativbewegung. Der aktive Bürger als rechts- und politikwissenschaftliches Problem.* Reinbek bei Hamburg: Rowohlt, 1976.

Mazower, Mark. *Dark Continent: Europe's Twentieth Century.* New York: Vintage, 1998.

McNeill, J. R. *Something New Under the Sun: An Environmental History of the Twentieth Century World.* New York: Norton, 2000.

Meadows, Donella H., Dennis L. Meadows, and Jørgen Randers. *The Limits to Growth: A Report for the Club of Rome's Project on the Predicament of Mankind.* New York: Universe Books, 1972.

Mende, Silke. "Asterix in Musterländle? Zur Entstehung und Geschichte der baden-württembergischen Grünen." In *Aufbruch, Protest, und Provokation. Die bewegten 70er- und 80er-Jahre in Baden-Württemberg.* Reinhold Weber, editor. Stuttgart: Theiss, 2013.

"'Enemies at the Gate:' The West German Greens and Their Arrival at the Bundestag—Between Old Ideals and New Challenges." *German Politics and Society* 33, no. 4 (Winter 2015).

"Nicht rechts, nicht links, sondern vorn." Eine Geschichte der Gründungsgrünen. Munich: Oldenbourg: Wissenschaftsverlag, 2011.

and Birgit Metzger. "Ökopax. Die Umweltbewegung als Erfahrungsraum der Friedensbewegung." In *Entrüstet Euch! Nuklearkrise, NATO-Doppelbeschluss und Friedensbewegung.* Christoph Becker-Schaum, editor. Paderborn: Schöningh, 2012.

Menke-Glückert, Peter. "Der Umweltpolitiker Genscher." In *In der Verantwortung. Hans Dietrich Genscher zum Siebzigsten.* Klaus Kinkel, editor. Berlin: Siedler, 1997: 155–168.

van Merriënboer, Johan. *Mansholt: Een biografie.* Amsterdam: Boom, 2006.

Metzger, Birgit, Annette Lensing, and Olivier Hanse, editors. *Die Ökologie im linken und rechten Spektrum: Konvergenzen und Divergenzen zwischen Deutschland und Frankreich von 1970 bis heute.* Hamburg: Peter Lang, forthcoming.

Meyer, Jan-Henrik. "Challenging the Atomic Community: The European Environmental Bureau and the Europeanization of Anti-Nuclear Protest." In *Societal Actors in European Integration: Polity-Building and Policy-Making, 1958–1992.* Wolfram Kaiser and Jan-Henrik Meyer, editors. Houndmills, Basingstoke: Palgrave Macmillan, 2013.

Mez, Lutz, editor. *Der Atomkonflikt. Atomindustrie, Atompolitik und Anti-Atom-Bewegung im internationalen Vergleich.* Hamburg: Olle & Wolter, 1979.

Milder, Stephen. "Between Grassroots Protest and Green Politics: The Democratic Potential of 1970s Anti-nuclear Activism." *German Politics and Society* 33, no. 4 (Winter 2015).

"Harnessing the Energy of the Anti-Nuclear Activist: How Young European Federalists Built on Rhine Valley Protest, 1974–77." *Perspectives on Global Development and Technology* 9, no. 1–2 (2010): 119–136.

"Protest and Participation: The Transformation of Democratic Praxis in the FRG, 1968–1983 Forthcoming in Michael Meng and Adam Seipp, editors. *German History in Transatlantic Perspective*. New York: Berghahn, 2017.

"Thinking Globally, Acting (Trans-)Locally: Petra Kelly and the Transnational Roots of West German Green Politics." *Central European History* 43, no. 2 (June 2010): 301–326.

and Konrad Jarausch. "Renewing Democracy: The Rise of Green Politics in West Germany." *German Politics and Society* 33, no. 4 (Winter 2015).

Miller, Byron A. *Geography and Social Movements: Comparing Anti-nuclear Acitivism in the Boston Area*. Minneapolis: University of Minnesota Press, 2000.

Miller, James. *Democracy Is in the Streets: From Port Huron to the Siege of Chicago*. Cambridge, MA: Harvard University Press, 1987.

Miller, Kyle. "The Bavarian Model? Modernization, Environment, and Landscape Planning in the Bavarian Nuclear Power Industry 1950–1980." PhD Dissertation, University of Missouri-Columbia, 2009.

Moldenhauer, Gerd and Hans-Helmuth Wüstenhagen. *Atomindustrie und Bürgerinitiative gegen Umweltzerstörung*. Cologne: Pahl-Rugenstein Verlag, 1975.

Morgan, Roger and David Allen. "The European Parliament: Direct Election in National and Community Perspective." *The World Today* 34, no. 8 (August 1978): 296–302.

Morstadt, Sibylle. "Die Landesregierung von Baden-Württemberg und der Konflikt um das geplante Kernkraftwerk in Wyhl." Diploma Thesis, University of Freiburg, 2002.

Moses, A. Dirk and Elliot Neaman. "West German Generations and the *Gewaltfrage*: The Conflict of the Sixty-Eighters and the Forty-Fivers." In *The Modernist Imagination: Intellectual History and Critical Theory*. Warren Breckman, Peter E. Gordon, A. Dirk Moses, Samuel Moyn, and Elliot Neaman, editors. New York: Berghahn Books, 2009.

Mossmann, Walter. *Realistisch sein: das unmögliche verlangen. Wahrheitstreue gefältschte Errinerungen*. Berlin: edition der Freitag, 2009.

and Cornelius Schwehr, editors. *Die Störung. Tonstück und Texte zur Anti-AKW-Bewegung*. Emmendingen: verlag die brotsuppe, 2000.

and Peter Schleunig, editors. *Alte und neue politische Lieder. Entstehung und Gebrauch, Texte und Noten*. Reinbek: Rowohlt, 1978.

Moyn, Samuel. *The Last Utopia: Human Rights in History*. Cambridge, MA: Harvard University Press, 2010.

Müller, Jan-Werner. *Contesting Democracy: Political Ideas in Twentieth Century Europe*. New Haven: Yale University Press, 2011.

Müller-Hill, Benno. *Tödliche Wissenschaft. Die Aussonderung von Juden, Zigeunern und Geisteskranken, 1933–1945*. Reinbek bei Hamburg: Rowohlt Taschenbuch Verlag, 1984.

Müller-Rommel, Ferdinand. "Ecology Parties in Western Europe." *West European Politics* 5 (1982): 68–74.

New Politics in Western Europe: The Rise and Success of Green Parties and Alternative Lists. Boulder: Westview Press, 1989.

Nader, Ralph. *Crashing the Party: Taking on the Corporate Government in an Age of Surrender.* New York: Thomas Dunne Books, 2002.

Nehring, Holger. "National Internationalists: British and West German Protests Against Nuclear Weapons, the Politics of Transnational Communications and the Social History of the Cold War, 1957–1964." *Contemporary European History* 14, no. 4 (November 2005): 559–582.

Politics of Security. British and West German Protest Movements and the Early Cold War, 1945–1970. Oxford: Oxford University Press, 2013.

Nelkin, Dorothy and Michael Pollack. *The Atom Besieged: Extraparliamentary Dissent in France and Germany.* Cambridge, MA: MIT Press, 1981.

Nicolon, Alexandre, Francis Fagnani, and Marie Josèphe Carrieu, editors. *Nucléopolis: matériaux pour l'analyse d'une société nucléaire.* Grenoble: Presses universitaires de Grenoble, 1979.

Nolte, Paul. *Riskante Moderne. Die Deutschen und der neue Kapitalismus.* Munich: Beck, 2006.

Was ist Demokratie? Geschichte und Gegenwart. Munich: Beck, 2012.

Nössler, Bernd and Margret de Witt, editors. *Wyhl. Kein Kernkraftwerk in Wyhl und auch sonst nirgends. Betroffene Bürger berichten.* Freiburg: inform-Verlag, 1976.

Notz, Gisela. "Die autonomen Frauenbewegungen der Siebzigerjahre. Entstehungsgeschichte – Organisationsformen – politische Konzepte." *Archiv für Sozialgeschichte* 44 (2004): 123–148.

Nullmeier, Frank, Frauke Rubart, and Harald Schulz, editors. *Umweltbewegung und Parteiensystem: Umweltgruppen und Umweltparteien in Frankreich und Schweden.* Berlin: Quorum, 1983.

Offe, Claus. "New Social Movements: Challenging the Boundaries of Institutional Politics." *Social Research* 52, no. 4 (Winter 1985): 817–868.

Oppenheimer, Andrew. "Conflicts of Solidarity: Nuclear Weapons, Liberation Movements, and the Politics of Peace in the Federal Republic of Germany, 1945–1975." PhD Dissertation, University of Chicago, 2010.

Ortsverein Wyhl. *10 Jahre SPD-Ortsverein Wyhl.* Wyhl: 1985.

Osif, Bonnie, Anthony Baratta, and Thomas Conkling. *TMI 25 Years Later: The Three Mile Island Nuclear Power Plant Accident and its Impact.* University Park: Pennsylvania State University Press, 2004.

Osterhammel, Jürgen, and Niels P. Petersson. *Globalization: A Short History.* Princeton: Princeton University Press, 2005.

Parkin, Sara. *Green Parties: An International Guide.* London: Heretic Books, 1989.

The Life and Death of Petra Kelly. London: Pandora, 1994.

Paul, Reimar. *. . . und auch nicht anderswo! Die Geschichte der Anti-AKW-Bewegung.* Göttingen: Verlag Die Werkstatt, 1997.

Peter-Davis, E., A. Albrecht, and F. Bucher. *Fessenheim vie ou mort de l'Alsace.* Mulhouse-Riedelsheim: Schmitt-Lucos, 1970.

Pettenkoffer, Andreas. *Die Entstehung der grünen Politik. Kultursoziologie der westdeutschen Umweltbewegung.* Frankfurt: Campus, 2014.

Pfau, Richard. *No Sacrifice Too Great: The Life of Lewis L. Strauss.* Charlottesville: University of Virginia Press, 1984.

Pichavant, René. *Les pierres de la liberté: Plogoff, 1975–1980: chronique.* Douarnenez: Editions Morgane, 1981.

Plogstedt, Sibylle, editor. *Der Kampf des vietnamesischen Volkes und Globalstrategie des Imperialismus.* West Berlin: Internationales Nachrichten- und Forschungs-Institut, 1968.

Pohl, Natalie. "Catte-NON. Atomprotest in der Saar-Lor-Lux-Region." *Forum für Politik, Gesellschaft, und Kultur in Luxemburg* 323 (2012): 51–54.

Poiger, Ute. *Jazz, Rock, and Rebels: Cold War Politics and American Culture in a Divided Germany.* Berkeley: University of California Press, 2000.

Prendiville, Brendan. *Environmental Politics in France.* Boulder: Westview Press, 1994.

"France: Les Verts." In *New Politics in Western Europe: The Rise and Success of Green Parties and Alternative Lists.* Ferdinand Müller-Rommel, editor. Boulder: Westview Press, 1989.

Pronier, Raymond and Vincent Jacques le Seigneur. *Generation Verte: Les ecologistes en politique.* Paris: La Renaissance, 1992.

Radkau, Joachim. *Aufstieg und Krise der deutschen Atomwirtschaft, 1945–1975.* Reinbek bei Hamburg Rowohlt, 1983.

Natur und Macht. Eine Weltgeschichte der Umwelt. Munich: Beck, 2000.

Raschke, Joachim. *Die Grünen. Wie sie wurden, was sie sind.* Cologne: Bund-Verlag, 1993.

"Politik und Wertewandel in den westlichen Demokratien." *Aus Politik und Zeitgeschichte* 36 (1980): 23–45.

Reichardt, Sven. *Authentizität und Gemeinschaft. Linksalternatives Leben in den siebziger und frühen achtziger Jahren.* Berlin: Suhrkamp 2014.

Reid, Donald. "Larzac in the Broad 1968 and After." *French Politics, Culture, and Society* 32, no. 2 (Summer 2014): 99–122.

Renn, Ortwin, M. Brooke Rogers, Kristian Krieger, and Ragnar Löfstedt. "Nuclear Accidents and Policy Responses in Europe: Comparing the Cases of France and Germany." In *Policy Shock: Regulatory Responses to Oil Spills, Nuclear Accidents, and Financial Meltdowns.* Edward Balleisen, Lori Bennear, Kim Krawiec, and Jonathan Weiner, editors. Cambridge: Cambridge University Press, forthcoming.

Richter, Manfred. *Bürger, helft Euch selbst, Wyhl – ein Beispiel.* Reinach: Manfred Richter Fine Photography, 2015.

Richter, Saskia. *Die Aktivistin. Das Leben der Petra Kelly.* Munich: Deutsche Verlags-Anstalt, 2010.

"Petra Kelly, International Green Leader: On Biography and the Peace Movement as Resources of Power in West German Politics, 1979–1983." *German Politics and Society* 33, no. 4 (Winter 2015).

Rodgers, Daniel T. *Age of Fracture*. Cambridge, MA: Belknap Press of Harvard University Press, 2011.

Rodgers, Daniel T. *Atlantic Crossings: Social Politics in a Progressive Age*. Cambridge, MA: Belknap Press of Harvard University Press, 1998.

Rollins, William H. *A Greener Vision of Home: Cultural Politics and Environmental Reform in the German Heimatschutz Movement, 1904–1918*. Ann Arbor: University of Michigan Press, 1997.

Rome, Adam. *The Genius of Earth Day: How a 1970 Teach-In Unexpectedly Made the First Green Generation*. New York: Hill and Wang, 2013.

Rootes, Christopher, editor. *Environmental Protest in Western Europe*. Oxford: Oxford University Press, 2007.

Roth, Roland and Dieter Rucht, editors. *Neue soziale Bewegungen in der Bundesrepublik Deutschland*. Frankfurt am Main: Campus, 1987.

Rowe, David E. and Robert Schulmann, editors. *Einstein on Politics: His Private Thoughts and Public Stands on Nationalism, Zionism, War, Peace, and the Bomb*. Princeton: Princeton University Press, 2007.

Rucht, Dieter. *Von Wyhl nach Gorleben. Bürger gegen Atomprogramm und nukleare Entsorgung*. Munich: C. H. Beck, 1980.

Rucht, Dieter, editor. *Protest in der Bundesrepublik. Strukturen und Entwicklungen*. Frankfurt am Main: Campus, 2001.

Rucht, Dieter and Roland Roth. *Die Soziale Bewegungen in Deutschland seit 1945. Ein Handbuch*. Frankfurt am Main: Campus, 2008.

von Rudloff, Hans. *Die Schwankungen und Pendelungen des Klimas in Europa seit dem Beginn der regelmäßiger Instrumenten-Beobachtungen (1670)*. Braunschweig: Friedr. Vieweg & Sohn, 1967.

Rusinek, Bernd-A. "Wyhl." In *Deutsche Erinnerungsorte II*. Etienne François and Hagen Schulze, editors. Munich: Beck, 2001.

Sarkar, Saral. *Green-Alternative Politics in West Germany: Volume II: The Greens*. Tokyo: United Nations Press, 1994.

Sattler, Karl-Otto. *Im Streit für die Umwelt: Jo Leinen, Basis-Aktivist und Minister: Bilanz und Ausblick*. Kirkel: Edition Apoll, 1995.

Schildt, Axel and Detlef Siegfried, editors. *Between Marx and Coca-Cola: Youth Cultures in Changing European Societies, 1960–1980*. New York: Berghahn, 2006.

Schleunig, Peter. "'Hoch die rote Blaskapelle?' Über die Entwicklung und Arbeit einer linken Freiburger Blaskappele aus der Sicht des Tubaspielers." *Anschläge* 4, no. 1 (December 1978): 43–64.

Schmitt, Rüdiger. *Die Friedensbewegung in der Bundesrepublik Deutschland. Ursachen und Bedingungen der Mobilisierung einer neuen sozialen Bewegung*. Opladen: Westdeutscher Verlag, 1990.

Schnieder, Frank. *Von der sozialen Bewegung zur Institution? Die Entstehung der Partei DIE GRÜNEN in den Jahren 1978 bis 1980. Argumente, Entwicklungen und Strategien am Beispiel Bonn/Hannover/Osnabrück*. Münster: Lit Verlag, 1998.

Schwarzer, Alice. *Eine tödliche Liebe. Petra Kelly und Gert Bastian*. Cologne: Kiepenheuer und Witsch, 1993.

Schregel, Susanne. *Der Atomkrieg vor der Wohnungstür. Eine Politikgeschichte der neuen Friedensbewegung in der Bundesrepublik, 1970–1985.* Frankfurt am Main: Campus, 2011.

Schroeren, Michael, editor. *Die Grünen. 10 bewegte Jahre.* Vienna: Ueberreuter Carl Verlag, 1990.

Schroeren, Michael. z. B. *Kaiseraugst: Der Gewaltfreie Widerstand gegen das Atomkraftwerk: Vom legalen Protest zum zivilen Ungehorsam.* Zürich: Verlag Schweizerischer Friedensrat, 1977.

Schulthess, Elisabeth. *Solange l'insoumise: ecologie, feminisme, non-violence.* Barret-sur-Méouge: Y. Michel, 2004.

Schwab, Günther. *Der Tanz mit dem Teufel: ein abenteurliches Interview.* Hanover: Adolf Sponholtz Verlag, 1958.

Serne, Pierre. *Des verts à EELV: 30 ans d'histoire de l'écologie politique.* Paris: Les petits matins, 2013.

Shepard, Mark. *The Community of the Ark.* Sante Fe: Ocean Tree Books, 1990.

Simon, Armin. *Der Streit um das Schwarzwald-Uran. Die Auseinandersetzung um den Uranbergbau in Menzenschwand im Südschwarzwald, 1960–1991.* Bremgarten: Donzelli-Kluckert, 2003.

Simon, Gilles. *Plogoff: L'apprentissage de la mobilisation sociale.* Rennes: Presses universitaires de Rennes, 2010.

Slobodian, Quinn. *Foreign Front: Third World Politics in Sixties West Germany.* Durham, North Carolina: Duke University Press, 2012.

Sperr, Monika. *Petra Karin Kelly. Politikerin aus Betroffenheit.* Munich: C. Bertelsmann Verlag, 1983.

Spretnak, Charlene and Fritjof Capra. *Green Politics.* Santa Fe, NM: Bear, 1986.

Stadelbauer, Jörg. "Der Weinbaukomplex Kasierstuhl. Überprüfung des sowjetischen Konzeption des agro-industriellen Komplexes und der wirtschaftsräumlichen Gliederung an einem Beispiel aus dem Oberrheingebeiet." *Regio Basiliensis* 19 (1978): 143–171.

Steffen, Michael. *Geschichten vom Trüffelschwein. Politik und Organisation des Kommunistischen Bundes, 1971 bis 1991.* Berlin: Assoziation A, 2002.

Sternstein, Wolfgang. *Mein Weg zwischen Gewalt und Gewaltfreiheit.* Norderstedt: Books on Demand, 2005.

Überall ist Wyhl: Bürgerinitiaitven gegen Atomanlagen: Aus der Arbeit eines Aktionsforschers. Frankfurt: Haag + Herchen Verlag, 1978.

Stöss, Richard. *Vom Nationalismus zum Umweltschutz. Die Deutsche Gemeinschaft / Aktionsgemeinschaft Unabhängiger Deutscher im Parteiensystem der Bundesrepublik.* Opladen: Westdeutscher Verlag, 1980.

Stöss, Richard, editor. *Parteien-Handbuch. Die Parteien der Bundesrepublik Deutschland, 1945–1980.* Opladen: Westdeutscher Verlag, 1983–1984.

Strote, Noah. *Lions and Lambs: Chaos in Weimar and the Creation of Post-Nazi Germany.* New Haven: Yale University Press, 2017.

Summers, Sarah E. "Reconciling Family and Work: The West German Gendered Division of Labor and Women's Emancipation." PhD Dissertation, University of North Carolina at Chapel Hill, 2012.

"'Thinking Green!' (and Feminist): Female Activism and the Greens from Wyhl to Bonn. *German Politics and Society* 33, no. 4 (Winter 2015).

Suri, Jeremy. "The Rise and Fall of an International Counterculture, 1960–1975." *American Historical Review* 114, no. 1 (February 2009): 45–68.

Tarrow, Sidney. *Power in Movement: Social Movements and Contentuous Politics*, (2nd Ed.). Cambridge: Cambridge University Press, 1998.

Tauer, Sandra. *Störfall für die gute Nachbarschaft? Deutsche und Franzosen auf der Suche nach einer gemeinsamen Energiepolitik (1973–1980)*. Göttingen: Vandenhoeck & Ruprecht, 2012.

Tokar, Brian. *The Green Alternative*. San Pedro, CA: R. and E. Miles, 1987.

Tompkins, Andrew. *Better Active than Radioactive! Anti-Nuclear Protest in 1970s France and West Germany*. Oxford: Oxford University Press, 2016.

"Grassroots Transnationalism(s): Franco-German Opposition to Nuclear Energy in the 1970s." *Contemporary European History* 25, no. 1 (2016): 117–142.

"Transnationality as Liability? The Anti-Nuclear Movement at Malville." *Revue belge de philologie et d'histoire* 89, no. 3–4 (2011): 1365–1379.

Touraine, Alain. *Anti-Nuclear Protest: The Opposition to Nuclear Energy in France*. Cambridge: Cambridge University Press, 1983.

Trouillet, Bernard. *Das Elsaß – Grenzland in Europa. Sprachen und Identitäten im Wandel*. Frankfurt: Deutsches Institut für Pädagogische Forschung, 1997.

Tucker, William. *Progress and Privilege*. Garden City, New York: Anchor/ Doubleday, 1982.

Uekötter, Frank. *The Greenest Nation? A New History of German Environmentalism*. Cambridge, Massachusetts: MIT Press, 2014.

Naturschutz im Aufbruch. Eine Geschichte des Naturschutzes in Nordrhein-Westfalen, 1945–1980. Frankfurt am Main: Campus, 2004.

Umweltgeschichte im 19. Und 20. Jahrhundert. Munich: Oldenbourg, 2007.

Vadrot, Claude-Marie. *L'Ecologie, histoire d'une subversion*. Paris: Syros, 1978.

Historique des mouvements écologistes. Paris: Association française de science politique, 1980.

Varon, Jeremy. *Bringing the War Home: The Weather Underground, the Red Army Faction, and Revolutionary Violence in the Sixties and Seventies*. Berkeley: University of California Press, 2004.

Walker, J. Samuel. "Nuclear Power and the Environment: The Atomic Energy Commission and Thermal Pollution, 1965–1971." *Technology and Culture* 30, no. 4 (October 1989): 964–992.

Three Mile Island: A Nuclear Crisis in Historical Perspective. Berkeley: University of California Press, 2004.

Weitz, Eric. *Creating German Communism, 1890–1990: From Popular Protests to Socialist State*. Princeton: Princeton University Press, 1997.

West, Cornell. *Democracy Matters: Winning the Fight Against Imperialism*. New York: Penguin, 2004.

Wette, Wolfram. *Filbinger. Eine deutsche Karriere*. Springe: zu Klampen, 2006.

Wewer, Göttrik, editor. *Parteifinanzierung und politischer Wettbewerb. Rechtsnormen – Realanalysen – Reformvorschläge*. Opladen: Westdeutscher Verlag, 1990.

White, Richard. "'Are You an Environmentalist or Do You Work for a Living?': Work and Nature." In *Uncommon Ground: Toward Reinventing Nature.* William Cronon, editor. New York: Norton, 1995.

Williams, Gwyn. *Struggles for an Alternative Globalization: An Ethnography of Counterpower in Southern France.* Aldershot: Ashgate, 2008.

Winkler, Heinrich August. *Der Lange Weg nach Westen. Deutsche Geschichte.* Munich: Beck, 2000.

Wittner, Lawrence. *The Struggle Against the Bomb.* Stanford: Stanford University Press, 1993.

Wöbse, Anna-Katharina. "Die Bomber und die Brandgans. Zur Geschichte des Kampfes um den 'Knechtsand'—eine historische Kernzone des Nationalparks Niedersächsisches Wattenmeer." *Jahrbuch Ökologie* (2008): 188–199.

Wolff, Jocelyn, editor. *Le patrimoine des communes de la Meuse.* Paris: Flohic Editions, 1999.

Wolfrum, Edgar. *Die Geglückte Demokratie: Geschichte der Bundesrepublik Deutschland von ihren Anfängen bis zur Gegenwart.* Stuttgart: Klett-Cotta, 2006.

Rot-Grün an der Macht. Deutschland 1998–2005. Munich: Beck, 2013.

Wüstenhagen, Hans-Helmuth. *Bürger gegen Kernkraftwerke. Wyhl – der Anfang?* Reinbek: Rowhohlt, 1975.

Umweltmisere, Bürgerinitiative und die Verantwortung der Wissenschaftler Cologne: Pahl-Rugenstein, 1976.

Zaretsky, Natasha. "Radiation Suffering and Patriotic Body Politics in the 1970s and 1980s." *Journal of Social History* 48, no. 3 (2015): 487–510.

Ziemann, Benjamin. "A Quantum of Solace? European Peace Movements During the Cold War and their Elective Affinities." *Archiv für Sozialgeschichte* 49 (2009): 351–389.

Zelko, Frank. *Make It a Green Peace! The Rise of Countercultural Environmentalism.* Oxford: Oxford University Press, 2013.

Zetti, Daniela. "Three Mile Island und Kaiseraugst. Die Auswirkungen des Störfalls im US-Kernkraftwerk Harrisburg 1979 auf das geplante KKW Kaiseraugst." *Preprints zur Kulturgeschichte der Technik* 13 (2001).

Index